Clear As Mud

Planning for the Rebuilding of New Orleans

Robert B. Olshansky, AICP,
and Laurie A. Johnson, AICP

American Planning Association
Planners Press

Making Great Communities Happen

Chicago | Washington, D.C.

Copyright © 2010 by the American Planning Association
122 S. Michigan Ave., Suite 1600, Chicago, IL 60603
1776 Massachusetts Ave., NW, Suite 400, Washington, DC 20036
www.planning.org/plannerspress

ISBN: 978-1-932364-80-4 (pb)
       978-1-932364-79-8 (cloth)

Library of Congress Control Number: 2009941508

Printed in the United States of America

Contents

Figures

Tables

Preface

After Hurricane Katrina, New Orleans became a city filled with hundreds of thousands of dramatic tales of survival and suffering. Everyone in the city's planning and development community and every public official, civic leader, and politician has a story to tell. We met as many as we could. We found that, without exception, each one worked earnestly, overtime, and without much pay to save the city in ways they thought best, based on their experience and their perceptions. We want to tell these stories in the hope they provide lessons for other cities struck by disaster.

This book is about local government in post-Katrina New Orleans, examined through the lens of professional planning. It is about the administrative and political worlds in which planners operate after a disaster. This is not a confessional "tell all" book. Rather, we describe as many details as possible, because we want readers to understand the environment that made decision making and planning so difficult. This can help readers to place themselves in the story. We studied this postdisaster recovery process as it happened, and in general we present the story chronologically to help readers consider each decision in its specific context. Each planning decision had to be as effective as possible, given its context in time as well as the availability of federal assistance and other resources. We encourage readers to think about what they would do if their cities were struck by catastrophic disaster and how they would organize, finance, and facilitate rebuilding a city under such circumstances.

We have studied postdisaster recovery for many years and in several countries. For us, this story began over a decade before the hurricane, when we began to study and compare the recovery processes following the 1994 Northridge earthquake in Los Angeles and one that struck Kobe, Japan, exactly one year later. With Ken Topping, former planning director of Los Angeles, we began to study how the Kobe earthquake could help us think about managing a catastrophic urban disaster in the United States. As we write this, Laurie is completing her doctorate at Kyoto University, and both of us continue to learn from and share insights with our Japanese colleagues as they continue to reflect on the earthquake and think about the disasters that lie ahead. From 2004 to 2005, Rob spent a sabbatical year in Kobe and at Kyoto University, reading and reflecting on recovery processes from disasters around the world. In January 2005, a series of conferences in Kobe that marked the 10th anniversary of the earthquake provided a forum for Rob, Laurie, Ken, and many of our disaster-planning colleagues to think about sustainable recovery and collaborate on developing theories of how communities recover from disaster.

When we began researching recovery, we were primarily interested in reducing a community's vulnerability to natural hazards, a process known as disaster mitigation. Over the years, our interest has expanded to the process of managing rebuilding and long-term recovery from disaster, of which mitigation is but one part. We know full well that communities are complex and that the challenges of disaster recovery are enormous, requiring the skills of professionals working in many different disciplines, such as land-use planning, economic development, community development, public administration, finance, law, and social work. But our profession is planning, so we have taken that perspective in our research. In publishing this through the American Planning Association, we expect the readers to be planners or professionals who share our interests.

In the days that followed Katrina, we had two goals. First, we thought it was important to communicate the lessons we had learned from other disasters to the media and fellow planners. Second, we wanted to study the recovery from this catastrophic disaster firsthand as it happened and unfiltered by the cultural and language differences we had experienced in Japan. In short, this was an unparalleled opportunity for both research and action. Indeed, we ourselves became actors in our study.

When Katrina struck in August 2005, Laurie was a vice president at Risk Management Solutions (RMS), an international catastrophic-risk modeling company. With the press dwelling on the immediate aftermath of the flood and the federal government's failed response, she thought it was important to make clear to the world the massive scale of the damage and the immense need for rebuilding and recovery. Laurie and staff at RMS worked day and night to put out the most defensible loss estimate possible and, within a few days, announced an estimate of $100 billion, which was sent out over the international wire services.[1] It was clear that the costs of this disaster far exceeded anything seen before; RMS increased its loss estimate to at least $125 billion one week later. Meanwhile, in November, Rob was invited to lead Jed Horne, city editor of the *New Orleans Times-Picayune*, and photographer Ted Jackson on a weeklong tour of Japan, in order to tell the Kobe story to the residents of New Orleans. This led to a front-page spread in the *Times-Picayune* on Sunday, December 4, which subsequently led to several ongoing, formalized exchanges between New Orleans and Kobe.[2] Laurie later became a key member of the Unified New Orleans Plan team, which in autumn 2006 through early 2007 drafted the citywide plan, and Rob became a member of its National Advisory Team, which worked on what the plan should be called, how the district plans should relate to the citywide plan, what information should be on maps, and how it would all relate to a new master plan for the city.

We have made this story as personal as possible; it is, ultimately, about a collection of individual actors. The motives, character, and interpersonal skills of individuals are important factors in historic events. Planners usually do not bear witness to historic events, so this came as a surprise to us. While researching planning in New Orleans after the hurricane, we became fascinated by how the personal characteristics of all the key players mattered just as much as the circumstances of the crisis did. Events could have played out very differently had there been a different mayor, president, governor, chief of staff, city planning commission director, and so on.

We invite readers to think about the following questions. How does one organize and finance the rebuilding of a city in the accelerated timeframes expected by its public officials and citizens? What should a planner, local or state government official, or involved citizen do when faced with such circumstances? To what extent can planning policies and strategies help to facilitate a successful recovery? How important are government-led planning efforts, as opposed to self-organized efforts by neighborhood organizations or nonprofits?

As a result of our observations, we want to leave readers with the messages that individuals and their actions make a difference and that leaders matter. We hope this makes the lessons gleaned from this book even more meaningful.

Clear As Mud

1

The Hurricane Katrina Catastrophe

Shortly after six in the morning on Monday, August 29, 2005, the center of Hurricane Katrina crossed the southeastern tip of coastal Louisiana, near the small town of Buras in Plaquemines Parish, where the mouth of the Mississippi River opens into the Gulf of Mexico.[1] By this time, there was very

NOAA

Fig. 1.1. Hurricane Katrina, August 29, 2005, at 10:15 a.m. EDT

3

little left of Buras. Structures had already been pounded for many hours by Category 3 hurricane-force winds of up to 127 miles per hour, and the storm's massive size had set up a deadly surge that had already overtopped nearby levees, flooding every building and surrounding lands with more than 20 feet of saltwater.[2] A nearby offshore buoy measured waves in excess of 47 feet.[3]

About 60 miles upriver to the northwest, most of the 1.3 million residents of the New Orleans metropolitan region had already left the area. Louisiana's governor, Kathleen Blanco, had initiated a statewide, voluntary evacuation on Saturday, August 27, two days before Katrina's landfall. On Sunday morning, the mayor of New Orleans, Ray Nagin, ordered the city's first-ever mandatory evacuation. The city also opened the Superdome in downtown New Orleans as the "refuge of last resort" for anyone unable to leave.[4] As many as 100,000 people remained in New Orleans; approximately 10,000 were inside the Superdome. Many of them had medical and special needs.

Mayor Nagin and key management personnel had checked into the Hyatt Regency hotel in downtown New Orleans and split their time between an operations center set up in the hotel and the city's emergency operations center, located on the ninth floor of city hall, across the street. Both buildings were just a block away from the Superdome. Most nonessential city personnel joined the mass evacuation. Several members of the city's executive team were prepared to set up "city hall west" in Baton Rouge, the state capital, about 90 miles northwest of New Orleans.[5] The state's emergency operations center and a major command post of the Federal Emergency Management Agency (FEMA) were also in the capital.

The eye of Katrina passed offshore and east of New Orleans, battering the city for several hours with rainfall and winds exceeding 90 mph. Katrina made its final landfall around 9:12 a.m. about 60 miles northeast of the city, near the mouth of the Pearl River in southwestern Mississippi. It was still officially a Category 3 hurricane, with winds topping 120 mph but with a much stronger storm surge exceeding 28 feet in depth along some parts of the coast from Gulfport to Biloxi, Mississippi.[6]

By late Monday morning, the worst was apparently over in New Orleans. Reporters and news crews who had descended upon the city to witness Katrina's impact cautiously emerged, along with many remaining residents, and took to the streets in search of damage. Throughout the day and into the early evening, news media projected relatively banal images of shattered windows, fallen bricks, and roofing torn from the familiar tourist areas in the city's downtown and French Quarter, both located on higher ground along the Mississippi River. The media were of the general opinion that

New Orleans had managed yet again to avoid the catastrophic flooding and devastation that hurricane experts had been predicting for years.[7]

In the days and weeks that followed, investigative reporters, emergency managers, and other government officials would debate what happened when and who knew what when, often presenting conflicting and contradictory stories.[8] Detailed testimonies and forensic studies would later confirm that even in those early Monday morning hours, eastern parts of New Orleans were already under as much as 14 feet of water. Levees and floodwalls along the city's canals were being overtopped by or collapsing under Katrina's immense surge.[9]

On Monday evening, a private helicopter company began feeding the first aerial images of the progressive and devastating flooding to major media outlets.[10] By August 31, two days after Katrina's landfall, over 80 percent of the city was underwater. The lowest areas were under more than 20 feet of water (see fig. 1.2).[11] Katrina's storm surge heights were well above the design standards for New Orleans's 350-mile levee protection system; overtopping, erosion, and other failures caused more than 50 breaches across the system.[12]

It took a week to plug the major breaches, the most destructive of which were along the 17th Street, Industrial, London Avenue, and Orleans Avenue

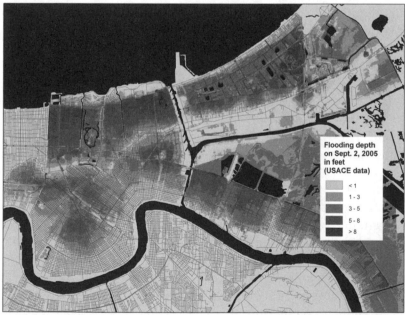

Timothy F. Green; flood data distributed by LSU GIS Information Clearinghouse: CADGIS Research Lab, LSU, Baton Rouge, La., 2005/2006

Fig. 1.2. Katrina flood depths in New Orleans

canals. During this time, the U.S. Coast Guard and others rescued thousands of people from rooftops in flooded neighborhoods. Thousands more lined up at the heavily damaged Superdome, the city's convention center, elevated freeway bridges, and any other place of higher ground seeking water, food, and shelter. With time, the floodwaters engulfed most of the city and downtown, creating islands of refuge at the Superdome and the convention center and further challenging the response efforts of all levels of government.

By September 5, a massive, federally coordinated evacuation that began on September 2 was nearing completion. The majority of the city's remaining residents were either bused or flown out of state to shelters set up at the Astrodome in Houston and elsewhere; only about 10 percent of the city's prestorm population remained. With power, communications, water, and sanitation services out, the city and other agencies enforced the mandatory evacuation and a nighttime curfew for the next weeks. Pumping stations worked around the clock to drain the city.

Before city, state, and federal officials could decide when and how residents would be allowed to return, the city was hit with another storm. In the Gulf of Mexico, Hurricane Rita grew to Category 5 strength, with possible trajectories including New Orleans and the Louisiana coastline.[13] On September 24, Rita veered west and made landfall as a Category 3 storm near the border between Texas and Louisiana.[14] Another wave of storm-related flooding inundated the lowest parts of New Orleans, especially the Lower Ninth Ward. With the exception of Rita, there was very little rainfall during September and October 2005, which helped expedite the pumping of nearly all of the water—about 225 billion gallons total—out of the city by October 14.[15]

By nearly every measure, Hurricane Katrina was the most destructive and costly natural disaster in American history (see fig. 1.3). Hurricane Rita was the third most costly—a devastating double punch for Louisiana. Combined, the storms affected a five-state area of 90,000 square miles along the U.S. Gulf Coast—an area larger in size than Great Britain.[16] They also caused more than 1,800 deaths and destroyed more than 300,000 housing units.[17] FEMA had more than 1.7 million registrants for its Individuals and Households programs, and more than 400,000 applied for transitional housing.[18] More than 400,000 jobs were initially lost, and the Congressional Budget Office estimated capital losses at $70 billion to $130 billion, with other estimates topping $150 billion.[19]

An estimated two million Louisianans in 22 parishes were affected by the storms. More than 1.3 million residents were displaced and over 1,500 lives were lost in that state alone. More than 200,000 homes were damaged in the state; out of the total number of houses damaged by the storms in the Gulf

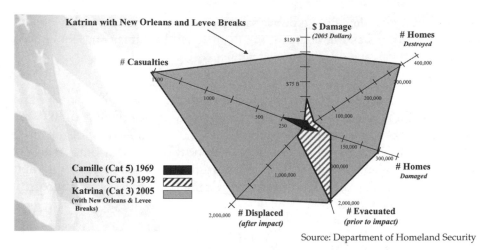

Source: Department of Homeland Security

Fig. 1.3. Impact of Hurricanes Camille and Andrew compared to Hurricane Katrina

Coast, 77 percent were in Louisiana. Additionally, 81,000 businesses and 870 schools were damaged. Thirty hospitals were closed, 10 of them permanently. An estimated 127,000 jobs were lost. Property damages totaled about $100 billion across every sector of the state:

- $35 billion in damages to residential homes, vehicles, and personal property
- $34 billion in damages to commercial structures, property, and inventory
- $17 billion in damages to public infrastructure (e.g., utilities, roads, ports, rail, and water)
- $8 billion in damages to public facilities (e.g., schools, hospitals, and government buildings)
- $6 billion in damages to levees[20]

In addition, 217 square miles of coastal lands were destroyed by the storms, causing massive environmental destruction and damage to the state's agriculture, forestry, wildlife, fishing, and recreation industries.[21] The cascading effects likely caused another $200 billion in economic losses statewide.[22]

The city of New Orleans sustained over a billion dollars in damage to city-owned property.[23] It included:

- $729 million in damages to road, bridges, catch basins, and sanitation systems
- $183 million in damages to parks and parkways, recreation and cultural facilities, libraries, and health clinics

- $109 million in damages to public safety facilities, such as the police department buildings and equipment, fire department buildings and equipment, courts, prison, and telecommunications
- $14 million to city hall, vehicles, and contents

Within the city, over 80 percent of all the buildings sustained some damage from high winds and water. Over 70 percent of housing units were either damaged or destroyed.[24] More than 100,000 homes (half of the city's total) were under more than four feet of floodwater.[25] With time, many of the evacuees were able to return, but more than 200,000 of New Orleans' residents were displaced long-term and became known as part of the great "diaspora" (see fig. 1.4).[26]

HOW KATRINA BECAME A CATASTROPHE

Formed as the 12th tropical depression in the record-setting 2005 Atlantic hurricane season, Katrina began its lifecycle on August 23 about 175 miles southeast of Nassau, Bahamas, and lasted a mere eight days.[27] The catastrophe of August 29, 2005, however, was decades in the making. After all, the Gulf Coast and southeast Louisiana had experienced many strong storms before. But the damage from Katrina was exacerbated by a number of factors that made New Orleans and its residents especially vulnerable this time.

New Orleans's Vulnerability of Place

New Orleans was founded by French settlers in the early 1700s on a narrow, crescent-shaped ridge formed by centuries of repeated flooding of the Mississippi River. For the first few centuries, development was limited to this higher ground and surrounded by coastal marshes and swamplands of the Mississippi River Delta (see fig. 1.5). After major flooding along the Mississippi River in 1927, an extensive and intricate system of levees, floodwalls, pumping stations, and drainage canals was constructed along the entirety of the river. This effectively stopped the soil replenishment that had historically been gained from repeat flooding. Much of this construction was financed by the draining and subsequent subdivision and development of the surrounding marsh and swamplands.[28]

As the population of southeast Louisiana boomed during the early decades of the 20th century, the city expanded its geographic limits, with residents moving into lower elevation areas. In 1919, approximately 90 percent of New Orleans's 339,000 residents lived above sea level; but by 1960, when the city's population peaked at 627,535 residents, only 48 percent (or 306,000) did.[29] Economic pressures also drove the expansion of the city's port and shipping capacity, with the creation in 1923 of the Industrial Canal—a shortened barge passage between the Mississippi River and Lake

Katrina's Diaspora

One of the best snapshots of how New Orleans area residents were scattered by Hurricane Katrina may come from the post office. Since the storm struck last year, more than 270,000 households have filed change of address forms, including about 200,000 that still listed an address outside New Orleans and its surrounding parishes as of July 1.

Current population estimates vary, but most put the city's population between 200,000 and 250,000, down from 480,000 before the hurricane. Estimates suggest that tens of thousands have also left nearby parishes.

Many evacuees stayed relatively close to home, moving to less hard-hit areas in Louisiana, but Southern cities like Houston, Dallas and Atlanta also saw a large influx of people.

The number of households having mail forwarded outside the New Orleans area peaked at the start of the year, and has come down slightly as some displaced residents have begun to return.

Number of New Orleans area households that had mail forwarded outside the area

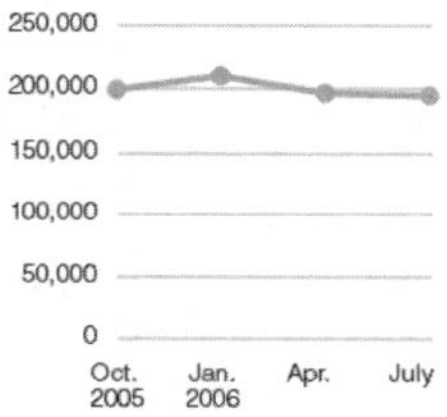

250,000

200,000

150,000

100,000

50,000

0

Oct. 2005 · Jan. 2006 · Apr. · July

Where New Orleans area residents moved, based on change of address forms filed with the post office

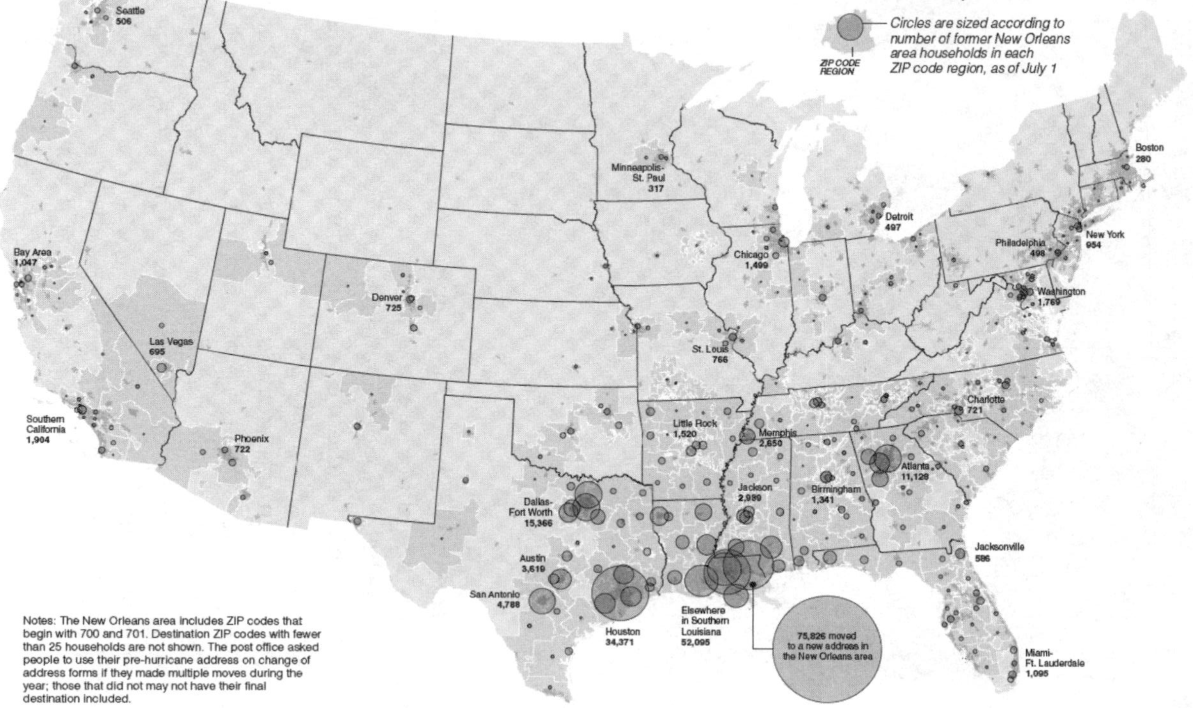

Circles are sized according to number of former New Orleans area households in each ZIP code region, as of July 1

ZIP CODE REGION

Boston 290
New York 654
Philadelphia 498
Washington 1,769
Detroit 497
Charlotte 721
Atlanta 11,129
Jacksonville 586
Miami–Ft. Lauderdale 1,095
Birmingham 1,341
Memphis 2,550
Jackson 2,990
Elsewhere in Southern Louisiana 52,095
Little Rock 1,520
St. Louis 766
Chicago 1,469
Minneapolis–St. Paul 317
Houston 34,371
Dallas–Fort Worth 15,366
Austin 3,516
San Antonio 4,789
Denver 725
Phoenix 722
Las Vegas 695
Seattle 506
Bay Area 1,047
Southern California 1,904

75,826 moved to a new address in the New Orleans area

Notes: The New Orleans area includes ZIP codes that begin with 700 and 701. Destination ZIP codes with fewer than 25 households are not shown. The post office asked people to use their pre-hurricane address on change of address forms if they made multiple moves during the year; those that did not may not have their final destination included.

Matthew Ericson / The New York Times

Fig. 1.4. Katrina's diaspora

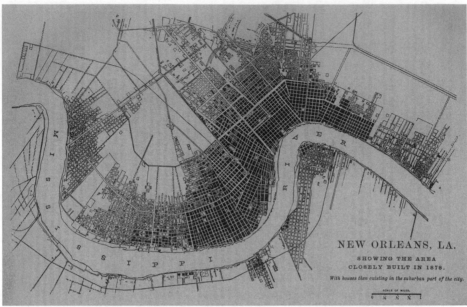

Courtesy of the University of Texas Libraries, The University of Texas at Austin

Fig. 1.5. New Orleans, 1878

Pontchartrain—and in 1965 of the Mississippi River Gulf Outlet (MRGO), a shortened route to the Gulf of Mexico.[30]

When Hurricane Betsy flooded the region in 1965, Congress passed the Flood Control Act, which authorized the U.S. Army Corps of Engineers (the "Corps of Engineers") to construct 350 miles of levees and floodwalls, known as the Lake Pontchartrain and Vicinity, Louisiana Hurricane Protection system. The system was designed to protect all of Orleans Parish and parts of neighboring Jefferson Parish from the storm surge and related flooding associated with a "standard project hurricane."[31] On the five-rung scale now used to categorize tropical storms, this "design storm" was roughly comparable to a fast-moving Category 3 hurricane. The design parameters for the "standard project hurricane" were first developed by the Corps of Engineers and the National Weather Service in 1959, using historic storm data up through that year; but the historic data lacked large-sized and strong storms, such as the later hurricanes Betsy (Category 4, 1965) and Camille (Category 5, 1969).[32]

In 2005, the hurricane protection system was still incomplete due to design-related delays, environmental concerns, and funding cuts. By some estimates, adequate protection from a Category 3 hurricane was still another 10 years away.[33] Furthermore, the complex construction and maintenance arrangement between the Corps of Engineers and the multitude of local levee boards resulted in reductions in design standards and construction quality, as well as ongoing maintenance problems, which all contributed to the system's failure in Katrina.[34]

Complicating matters, both New Orleans and the surrounding Mississippi River Delta plain were sinking as the soils naturally compacted. The process accelerated as cities tapped underground aquifers for freshwater supplies. The added weight of buildings, roads, and other urban development packed down the soil.[35] Areas of New Orleans that had been above sea level during the middle 19th century were an average of six feet below sea level by 2005. Levees constructed as recently as 2000 were more than a foot lower than design intentions.[36] In effect, the city had been transformed into a series of sinking bowls, each surrounded by a ring of levees and floodwalls still vulnerable to flooding from major hurricanes, as well as seasonal flooding on the Mississippi River and heavy spring rains.

Furthermore, as exploration and production of oil and natural gas in the Gulf of Mexico expanded during the 20th century, much of Louisiana's southeast coastal marsh was dredged for oil and gas transport canals and pipelines. As a result, saltwater intruded into the marshes; southeastern Louisiana's coastline and its wetlands, which naturally dampen storm surge waves, were eroding at a rate of 25 square miles annually.[37] Without this natural line of defense, New Orleans was subject to increasingly higher storm surge levels as the coastline inched closer and closer to the city.

Beginning in 1960, New Orleans's population began a slow decline to 484,674 in 2000. During this same period, however, the city continued to expand in area, as many residents continued their migration from higher to lower elevation land as it was opened up for development. In 1960, 627,535 people lived mostly within 36.8 square miles of developed land, which equates to 17,053 people per square mile. By 2000, the city's "footprint" of occupied and developed land had expanded to 66.7 square miles, but the population density had declined to 7,266 people per square mile. By 2000, only 185,000 (38 percent) of New Orleans's residents lived above sea level.[38] The city limits had expanded until they were contiguous with the Orleans Parish boundaries and effectively became one governing unit.

Construction of the hurricane protection system provided the city with a false sense of security that was further reinforced by national risk management policy. The city of New Orleans participates in the National Flood Insurance Program (NFIP), which was created in 1968. The program enables—and in some cases requires—households and businesses located in designated floodplains to obtain federally backed insurance for flood-related damages. Federal law only requires that mortgage holders of properties within NFIP Special Flood Hazard Areas (SFHAs)—more commonly referred to as 100-year floodplains—purchase flood insurance. Properties within SFHAs that do not have mortgages, as well as all other properties outside SFHAs, are not required to purchase insurance. The flood-insurance rate maps issued by the NFIP establish base flood elevations (BFEs)—the water-surface elevation resulting from a flood that has a 1 percent chance of equaling or exceeding that level in any given year—that the NFIP uses to price insurance and NFIP-participating communities must follow when setting elevation requirements for new buildings.[39]

In New Orleans, the BFEs and SFHAs have been calculated on the assumption that the federally certified hurricane protection system would perform to its design standard; they did not account for the effects of regional subsidence or the potential for catastrophic levee failure.[40] Thus, it was possible to build NFIP-compliant homes (eligible for flood insurance) in many of the city's lowest-lying areas with only a few feet of elevation required; many of these structures would sustain flooding from Katrina up to 15 feet above the BFEs.[41] In 2005, prior to Katrina's landfall, much of the city's land area was outside the SFHA zone, and there were about 84,000 NFIP policies in force (covering about 40 percent of residential housing).[42]

In the decade after Congress authorized the hurricane protection system and launched the NFIP, New Orleans grew by 29,000 housing units, many of which were located in the city's lowest elevation areas.[43] In particular, the east end of the city, beyond the Industrial Canal, grew tremendously. It was envisioned that this area would soon be enclosed in the hurricane protection system; indeed, the expansion was used to justify the system's funding.[44] New Orleans East—a housing subdivision developed in the 1980s on former marshland—was originally planned to have 22,000 new housing units and a population of 250,000. Even as late as 1999, after the city's population had declined and the economy slowed, city plans still called for thousands more residences in New Orleans East.[45] Flooding in much of this area exceeded the BFEs.

Prior to Katrina, the state of Louisiana required neither local comprehensive plans nor the adoption and enforcement of building codes. Nonetheless, the city of New Orleans had a master plan, a comprehensive zoning ordinance, subdivision regulations, and a building safety department that was charged with, among other things, enforcing compliance with the NFIP standards.[46] The city also had a comprehensive emergency management plan and, in 2005, was developing a mitigation plan to reduce its vulnerability to storms and flooding in compliance with the Disaster Mitigation Act of 2000. It did not have a postdisaster recovery plan or recovery management structure in place before Hurricane Katrina. Two of the only legal references to recovery management are contained in the city's Home Rule Charter:[47]

- Section 4-206 authorizes the mayor to study, devise, and implement programs to improve housing and neighborhood conditions in the city and to implement plans to foster recovery and economic development there.
- Section 5-402(3)(e) states that the City Planning Commission shall prepare and recommend to the City Council "plans for the replanning, improvement, and reconstruction of neighborhood and community centers and of areas or districts destroyed or seriously damaged by fire, earthquake, flood or other disasters."

Implementation and enforcement of this regulatory and disaster planning framework wasn't without its problems and criticisms.[48] For one, the master plan had no authority to enforce compliance. The city's zoning was inconsistent with the land use component of the master plan. Furthermore, in the 1980s the Federal Insurance Administration (FIA) waged and won a lawsuit against Orleans, Jefferson, and St. Bernard parishes for failing to maintain levees and enforce NFIP requirements for new construction; the FIA contended that these failures had led to repetitive and unnecessary flood insurance claims and payments.[49]

Social and Economic Vulnerability in New Orleans

Beginning in 1960, New Orleans's population and economic strength began to decline as Houston increasingly became the corporate hub for oil and gas industry.[50] In 2005, New Orleans's population was roughly 455,000.[51] That year, the city's median household income was $27,000 (versus $41,000 nationally), and it had one of the nation's highest poverty rates of 23.2 percent (compared to 12.7 percent nationally). The home ownership rate was about 46 percent; the rate nationally was 68 percent. There were an estimated 40,000 vacant lots or abandoned residential properties in the city, which caused significant blight even before Katrina.[52]

The city's history of racial segregation had grouped large numbers of low-income African-Americans in public or government-subsidized rental housing. This social stratification also affected the city's social vulnerability and residents' abilities to prepare for, respond to, cope with, and recover from a disaster.[53] A study that used tract-level data from the 2000 census identified areas with higher concentrations of minorities, lower-income households, young families, and public housing projects as being the most vulnerable to natural hazards and having the fewest resources to prepare for and recover from a disaster.[54] Another study estimated 29 percent of city residents (or 134,000 people) did not have a car and depended upon buses, relatives, and friends for transportation.[55] This created tremendous logistical challenges for mass evacuation, short- and long-term sheltering, and other means of disaster response and recovery.

Forty years of population decline prior to Hurricane Katrina also severely reduced city coffers and the quality of local services and public facilities maintenance. For example, in 2001, the Housing Authority of New Orleans was taken into federal receivership by the U.S. Department of Housing and Urban Development (HUD). The state of Louisiana began taking control of failing schools in the New Orleans Public School district—a special district separate from the city's government—in early 2005.[56]

However, in the five years prior to Katrina, the city government was showing signs of an upturn. Between fiscal years 2001 and 2004, the city's general fund revenue increased more than 18 percent—from $405 million to $479 million annually. This was sufficient to pay both general fund expenses and its annual debt service of nearly $39 million (on a total bond debt of $879 million).[57] The city had approximately 6,000 employees, operated more than 400 buildings, and maintained more than 1,600 miles of streets.[58] All utilities—sewer, water, electricity, gas, and telecommunications—were owned and operated by separate entities, some of which were public entities, such as the Sewerage and Water Board. Others were private, such as Entergy, which provides electricity and gas.

New Orleans's economic growth was outpaced by other Louisiana cities such as Baton Rouge, but it was still growing, albeit slowly, in the years before Katrina. The city's main industries were tourism, port-related shipping and transportation, medical research, and higher education. The tourism industry was attracting more than 10 million visitors annually and produced more than 80,000 jobs. The Port of New Orleans accommodated an average of 2,000 vessels per year and supported more than 160,000 jobs in the metropolitan region. The New Orleans metropolitan area was also home to a growing health care sector, which employed around 80,000 people.[59] The Tulane School of Medicine and the Louisiana State University (LSU) Health Sciences Center, both located in New Orleans, were major contributors to this sector of the economy.

With a stronger balance sheet, in November 2004 the city sought voter approval for its largest referendum ever: $260 million in general obligation bonds to improve, upgrade, and expand city infrastructure and facilities; voters agreed.[60] Just before Katrina, the city was preparing to sell the bonds to take advantage of its improved investment grade rating.[61] The city planned to use more than half of the proceeds to repave and repair streets. There were plans to upgrade police, fire, and judicial facilities; parks and recreation facilities; libraries; and other public buildings.[62] All were in need of upgrade and repair; all would be devastated by the 2005 storms and flooding.

FORESHADOWING THE KATRINA CATASTROPHE

On March 8, 2005, less than six months before Hurricane Katrina, the National Academy of Sciences hosted a workshop in Washington, D.C., entitled "Lessons Learned Between Hurricanes: From Hugo to Charley, Frances, Ivan, and Jeanne."[63] The workshop was part of the Academy's Disasters Roundtable—an open forum held three times a year and designed to facilitate communication among scientists, practitioners, and policymakers on important issues related to natural, technological, and other disasters. The March workshop was organized after an unprecedented and devastating series of four hurricanes struck Florida and the southeastern United States in 2004. Its speakers were asked to consider what lessons had been learned since Hurricane Hugo struck South Carolina in 1989 and what disaster management challenges remained in combating future disasters. Many in attendance likely did not appreciate the truly paradoxical and prophetic nature of that day, just weeks in advance of one of the most active, costly, deadly, and catastrophic hurricane seasons in U.S. history.[64]

At the workshop's morning session, FEMA's director, Michael Brown, reviewed the agency's response to the 2004 hurricane season and the lessons learned from this and previous year's emergencies.[65] Brown observed that post-9/11, FEMA's major challenges had been to maintain a multiperil (both man-made and natural) focus and to prepare and train for a truly catastrophic disaster. Following the September 11, 2001, terrorist attacks, Congress and the White House made many legislative changes and organizational reforms to try to ensure that the nation was better capable of dealing with a catastrophic event.[66] The most notable change was the creation of the Department of Homeland Security (DHS) and designation of the DHS secretary as the "principal Federal official for domestic incident management."[67] FEMA and many other federal agencies were absorbed into the Emergency Preparedness and Response (EPR) Directorate of DHS, which had responsibility for (among others): consolidating existing federal response plans into one plan; creating an intergovernmental national incident management system; enabling seamless communication among responders; and aiding disaster recovery.[68]

In December 2004, DHS also released a new National Response Plan (NRP) that integrated the previous functions of FEMA within a new "all-discipline, all hazards" national framework. Many critical new response positions and coordinating bodies were created, including the required designation of a primary federal official (PFO) as an on-scene representative of the president, in addition to the federal coordinating officer.[69] The NRP also added a new Emergency Support Function, #14, Long-Term Community

Recovery and Mitigation, which had the potential to significantly alter the federal government's involvement in local recovery.

Formation of DHS and the development of the new national response system had significant impacts on FEMA. While it kept its name, FEMA lost its independent agency status, and its cabinet-level status had already ended in early 2001 with the start of the Bush administration. FEMA's emphasis significantly shifted away from natural hazards to the consequences of man-made disasters. The resulting departmental reorganizations shuffled staff into new and unfamiliar roles, added new personnel with military backgrounds who were unfamiliar with the previous emergency management system, and ultimately may have led to the departure of many of the agency's senior and middle managers who had risen through the ranks during the agency's previous decades.[70]

New positions of authority and coordination mechanisms defined by DHS and within the NRP were not fully operational in the 2004 or even the 2005 hurricane season. Yet it is generally agreed that the state and federal response operations performed adequately in the 2004 season, when four major hurricanes—Charley, Frances, Ivan, and Jeanne—and one tropical storm struck the state of Florida. Florida's emergency management agency, one of the best in the country, worked closely with FEMA, which maintained federal coordination responsibility and stuck to its established guidelines.

At the March 2005 workshop, Brown described FEMA's response to the 2004 storms as unprecedented; the agency's prepositioning of manpower and equipment in Orlando, Florida, and throughout the southeastern United States helped to facilitate quicker responses to the four major hurricanes.[71] Yet as one hurricane headed directly toward Orlando, FEMA had been forced to evacuate personnel and equipment out of the state. Brown reported that, as a result, FEMA was developing policies and procedures to reduce what he called "excess preparation" while maintaining a quick response time "crucial for success in reducing the impacts of disasters."[72]

Brown was optimistic about the agency's readiness for the 2005 hurricane season. He credited some of this readiness to catastrophe planning efforts under way across the country. He briefly described a catastrophe planning pilot project known as the "Hurricane Pam" exercise, which centered on the New Orleans metropolitan region. FEMA had cosponsored a five-day response and coordination simulation in Baton Rouge in July 2004; more than 300 participants came from multiple agencies and levels of government, as well as a vast array of nonprofit, voluntary, and community- and faith-based organizations.[73] Brown said that the lessons learned from this exercise would be applicable nationwide.[74]

Dr. Shirley Laska, professor of sociology at the University of New Orleans, also referenced the Hurricane Pam exercise at the 2005 workshop.

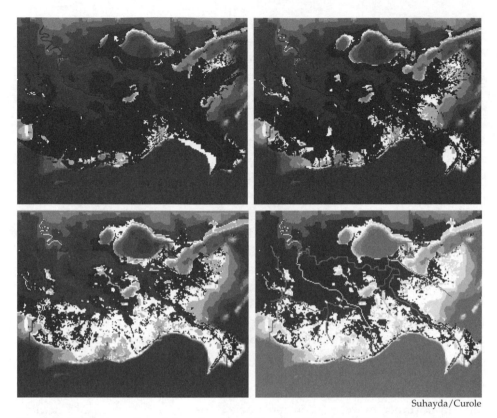

Suhayda/Curole

Fig. 1.6. Historic and envisioned wetland loss in Mississippi River Delta (left to right and top to bottom, 1839, 1870, 1993, 2020); white indicates areas of saltwater intrusion and land loss.

She pointed out that the exercise presented a scenario in which a slow-moving, Category 3 hurricane hit the city. It assumed that the storm would produce more than 20 inches of rain, result in 10 to 20 feet of flooding in New Orleans, more than 50,000 fatalities, and 100,000 casualties. It would leave one million metropolitan region residents homeless and 80 percent of structures in 13 parishes damaged.

Laska then proceeded to describe what would happen to the city if it were struck by a Category 5 hurricane. In this scenario, the hurricane protection system would likely fail and the entire city would be inundated with five feet or more of water for many weeks. Laska estimated it would take at least nine months to drain New Orleans, and, during that time, evacuees would have to be relocated to sites in other parts of the country.

Laska concluded that "New Orleans [was] holding its breath waiting to see if the worst case scenario happens" instead of investing in coastal wetlands restoration and the types of long-term mitigation that would restore the region's deteriorating environment. And she questioned whether the city might "be open for redevelopment as other coastal areas have been" after such storms. She speculated that it would not. In her scenario, the postdisaster environmental conditions were so dire that they would hinder redevelopment. Instead, she speculated that many of the city's residents and business would move to the north shore of Lake Pontchartrain. Only a much smaller urban area would remain, centered on the city's historic port of commerce.[75]

It wasn't just New Orleans that was "holding its breath," and Laska's graphic presentation wasn't the only time such grim predictions were made in Washington, D.C., in Baton Rouge, or to the general public. The first warning came from Hurricane Camille in 1969, and recognition of the potentially catastrophic flooding conditions increased in the 1990s, after Hurricane Andrew (1992) and Hurricane Georges (1998) narrowly missed New Orleans. Following Hurricane Andrew, Louisiana made evacuation planning a priority of its newly formed state office of emergency management.[76]

During the 1990s, a consensus emerged among researchers as well as federal, state, and local emergency planners that mass evacuation would be critical to a successful hurricane response in southeast Louisiana. In 2004, the state revealed its "contra-flow plan" that turned the interstates and other major highways into one-way routes out of the potential impact zones of an approaching hurricane. Raising public awareness about the hazards and importance of evacuation remained difficult, however, as did dealing with the large proportion of New Orleans's residents without cars or other means of transport.[77]

In addition, some mitigation initiatives had already begun. After Hurricane Camille, the Corps of Engineers and an array of hurricane researchers began studying the region's vulnerability to tropical storms, and they developed proposals both to fortify New Orleans's protection system and restore the surrounding region's wetlands. However, the political support for funding coastal wetland protection or Category 5 levees did not exist until the 1990s and early 2000s, when researchers and emergency managers finally had the ability to show computer simulations of the impact of Category 4 and 5 storms on southeast Louisiana.

Even then, efforts to get the federal government further involved in such an enormous project had mixed results; Congress took a more incremental approach. For example, in 1990, Senator John Breaux (D-La.) won passage of the Coastal Wetlands Planning, Protection, and Restoration Act, which secured $50 million annually for coastal restoration projects. Although this was an important initiative, the funding was insufficient to address the high erosion rates across vast stretches of the coastline. Then, in 1999, Congress finally approved funding for the Corps of Engineers to initiate a

NOAA

Fig. 1.7. New Orleans flooding after Katrina

reconnaissance study—the first step in what is normally a 10-year design process required by the Water Resources Development Act—of how to provide protection against the effects of Category 4 or 5 hurricanes in southeastern Louisiana. The reconnaissance study was completed in 2002. As the next step, the Corps of Engineers proposed a five-year, $12 million feasibility study, which was yet unfunded as of August 2005.[78]

In 1998, Louisiana politicians, the Corps of Engineers, the Environmental Protection Agency (EPA), and several other corporate, environmental, and public interest groups began to work together to gain congressional support for "Coast 2050," a $14 billion plan called to restore "America's Wetland," as the group branded the state's coastline. They were successful in getting legislation developed and in front of Congress for consideration. Late in 2004, as Representative W. J. Tauzin (R-La.) testified in support of such a bill to more fully fund coastal restoration, he reportedly threw aside his script and said, "We'll be faced one day with thousands of our citizens drowned and killed, peopled drowned like rats in the city of New Orleans. . . . Our paradise is about to be lost. . . . Please don't let's have a commission where all of us, red-faced, say we saw it coming and didn't do anything. . . . Please don't let that happen."

Subsequent changes in the state's congressional delegation, growing budget deficits, and a controversial provision added by Senator David Vitter (R-La.) to help loggers deforest cypress swamps stalled and eroded support for the bill. In 2005, the Bush administration's most recent pre-Katrina budget proposed just $540 million total for coastal restoration for the next four years. Just two months prior to Hurricane Katrina's landfall, at a Senate hearing Vitter showed a Category 4 storm simulation flooding all of New Orleans and said, "It's not a question of if; it's a question of when. . . . Instead of spending millions now, we are going to spend billions later."[79]

THE CHALLENGES AHEAD

After the hurricane, damage to city hall forced the emergency operations center and other key government functions across the street to a ballroom at the Hyatt for several weeks. With time, staff returned to the city and sufficient repairs were made so that city hall could reopen. The office of the mayor's chief administrative officer (CAO) became the hub for federal, state, and city recovery activities. The CAO's office managed most of the city's insurance claims and FEMA-related activities, particularly its Public Assistance (PA) applications. One year after the hurricane, various federal, state, and local agencies were still working out of cubicles in the CAO's office. Other city departments active in the early recovery included: building permits and safety, public works, and planning. It wasn't until December 2006, 16 months after Katrina's landfall, that Mayor Ray Nagin formed the Office of Recovery Management (later called the Office of Recovery and Development Administration) to lead the city's recovery efforts.

During the rest of 2005 and throughout 2006, FEMA was consumed with an unprecedented recovery effort; at the same time, it was facing intense political scrutiny for its failure to quickly and effectively respond to the disaster. Numerous federal and state agencies, academic institutions, and media organizations launched investigations into the failings of the local, state, and national responders. Two key federal government reports resulting from these investigations are the White House's report, "The Federal Response to Hurricane Katrina—Lessons Learned, February 2006," and the report of the U.S House of Representatives' Select Bipartisan Committee to Investigate the Preparation for and Response to Hurricane Katrina, "A Failure of Initiative."[80] The U.S. Government Accountability Office (GAO) has also issued more than 100 reports on various elements of the federal agencies' responses, lessons learned, and recommendations for legislative and programmatic changes.[81]

The post-Katrina studies concluded that there was an absence of strong response leadership at all levels of government. Furthermore, FEMA's subordination to DHS and its recent focus on terrorism had severely affected the nation's capability to respond to natural disasters.[82] Before Katrina, FEMA had to adopt new guidelines for integrating emergency response functions into one unified disaster management structure that all organizations were supposed to follow. But "some federal agencies and key state and local organizations had not yet implemented the structure" or were not trained in the new command and control system.[83] Also, the new structure added bureaucratic layers that confused decision making and caused many breakdowns in communications.[84] In all, Katrina demonstrated to the nation and the world the inadequate preparation of the affected localities and states, as well as the tragic inability of the new national system to help them respond to and recover from a catastrophic event.[85]

Organizational changes in DHS and FEMA began soon after Katrina, and there was immense media and political pressure on them to fix problems before the 2006 hurricane season. To carry out the expansive Gulf Coast response and recovery operations, FEMA augmented its permanent staff of about 2,500 with employees from other federal agencies, its reservists, and a vast network of contractors. FEMA's director, Michael Brown, resigned. Although he had exuded confidence at the March 2005 workshop about the nation's readiness, he later said, "There was a complete breakdown of government at every level—federal, state, and local" from the very start of Hurricane Katrina disaster.[86]

Shortly after Katrina, Congress approved funds directed to short-term needs, such as emergency housing, relocation assistance, immediate levee repair, and debris removal.[87] The city was optimistic about receiving large sums of federal funds to cover both its immense response and recovery-related expenses. This was reinforced about two weeks after Katrina, when President Bush toured the devastated Gulf Coast and made a nationwide, televised address in front of Jackson Square in New Orleans's fabled French Quarter. He declared, "We will do what it takes; we will stay as long as it takes, to help citizens rebuild their communities and their lives. . . . This great city will rise again."[88] These words would be remembered, retold, rebuked, and possibly regretted in the months and years ahead. Never before had a modern U.S. city been brought to the brink of complete collapse like New Orleans had. Elected officials, government staff, engineers, and planners had no precedent to rely on for triaging and jumpstarting a lifeless city. While trying to figure out the sequence for rebuilding the city's social, economic, and physical infrastructure systems, they also had to face the immediate threat of another hurricane, the possibility the city's residents might not return, and the prospect that a regional flood risk management solution would never materialize. It is within this chaotic and uncertain environment that the planning for the rebuilding of New Orleans began.

2

Order from Chaos

Planning at the State and Federal Levels

The extent of the devastation was clear very soon after the storms hit, as was the fact that the State of Louisiana would need an enormous amount of money to rebuild and restore New Orleans and the surrounding parishes. After Hurricane Rita struck three weeks later, the disaster area grew to encompass the entire southern third of the state. It added to the uncertainty surrounding even the most basic of questions: How much money would it take to rebuild the city? Where would it come from? And how would it be allocated for restoring infrastructure, businesses, and homes?

The first reliable estimate put the direct damages at $100 billion.[1] Later, on September 22, 2005, Senators Mary Landrieu (D-La.) and David Vitter (R-La.) introduced a bill asking for $250 billion in assistance, which included funding for levees and coastal restoration.[2] But no one knew what the actual costs would be, nor were there any mechanisms for allocating and spending recovery money. This would be left up to the state and federal governments to figure out.

MONEY, POLITICS, MISTRUST

The nation, however, was wary of sending money to Louisiana. It is important to appreciate the cloud of suspicion that hung over the state and its requests for federal assistance in the fall of 2005. From the days of Huey Long, Louisiana has had a colorful and systemic history of corruption, and its political, governmental, and economic environments have frequently been compared to those of a third world nation.[3] Some claim that 21st-century

Louisiana is no more corrupt than other states and its reputation rests more on its history than on present reality. But there are grounds for the suspicion: Edwin Edwards, who was popular enough to be elected governor four times, has been in prison since 2001 on a federal racketeering charge; and nine months before Hurricane Katrina, three Louisiana emergency preparedness officials were indicted for mishandling $30.4 million in FEMA funds designated for floodplain buyouts.[4] It was perhaps unsurprising when, in early September, then-Representative Tom Tancredo (R-Colo.) urged congressional leaders not to give money to Louisiana because of the "state's long history of corruption."[5] While none of Louisiana's political leaders at the time was surrounded by charges of corruption, three former governors of Louisiana proposed a commission of citizens, rather than politicians, to administer any recovery funds.[6]

Thus, when Louisiana's senators introduced their bill asking for $250 billion, there was already a strong sensitivity to the potential for misdirection and waste.[7] For example, a *Washington Post* editorial entitled "Louisiana's Looters" declared, "Louisiana legislators are out to grab more federal cash than they could possibly spend usefully."[8] The editorial argued legislators should teach a lesson to Louisiana and other states: political patronage leading to poor decisions regarding flood control and development would not be federally subsidized. Then-Senator Barack Obama (D-Ill.) and conservative Senator Tom Coburn (R-Okla.) reflected the concerns of many in a joint statement that declared the importance of "protect[ing] both taxpayers and citizens of the Gulf Coast with strict accountability and oversight about how the money is spent and whether it is most efficiently directed to help rebuild lives."[9]

It was telling that President Bush's choice for the post of Gulf Coast recovery coordinator was Donald Powell, a banker and former chair of the Federal Deposit Insurance Corporation. Powell's appointment in November 2005 was a clear signal that, in the eyes of the White House, one function was preeminent: to ensure that federal funds were well spent. Many pundits and politicians had called for an independent recovery commission run by a recovery "czar," but Powell's role within the Department of Homeland Security (DHS) was more modest. He was charged instead "to help state and local leaders reach a consensus plan; bridge regional, racial and partisan divides; and persuade a debt-leery and gridlocked Washington to pay for it."[10]

Post-Katrina recovery also took shape within a much larger, high-stakes political context. While Hurricane Katrina was a catastrophic disaster for the residents of the Gulf Coast, the bungling of the immediate response to the flooding of New Orleans was a political disaster for the White House. Nothing could erase the administration's black eye from that first week in

September, not even a successful recovery brought about by cooperative effort. As such, the White House saw Hurricane Katrina as a political problem, and Senior Advisor Karl Rove became the point person to address it.[11] In author Paul Alexander's concise words, "Rove was going to blame [Governor] Blanco for the failure of the response in Louisiana, and to do that he was going to use [Mayor] Nagin."

In other words, the White House's strategy was to shift the blame for the bungled response rather than solve the recovery problem at hand. To succeed, this strategy required driving a wedge between Mayor Nagin and Governor Blanco; not only would they be less likely to accomplish anything, but the two Democrats would be seen as petty, bickering children.

Louisiana and New Orleans had other detractors as well. In the days after the storm, while residents were still being rescued, Speaker of the House Dennis Hastert (R-Ill.) said it didn't make sense to rebuild a low-lying, hurricane prone city.[12] "There are some real tough questions to ask about how you go about rebuilding this city," Hastert said. "It looks like a lot of that place could be bulldozed." This sentiment was echoed in a *60 Minutes* feature in late November, which suggested the homes, businesses, and industry that made up the city should gradually and permanently retreat from the area because of steady coastal erosion.[13] Senator Larry Craig (R-Idaho), then a member of the Senate Appropriations Committee, bluntly declared in mid-October that flooded parts of New Orleans should be abandoned and that "Louisiana and New Orleans are the most corrupt governments in our country and they always have been."[14] He claimed growing Senate support for abandoning entire sections of New Orleans such as the Lower Ninth Ward. "I'm not humorous when I suggest we should turn it back to what it was, a wetland."[15] With these kinds of signals from Washington, it was clear that New Orleans's access to long-term reconstruction funding would not be easy.

Mutual Mistrust

Beyond the federal government's mistrust of Louisiana, New Orleans itself is a veritable petri dish of mistrust and enmity. The biggest gulf is between the races. Long-resident white families have had the most power and money in New Orleans historically, and they have a deep-rooted reputation for using this power over African-Americans and new arrivals. Whites are also more likely to afford the gracious homes on the higher ground of the Mississippi River's natural levees and were usually untroubled by the flooding that plagued other residents.[16] The white elites tend to be suspicious of the ethics and governing ability of many of the city's African-American politicians, who assumed greater political power with the 1977 election of Ernest Morial as the city's first black mayor. In 2007, for example, Representative William

Jefferson, whose district encompassed greater New Orleans, was indicted for money laundering and racketeering. That same year, city council member-at-large Oliver Thomas, who was widely expected to be the city's next mayor, also pleaded guilty to accepting illegal payments. Certainly, these incidents did nothing to improve the city's reputation for corruption.

On the other hand, the city's African-Americans have some very good reasons to be suspicious of their fellow white citizens. Many African-Americans know that during a flood in 1927 members of the white elite ordered the destruction of a levee protecting a poor area downstream in order to save New Orleans.[17] Consequently, in 2005, it was not difficult for people to believe that the levee on the Industrial Canal was destroyed on purpose to drive African-Americans from their homes. African-American New Orleanians also tend to be suspicious of promises that neighborhoods will be improved through redevelopment—suspicions that are based on their recent experiences of broken agreements. For example, when the St. Thomas public housing project was redeveloped earlier in this decade under HOPE VI, the project became largely a market-rate development with insufficient units for previous residents.[18] This was despite promises of new housing for all the low-income residents displaced by the project. Amity between the races was not improved when, just days after the storm, Jimmy Reiss, the head of the New Orleans Business Council, was quoted in *Newsweek* and the *Wall Street Journal* as saying the diaspora after Katrina created an opportunity to build a city with fewer poor people.[19]

There is also a history of mutual mistrust between New Orleans and the rest of the state, especially its capital, Baton Rouge. New Orleans is sometimes described as an island in Louisiana; its urban, Catholic culture has long been at odds with the upstate, Protestant culture that dominates the bulk of the state. New Orleanians have also been at odds with rural, Catholic Cajuns. The economic growth of Baton Rouge in recent decades, coupled with the steady population decline of New Orleans, has further fueled New Orleans's resentment of Baton Rouge.

Needless to say, all of these levels of mistrust made it exceedingly difficult to mount a cooperative rebuilding effort on the scale required by Hurricane Katrina. Still, a strong federal response could have overcome some of these differences; instead, Rove's political strategy fanned the flames.

STATE AND FEDERAL PLANNING INITIATIVES

Despite the intrigue, some federal, state, and private-sector professionals came together in various venues to attempt to create a coherent planning strategy for rebuilding the state. At the center of it all was the Louisiana Recovery Authority, which grew to be the most powerful player in the rebuilding of southern Louisiana.

The Birth of the Louisiana Recovery Authority

In September 2005, Andy Kopplin, Governor Blanco's chief of staff, was faced with the task of figuring out how to rebuild his devastated state.[20] He was highly experienced in state government, having also served as chief of staff for Blanco's Republican predecessor. The day after the flood, he began to receive phone calls from all over the country offering advice, assistance, and condolences. Initial offers of assistance focused on the response effort, but many callers, such as Bill Leighty, the Virginia governor's chief of staff, also came to help with long-term recovery. One of the most helpful initial offers came from Jay Altman, a friend who had run a charter school in New Orleans and had just moved to London in July. Altman showed up in Baton Rouge within days of the storm. One of his first tasks for Kopplin was to set up a mechanism for receiving donations, an effort that eventually led to the Louisiana Disaster Recovery Fund, and he helped Kopplin to think about best practices for rebuilding communities. Like everyone else's, Kopplin's life was complicated by Katrina at many levels, as home and work merged. His children's rooms were given over to guests: Altman, Leighty,

LRA

Fig. 2.1. Andy Kopplin, Donald Powell, and Louisiana governor Kathleen Blanco, November 29, 2005

and two Ford Foundation representatives. He was also housing a cousin's family, who had evacuated from Slidell, a suburb north of New Orleans, as well as a Plaquemines Parish family of five that his wife brought home from a shelter.

Kopplin called on Louisiana leaders whom he knew to be "good thinkers." He set up an informal think tank to begin identifying long-term recovery issues while his office was still involved in day-to-day response and recovery activities. A key member of this group was Sean Reilly, a former state legislator, civic leader, and president of Lamar Advertising. Soon, this group was holding brainstorming sessions in Reilly's spacious home, away from the chaos at the governor's office. The group's members sought out advice from people with disaster recovery experience, such as former White House chief of staff Leon Panetta. One particularly helpful call came from New York governor George Pataki's chief of staff, who offered advice on how set up something like the Lower Manhattan Development Corporation (LMDC), which was created after September 11, 2001. Stefan Pryor, the director of the LMDC, was invited to Baton Rouge and stayed at Reilly's home. Another key addition was a small team from international management consultants McKinsey & Company, who provided pro bono management consulting services for more than six months after the storm.

During the first week after Katrina, Kopplin's group of "good thinkers" considered some fundamental questions: How should the governor's cabinet be organized to respond to the challenge of rebuilding? Is an extra agency needed? If so, what would be its responsibilities and how would it be constructed? Would it be advisory or administrative? How long should it last? It became clear that the LMDC provided a model for a citizen-led, bipartisan organization that bridged local, state, and federal governments in order to receive and direct recovery funds. At the request of Kopplin, Pryor stayed in Baton Rouge for two weeks and worked with Reilly and others to draft an executive order creating this new organization.

Looking at the LMDC's experience, Reilly's group concluded that in order to facilitate a smooth flow of federal aid, it was important to design an entity that could identify, secure, and receive federal recovery dollars, especially HUD community development block grant (CDBG) funds and FEMA Public Assistance funds, which would be based on project-by-project applications. They also decided the organization should have powers to establish priorities for spending those funds, as well as monitor and audit their use. The makeup of such an agency would be critical. It needed to represent everyone in the affected areas and, in Kopplin's words, "unite the face of recovery." Its membership needed to be bipartisan and include people who were influential in their communities as well as nationally prominent leaders with Louisiana roots. Most important, the members needed to be people who would fight for the interests of Louisiana as a whole. The first thing on their agenda would be making a rational, persuasive, and influential argument to Congress and the American people for providing the money. Kopplin hoped that a diverse and influential LRA board "could reach everyone in the country, regardless of party."

One Sunday in late September, shortly after Hurricane Rita delivered a second blow to the state, Kopplin, Reilly, Altman, Pryor, and Bryan Begley of McKinsey & Company presented their ideas to the governor. On October 17, 2005, Governor Blanco created the Louisiana Recovery Authority by executive order.[21] Until it was made a permanent entity by the Louisiana legislature on February 23, 2006, it operated out of the governor's office.[22]

At the very beginning, the LRA had no budget—indeed, it had no money at all. The state was broke. Its main economic engines had come to a halt, and the citizens of its largest city were scattered across the country, homeless and jobless. Nor was there yet a single penny of federal money for permanent reconstruction and economic recovery. Thus, the LRA began with a single staff employee, Andy Kopplin. But the LRA could use staff and resources from other agencies. Kopplin compared it to "draft day in the major leagues," as he sought the best talent from across state government.

The LRA board members were selected to be bipartisan, socioeconomically and racially diverse, and influential. For example, Mary Matalin, a nationally prominent Republican political advisor, was balanced by Donna Brazile, who had been Al Gore's campaign manager. Members also represented each part of the state, regardless of whether it was affected by the hurricane or not. Governor Blanco was so convinced that Norman Francis, the venerable president of New Orleans's Xavier University since 1968, needed to be chairman that she called him for three straight days until he agreed. New Orleans native Walter Isaacson, president of the Aspen Institute and former president of CNN, was appointed vice chairman. Sean Reilly was also appointed to the board, and he continued to be influential in charting the agency's course.

In late October, very soon after their appointment to the board, Francis, Isaacson, Reilly, Kopplin, and other Louisiana leaders flew to Washington, D.C., in Reilly's jet to meet with Senators Landrieu and Vitter. They also met with White House chief of staff Andy Card, staff from the Office of Management and Budget, and Al Hubbard, who led the Domestic Policy Council staff.[23] They also had a luncheon meeting with DHS secretary Michael Chertoff and held a press briefing. The Louisianans asked for stronger levees to protect against Category 5 hurricanes and money for housing and economic development. They promised to develop a detailed, defensible request for funding. They also promised to provide damage estimates, which were still unknown. This was the first significant step in what would become a long dance with the White House to obtain an appropriate level of funding for long-term rebuilding.

Federal Planning Assistance: ESF #14

FEMA was also concerned about helping to plan the long-term recovery of Louisiana communities affected by the storm. Even amid its many response-related activities in mid-September and early October, FEMA staffers, contractors, and reservists began to arrive in Baton Rouge to begin the Long-Term Community Recovery (LTCR) Emergency Support Function (ESF #14) of the National Response Plan. ESF #14 was added to the National Response Plan in 2004 as a way to coordinate the resources of federal agencies to assist the long-term recovery of states and communities following disasters.[24] FEMA describes LTCR planning as "the process of establishing a community-based, [postdisaster] vision and identifying projects and project funding strategies best suited to achieve that vision, and employing a mechanism to implement those projects."[25] In FEMA's view, ESF #14 was a temporary, short-term technical assistance program offered to help the State of Louisiana better access federal services, which is why it was headquartered in Baton Rouge.

In 2005, ESF #14 was still an experiment. It had been used on a trial basis two times in 2004—in Florida after Hurricane Charley and in Utica, Illinois, after a tornado. But neither of those areas had experienced devastation on the scale caused by hurricanes Katrina and Rita. The catastrophe in Louisiana provided the conditions for ESF #14's rapid evolution. By late 2005, it had grown into a means of proactively trying to help communities develop a postdisaster vision, prioritize projects to achieve that vision, and identify funding sources. This was mostly unfamiliar territory for FEMA, both in terms of the local community planning process and the involvement in long-term recovery. Over time it became clear that these new roles made parts of the agency very uncomfortable.

At its peak, ESF #14 employed approximately 325 temporary staff across Louisiana's 19 hurricane-affected parishes. To create the LTCR plans, ESF #14 staff solicited input directly from communities to create a community-specific list of projects that its residents thought important for recovery. In November and December, ESF #14 staff held meetings and workshops with officials in the 20 most heavily affected parishes. In many parishes, a few daylong meetings (with food and entertainment provided) were all that was needed to bring the community together to develop an ESF #14 project list.[26] Although the postdisaster chaos, parade of temporary workers, and lack of information made coordination difficult,[27] the process was helpful in many rural parishes, especially those with little planning capacity.[28]

Fig. 2.2. The ESF #14 office in Plaquemines Parish, Louisiana

However, one ESF #14 plan in particular—Orleans Parish—was especially difficult to accomplish because of the severity of damage, the absence
of municipal employees, and the lack of established postdisaster planning
processes or information on postdisaster priorities. The best information
available to the Orleans Parish FEMA office was the Bring New Orleans
Back plan (see Chapter 3). Work on the Orleans Parish plan continued in
the New Orleans FEMA office through the summer, and the final version
was released in mid-August 2006, approximately four months later than the
plans of the other hurricane-damaged parishes.[29]

But after the planning processes were completed, little happened in most
parishes. ESF #14 wound down as quickly as it had ramped up; it ended
suddenly in March 2006 when FEMA stopped funding the program. At this
time, the state's planning process was not yet fully operational. The termination of ESF #14 placed the entire parish planning function back into the
state's hands, but there was nobody yet to receive it.

GETTING PROFESSIONAL HELP:
THE ROLE OF THE PRIVATE SECTOR

For three days, starting on November 10, around 650 people came together in devastated and still mostly vacant New Orleans to talk about planning.[30] The event—the Louisiana Recovery and Rebuilding Conference— was hosted by the American Institute of Architects (AIA) in collaboration with the American Planning Association (APA) and was cosponsored by the National Trust for Historic Preservation and the American Society of Civil Engineers.[31] Participation was by invitation only, but organizers intended to include "a broad range of local and state organizations, Louisiana citizens, religious and civic groups, community leaders, and public officials."[32] This event had 650 attendees and featured presentations by local and national planners about how to approach long-term recovery. The postconference summary presented a set of core policy goals and planning principles formulated during the event:[33]

Create infrastructure that supports recovery by restoring confidence, enhancing quality of life, and withstanding future disasters by:

- Constructing Category-Five-strength levees, restoring wetlands, and creating an independent authority to ensure ongoing maintenance and funding
- Improving services including communications, energy, and other key elements
- Supporting sustainable, equitable, and transparent approaches to rebuilding and future development

Promote economic growth that benefits everyone through:

- An economy encompassing traditional and emerging industries supported by respect for the region's historic character and innovative funding strategies
- Quality education and job training, housing, transportation, and other key services accessible to all income levels
- Equity that includes living wages and career tracks, and long-term economic opportunity

Provide public services that enhance quality of life for everyone through:

- High-quality education at every level and in every community
- Regional transit, coordinated with opportunities for community development
- Great parks and other public spaces that serve communities and support flood control

Pursue policies that promote a healthy environment and healthy people by:

- Deciding where to rebuild, investing in protecting these areas, and dedicating remaining areas to open space and parks
- Using sustainable approaches in every facet of rebuilding—energy, transit, land use, and building design
- Creating walkable communities that through their planning and design promote healthy lifestyles

Plan and design communities that advance livability by:

- Preserving the best of the past as the core for rebuilding while anticipating future needs
- Creating mixed income, mixed use neighborhoods that foster diversity and social equity
- Smart growth at urban, suburban, and rural scales that balances recovery and sustainability

For professional planners, this conference turned out to be an important event, with many later tracing the genesis of key post-Katrina planning ideas and professional collaborations to it. It also turned out to be significant for subsequent state planning efforts. The Louisiana Recovery Authority held its second board meeting at the conference and the following month adopted the AIA/APA planning principles.[34] Later, it began citing those principles as its criteria for its decisions regarding postdisaster plans and planning processes, the allocation of CBDG funds from HUD, and its approach to rebuilding and planning in New Orleans.

Furthermore, at the board meeting, LRA board members Donna Fraiche, a New Orleans attorney and head of the LRA's Long-Range Planning Task Force, and David Voelker, a New Orleans businessman, introduced the idea of creating a privately funded organization, the LRA Support Foundation, to help the LRA find and hire experienced community planning and design firms. Fraiche and Voelker told the LRA board the state already had a promising partner in the Baton Rouge Area Foundation (BRAF), which had been advocating smart growth for nearly a decade. In 1998, BRAF cofunded (along with the city and state) preparation of a downtown plan for Baton Rouge by the firm of Duany Plater-Zyberk (DPZ). By the summer of 2005, BRAF had extended its planning activities beyond Baton Rouge by holding smart growth workshops throughout the state. BRAF's point person for planning, Elizabeth "Boo" Thomas, was seeking more money to expand the initiative across the state. She even had a business plan for a new statewide program by the time that Katrina struck. Shortly after the storms, BRAF began identifying planners to assist in rebuilding southern Louisiana in order to use the postdisaster reconstruction as an opportunity to promote smart growth planning principles.[35] In late October, at BRAF's recommendation, Fraiche's Long-Range Planning Task Force met with Peter Calthorpe, the principal of one of the nation's most prominent urban design firms, Calthorpe Associates, as well as a founding member of the Congress of the New Urbanism. After that meeting, Fraiche became supportive of the regional planning effort Calthorpe proposed, which would guide posthurricane investments toward smarter and more sustainable development patterns.

Fraiche and Voelker suggested to the LRA board that the agency work with BRAF to help the state find "firms that are recognized in regional planning strength, [have] experience with post-disaster planning, and [are experienced in] working with local, state, and federal agencies."[36] To this end, BRAF created the LRA Support Foundation (LRASF) as a separate legal entity supporting the work of the LRA.[37] Until May 2006, the planning staff assistance for LRA was provided by the LRASF through BRAF. LRA board members Sean Reilly and David Voelker assumed positions on the LRASF board.

In December, it was Boo Thomas's turn to address the LRA board. She revealed which firms LRASF had selected to be a part of the regional planning effort. Thomas said LRASF solicited proposals from 39 firms, received proposals from 14, and selected three: Calthorpe, DPZ, and Urban Design Associates (UDA).[38] These were firms they already knew from their work on smart growth and new urbanism. The team was also to include research and technical support from several research institutions, such as the Brookings Institution (a Washington, D.C., think tank), PolicyLink (a research institute in Oakland, California, which would assist in outreach to displaced populations), and Louisiana State University. Although the LRASF didn't yet have the money to execute this project, the LRA board voted unanimously to accept its recommendation of planners and designers.

On January 19, 2006, the governor and the LRA announced a regional planning effort led by a "team of world-renowned planners, designers and architects" who would "develop a long-term regional vision for rebuilding" all of southern Louisiana.[39] DPZ would conduct charrettes to help localities develop planning ideas; UDA would produce a set of "pattern books" with designs for affordable housing suitable for southern Louisiana;[40] and Calthorpe Associates would tie it all together with a regional plan, the content and timeframe of which were not yet clear. Nor was it clear how this effort would relate to the ongoing planning process in New Orleans, which was, at this time, confident it could rebuild without the help of Baton Rouge (see Chapter 3).

"LOUISIANA SPEAKS": MERGING STATE, FEDERAL, AND PRIVATE-SECTOR PLANNING

The way in which the state-level planning effort evolved over December and January was confusing to most outside observers. It was not even clear to those involved. What happened was that, without any official, public notification, the LRASF's regional planning effort and the ESF #14 parish plans were incorporated into one statewide recovery planning process called "Louisiana Speaks," which was paid for by FEMA and LRASF and coordinated by the LRA.

The Louisiana Speaks branding happened in early January. FEMA had proposed holding a "Recovery Planning Day" later that month to involve Louisiana residents in the planning process. The LRASF supported this idea. At this point, the LRASF had not yet articulated the type of planning work it was going to do except to say it would involve a regional plan by Calthorpe, some local planning charrettes by DPZ, and design resource guides by UDA. While the LRASF was still trying to raise sufficient funds for these endeavors, FEMA was already providing planning guidance to communities through ESF #14, so it made some sense to try to merge these planning efforts. At a joint meeting between FEMA's Louisiana ESF #14 leader, Boo Thomas, and the LRA communications director, everyone agreed on the partnership, the Louisiana Speaks name, and a logo consisting of four interlocking puzzle pieces.

Not surprisingly, this marriage of convenience had its problems, primarily because all the parties had different goals, approaches, and time frames.

LRA

Fig. 2.3. Attendees at the Louisiana Recovery and Rebuilding Conference

From FEMA's point of view, ESF #14 was designed to provide immediate, short-term assistance to help localities identify projects and potential funding sources. The LRA, in contrast, was interested in long-term, regional planning but lacked the capacity to accomplish this. When FEMA wrapped up ESF #14 in March, the entire planning function was back in the state's hands. The LRA lacked planning staff, so it contracted with LRASF-recommended planners.[41] But the design-oriented planners lacked the breadth needed for this situation, such as experience in housing, economic development, hazard mitigation, and postdisaster recovery planning. Eventually, the state's recovery planning function was taken over by professional planners—Hal Cohen at the LRASF in March and Jeff Hebert, hired by the LRA in May— and the two of them worked together to turn Louisiana Speaks into a more coherent planning program.

DPZ's work came first. They conducted a series of three seven-to-10 day charrettes in March 2006 in various parts of the state: Lake Charles, a western Louisiana city affected primarily by Hurricane Rita; Vermilion Parish, a rural coastal county; and St. Bernard parish, immediately to the east of New Orleans.

UDA's *Pattern Books* were released in early July 2006.[42] The LRASF printed 100,000 copies and distributed them for free in home improvement stores throughout southern Louisiana. In February 2007, UDA released its second product, the *Planning Toolkit*, designed to be a guide to preparing community plans.[43]

The regional planning effort ("Louisiana Speaks Regional Vision") was more systematic and data-rich than the other components of Louisiana Speaks, so it took much longer to launch and to complete.[44] In the end, it became the most visible manifestation of Louisiana Speaks, and to most people the term "Louisiana Speaks" signifies this regional planning process. From January to June 2006, the regional planning work was technical and out of the public eye as the consultants prepared maps and data to describe the base conditions. Consultants also polled 2,500 Louisianans (some of whom were displaced and out of state) and held a series of six stakeholder workshops that solicited more than 1,000 participant opinions on coastal protection, transportation, land-use alternatives, economic development, and infrastructure.[45] To ensure representation from New Orleans, they also surveyed 100 neighborhood leaders in the city. The consultants used this information to develop a questionnaire, which asked the following multiple-choice questions: (1) "What are your top priorities for economic development in Louisiana?" (2) "Which values in the state's proposed plan are most important to you?" (3) "How important do you think funding and implementation of the state's proposed plan is to the recovery?" (4) "How

a

b

c

d

Figs. 2.4a–d. Four images from the UDA's Planning Toolkit.

should we grow?" and (5) "What is the right mix of property rights and community risk?"

The questionnaire was announced in Baton Rouge on January 22, 2007, at a kickoff event of a three-week, million-dollar public outreach campaign funded by the LRASF. The questionnaires were distributed as newspaper inserts and via the Internet; Louisiana Speaks programs aired on public television stations throughout the state, as well as in Atlanta, Dallas, and Houston. Citizens were asked to mail in their completed questionnaires, drop them off at their nearest public library, or take the poll online or by phone.[46] By the February 10, 2007, deadline, about 23,000 citizens participated in the poll, including 1,200 people out of state.

The Louisiana Speaks Regional Plan was released to the public on May 2, 2007, and endorsed by the LRA one week later.[47] The plan emphasizes smart growth and investment in coastal restoration. It also advocates thinking regionally about economic development to create a more stable and robust economy. New Orleans's recovery plan came out at virtually the same time (see Chapter 7). To planners, the Louisiana Speaks process seems like a textbook example of good planning, incorporating regional planning, smart growth, environmental protection, hazard mitigation, transportation improvement, economic development, and broad public involvement. But in the political environment of southern Louisiana, it added to suspicions that conservative Baton Rouge was meddling in New Orleans's recovery.

3

Planning for New Orleans

October 2005–March 2006

In the fall of 2005, New Orleans was a ghost of a city. Out of an estimated population of 455,000 residents, 353,000 had been displaced by flooding.[1] For those planning to return, Hurricane Rita's landfall on September 24 gave them pause. The city's six major universities, including the University of New Orleans and Tulane University, were closed for the fall semester; their 44,000 students went elsewhere.[2] When we first traveled to New Orleans in early October and November, we found that outside of downtown and the French Quarter the city was completely empty—no traffic, no lights, no open stores or gas stations. Debris and dead automobiles were scattered over the cityscape, and a gray layer of dust and mud coated everything. Even in downtown most of the office towers and hotels were dark.

The lack of residents posed immense fiscal challenges to the city. Its sales and property tax revenues were down more than 50 percent, and neither the state nor federal government had promised any loans or major rebuilding grants.[3] In October, Mayor Nagin announced the city had to make drastic budget cuts by reducing citywide operations by 30 to 60 percent and cutting half of his administrative workforce, excluding public safety positions. More than 3,000 city employees were furloughed.[4] The city's bond rating was also downgraded to junk status, and it was no longer able to sell the 2004 voter-approved bonds to conduct long-needed repairs of city streets and public facilities.[5] In October 2005, Congress passed the Community Disaster Loan Act of 2005, authorizing FEMA to manage the distribution of up to $1 billion in loans to "assist local governments in providing essential

Fig. 3.1. Visible waterline on a house that had been flooded

Fig. 3.2. Post-Katrina destruction

services." It also gave the president authority to "make loans to any local government."[6] Later that month, FEMA approved an initial loan of $120 million to New Orleans.

This was the environment in which planning discussions began in late 2005. Most of the remaining residents lived in areas at higher elevations along the Mississippi River in neighborhoods that were generally whiter and wealthier than the rest of the city. It was a city full of anxiety and uncertainty. How would it rebuild? Where would the money come from? Would major employers stay in the city? Would the levees be repaired? How does one even begin to approach such a problem?

The Brookings Institution called for a systematic planning effort led by the federal government:

> The federal government should take the lead in convening a world-class deliberation of the region's top federal and other experts to assess the situation, and consider where rebuilding may and may not make sense, based on the best environmental and engineering research. Once that basic work is done, this process should distill the trade-offs between different scenarios, and convey it all—in full public view—to policymakers and the local citizenry for deciding the right path. Do this well, with clarity and transparency and objectivity, and metro New Orleans as well as the nation will gain something critical: a solid foundation on which to build. . . . [G]overnment needs to invest generously in the creation of a world-class public involvement dialogue to inform the crucial decisions about New Orleans' future that policymakers are already beginning to make.[7]

In October, the New Orleans City Planning Commission and the American Planning Association's Louisiana Chapter requested APA send a team of six urban planners to assess the ability of the city to plan for recovery.[8] The team's primary finding was that the city's planning staff was woefully inadequate for the massive job in front of them. Before the hurricane, New Orleans had a planning office that was small for a city of its size, and out of a staff of 24 only half were professional positions. The city budget cuts reduced the office to eight and retained only four professional planners. The team also observed that prior to Katrina, the City Planning Commission lacked a central role in the city's planning, the master plan was incomplete, and there was no formal channel for meaningful public involvement. The team recommended the city add planning commission staff (funded by private sources if need be), create a formal neighborhood planning program, finish the master plan, and involve the commission in capital improvements planning. The team observed that the city lacked a typical big-city planning function and that it was high time to add one. The city took on these types

of planning challenges over the following months, and eventually the functions of planning were restored to the City Planning Commission—but it
was a long and complicated road.

THE BRING NEW ORLEANS BACK COMMISSION

Two weeks after the storm, Mayor Nagin began to consider how to organize
the reconstruction of the city. On September 10, he led a meeting in Dallas
with approximately 60 business and public leaders from New Orleans to
discuss some of the challenges that lay ahead. Nagin announced his intention to appoint a racially balanced group to plan the city's recovery and
declared that New Orleans's rebirth would be led by New Orleanians.[9]
Rumors quickly began to swirl about who would be asked to serve on Nagin's commission as well as who would serve on the commission the governor intended to form.

Soon after the mayor's announcement, the city council unanimously
approved a resolution for its own 11-member Advisory Committee on Hurricane Recovery consisting of the state's two senators, the parish's two congressional representatives, and seven additional members appointed by the
council.[10] The council pledged to provide the committee with adequate staff
resources and set a date for the first meeting for mid-October. That meeting
was never held, and there were no subsequent announcements regarding
the existence or intentions of this committee.

On September 30, Mayor Nagin announced who would serve on the Bring
New Orleans Back (BNOB) Commission. The 17-member team included
attorneys, academics, business people, and church leaders. It was tasked
with overseeing the development of a rebuilding plan for New Orleans. It
had only until the end of 2005 to complete its work.[11] Nagin emphasized the
members' high ethical standards, and he promised a transparent process
for spending any federal recovery money the city might receive. Besides the
city's reconstruction, the commission would address other issues such as
health care and education. The mayor also announced he had sent an email
to the White House with the following requests: an improved levee system,
light rail to the airport and to Baton Rouge, and a package of incentives for
businesses in New Orleans.

The BNOB commission first met on October 10, 2005, and divided its
work among several committees focused on city planning, infrastructure,
culture, education, health and social services, economic development, and
government effectiveness.[12] Each committee was led by a BNOBC member
but filled by volunteers. The city planning committee was widely regarded
as the most important group and was chaired by Joe Canizaro, a well-known
conservative white developer with connections to the White House. The
planning committee was divided further into six subcommittees on land

use, housing, infrastructure, historic preservation, sustainability, and urban design. In all, it included 235 volunteer participants. Each committee had its own chair and freedom to access whatever resources it could. Canizaro was able to use private donations to retain the services of the Philadelphia planning firm Wallace Roberts & Todd (WRT), which would provide professional support to the committee's efforts. Both WRT and its principal working on the project, John Beckman, had decades of planning experience in New Orleans.

Canizaro also requested help from the Urban Land Institute (ULI), a nonprofit research organization specializing in land-use issues and real estate development. ULI sent a team of 50 of its members to New Orleans for one week in mid-November to interview more than 300 residents and hold a town hall meeting that was attended by 250 people.[13] They released a preliminary report after a week and a full report a month later.[14] Their chief recommendation was for "officials at all levels to quickly establish one unified request to Congress for federal support." They also recommended creating a redevelopment corporation and a diversified economic development strategy. Finally, ULI recommended rebuilding strategically and "encouraging those areas that sustained minimal damage to begin rebuilding immediately and those areas that have more extensive damage to evaluate the feasibility for reinvestment and proceed in a manner that will ensure the health and safety of the residents of each neighborhood and proceed expeditiously." ULI also recommended that "people who cannot rebuild should be given fair compensation for their property."

The ULI study was comprehensive and sophisticated, which was all the more remarkable given that it was prepared in just one month. It addressed governance, financing, economic development, job training, physical redevelopment, and other issues. It recognized New Orleans was a "city of neighborhoods" and called for assistance to all of them. But it also made the sensible argument that neighborhoods with different elevations and degrees of flood damage would require different redevelopment strategies. Thus, the most heavily affected areas would require the greatest commitment of effort, planning, funds, and time to re-create livable, sustainable neighborhoods. According to ULI, some of that redevelopment would likely include wetlands and parks in order to improve stormwater management and increase neighborhood access to open space.

The ULI team saw that the city required a continuum of strategies: areas with the heaviest damage needed the most effort and collective action, and areas with the least damage could rely more on individual initiatives. The areas that could rebuild most easily should do so "with all haste," and the most heavily flooded areas would need additional analysis and planning efforts that took "great care . . . to work with the residents closely to determine the exact patterns of reinvestment to restore and create a functional and aesthetic neighborhood."[15] ULI predicted an informed planning process would recognize the need to reconfigure lots and allocate open space for stormwater to successfully rebuild the most damaged areas. ULI also said it was likely that most neighborhoods would benefit from additional open space.

Unfortunately, many people in New Orleans did not interpret the ULI study, meant to be a starting point for discussion, this way. For example, an article in the *Times-Picayune* emphasized ULI's recommendation to delay development in the most flooded areas. The newspaper claimed ULI suggested the city "use its original footprint, as well as lessons learned from Hurricane Katrina, as a guide in determining what areas are most logical for redevelopment."[16] The newspaper also referred to "the potential for mass buyouts" in the most flooded areas. "Buyout," however, was not a term that was used in the ULI documents.

Following the November ULI visit, the public debate was redirected, and there was widespread public concern about the city's "footprint," "shrinkage," mass buyouts, and the forced abandonment of parts of the city. ULI bore the brunt of this anxiety, although it made it very clear it supported rebuilding "equitably and without delay" and strengthening and empowering neighborhoods.[17] On November 29, citizens and elected

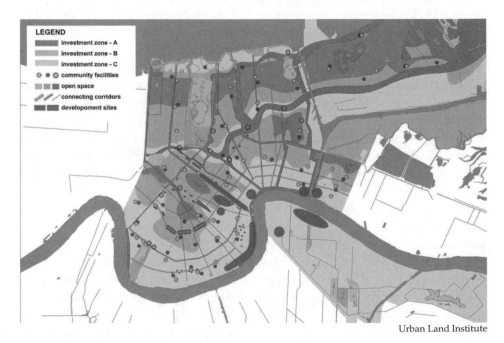

Urban Land Institute

Fig. 3.3. A map from the Urban Land Institute's report

officials—particularly city council members Cynthia Hedge-Morrell and Cynthia Willard-Lewis, who represent the heavily flooded Gentilly, New Orleans East, and Lower Ninth Ward sections of the city—reacted with hostility to the "controversial proposal to eliminate their neighborhoods from post-Katrina rebuilding efforts."[18] One eastern New Orleans developer, Sherman Copelin, was quoted as telling ULI representatives, "We don't need permission to come back! We are back!"

The mayor was on vacation in Jamaica during the pivotal week of planning activities in mid-November. He refrained from commenting on the ULI study.[19]

November 2005 was a time of numerous initiatives and conferences in New Orleans. There was the Louisiana Recovery and Rebuilding Conference, followed by the ULI team visit and a community forum on rebuilding New Orleans, sponsored by the national community-organizing group ACORN, in Baton Rouge on November 7 and 8.[20] Tulane, Xavier, and Loyola universities sponsored a conference called "Reinhabiting NOLA" on November 29 and 30. There were federal hearings on the Baker bill, which proposed establishing a federally supported redevelopment corporation. Communication among all of these efforts was inconsistent or nonexistent, although the LRA and the BNOBC had an official liaison at the other's meetings to keep each organization informed of their activities.[21]

In contrast, December was a time of public discussion, albeit often disconnected, chaotic, and unevenly documented. APA assisted in some of the conversations and helped ULI organize "town hall" meetings for displaced New Orleanians in Memphis, Atlanta, Fort Worth, Dallas, Houston, and Baton Rouge on December 4–10. Several hundred people attended these meetings, and many were frustrated by the lack of news and information about when they might be able to return home and the services available to them.[22]

The public discussion centered on whether some parts of the city should be abandoned or rebuilt. "Footprint" and "shrinkage" were the words of the hour, but it was still unclear in what ways the city might diminish in size and population. Some city council members portrayed the ULI plan as a proposal to completely abandon large portions of districts such as New Orleans East. But even Joe Canizaro (who was later cast by many as the villain of the story) was quoted by the press as saying, "I don't envision the elimination of neighborhoods, I see the shrinkage of neighborhoods." He said he expected vibrant communities throughout the city, including the Lower Ninth Ward.[23]

Numerous voices were weighing in on the efficacy of rebuilding the entire city. Many of these conversations focused on two big (and somewhat conflicting) questions. The first question was whether or not the risk of catastrophic flooding could be substantially reduced. Many residents viewed the reconstruction of New Orleans as a simple problem: if the U.S. Army Corps of Engineers could repair all the levees and protect New Orleans from storms even larger than Katrina, then all parts of the city would be equally safe for reconstruction. This, however, ignored several points. First, the city's population had been declining for four decades and would likely remain significantly smaller than it was in 2004. It would be difficult to pay for the infrastructure of a city that accommodated 455,000 people in 2005 (and 630,000 in 1960) if the rebuilt city contains only 300,000 to 350,000 people. Second, even if New Orleans were never hit with another strong hurricane, the low areas of the city would still frequently flood during heavy rains and continue to depend excessively on pumps for their drainage. Thus, even if the Corps of Engineers could protect the entire city, this would not solve all the flood problems in low-lying areas, and significant local infrastructure costs would remain a problem.

The second question was whether or not it was desirable to let the free market decide which areas were the most economically viable for reconstruction. After the ULI controversy, Canizaro proposed the city should encourage everyone to return in order to see what would happen. He also suggested it wait for three years before making decisions regarding public investments. The areas that turned out to be most viable would benefit from scarce public resources, and returning residents who instead found themselves all alone in a sea of blight would be given the opportunity to sell their properties back to the city or a development corporation.[24] This proposal was also castigated at the time for being unduly pessimistic, but it accurately anticipated conditions in New Orleans in 2009.[25]

In mid-December 2005, the BNOB city planning committee modified Canizaro's proposal to a one-year test of viability to avoid the "jack-o'-lantern effect" of scattered houses in largely abandoned neighborhoods.[26] (That phrase, which first appeared in a presentation by ULI in November, soon became another term du jour.) The adverse reactions to the notion that government policies would designate certain areas for preferential reconstruction prompted the committee to endorse first letting the free market decide what areas were most viable and then targeting those areas with financial assistance. The BNOB planning committee suggested property owners should decide carefully where to settle based on issues such as future flood risk, FEMA elevation requirements, and environmental contamination. The committee argued one year should be long enough to see which areas were most likely to rebuild. It also suggested that the city should promise basic utility services everywhere but only facilitate the reconstruction of retail, schools, and medical facilities in areas that were repopulating. An important element of this proposal was an offer to buy out anyone who had already rebuilt areas that weren't viable. It is noteworthy that proposals for rehousing the rental population were not yet well formed. Throughout the process, Canizaro frequently reminded participants he had a close relationship with the White House and would have an inside track to sell the completed plan to the administration and obtain the funds to implement it.[27]

While the BNOB planning committee worked on the details of this plan, many residents and evacuees continued to protest what they saw as an attempt to drive poor people from the city.[28] They repeatedly asked for promises that all residents would be welcome to return. ACORN, which has long had a significant presence (and its national headquarters) in New Orleans, created a Katrina Survivors Association to advocate for more effective relief efforts and provide a voice for the displaced in the reconstruction decision process.[29] Among its demands were rights of return for all displaced families and a right to vote in the upcoming New Orleans mayoral and city council elections.[30]

In contrast, other organizations such as the Bureau of Governmental Research (BGR), a nonprofit city policy watchdog group, argued the city simply must make hard decisions about which areas were the most suitable for rebuilding.[31] Given the reality of a smaller city, they argued,

> The City of New Orleans owes its residents a plan laying out exactly which parts of the city can be rebuilt and when. The plan must be based, not on political considerations, but on careful analysis of the physical and demographic realities facing the city. The criteria should be relevant, objective, clearly articulated, and applied in an even-handed manner. The analysis should be supported by hard scientific data, expert projections, realistic predictions of outcomes, sophisticated financial analyses, and comparisons of alternative plans.

BGR argued that Canizaro's proposal to let citizens vote with their feet was "no plan at all." Not so, countered the BNOB planning committee, contending that its intent was to conduct a bottom-up process in which residents would participate in neighborhood planning meetings and collect information on flood risk, sources of funding, reconstruction standards, and the actions and intentions of their neighbors to help them make up their minds about what to do.[32] It might turn out that some neighborhoods would see taking buyouts as the best choice, but this decision would need to come out of discussions between residents rather than from top-down analysis.

By December, some people had indeed started to vote with their feet, or at least hedge their bets. By December 10, 2005, the city had issued 88,000 electrical, mechanical, residential, and commercial permits valued at $164 million.[33] It is not clear, however, to what extent these permits reflected actual reconstruction plans or anticipation of a moratorium on permits for certain areas. In order to obtain a building permit, a home owner must raise his or her house to current FEMA base flood elevation (BFE) requirements if the cost to repair exceeds 50 percent of the cost to rebuild. Given the expectation that FEMA would soon release stricter flood maps and raise the elevation requirements, many owners hurried to have their permits grandfathered at the current BFEs. Moreover, city hall was being extremely cooperative in responding to applicants' appeals to reduce their damage estimate to less than 50 percent, thereby relieving them of the obligation to elevate.[34]

Meanwhile, the reality that the displaced population was disproportionately African-American continued to feed distrust and resentment. Many evacuees were just impatient for actions that could facilitate their return, but some believed the lack of proactive support for their plight was in fact an attempt to transform the racial and political power base of the city and state. One African-American community leader described distrust of the BNOBC in this way: "This is not like your mom or your dad trying to take care of your best interests while you happen not to be there. Folks don't feel that way. They feel like their absence is an opportunity for [other] people to put them out. That's far from trust."[35] In this environment, race was seen as influencing every decision about which areas could rebuild, which areas might receive preferential treatment by policy makers, to how much assistance would extend to renters. This tension made it uncertain whether damaged homes were being demolished for public safety reasons or as the first step to clear out large sections of the city.[36] These fears were manifest in local politics. Cynthia Hedge-Morrell and Cynthia Willard-Lewis, the two city council members with the largest number of displaced constituents, were understandably concerned for their own political futures. To help to quell such fears, city council president Oliver Thomas asked the BNOBC at its October 24 meeting to promise that the Lower Ninth Ward and New Orleans East would officially be included in the rebuilding process. Mayor Nagin seconded the motion, and all supported it except for the chair, Canizaro, who abstained "because he felt it important that we make sure that all of the people in New Orleans East and the Lower [Ninth] Ward have an opportunity to have a safe, secure, environmentally sound, and quality home in a location that would not be susceptible to destruction in future disasters."[37]

By and large, most people in New Orleans were living on the "sliver by the river"—the unflooded areas ranging from the French Quarter to Uptown—and on the West Bank, where the levees held. Even these areas, however, were incompletely populated and had limited retail, medical care, and schools. Regardless of where one lived, uncertainty reigned, and a typical resident was filled with anxieties: Will I get enough money from my insurance company? How can I find a contractor to rebuild my home? How do I replace everything that was lost in the flood? Can I find an affordable place to rent? What do the other people on my block intend to do? When will the schools open, where will they be, and will they be suitable places for my children? Do I still have a job? If not, will I be able to find one? What are my friends and family members planning to do? Is New Orleans going to be a viable place to live again, or is this the time to start fresh somewhere else?

Given all these uncertainties, how does a city develop an overall strategy for recovery? No one knew when residents would return. There was a great need for money to rebuild infrastructure and housing, restart businesses, and strengthen the levees, but specific needs were still unclear. Where would the money come from? Who would decide how to spend it? By what means would the most heavily flooded areas be rebuilt, and would funding providers be willing to finance it? Would reconstruction decisions come from Washington? Baton Rouge? The city council or mayor? High-powered consultants and urban "experts" from far-off cities and universities? Individuals acting on their own? Would lower-income neighborhoods ever be able to repopulate, and would there be sufficient employment for their residents?

MAKING THE CASE FOR FEDERAL FUNDS

The general consensus was that it was important to have a plan as soon as possible in order to make an argument for federal assistance. The BNOBC set the end of the year as a goal. On December 23, Congress appropriated $6.2 billion in community development block grants (CDBG) funds to help Louisiana communities rebuild.[38] The funds were part of a larger aid package dedicated to the entire Gulf Coast region: $2.9 billion was set aside for levee repairs, $1.6 billion to help repair damaged schools, $11.5 billion in CDBG funding for the region, $2.75 billion to repair roads and bridges, $1.7 billion for Gulf Coast shipbuilders, $618 million to help farmers and ranchers, $441 million for Small Business Administration (SBA) disaster loans, $350 million to repair NASA facilities, $135 million to repair damage in national parks, wildlife refuges, and forests, and $30 million to repair waterways or watersheds.[39] President Bush signed this into law on December 30, 2005.

It was clear to state and local politicians that Louisiana's $6.2 billion share of the CDBG funding was far from enough to permanently rebuild communities. The state knew that it and the City of New Orleans would need to provide additional evidence to make the case for more funding. Exactly how to accomplish this was unclear, and there were competing proposals for how to receive and spend both the $6.2 billion and any additional funds. The LRA was established as a mechanism for receiving the federal funds, but it was not yet clear to what extent the LRA or New Orleans would control the money.

The amount, source, and application of rebuilding funding were not the only questions. The way these funds would be distributed was also being hotly debated in the political arena, in the newspaper, and on talk radio. One of the leading proposals was the so-called Baker bill, legislation first introduced on October 20 by Representative Richard Baker (R-Baton Rouge) that would create the Louisiana Recovery Corporation (LRC) to fund rebuilding through the sale of federal bonds over 10 years.[40] It seemed clear at the time that tens of thousands of home owners who were unable to return to or fix their homes quickly and affordably would soon face foreclosure as lenders' standard 90-day grace periods for mortgage payments ran out.[41] This would not be a happy result for either home owners or the banks, which would find themselves the owners of thousands of flood-damaged properties. Baker proposed that owners facing foreclosure could instead choose to sell to the LRC, which would give them approximately 60 percent of their equity.[42] The banks would receive something like 40 percent of the unpaid mortgage value. The LRC would then offer bundles of properties to developers, though the original home owners would have right of first refusal to buy back into the developments. The proposal was strongly supported by Mayor Nagin, Governor Blanco, and the Louisiana congressional delegation. It was also viewed favorably by mortgage and banking industries. Congress held a hearing on the bill on November 17, it was reported out of committee on December 15, and Senator Landrieu introduced a Senate version on December 21. Thus, by the end of the year, there was every reason to believe that legislation to create the LRC could soon be enacted into law.

In New Orleans, ULI and BNOB had a different idea: instead of giving the LRA or any other state agency control of the funding, create a more local entity controlled by people appointed by the president, governor, mayor, and city council. ULI called this concept the Crescent City Rebuilding Corporation (CCRC) and envisioned it as a vehicle for receiving public and private funds and applying them to a variety of redevelopment projects. The CCRC would also compensate those who had "unusable" properties. However, ULI was unclear about exactly what the CCRC would do aside from being a means to accomplish whatever goals eventually emerged from the planning process. And its proposal didn't recognize the role the LRA had already staked out as the conduit for federal funds, although there is no reason why the LRA could not have directly passed those funds to the CCRC. The proposal also overlooked the existence of the New Orleans Redevelopment Authority (NORA). NORA was created by the Louisiana state legislature in 1968 to obtain and dispose of blighted properties for "community improvement projects." It already had most of the elements ULI called for, but it was controlled only by the mayor and the state legislature.

It was expected that one of these organizations, or something similar, would supply the means for property owners to demonstrate which neighborhoods were most viable for limited public investment (even though the city council continued to dispute that any prioritizing was needed at all).

The gorillas in the room were the FEMA BFE requirements as well as future private insurance and national flood insurance program rates. FEMA was expected to produce new flood maps and new elevation requirements soon. If the new elevation requirements were substantially higher, they could effectively define where it was infeasible to rebuild. These new requirements and increases in insurance rates could be deal breakers. The most flood-prone areas would be shunned by public and private investment alike and become the most likely targets for buyouts. The various parties proposing recovery actions for New Orleans, such as ULI and Representative Baker, assumed these pressures would convince most property owners in low-lying areas to sell and move.

Curiously, no one seemed to appreciate the contradictions inherent in the proposals by Baker, ULI, and BNOB. They were designed to relieve property owners of the most flood-prone tracts and encourage investments in a city that would be smaller than before. But what would happen to the bad properties? "Redevelopment" implies turning properties into something profitable. But, given a smaller city, all the least-desirable properties would end up permanently in the hands of the redevelopment corporation. Presumably, these would become permanent open space. But who would pay for them? Who would manage them? And what if the properties turned out to be scattered and impossible to consolidate?

Finally, it is worth noting that none of these proposals addressed the rental properties that had housed 34 percent of the city's households, according to the 2000 census. It was assumed CDBG funds, SBA loans, insurance funds, or other private resources would be available for the reconstruction of rental properties. As a result, how rental units would be permanently recovered was not a large part of the public policy discussion. However, by the end of 2005, many renters who came back to the city were met with inflated rents. Even worse, many were coming back to their rented homes only to discover they had been evicted.[43] In many of these cases, the landlords did not have financial means to repair or rebuild and thus had little choice but to evict their tenants.

PUBLIC UNVEILING OF THE BNOB PLANNING STRATEGY

Such was the situation on January 11, 2006, when the BNOBC urban planning committee revealed its strategy for the city's long-term reconstruction and recovery. The strategy, developed by WRT, proposed a citywide framework with four elements: flood and stormwater protection, transit and transportation, parks and open space, and neighborhood rebuilding.[44] It asked for multiple lines of defense against flooding, which included regional coastal wetland restoration. It proposed a light-rail network to connect the city with the airport, Baton Rouge, and other activity centers. It's worth noting that the first phase of this proposed network would have extended to New Orleans East and serve the Lower Ninth Ward. The proposal called for parks in every neighborhood, and it recognized the large regional parks did not serve all parts of the city. The plan also proposed creating multi-functional open spaces, including "neutral ground" (the local term for road-way median strips), covered canals, and stormwater protection areas (see fig. 3.4). A map identified "a number of areas, shown by dashed circles, within which there is potential for future parkland. The circles are large to indicate that we have not identified properties; those will be determined with citizen involvement in a process described later." The proposal called for a "neighborhood center model," in which neighborhoods would contain activity centers supported by public investments. The committee presented this element's underlying principle as follows: "Because the Committee wants everyone to return and new people to come, we have to support and create great neighborhoods."[45]

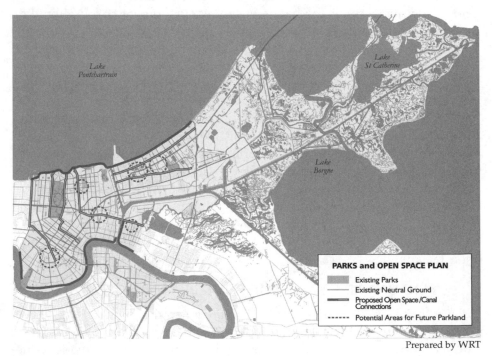

Prepared by WRT

Fig. 3.4. WRT's map of parks and open spaces

The plan also recognized the reality of New Orleans in January 2006. Although the plan determined that temporary housing was the highest priority for the city in the short term, it also needed to begin establishing "neighborhood-planning teams to complete plans for the neighborhoods by May 20, 2006" in order to build the city in the long term. It acknowledged those teams would face difficult decisions:

> We must face the fact that there may have to be some consolidation of neighborhoods that have insufficient population to support the equitable and efficient delivery of services. In the short-term, there will be half the population of July 2005. We have no choice but to be responsible with use of limited City resources. We must provide public facilities and services where population is concentrated so these resources can be used in the most equitable and efficient manner possible.[46]

Consistent with the ULI plan, the BNOB strategy laid out three approaches to neighborhood planning based on the physical needs of the neighborhoods and their placement into one of three categories: immediate opportunity areas, neighborhood planning areas, and infill development areas. The "neighborhood planning areas" were the most heavily flooded areas and posed the greatest challenges:

> The difference in these areas is that individual decision making will be more difficult because of the severity of damage and the effect of rules imposed from outside the city. When released, the revised Base Flood Elevation maps will likely have a significant effect on many residents' decisions. Because these maps are not now available, it would be irresponsible to guess their effect. The planning with these areas will be especially intense and expeditious.[47]

The BNOB planning committee stressed that neighborhood planning would occur throughout the city based on the City Planning Commission's 13 planning districts. However, because of differences in damage,

> some planning districts will require more in-depth attention than others, with the most heavily damaged requiring additional effort. It is the intent of the neighborhood planning process to level the playing field for recovery, regardless of the internal resources in any neighborhood. In fact, many neighborhoods had pre-Katrina plans that can serve as the basis for this effort. Some have already initiated post-Katrina efforts that, likewise, can facilitate completion of the neighborhood planning work.

The committee articulated its vision of neighborhood planning with specificity:

Neighborhood Planning will be conducted by teams which will be assigned to every planning district and charged to begin work by February 20, 2006. The team members will include neighborhood residents, plus experienced professionals (planner, urban designer, historic preservation expert, City Planning Commission representative, environmental/public health consultant, mitigation planner, housing and finance expert, hydrologist, civil engineer, administrative/technology support). It is very important that each have community outreach support to work with displaced residents as well as those who have already been able to return. Clearly, the greatest challenge will be to contact and involve residents who have not yet returned. The team will use a variety of techniques to accomplish this which may include remote meetings and work sessions, virtual internet neighborhoods, and others. The importance of outreach and follow-through cannot be overemphasized.[48]

The BNOB report described the brief four-month schedule as ambitious but necessary. It also anticipated the release of the FEMA flood maps early in the process and considered them critical pieces of information for each neighborhood.[49]

The third category, "infill development areas," consisted of a variety of areas that had immediate development potential because they contained preexisting blighted or tax-adjudicated properties, underutilized land, publicly owned land, or areas of heavy damage that would likely require demolitions. These areas could be developed into housing, commercial, or industrial space depending on the results of the neighborhood plans.

Finally, the BNOB planning committee recommended a citywide coordination plan that would be "the glue that holds the neighborhood planning efforts together and leads to a draft Master Plan recommendation to the City Planning Commission."[50] They recommended this effort begin immediately so the citywide coordinators could create standards and gather information to help the neighborhoods meet the tight planning deadline.

To help implement the completed master plan, they recommended creating the New Orleans Recovery Corporation (NORC), which could be a subsidiary of the Baker bill's federal corporation, a modified version of the NORA, or a new state-created entity. NORC would receive and dispose of funds and property, and it would coordinate with both the city council and the City Planning Commission to enhance the city's planning capacity and ensure its work was consistent with a new master plan. The only unresolved issue was its source of funds. Possible funders included FEMA, CDBG funding, and "other governmental sources." To facilitate housing reconstruction if the Baker bill fell through, the BNOB planning committee recommended using CDBG funds for gap financing, streamlining home improvement loans, extending mortgage forbearances, and issuing tax credits for new apartment developments. To help placate citizens concerned about buyouts, they proposed paying for the full value of homes up to $150,000, presumably by using CDBG funds in combination with the less-generous Baker bill.[51] The BNOB plan estimated meeting the immediate needs of New Orleanians and completing the activities leading up to the master plan would cost around $6.1 billion in addition to money expected from the Baker bill. It said long-term projects, such as the light-rail system, would eventually cost $3.8 billion more. Contacts with Gulf Coast recovery coordinator Donald Powell and Canizaro's access to the White House made committee members optimistic that the funds might flow into New Orleans now that the city's needs had been documented.[52] The plan would need to be approved first by the LRA and then forwarded to Washington.

The most obvious land mine hiding in the proposal was the recommendation that

> the City not issue any permits to build or rebuild in heavily flooded and damaged areas until the advisory Base Flood Elevations maps have been issued by FEMA, until the neighborhood planning teams have completed their plans and made their coordinated recommendations in a [citywide] plan to the city, and until adequately delivered utilities and city services are available.[53]

Thus, the plan proposed a moratorium on building permits for at least four months. Rather than formalize the "voting with their feet" proposals floated by the committee in the preceding weeks, the proposal said neighborhood viability would be determined primarily by a neighborhood planning process and by property owners' individual decisions. Committee members had balked at the laissez-faire approach because they thought it unfair to enable some individuals to rebuild their homes only to later find out their neighborhood would not be a priority rebuilding area.[54]

The proposal was unveiled to the public in a large, packed ballroom at the Sheraton hotel in downtown New Orleans on January 11. But the verdict was in even before the committee spoke a word. Just before the presentation, the city council held a press conference in another room in the same hotel to denounce BNOB's proposal. The council had been pushing its own neighborhood planning process, which reflected the estrangement between the city council and the mayor. The ballroom and adjacent hall were filled with approximately 1,200 citizens and many angry representatives from neighborhood groups and organizations such as ACORN and the NAACP.

Opponents of the BNOB proposal saw it as business as usual in New Orleans: an unrepresentative group, dominated by white elites, led by a prominent developer with close ties to the Bush White House, were saying low-income African-American neighborhoods should be sold to a redevelopment corporation. Wade Rathke, chief organizer of ACORN, said,

> The arrogance of the ULI's [*sic*] recommendations is breathtaking. People like Canizaro, the ULI and the commission itself are unelected and unaccountable. They rejected the idea that home owners and citizens should have a voice and instead wanted decisions to be made in bulk at the community level, rather than individually. . . . The "whitewashers" and ULI promoters have argued with the support of the *New Orleans Times-Picayune*, for bad medicine to be swallowed and neighborhoods written off, particularly in the hardest hit lower-income areas where ACORN members have lived forever. . . . We realize that without resources or leadership or any kind of plan that gives the majority of residents input and the means to move forward, the developers' bulldozers will win. Our members and hundreds of thousands of people like them will be stuck in the New Orleans Diaspora, homeless and unable to return.[55]

Opponents also objected to the notion that some places would be favored over others and that the government might not support the right of some residents to rebuild. Mtangulizi Sanyika of the African American Leadership Project alleged the mayor was deferring to moneyed interests and said that basing public investments on neighborhood viability amounted to "Katrina cleansing—the removal of Blacks from the city."[56]

The large crowd at the Sheraton didn't condemn all aspects of the plan. They generally welcomed the idea of the four-month, citizen-based planning process but not the accompanying moratorium.[57] Some groups such as ACORN even said the planning process needed to be longer. After the meeting, the mayor again recommended residents wait before rebuilding in the most devastated areas, but he said he was not inclined to support the moratorium.[58] Nagin also emphasized the preliminary nature of the recommendations, warned that hard decisions lay ahead, and implied people needed to listen more carefully to the facts being presented: "The realities are that we will have limited resources to redevelop our city. . . . The other reality is this report is controversial. It pushes the edge of the envelope. It probably says some things to some people they are probably misinterpreting."[59] Canizaro agreed that decisions about where the city should spend its resources were not his to make, but he reiterated his argument for the moratorium: it was intended to save home owners from rebuilding too quickly in areas that might turn out to be too weak to warrant substantial public investments.[60]

Presenters tried to stress that this was the beginning of a planning process, not its conclusion. During the introduction, Nagin reminded the crowd that the commission's proposals were just that, and no firm decisions had been made yet. John Beckman, the lead for WRT, asked the audience to dream of a great city with parks and transportation for all. He said the vision statement in the plan summed it up: "New Orleans will be a sustainable, environmentally safe, socially equitable community with a vibrant economy. Its neighborhoods will be planned with its citizens and connect to jobs and the region. Each will preserve and celebrate its heritage of culture, landscape, and architecture."[61] He also reminded them of President Bush's September 15 promise that the federal government would "do what it takes" to rebuild New Orleans and that Bush was scheduled to visit New Orleans the very next day. Beckman implied that this was the city's chance to make its case for the billions of dollars it needed to rebuild.[62]

But despite some of the positive aspects of the meeting, there is no doubt that on January 11 the BNOB process began to spin out of control. The mayor's weak statements of support did little to save it. The BNOB process was kept alive by continued promises of neighborhood planning, but it was certainly dealt a serious blow at what was supposed to be its grand unveiling. Canizaro, who was a conservative white developer, was a problematic messenger, however noble his intentions may have been. New Orleans resident Harvey Bender expressed a common sentiment toward the BNOB chair when he said, "Mr. Joe Canizaro, I don't know you, but I hate you. You've been in the background trying to scheme to get our land."[63] Furthermore, Jimmy Reiss—who had been quoted in September as saying the diaspora created an opportunity to build a city with fewer poor people—was the chair of the BNOBC's infrastructure committee. His presence did little to engender trust of the African-American community.

Nor did the press promote a nuanced understanding of BNOB's proposal. For example, the *Times-Picayune* printed a simplified graphic of WRT's land-use map in its morning edition that was no doubt in the hands of everyone at the Sheraton (see fig. 3.5). In the paper, the plan's open, dashed-line circles showing "potential areas for future parkland" became large, solid green dots showing "approximate areas of [sic] expected to become parks and greenspace." Although we certainly appreciate that nonplanners may not understand the tentative meaning of dashed-line circles, the solid green dots are not at all subtle. They suggest the BNOBC had targeted those entire areas for open space. Indeed, they are so memorable that residents and officials still speak of the infamous "green dot map." Furthermore, it is notable that out of all the low-lying and heavily flooded parts of the city, only Lakeview—a mainly white, upscale area—did not have a green circle. The proposal explained that the circles represented damaged areas that did not have enough access to parks and open space. Lakeview does not have a shortage of parks. But this conspicuous omission from the map was interpreted as another sign that flooded areas in only the African-American

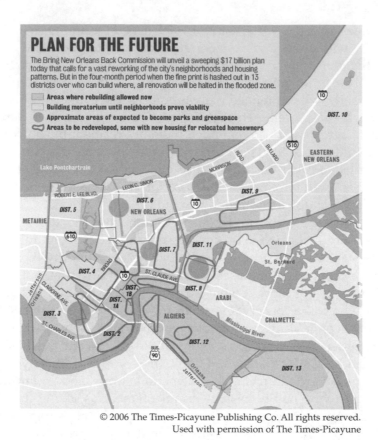

Fig. 3.5. The New Orleans Times-Picayune's *infamous "green dot" map*

neighborhoods would be bulldozed and transformed into permanent open space.

Based on the accounts of people who were at the meeting as well as numerous news articles, it is clear that the room was full of residents who were stressed from having to bear more than four months of the worst kind of uncertainty. They were anxious about their futures and narrowly focused on questions related to rebuilding their homes and their lives. They were interested in their homes first; any larger, more abstract issues could wait. Many people were suspicious of government and familiar with a history of planning in New Orleans that was almost always insensitive to lower-income African-American residents. They thought these outside experts' shining planning visions foretold future bulldozers and profiteers. Permanent open space was to them a code for more parks for the wealthy. The wealthier members of the audience were also impatient with their current situation, the government, and the pace of planning. They, too, simply wanted to know how and when they could start rebuilding. No one was receptive to discussions about a shrinking city or limited resources. Planners understood full well that New Orleans had been shrinking for 40 years and would not quickly build back to the size it was in the 1960s, but residents were still angry over levee breaches and a bungled federal response. They expected the city to be made whole. Moreover, most residents resented the notion of having to pass some "test" of viability before being allowed to rebuild their homes. Given this, the idea of having a dispassionate conversation about tough decisions and limited resources was simply off the table.

The tone here had been set by the White House and Congress: they would not promise any funds to New Orleans until they were satisfied the money would be spent wisely. This required a plan, a promise to reform city governance, and proof that New Orleans would rebuild sensibly, cost-effectively, and rationally. This message, however, was not introduced in a way or into a context conducive to promoting these admirable goals. Unlike planners and the LRA, the audience was not ready to discuss the "balance between . . . self-determination and tough choices."[64] To many, the proposal made planning look like a punishment rather than empowerment.

The leaders of the BNOB planning committee were only partially to blame. It is likely that Canizaro perceived he needed to deliver a plan to the White House as soon as possible in order to receive the money. He was probably trying to time the unveiling of his plan with President Bush's January 12 visit to New Orleans, which was the president's first visit in three months. As a result, the proposal may have been presented before it was ready for a full public viewing. But Canizaro may have also believed that the proposal met the White House's requirements.

Even so, it might have been possible to deliver the message in a more clear and sophisticated way that brought the public into the decision process rather than left them feeling like they were outsiders. Clearly, the Sheraton meeting was a communications disaster. The presenters summarized the solution before having fully sold the crowd on the problem. Furthermore, the mayor was ineffective in communicating to the public the difficult problems and decisions facing the city. He could have related the proposal to the personal struggles of the city's residents. He could have more forcefully clarified that this was only the beginning of the planning process rather than an endpoint. He could have announced that the city was going to provide technical support for the process. And he could have enthusiastically invited everyone to participate in the neighborhood discussions that were going to be the crucibles of the plan. He did none of these things and instead remained indecisive about the moratorium and about what would happen next.

In the end, if Canizaro's intended audience was the president, his tactics didn't work. The rushed spectacle of January 11 did little to improve New Orleans's standing in the eyes of the White House. Donald Powell, speaking for the president on Air Force One on January 12, distanced the White House from New Orleans by saying, "We're not going to weigh in. It will be their plan."[65] Bush also expressed reservations that day about the Baker bill.[66] WRT's John Beckman says the city was let down by the White House and the president's empty promise in Jackson Square in September. But Beckman also says he felt let down by Nagin, whom he describes as a client who never really knew what to do with the product he received. The jobs of ULI and WRT were to introduce factual planning information, alternative concepts, and cost estimates into a politicized environment, but there was no political leadership provided by the client.

MOVING FORWARD: ORGANIZING
FOR NEIGHBORHOOD PLANNING

Even so, all was not lost. Despite the conflict at the Sheraton, the BNOB proposal was still on the table. On January 13, Beckman and Nagin presented the plan at the LRA's monthly board meeting in Baton Rouge, a meeting that Donald Powell and Representative Baker also attended. The LRA enthusiastically supported the plan, and chairman Norman Francis approved of BNOB's decision to refrain from encouraging people to move back to the most vulnerable areas. He said, "I would not want somebody to put me in harm's way."[67] On the other hand, city council member Cynthia Willard-Lewis expressed concerns about the moratorium and repeated her plea for rebuilding the entire city. Nagin emphasized the city was still issuing building permits and stated he was "pretty uncomfortable" with the moratorium, although he otherwise supported the plan as "the way we are going to go."[68] (One week later, Nagin confirmed that he was opposed to a moratorium.)[69] Governor Blanco diplomatically said the details of the plan, such as the moratorium issue, were best decided in New Orleans. Baker was buoyed by Powell's statement that the administration "share[d] common goals" with Louisiana regarding the Baker bill. Baker asked the LRA to wait on allocating the $6.2 billion in CDBG funds approved by Congress in December; if his bill could provide the housing reconstruction and buyout funds, then the CDBG money could be spent in other ways.[70]

Thus, the stage was set. The reconstruction funding process was well on its way. It seemed likely that some modified version of Baker's proposal could be signed by the president to augment the CDBG funds. Despite the inauspicious start, many now believed the planning process would shift to the neighborhoods, and the result would be a consensus on how to spend the recovery funds.

Joe Canizaro tried to move the process forward by naming the two leaders of the neighborhood planning process. He appointed prominent New Orleans architect Ray Manning and the dean of Tulane University's School of Architecture, Reed Kroloff.[71] They worked out a design process based on a work scope and schedule prepared by WRT. Neighborhood meetings would begin on February 20; planning teams would identify residents who were committed to return by March 20; by April 20, they would finalize the mechanics of residential buyouts; and by May 20, the neighborhood planning teams would complete the plans and the buyouts would begin.[72] Kroloff and Manning began to assemble 12 teams of architects and planners (for the 13 planning districts in New Orleans) and another team to develop citywide principles to guide all of the neighborhood planners. Kroloff and Manning would direct the entire process. They estimated the planning process would cost six to eight million dollars based on New Orleans city government hourly rates and a 10 to 15 percent margin to cover any unanticipated costs.[73]

In a January 22 interview with the *Times-Picayune*, Kroloff and Manning said the planning process was an opportunity to make the city better than before and emphasized that they were relying on the neighborhoods to provide the ideas.[74] They estimated that they would have the planning teams assembled and ready to go in approximately one month. The *Times-Picayune* reported "the cost will run to several million dollars, money they've been assured will be available from private, philanthropic and government sources." Every planning district in New Orleans was going to prepare a plan whether it was flooded or not. The explicit goal of the process was to "roll up" the neighborhood plans into a citywide plan that would then become part of the LRA's statewide plan. This LRA plan would guide decisions about the disbursement of "billions of dollars in federal aid to the communities affected by Hurricanes Katrina and Rita."[75] Presumably, the citywide plan would be the equivalent of the FEMA ESF #14 and Louisiana Speaks plans for Orleans Parish.

Although the details were not yet clear, it was apparent that the BNOB process was meant to align with funding from the Baker bill, which would be in front of Congress in February. It also would rely on some of the CDBG funds. Furthermore, it was assumed that the new FEMA BFE maps would be released early in the process, probably in March. The neighborhood conversations would help residents develop a sense of who intended to stay, who planned to take the buyout money and leave, and who planned to move to other parts of the city. A key challenge would be how to bring the displaced residents into these conversations. Some options included electronic communications and holding some meetings in cities with large numbers of displaced New Orleanians. Other challenges included how and when to determine whether a neighborhood had a viable number of returnees, as well as what exactly constituted a "neighborhood."

One important quality of the process was that locals were in charge of it. It was clear that most citizens did not understand how the planning process was supposed to work, and they feared outside professionals would make important decisions about their lives. In some sense, Kroloff was such an outsider. He was a nationally prominent architecture intellectual and former editor of *Architecture* magazine who had lived in New Orleans for only a year. Still, he emphasized, "If we don't do the planning here, designed by our own local architects, planners and designers, someone else will do it for us."[76]

The city's mid-January vision of the planning process presented an attractive, rational, citizen-driven model for the rebuilding of New Orleans. The BNOB planners, despite some public resistance, were convinced they had the right formula. FEMA would fund the neighborhood planning process, and the new FEMA flood maps would inform those discussions. Individuals in low-lying areas would begin to appreciate the wisdom of relocating. Those with properties worth $150,000 or less would be compensated in full if they decided to move. The CDBG funds, the Baker bill, and private insurance would make such voluntary relocations possible and save the New Orleans housing market from collapse.

Unfortunately, the entire edifice came crashing down in spectacular fashion during the ensuing month.

THE FEDERAL FUNDING BATTLE, ACT 2

In late January 2006, Louisiana officials were stunned by the White House's sudden and fierce rejection of the Baker bill. The first hint came on January 18 while LRA vice chair Walter Isaacson was having lunch in the West Wing with Al Hubbard, President Bush's economic advisor.[77] Karl Rove joined them for a while and made it clear the administration was dead set against setting up a federal corporation. The best Louisiana could expect would be something similar to the home owner compensation program announced in Mississippi earlier that month that would pay uninsured home owners outside of federally designated floodplains up to $150,000.[78] On January 24, the administration made it official that it would give the State of Louisiana nothing more than the $6.2 billion in CDBG funding it had set aside on December 30, 2005.[79] Donald Powell emphasized that the funds should assist only home owners who sustained flood damage outside of federally recognized floodplains and did not carry flood insurance. His estimate of the number of those owners was far smaller than Louisiana's figures.

Louisiana officials, from the governor on down, insisted $6.2 billion was not enough to cover home owners, much less renters and businesses, all of whom had suffered as a result of the failure of federal levees.[80] They argued that their situation was far worse than Mississippi's and that most of the damage to New Orleans occurred because federal levees failed to perform as designed. Finally, they argued that the federal government's policy would just start the cycle of disaster again: without a buyout option for insured home owners, they would likely rebuild in the same flood-prone locations.

Despite the official statement, both Canizaro and Baker remained optimistic that Congress would pass some form of the Baker bill.[81] Without additional funding, the entire planning concept for New Orleans would be in jeopardy. Meanwhile, the LRA began to explore how it would implement an underfunded housing program and began to make tough decisions that would fall short of making any home owner close to whole. Powell had said there could be additional money later on, but only after the $6.2 billion was allocated and reconstruction plans were more clear: "After that plan is in place, and there is need for more money . . . I can assure you we will go back after that's done and work hand in hand with the leadership of Louisiana to ask for more money."[82] And yet Mayor Nagin had just returned from Washington, where he had stressed that New Orleans had a plan that estimated recovery costs of $10 to $15 billion.[83] White House officials had told him that the costs were too high.

Thus, multiple discussions began about how to obtain sufficient funds to meet Louisiana's housing needs. The Bush administration maintained that it had already provided $85 billion for recovery in the Gulf Coast, including $24.5 billion for housing in Louisiana. However, these claims were a bit disingenuous because the housing money included the federal government's NFIP payouts and the costs of temporary postdisaster housing. In fact, the only discretionary money that Louisiana could use for permanent housing rebuilding was the $6.2 billion in CBDG funds.

The LRA decided to move forward anyway. On January 27, 2006, Donald Powell and LRA board member Sean Reilly met in Powell's hometown of Amarillo, Texas, to discuss how the CDBG funds would be used.[84] In an informal local restaurant, they delineated a plan on a paper tablecloth. Home owners would be paid the full pre-Katrina value of their property up to $150,000, less any insurance payouts they had received. Long-distance negotiations continued for the next several days. Governor Blanco met with Powell personally on February 1 while she was in Washington for President Bush's January 31 State of the Union address.

The State of the Union address provided more insight into the White House's thinking about post-Katrina funding. It was seen as an opportunity for the president to repair some of the political damage from the embarrassing federal response in the days after the storm. Many observers expected a bold statement regarding the government's commitment to rebuilding. Instead, Bush never mentioned the word "Katrina," and his most substantive statement reiterated that the government had already pledged $85 billion to the region.[85]

Powell then chose to put an exclamation point on the administration's position in case there was any doubt about the viability of the Baker bill. In a February 2 editorial in the *Washington Post*, he explicitly put the Baker bill to rest. He argued that local control of recovery dollars would be circumvented by Baker's proposed federal corporation.[86] Powell said such a corporation would lack congressional accountability, would be difficult to create and manage from an administrative standpoint, and would overwhelm the private real estate market. He also restated that planning was a precondition of receiving funds and that

> the LRC is not a long-term plan. As with any complex problem, the state must identify and prioritize its needs. The plans should include some key elements, among them: decisions on where, and where not, to rebuild; the creation of codes so that buildings can withstand future disasters; an examination of zoning issues; a rebuilding timeline; and a setting of priorities for housing and infrastructure needs.

This unexpected and conspicuous statement by Powell shocked Louisiana officials. Some wondered whether to expect any additional aid at all. In a meeting with Powell two days later, the governor declared she was going to start playing "hardball."[87] A few days later in a forceful speech kicking off the special session of the state legislature, she elaborated on this threat: the state would delay the planned August sale of federal offshore oil and gas leases unless the state was given its "fair share" of the royalties.[88]

State and federal officials eventually agreed on a program that was similar to the one that was proposed in Mississippi, so long as it also included homes located in mapped floodplains. The idea was to provide all damaged home owners with up to $150,000 (less insurance settlements) to help them rebuild, relocate, or sell to some yet-unnamed entity. WRT had already proposed this in its BNOB plan, and Reilly and Powell had apparently discussed the concept as well. In addition, several Louisiana officials talked about the idea at the White House on February 12, and the elected leaders of the five hardest-hit metropolitan parishes all threw their support behind such a plan.[89] The parish leaders were clear that they wanted to assist home owners first because they were the most critical investors who could stabilize neighborhoods. Additional requests for renters, businesses, and infrastructure would come later.

Mississippi had announced its program in early January, just days after the president signed the supplemental emergency funding bill that provided $5.5 million in CDBG funds to the state.[90] It promised up to $150,000 to home owners who lived outside of the federally designated flood hazard zones but were nevertheless swamped by unusually high floodwaters. The purpose was to assist unfortunate home owners who had been struck by an unexpected and catastrophic event and did not have, or were not required to have, federally backed flood insurance. Those households located within mapped floodplains should have taken out federally backed flood insurance; those that chose not to buy the policies were not entitled to federal funds because such a bailout would undermine the basic purpose of the NFIP. The origins of the $150,000 limit are unclear, though there seemed to be a broad consensus that it was enough to help low- and middle-income home owners but not enough to help people rebuild more upscale homes. The cap would help the money go further, to help cover as many people as possible.

Louisiana officials were uncomfortable about the ease with which Mississippi seemed to get its federal recovery funds. This discomfort continued to grow over the next two years. It was clear that Mississippi's line of communication to Washington was much more direct than Louisiana's. Mississippi governor Haley Barbour was the chairman of the Republican National Committee from 1993 to 1997. The Republicans won back both houses during that time. He was also one of Washington's most powerful lobbyists for two decades before he returned to Mississippi in 2003. Senator Thad Cochran (R-Miss.) was chairman of the powerful Senate Appropriations Committee at the time. Both Barbour and Cochran were well situated to argue effectively for Mississippi's post-Katrina needs. Louisiana officials were livid when they saw that Mississippi received 44 percent of the CDBG funds whereas Louisiana sustained well over 75 percent of the damage from Katrina.[91] And they resented that New Orleans was told it needed to have a plan in order to justify additional money while Mississippi's plan for spending its funds had been announced and accepted by the White House within days of the congressional appropriation.

Beleaguered Louisiana officials really only had one viable option left at this point: imitate Mississippi's plan. The state would manage the funds and payments would go directly to victims. But this plan didn't erase the fact that the CDBG funds wouldn't be enough to help home owners rebuild. Private and federally back flood insurance only went so far, and the state estimated that it would need about $10 billion to fill the gap and provide some type of assistance for affordable housing.[92] On top of this, they expected a second grant program from FEMA would pay to elevate homes to meet the new BFE requirements once they were updated.

The proposed home owner assistance program shared some similarities with the Baker bill. The idea was that home owners would go through the neighborhood planning process, get the new FEMA BFE requirements, find out what their neighbors' intentions were, and then decide whether to relocate or rebuild. At the time, most informed observers expected a considerable number of owners—possibly as many as half—to choose to sell out. Many would leave the state, and those who remained would likely relocate to higher areas into strengthened and elevated homes. Above all, it was critical that state obtain a commitment of funds so individuals could begin to make informed decisions and act. In mid-February 2006, Mayor Nagin expressed this urgency when he said, "I want to make sure we're not six months behind Mississippi. And I want to give hope and get the economy going right now . . . [to put] us in position to go back and get the money we need. Because if they're [federal officials] not going to do Baker, they've got to do something."[93]

Once it was clear that Louisiana was moving closer to Mississippi's plan, the White House quickly came around. On February 15, the president announced that he would ask Congress for an additional $4.2 billion to help rebuild homes in Louisiana.[94] Governor Blanco flew to Washington for the announcement and thanked the president. Furthermore, it appeared that the state had made some progress convincing Powell of the unusual nature and broad scope of its needs. State officials had also assured him the state was developing plans for managing its funds responsibly.[95] The LRA promised to develop, within the week, guidelines for how it would spend the CDBG money. They promised to iron out a number of details, such as how to calculate smaller payments for those who did not have private or federally backed flood insurance, how to compensate home owners who decided to leave the state, what the incentives for elevating might be, and so on. Not everyone was delighted with the proposal.[96] Unlike the Baker bill, the CDBG-funded housing repair program would not cover commercial properties. Senator Landrieu identified many other unmet needs, such as public safety, schools, economic development, and infrastructure. And, of course, the funds were not guaranteed but would still need congressional approval and appropriation. Finally, Powell reminded everyone that "the onus is in the hands of the local people. The federal government is ready to disburse the money, subject to a plan."[97] Clearly, a coherent plan would be critical to persuade Congress.

Many issues still remained. Should Louisiana start spending the $6.2 billion now or develop a strategy for spending the entire package whenever it arrived? Should it reimburse everyone for up to $150,000, or should some home owners only receive 60 to 80 percent of the gap left by private and federal insurance? Should insured owners be treated better than uninsured owners? The mayor's expectation was that these issues would be sorted out quickly and the neediest home owners could start receiving checks within a month.[98] But to do so would still require a plan for how to spend the funds that was approved by the state legislature and the U.S Department of Housing and Urban Development, the agency that manages CDBG funds.

Another unresolved issue was whether the state or city would control the funds. The city hoped to get a set allocation from the state to cover buyouts and renovations. Powell had asked only for a "transparent vehicle" at the state level to allocate funds in an equitable and systematic manner.[99] Blanco was emphatic that all hurricane-affected parts of the state needed to be treated by the same rules, and she proposed a state land trust as the vehicle. However, Nagin and Canizaro were hoping for some sort of a city subsidiary to this state organization but did not make it clear how such a mechanism would operate. How could the whole state be treated equally if there were a separate organization for New Orleans?

WHITHER THE NEIGHBORHOOD PLANNING INITIATIVE?

The news that the state was partially victorious in prying funds away from the federal government overshadowed the fact that on February 20—the start date for neighborhood planning in New Orleans—nothing happened. Neighborhood planning was a critical part of the BNOB planning process, but only hints of its progress appeared in the pages of the *Times-Picayune*. On February 26, the newspaper reported the BNOBC was still negotiating with FEMA over the expected cost of the planning effort.[100] Two days later it reported that the mayor's office said the final meeting of the BNOBC would be on March 8. It would be followed shortly thereafter by the publication of the final report and initiation of the neighborhood planning process.[101]

March 8 came and went without any final BNOBC announcement. However, on March 13, the bombshell appeared in the second half of a *Times-Picayune* article about how some neighborhoods had begun to plan on their own. It said that the BNOB planning effort had run "into money problems after FEMA denied a request for millions of dollars to pay for technical assistance."[102] This simple statement confirmed what had become increasingly obvious: Nearly two months after the ambitious neighborhood planning effort had been announced, there were no funds for it, and it was not going to happen.

How did something that had seemed so certain in mid-January reach this dead end? Ray Manning claims that high-ranking, experienced FEMA personnel led by ESF #14 leader Brad Gair told them in January that FEMA could provide somewhere between six and nine million dollars.[103] Beckman and several other New Orleanians were at that meeting with FEMA and HUD, and they claim they heard the same thing. We have seen no written records of the FEMA meetings, and Gair declined to be interviewed for this book. Some say it was all a misunderstanding: Gair had said, "Tell us what you need, so we can see what we can do," but representatives from

New Orleans heard, "We will give you whatever you ask." Apparently, all of the participating FEMA and HUD officials were rotated out to different posts shortly after this meeting. The new officials who arrived in their place claimed they knew nothing about a promise to fund the planning effort. Furthermore, they claimed that even if there was one, FEMA was simply not permitted under the 1988 Stafford Act (the key piece of legislation authorizing federal funding for disaster relief and recovery) to provide such funds for local municipal planning. The answer was "no" because it had always been "no." End of story.

But this administrative explanation is unsatisfying. Surely a matter of such significance wouldn't simply fail because of bureaucratic fine print. Surely a livid Canizaro would have been on the phone to the White House to demand an explanation. Surely it would have taken someone high up in the federal chain of command to say to him, "No, we are not going to help you to prepare the plan that you need, the plan that we are demanding as a condition of providing reconstruction funding." And surely there would have been more than a bureaucratic reason for saying so.

No one we have spoken to in Louisiana, including those directly involved in the negotiations with FEMA, fully understands how and why this apparent reversal occurred. But almost everyone has a theory.[104] One theory is that FEMA was simply applying standard practices that were inappropriate for the nature and scale of Louisiana's problems. We heard numerous complaints that FEMA's policy of frequently rotating staff created a highly problematic administrative environment. It exacerbated the inherently chaotic nature of postdisaster decision making and created a system with no institutional memory.

A variant of this theory suggests FEMA was simply too rigid and would not admit this situation warranted any new thinking, creativity, or reinterpretation of the rules. Proponents of this theory suggest the buck stopped at Michael Jackson, the deputy director of the Department of Homeland Security, who insisted that everyone in FEMA follow the regulations as he saw them and left no room for independent decisions at the local level.

A more cynical view is that if the bureaucracy had not killed it, the Bush administration surely would have as an intentional statement of policy. FEMA had been a bit schizophrenic about the entire ESF #14 effort. Long-term community recovery planning was not a task in the comfort zone of most longtime FEMA employees. Even today, many of its staffers continue to see FEMA mainly as a disaster response organization. FEMA was funding outside planning consultants in many of the parishes, but this was considered unusual. Although some within FEMA touted the value of this new community-building function, others ensured that it wasn't really comprehensive or long term at all. There was pressure within FEMA to pull the plug on the ESF #14 process even before it was completed. Given this, it is easy to believe that FEMA, Powell, and the White House were uncomfortable setting a precedent by involving FEMA too deeply in community planning. To do it correctly would require them to set standards, review plans, spend money, and likely become embroiled in local politics. Furthermore, funding New Orleans planning to the tune of $7 million or more would raise the ante and immediately increase the profile of what had been, to date, a relatively simple technical assistance program for the parishes. This view suggests Gair overstepped his authority, and Washington took the New Orleans request as a signal that it should instead move in the opposite direction by stopping all support for long-term planning everywhere. This may be why FEMA began winding down ESF #14 in mid-February 2006.

Another cynical, political view is that the White House did not want any federal funding from FEMA or HUD to become entangled in plans that might emanate from New Orleans. After the infamous January 11 BNOB meeting at the Sheraton, the White House may not have wanted to court any further controversy from a politically charged plan that could be linked to federal funding.

To some, the White House was simply dealing with New Orleans in bad faith. In September, President Bush stood in Jackson Square and promised to "do what it takes" to rebuild. But six months after the disaster, the White House seemed to be helping only reluctantly. Furthermore, after repeatedly stating that New Orleans needed a plan in order to receive significant federal funds, the administration refused to pay a relatively small but crucial sum that would help the city complete the plan it had begun. Virtually all the planning that had been done to that point by the BNOBC, the LRASF, and some self-organizing neighborhoods had been paid by private sources. This rankled many locals who believed it was time for Washington to step up and help. John Beckman of WRT said the White House's failure to follow through with its promise was one of the biggest disappointments of his professional career and put a heavy brake on recovery and reconstruction.

Others say the State of Louisiana was complicit in undermining New Orleans's plans. There is no doubt there is tension between New Orleans and Baton Rouge because they compete with each other economically and for political power in the state. Some say the state was determined to control the rebuilding process. Direct federal funding of the city's reconstruction might undermine the needs of the rest of the state. A variation of this theory is that Republicans in Baton Rouge with White House connections were happy to see a depopulated New Orleans because it would be good for business in Baton Rouge and would weaken the Democratic Party in Louisiana. It is unlikely that there was an active conspiracy in Baton Rouge, but certainly the age-old rivalry had many opportunities to assert itself.

FINAL CHAPTER IN THE BNOBC PROCESS

On March 20, the mayor released the BNOBC's "general guidelines" for rebuilding New Orleans.[105] Although he rejected the idea of even temporarily forbidding rebuilding in any part of the city, he also warned home owners that low-lying areas would be challenged by high insurance rates, limited federal assistance, and limited city resources:

> What I'm saying is: Look, here's the situations [*sic*] with the levees. Here's where I think it's safe, here's where I think it's still not safe. I don't recommend you going in areas I'm not comfortable with. Now, if you go in those areas, God bless you. We'll try to provide you with support as best we can. But understand we're concentrating city resources in the areas that are in the immediate recovery zone.[106]

Nagin said he still expected that neighborhood plans would somehow be completed by June 30 and that it would be up to residents to decide what parts of their community might become parks and open space. Nagin also stressed that the BNOBC's final recommendations were only "general guidelines." He said he would ask the city council to approve these recommendations and would forward the section on land use to the City Planning Commission. The report also contained a number of recommendations for school system reform and improved governance, many of which were eventually implemented. It also asked for an independent redevelopment entity to receive properties from home owners who had decided to sell rather than rebuild and to seek proposals to develop these properties. This has also come to pass, but under circumstances very different from the ones envisioned in early 2006.

By all accounts, Nagin—a political outsider who was elected to rid city hall of corruption—has been an honest mayor and has the city's well-being at heart. But many have complained that he did not provide decisive and inspiring leadership at a time when his city most needed it. Sally Forman, the mayor's communications director at the time of the storm, later noted some of his limitations such as his political isolation, his unwillingness to seek outside advice, and his excessive dependence on dedicated loyalists within city hall.[107] Furthermore, as the APA team found, Nagin's commitment to planning had been weak before the storm, and his laying off all of the planning staff at the most critical moment in the city's history demonstrated a lack of understanding about the important role city planning has in local government.

The release of the BNOB report helped to further inform public conversation. However, the BNOBC had no funding source, and its activities effectively came to a halt. After several months of operation, it had damaged the public's trust in the planning process and left the city without a parishwide recovery plan to guide the use of the CDBG money. The initiative that was the city's attempt to make quick decisions to efficiently access federal recovery funds was now dead.

Thus, New Orleans found itself in a tough spot in March 2006. After approximately five months of intensive planning efforts and tough negotiations with Washington, virtually all the best efforts of the city and state had gone up in flames. The city had no viable plan, and the draft plan it had was still too controversial to touch. The most contentious issues were punted to the neighborhood planning process, which was subsequently dealt a death-blow. The state had insufficient CDBG funds to prevent a wave of expected mortgage foreclosures or provide for rebuilding and voluntary buyouts. Bush had promised to ask Congress for $4.2 billion more, but the state had learned not to count on anything until it materialized. Two months earlier, New Orleans had optimistically dreamt of having both a plan and the money to realize it; now it had neither.

The collapse of the BNOB land-use plan had complex political fallout. Canizaro had assumed his connections to the White House would ensure fair treatment for New Orleans.[108] In fact, he had assured Nagin these connections would be all that was necessary to secure direct federal funding for a recovery planning process in New Orleans, effectively bypassing FEMA and the state. The city also didn't trust Baton Rouge and was concerned the state would try to control the rebuilding of New Orleans through the LRA. As a result, New Orleans had resisted planning assistance from the state, and the BNOB process had intentionally stayed independent of ESF #14 and Louisiana Speaks. Now the city was penniless and alone. Abandoned by Washington, New Orleans suddenly found that it needed to make up with Baton Rouge.

4

Return to Chaos

Spring 2006

New Orleans was starting to crawl back from the grave in the early spring of 2006.[1] The city's population was increasing rapidly throughout the first half of the year as residents began to return and more jobs became available. No one knew exactly how many people had returned, but estimates were

Robert B. Olshansky

Fig. 4.1. The service industry rebounds, in a way

Laurie A. Johnson

Fig. 4.2. Fresh house gutting, New Orleans East, 2006

as low as 135,000 and as high as 200,000.[2] By mid-February, 95 percent of households had electrical service, and 83 percent had gas service.[3] Although the population was growing, more than half of pre-Katrina residents were still displaced and had not returned. Only two pharmacies were open, and fewer than 15 percent of businesses were operating (although a third of the restaurants were open).

City finances were still strained in early 2006. As of January, the city had a budget shortfall of $168 million—half of its $324 million annual budget.[4] The city had received two Community Disaster Loans from FEMA totaling $240 million for operating expenses. It had already used the first loan of $120 million to help pay staff who were providing essential services such as law enforcement, schools, and fire protection.[5] The Orleans Parish schools, which had served 60,000 students before Katrina, enrolled only about 4,000 for the spring semester; the city's Catholic schools, however, enrolled about 12,000, compared to 18,000 before the storm.[6] Transit was free, but service was limited. Levee repair was proceeding rapidly but was only 40 percent complete, which made many residents uneasy as the 2006 hurricane season approached.[7]

Some significant institutions reopened early in the year, and their presence provided some sense that the city was no longer a disaster-struck wasteland. The major four-year universities—Tulane, the University of New Orleans (UNO), Loyola, Xavier, Southern University of New Orleans (SUNO), and Dillard—reopened for the spring semester, albeit with 30,000 students instead of a full complement of 45,000.[8] Because of flood damage, however, not all were in their normal facilities: Dillard and its 1,000 returning students (out of a student body of 2,200) were at the Hilton Riverside New Orleans Hotel, and SUNO was using government-provided trailers next to the UNO East Campus. Most universities were surprised by the high return rates, particularly among freshmen, who had been in school for only a few days before being evacuated in August. Resident universities, such as Tulane, provided a significant boost to the city's population. Still, due to reduced tuition revenues, most campuses needed to severely pare back their staff and services and make cuts to their academic departments in order to make ends meet.

Tourists and conventions were slowly returning, which brought back jobs for the hospitality industry. Louis Armstrong Airport had about half of its pre-Katrina scheduled flights back by mid-February, and Harrah's casino started up its 24/7 operations, supporting 1,200 employees.[9] The city rolled the dice and supported the annual Mardi Gras celebration; it was rewarded with crowds about 70 percent as large as normal.[10] Out of the city's 38,000 hotel rooms, 15,000 were open for tourists; an additional 10,000 were filled with recovery workers and displaced victims.

Although the West Bank and the "sliver by the river"—including the French Quarter, downtown, and uptown—were revitalizing rapidly, other parts of the city were not. The places that had been flooded with two feet or more of water hadn't changed very much since September. About 60 percent of the population had lived in those areas, and repopulating them was not going to be quick or easy. It would require substantial outside financial assistance and planning support. But in mid-March, no one knew where this would come from. The state was just beginning to develop ideas about where and how to direct $10.4 billion in CDBG funds, of which $4.2 billion were just a presidential pledge. It was not clear how the funds would be prioritized in New Orleans in the absence of an approved plan, nor was there an obvious institutional mechanism for spending the money. And the Bring New Orleans Back planning process was dead in the water due to FEMA's unwillingness to pay for it.

THE ELECTION

It was not at all clear what would happen next in New Orleans or who would lead the effort to plan the city's rebuilding. Mayor Ray Nagin gave up providing any leadership on this issue. Instead, he quietly backed away from the BNOB plan and concentrated on the upcoming April mayoral primary, in which 22 candidates were running. Nagin's strategy was to stay away from politically toxic land-use and planning issues and instead actively court the African-American vote. It seemed a logical path to success, assuming the diaspora population voted in sufficient numbers. The irony was that Nagin—a businessman and political unknown prior to 2002—won his first election with the support of the white business community. Most African-Americans had never trusted him, which was another reason for the widespread suspicion of the BNOBC.[11] He reinvented himself for this election, hoping that the African-American community would choose him as the least of 22 evils. His two strongest opponents were Ron Forman, a popular uptown white businessman, and Mitch Landrieu, Louisiana's lieutenant governor, son of a former mayor, member of a prominent political family, and a rare white politician who enjoyed significant African-American support.

On April 22, Nagin and Landrieu captured the top two spots in the primary with 38 and 29 percent of the vote, respectively.[12] With low turnouts in African-American neighborhoods and among the displaced, Landrieu was in a strong position to prevail in the runoff election scheduled for May 20. Remarkably, this referendum on who was to lead the city's reconstruction did not actually address the historic challenge at hand; all of the major candidates avoided contentious post-Katrina land-use issues.[13] Political rationality required demanding the right to rebuild for all citizens, more affordable housing, and full compensation for flooded properties, but to the rest of the world this surely seemed self-deluding. On the tough questions, both candidates deferred to the planning process, which was still stalled and unfunded.[14] In the end, the differences between the two men came down to Landrieu's argument that he could manage the city more effectively than had Nagin versus Nagin's arguments for continuity and for maintaining black leadership.

Many were surprised when Nagin was reelected on May 20 with about 52 percent of the vote.[15] It was the narrowest margin of victory ever for an incumbent mayor in New Orleans. Thirty-eight percent of the city's eligible voters cast ballots, and nearly 25,000 (22 percent) voted either absentee or at one of the 10 early voting centers around the state.[16] In the city council election, newcomers ousted four of the seven incumbents, dramatically changing the council's composition but not its racial composition.

Nagin immediately declared that he would be "dusting off" the BNOB plan and meeting with advisors to map out a recovery strategy over the next 100 days.[17] He also promised to reorganize city staff. He continued to avoid the issues surrounding how the city would deal with its diminished footprint but observed it would soon become clear which neighborhoods were rebuilding and which were not.

NEIGHBORHOOD PLANNING FROM THE BOTTOM UP

While the mayoral candidates had been avoiding planning issues for two months, others had not. As early as December, the idea that all neighborhoods might need to prove their "viability" spurred community organizations in flooded neighborhoods to hold meetings and spearhead their own independent recovery planning processes. In addition, groups began to form in areas that didn't have any established organizations because they anticipated the threat of forced redevelopment of their neighborhood. Even in January, when the BNOB neighborhood planning process seemed likely, many neighborhoods had begun to organize.[18] None of these residents knew who the BNOB neighborhood "planners" were going to be, but they were fearful of letting others determine their future.

The Broadmoor Improvement Association, for example, actively began to identify which residents were returning. The association's president, LaToya Cantrell, was quoted in the *Times-Picayune* as saying, "When this neighborhood planning team is assigned to our district, we want to already have a vision in hand. We want to craft our own vision, and this is our way of getting ahead of the game."[19] The Lakeview Civic Improvement Association

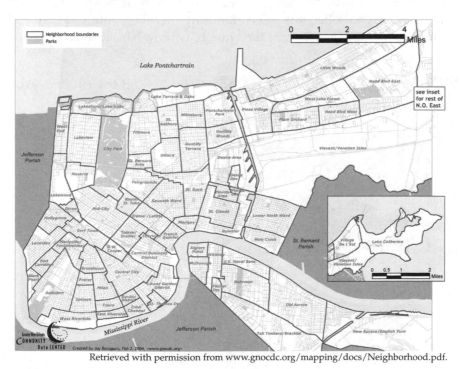

Retrieved with permission from www.gnocdc.org/mapping/docs/Neighborhood.pdf.

Fig. 4.3. The New Orleans City Planning Commission's neighborhood boundaries, adapted by the Greater New Orleans Community Data Center (2004).

(LCIA) and the Gentilly Civic Improvement Association (GCIA) also began to develop contact lists of residents and hold events to connect home owners with resources for rebuilding, rehabilitation, and financing. City council member Cynthia Hedge-Morrell helped residents in Pontchartrain Park find pro bono planning assistance through local architectural and planning firm Hewitt-Washington & Associates and Southern University at Baton Rouge.[20] In fact, many neighborhoods partnered with academic institutions to develop plans and conduct studies of their neighborhoods. Scores of universities from around the nation eventually established relationships with neighborhood organizations.

The Vietnamese community, which was associated with Mary Queen of Vietnam Church, simply rolled up its sleeves and started to rebuild. Its members did not wait for insurance but started to use their own savings to buy building materials. Neighbors supplied labor for one another. Their community had long been self-sufficient, and they had no inclination to wait for governmental help. They had arrived as refugees in the 1970s, settled into public housing at the farthest reaches of eastern New Orleans, and had lifted themselves up into a middle-class community by the time Katrina hit. According to Father Vien The Nguyen, they were asked to "look and leave" in early October, but 800 community members (out of about 6,000) chose to stay.[21] People slept in the church as they rebuilt their homes and

Fig. 4.4. Father Vien The Nguyen

Robert B. Olshansky

shared information with one another. They began data collection and planning in December, created a community development corporation in May, and were the first neighborhood in New Orleans to fully recover from the storms. They were also one of the most vocal opponents of the BNOB plan because they feared it might interfere with what they were doing.

The New Orleans East Vietnamese community, the neighborhoods of Broadmoor, Lakeview, and Holy Cross, and portions of Gentilly coordinated their own independent planning processes. In fact, by the time the mayoral election was complete, Broadmoor and the LCIA were putting the finishing touches on their neighborhood plans. Similar efforts flourished in the vacuum of official planning in post-BNOB New Orleans. Meeting notices appeared online, on local radio, and in the *Times-Picayune*, and people started to show up at regular meetings all over the city. In early April, a group that would eventually adopt the name Neighborhood Planning Network (NPN) started to meet every Wednesday night at the Musicians Union Hall on Esplanade Avenue. This venue soon became a place to trade information and learn about resources for neighborhood planning, as well as a place for local agencies to make announcements to the growing number of neighborhood groups. In the absence of reliable communication channels, the NPN meetings were an important way to develop support for neighborhood organizations.

THE CITY COUNCIL TAKES ACTION

In December 2005, simultaneous to the BNOB planning process, the city council had decided it needed to actively support neighborhood planning.[22] Not surprisingly, the council, which has constituents throughout the city, strongly advocated for rebuilding all of New Orleans and welcoming back every displaced resident. On December 15, the council passed Motion M-05-592, which stated its desire to assist neighborhoods "in the development of . . . housing and redevelopment plans with the explicit aim of hastening the ability of residents of those neighborhoods to return and enjoy a generally improved quality of life in part by insuring that revitalization and redevelopment is consistent with best practices in flood protection and mitigation to minimize the impact of future flood events."[23]

The council also reenlisted the services of Miami-based planning firm Lambert Advisory, which it had hired in 2004 under a $125,000 general services contract to advise the council on housing matters, such as the review of plans for redeveloping public housing complexes.[24] Motion M-05-592 directed the council president "to amend the scope of services, terms and fees for Lambert Advisory LLC to structure, organize and work with the certain neighborhoods" and help them develop neighborhood plans. It also authorized Lambert to hire additional subcontractors with "expertise in flood control and mitigation, urban design, architecture and engineering, construction contracting and cost estimating, and other disciplines" to help neighborhoods with planning. Paul Lambert, the principal of Lambert Advisory, had planning experience in the Miami area after Hurricane Andrew in 1992. After Katrina, he told council members about a neighborhood-based economic development effort that successfully rebuilt declining areas affected by Andrew. The idea of a bottom-up planning effort designed to revitalize all distressed neighborhoods had great appeal to the city council.

In December, the BNOB and ULI efforts weren't yet placing much public emphasis on neighborhood planning, so the council set out on what became a parallel path to the neighborhood planning initiative the BNOB city planning committee later attempted to pursue. The difference between the two approaches became clearer in time: the BNOB effort intended to use neighborhood planning as a way to determine neighborhood viability, whereas the council approached it as a proactive means of facilitating the survival of all neighborhoods.

The council's immediate task was to figure out how to pay for its neighborhood planning effort. Over the next two months, it identified nearly $3 million in pre-Katrina CDBG funds to which the city already had access. The money was moved from various accounts into the planning account via a series of ordinances—in full public view, that is, though the purpose of these ordinances was probably not clear to most observers. This effort accelerated as the stalemate over the BNOB plan became more pronounced. Finally, on February 16, 2006—the week in which the BNOB neighborhood planning process was originally slated to begin—the council approved a motion to hire Lambert to lead the effort for nearly $3 million.[25] Although this appeared to be a solution to the neighborhood planning stalemate, the local press didn't report on the motion immediately, probably because no one quite understood what was happening.

Lambert and his local, longtime partner, Sheila Danzey (a former director of the New Orleans Housing Authority), signed a contract with the city in late March, hired subconsultants, and began work on April 1. Lambert says he soon met with FEMA staff, and his intent was to meet the ESF #14 guidelines for parish plans, which would enable New Orleans to access the state's post-Katrina CDBG funds. In addition to producing a targeted list of projects to fund, just like other ESF #14 projects had done, they hoped to identify land-use strategies that would make neighborhoods more successful in the long term.

At its April 7 meeting, the city council announced it had started its planning process in 49 flooded neighborhoods (out of 73 in the city), adding to the confusion of those who were still wondering how the BNOB neighborhood planning process would be funded.[26] The *Times-Picayune* account of the meeting stated that the city council had "toyed with launching a neighborhood planning project of its own. . . . At this point, the council's effort appears to have no direct connection to the similar effort that Mayor Ray Nagin's Bring New Orleans Back Commission hoped to launch."[27] What role the City Planning Commission might play was also unclear; it was still understaffed and practically invisible. But the council stated it would submit its final plans to the planning commission before it was forwarded to the state and federal government. The city council also announced Lambert's subconsultants, which included 16 planners from New Orleans, Miami, and Boston. Some of them had been working with flooded neighborhoods already. Lambert's goal was to complete the process by the end of August. In March, Manning stated that a council planning process, should it occur, would complement the BNOB process, although it was not at all clear how, or if indeed the BNOB process would ever begin.[28]

ROCKEFELLER TO THE RESCUE

The city council's plan seemed to target many of the BNOBC's own neighborhood planning objectives, but the project lacked a clear road map. Many of the key players in the BNOBC and the LRA doubted the council's effort would produce a systematic and comprehensive recovery plan that would make a convincing case to the federal government. So, in March—after FEMA had denied its request for millions of dollars to fund neighborhood planning—the BNOBC turned to the LRA for help.

Before this, Mayor Nagin and BNOB planning committee chair Joe Canizaro had assured the LRA that the city had its planning situation under control, and the LRA had intentionally stayed out of New Orleans and deferred to the locals who were leading the process. This freed up the LRA to focus its efforts on the other parish plans. But after it became clear FEMA would not come through with the funding, members of the BNOBC met with LRA officials, including attorney Donna Fraiche, the chair of the LRA's long-range planning task force and the organization's designated point person for planning issues in New Orleans. Fraiche later announced that the LRA fully intended to find a way to fund the BNOB neighborhood planning process.[29] What ensued were more than two confusing months of behind-the-scenes wrangling.[30]

Canizaro also made calls to LRA director Andy Kopplin and board member Sean Reilly. Reilly was instrumental in fund-raising for the LRASF, so he was aware of potential sources. One person he had been talking to was Darren Walker, the vice president of the Rockefeller Foundation, which was looking for an opportunity to help New Orleans. Reilly now called him to offer such a chance.

The Rockefeller Foundation had been working with the Greater New Orleans Foundation (GNOF) since the days right after Katrina.[31] On September 8, just a week after the flood, Rockefeller had provided $3 million to GNOF's Katrina Disaster Relief Fund to support local organizations helping displaced residents.[32] The foundation saw this as an opportunity to strengthen the long-term capacity of local institutions for community development. The Rockefeller Foundation had a clear goal regarding its involvement: it wanted to build local capacity that would permanently improve institutions in the city rather than give a one-time, postdisaster donation. Its staff became convinced that supporting long-term neighborhood and city planning that addressed housing, community engagement, and open space would be a very cost-effective way for the foundation to leverage the value of its funding. In Walker's words, "The plan was a fulcrum through which we could support the generation of a tier of positive outcomes." The Rockefeller Foundation recognized the value of all the exciting new neighborhood-based activities that had recently sprouted, but it also believed that a well-funded, credible planning effort could provide cohesion to these disconnected strategies.

Representatives from Rockefeller, BNOBC, the LRA, and GNOF met in March to discuss how to fund continuation of the BNOB planning effort. One obvious model was to replicate the LRASF to use nonprofit funds to hire planners. Because of this, two key New Orleans LRA members, Donna Fraiche and businessman David Voelker, took the lead for the LRA on developing this fiduciary organization. Although the LRA had no interest in actually planning for New Orleans, it needed New Orleans to have a planning effort that would succeed in order to persuade Washington the city's needs were genuine and its funding requests were reasonable. To create something like the LRASF would give the city access to the best planners and help it perform a transparent, thorough, inclusive, and well-documented planning process to abet the ongoing struggle for federal funds. Over the subsequent months, the LRA kept repeating that it was following the planning principles adopted following the November 2005 AIA/APA rebuilding conference (see Chapter 2). In fact, it seems to have been following much more than these principles, which focus on specific outcomes; rather, it was being guided by the basic governance and recovery management goals that underlay the purpose of the LRA.[33]

The LRA was interested in parishwide plans—and New Orleans was no exception—because so many issues—transportation, housing markets, infrastructure systems, and financing—required thinking beyond individual neighborhoods. And the LRA thought the plan needed to have several degrees of freedom in order to consider alternative futures. Thus, a plan that focused only on rebuilding flooded neighborhoods in New Orleans would provide only part of the story. The challenge facing the LRA in March 2006 was how to guide New Orleans toward such a comprehensive planning effort. With respect to the ESF #14 parish planning approach that had begun in December, the LRA's thinking had evolved from listing projects toward instead emphasizing the value of the broad process needed to create a defensible list of projects.

A NEW PLANNING PROCESS BEGINS TO EMERGE

LRA director Andy Kopplin was in Baton Rouge, and, with the planning situation changing daily in New Orleans, he needed someone he trusted there to report on ongoing planning discussions. In March, Kopplin hired Steven Bingler as both LRA planning advisor and New Orleans liaison. Bingler was an architect Kopplin had known for several years. He was principal of Concordia, a New Orleans firm specializing in community-based planning and design. Concordia had conducted community-centered planning for school buildings in several cities across the nation. In 2004, the firm had prepared a community plan for the Central City neighborhood in New Orleans. In the fall of 2005, Bingler had started to advocate for a community-based model of rebuilding New Orleans and the school system in tandem, and he gave a presentation on this topic at the AIA/APA conference in November. He operated comfortably with philanthropic organizations, which had funded some of his projects. Kopplin thought this could help the LRA's search for the funds to carry out the neighborhood planning effort.

In early February 2006, Bingler organized weekly "planning alliance" meetings at the Ashe Cultural Arts Center in Central City to try to recharge the stalling, directionless planning process.[34] Regular attendees included representatives from the City Planning Commission and Lambert Advisory, FEMA, BNOB, and Louisiana Speaks. The meetings continued until mid-May, providing a valuable forum for the exchange of ideas during a confusing time. It also established Bingler as a critical link between locals, the LRA, and potential funders.

Two months later, the Rockefeller Foundation's Darren Walker held a meeting at the GNOF offices with Kopplin, Bingler, Barbara Major (a cochair of the BNOBC), and Ray Manning, one of the architects assigned to lead the BNOB neighborhood planning process.[35] Walker said that Rockefeller was willing to support the New Orleans planning effort with up to $3.5 million, but he wanted to avoid partisanship and wanted the effort to be inclusive of a broad range of community interests. He asked the LRA to figure out how to merge the BNOB process with the city council's Lambert process. Ben Johnson, the director of GNOF, asked Bingler to meet with Manning and Lambert to explore this merger and discuss what $3.5 million would buy.

Manning and Bingler were excited about moving ahead. Using what Bingler calls a "community trust model," they developed a budget and organizational chart that included representatives from all the relevant organizations. The idea was to convince the city council and the mayor to merge the two processes and match the Rockefeller money with the council money to create a broad, well-funded process involving everyone. From the BNOBC side, Manning would contribute his stable of neighborhood planners; Lambert would carry over his planners from the city council's process. They would agree on a common structure and common format set by the City Planning Commission that would cover all the neighborhoods of the city. Overseeing the whole operation would be a Community Support Organization (CSO), made up of delegates from the mayor's office (to represent the BNOB process), the city council (to represent the Lambert process), the LRA (to represent the state's parish planning process started by ESF #14), GNOF (to represent the funding agencies), and the City Planning Commission. GNOF also wanted to separate funding decisions from policy decisions, so it would create a subsidiary fiduciary organization, the New Orleans Community Support Foundation (NOCSF), composed of five past and present GNOF board members.[36] Bingler would be hired by GNOF as the coordinator and project manager. There was also discussion of a staff working group, consisting of staff-level representatives from each of the CSO entities. Meetings were held with city council members and City Planning Commission staff, and it appeared that the major stakeholders were seriously considering the idea of the merger in April.

The merger was not yet complete when, on April 20, the Rockefeller Foundation officially announced an award of "$3.5 million to support the development of a comprehensive rebuilding plan for New Orleans."[37] The foundation made it clear that this was only part of the money needed

> to fund the estimated $7.9 million planning process for rebuilding New Orleans. The grant . . . represents the first commitment of private funds to this planning process, and will make it possible for city and state representatives and neighborhood organizations to work together to craft the detailed plans necessary to trigger national funding of full-scale redevelopment efforts. . . . It will include the development of a detailed [citywide] framework to be integrated into the Louisiana Recovery Authority's statewide plan, and the preparation of neighborhood plans throughout the city.

This was a significant moment. The structure was now official. But more money was still needed, and the shape of the planning process was still unclear.

A huge wrench was thrown into the proposed planning structure in early May. Janet Howard, president of the Bureau of Governmental Research

(BGR), a government watchdog group, issued a report on May 8, claiming the $3 million contract awarded to Lambert Advisory by the city council violated city rules.[38] Although Lambert had responded to a Request for Qualifications (RFQ) in 2004, Howard claimed that the current contract, which called for neighborhood concept plans, was sufficiently different from the public housing consulting terms specified in the 2004 contract. Howard claimed that, according to council rules, this required a new competitive selection process: "It is absurd to suggest that one of the most significant urban planning contracts in American history can be awarded in 2006 under an RFQ issued in 2004 for totally different purposes under totally different circumstances."[39] Furthermore, Howard pointed out that the city charter explicitly gives the City Planning Commission responsibility for preparing reconstruction plans following disasters. If the city intended to spend money on planning, "those funds should be allocated to the City Planning Commission to rebuild its capacity and hire the necessary contractors, rather than awarded by City Council to its own contractor." Howard concluded that, although everyone was understandably frustrated by the pace of post-Katrina planning, "the citizens of New Orleans are entitled to a serious, transparent search for the most talented, experienced urban planners in the world."

The two at-large members of the city council, Oliver Thomas and Eddie Sapir, vigorously defended their actions, stating it was legal to expand the terms of the 2004 contract, which broadly covered a variety of housing matters.[40] Furthermore, they asserted these were extraordinary times, and BGR's claim "only serves to confuse the public and slow down a critical process that is directly tied to the release of federal and state revitalization funds." Four days later, BGR posted both the 2004 and 2006 contracts on their website, inviting readers to judge for themselves whether the two contracts were similar enough to be covered by the first RFQ process alone.[41]

The BGR report caught the attention of GNOF. The larger planning process it was about to orchestrate involved not only Lambert but also the Manning team, which had not been hired through an open and competitive process either. Howard promised to start asking some hard questions about the entire GNOF process if it continued to proceed as it was.

The BGR report was not the only complication. As merger negotiations continued into May, the Lambert process continued as originally planned with the strong support of the city council. This cast doubt on how committed the council was to the merger. Moreover, in the last weeks of the election campaign, several incumbent council candidates declared they wouldn't necessarily support a merged process that lacked their input.

On the other side, the LRA continued to doubt the council's process would be comprehensive enough to meet its goals. Further, the difference between the two approaches became intractable. After the election and the new city council was in place, the primary champions of the Lambert approach remained Cynthia Hedge-Morrell and Cynthia Willard-Lewis, who continued to insist that the "viability" issue be taken off the table. Canizaro, representing the BNOBC, maintained the central issue was how to design the city with a fundamentally different footprint. It also became increasingly clear after the election that the mayor did not relish fighting with the city council over this. Thus, the merger never occurred.

The Rockefeller-funded process began to move forward anyway. Thus, even though the city council had not yet agreed, GNOF and the LRA decided that the City Planning Commission should go ahead and issue an RFQ for the Rockefeller-funded planning team.[42] Manning would be invited to submit his qualifications, as would Lambert. Manning was not happy at all about this, having been involved since January, when he had carefully designed the neighborhood planning process with BNOBC colleagues. He had created a structure, identified neighborhood consultants, and expected to lead the plan. He agreed to step down as the lead planner but ultimately decided not to submit his firm's qualifications in response to the RFQ. Lambert also declined to submit his qualifications on the grounds that he was already conducting a fully funded neighborhood planning process.

In such an environment, creating the CSO to oversee the process also became quite complicated. GNOF attempted several different combinations of nonprofits and neighborhood organizations, but each combination brought complaints from those not included. By the end of May, the working concept was to include three representatives from neighborhoods and two from communitywide nonprofits. But there was no agreement on the method for selecting them.

Pity the citizens of New Orleans who were trying to understand the direction planning would take. As a May 27 *Times-Picayune* article observed, "Many New Orleans residents are confused about how neighborhood planning under the direction of the Blanco-appointed Louisiana Recovery Authority, or LRA, will mesh with work begun weeks ago by planning consultants hired by the City Council."[43] A spokesman for the Rockefeller Foundation described the process as "unfolding," and Ben Johnson of GNOF said it was "a complicated conversation." As for the mayor, he said nothing. Council president Oliver Thomas said he had met recently with the governor, "and the two agreed that all recovery plans must be tied together." Talking about the status of the merger, Lambert stated, "The details of that, there isn't a lot of clarity. . . . We're forging ahead because the last thing that needs to happen is a delay in the process."[44] In a June 1 interview, LRA board member David Voelker said Mayor Nagin and city council members were "considering a compromise plan crafted by the Greater New Orleans

Foundation, the fiduciary agent for the Rockefeller grant, that would create a board to oversee a single planning effort and would create a competitive process for hiring consultants."[45] This plan would halt the council planning process but provide opportunities for neighborhood planning consultants to participate in the effort. The mayor's office, however, offered no comment.

REQUEST FOR QUALIFICATIONS

The task now became how to construct an RFQ and a process for reviewing the applications as quickly as possible. To do this, more details of the proposed planning process needed to be ironed out. One important aspect was to formalize the role of the City Planning Commission. Thus, GNOF asked Yolanda Rodriguez, the planning commission director, and her staff to develop the RFQ. They also prepared a set of "neighborhood planning guidelines," which were issued along with the RFQ to provide a common framework for all the neighborhood plans.

On June 5, 2006, the NOCSF, the subsidiary to the GNOF, issued two RFQs for qualified, nationally recognized planning firms. One was to select a citywide planning team, and the other was for selection of multiple neighborhood planning teams.[46] The goal was to find the best planners the nation could offer. Questions were referred to Steven Bingler at Concordia, which

Fig. 4.5. Yolanda Rodriguez, director of the City Planning Commission

New Orleans City Council

was staffing the management of the planning effort for NOCSF/GNOF. According to the RFQs, the neighborhood planners were to create and integrate "approximately 73" neighborhood plans into 13 district plans, based on the City Planning Commission's 13 districts. The citywide team would "work with the City Planning Commission to develop a plan for [citywide] infrastructure" by integrating the 13 district plans into "a single [citywide] Post Disaster Recovery & Rebuilding Plan" that would "support the comprehensive rebuilding of New Orleans that will foster racial and economic equity and provide neighborhood-guided proposals for future development." The RFQ also defined the role of NOCSF as supporting "the City Planning Commission, the Mayor's Office and City Council in developing a rebuilding plan that will be used to seek funding and technical support for the city's recovery, growth and prosperity after Hurricane Katrina."[47] Although this was a nationwide call, nonlocal applicants were asked to "demonstrate a willingness to hire and work with local planning and design professionals, as well as students," who would be familiar with the plans and regulations in New Orleans.

The RFQs announced an ambitious schedule. They asked prospective applicants to submit questions to Concordia by June 12; answers would be published and distributed by June 15. Submissions were due by June 26, finalists would be notified by July 10, and interviews were scheduled during the first half of July. The final decisions would be made immediately after the interviews, and the consultants would be expected to start work in mid-July.

The release of the RFQs, as with so many other planning events in post-Katrina New Orleans, had a strange *Alice in Wonderland* quality to it; nothing was what it seemed, and the usual points of reference in a planning process were elusive. If an out-of-town planning firm had read only the RFQs, it would have been mystified as to what this planning process was all about. A foundation was looking for firms to plan the rebuilding of New Orleans? Who was in charge? Who was the audience for this plan? What authority would it have? Does the foundation have enough funds to sufficiently support this effort? When is the expected completion date?

New Orleanians, too, might have wondered how this effort could be moving forward even though it lacked the support of the mayor, whose BNOB process was its foundation. And they certainly may have wondered how it related to the council's process, which was well under way by now. The RFQs referred only obliquely to the Lambert process, lumping it in with all the various homegrown neighborhood initiatives and referring readers to the NPN website for further information.[48]

According to the RFQ, the one local governmental entity that explicitly supported this new effort was the City Planning Commission.[49] Thus, the

RFQs represented the introduction of a third entity into the planning arena. The first plan was the mayor's; the second, the council's; and now, belatedly, the City Planning Commission had stepped into the ring (though one might also call this the LRA's plan).

Prospective applicants sent in many questions to Concordia.[50] Here are some of the more salient answers:

- The plan was expected to be complete by December 2006. It would be adopted sometime in 2007.
- The NOCSF and City Planning Commission (not Concordia) would jointly oversee the planning process. Contracts would be with the NOCSF.
- Both neighborhood and citywide planning would begin immediately once applicants were selected.
- Incorporation of existing neighborhood plans into this process would be on a case-by-case basis; "Any creative thoughts or ideas would be welcome at any time."
- The organizational mechanism for coordinating citywide and neighborhood teams would be determined after the teams are selected. They would work collaboratively throughout the process.
- All budgets and work plans would be determined during the procurement process, which would begin immediately once applicants were selected.
- The planning process "will enhance and incorporate existing planning projects into an overall [citywide] plan" that would be reviewed by the mayor's office, submitted to the City Planning Commission and city council, and then passed on to the LRA and other funding entities.
- The Lambert planning work would be "incorporated into a comprehensive neighborhood, district-level and [citywide] infrastructure plan."
- Regarding selection of the planning teams, a review panel of nationally recognized planners would provide recommendations, as would the CSO. The NOCSF would make the final selection.
- "The Office of the Mayor will appoint a representative to the New Orleans Community Support Organization and will be integrally involved in the planning process through the City Planning Commission and the various agencies of City Government."
- "The City Council will appoint a representative to the New Orleans Community Support Organization (Advisory Committee) and will be responsible for review and approval of the final plan."

Clearly, this was still a very fluid situation, and a highly uncertain one for planning consultants. But the temptation to work in this historic and highly visible situation was strong. Several dozen consultant teams incorporating scores of planning firms responded.

A WEEK IN JUNE

We visited New Orleans and Baton Rouge for one week in the middle of June 2006.[51] We felt as if we had signed on for a version of one of those murder mystery weekends, in which participants meet all the characters, ascertain their motives, and try to identify the killer by Sunday. In this case, we just wanted a clear understanding of the current status of the planning process and its players. At the beginning of the week, we found that even the most astute New Orleanian planners knew only what they could glean from the mysterious RFQ and what they heard from rumors.

During the course of the week, we met with five knowledgeable and respected planners, and they presented five different accounts of the previous three months and a variety of interpretations of the current situation. Our conversations were full of questions, speculation, and, sometimes, nascent conspiracy theories. Some planners were trying to decide how they would respond to the RFQs, which were vague about the exact nature of the work. One planner said he thought the city council had tentatively agreed to cut off the Lambert process, merge it into the new process, and reallocate the city's CDBG money for other purposes. But, he said, there was still considerable debate regarding how to structure the neighborhood and non-profit representation on the CSO. There was also a rumor (supposedly from a source inside the mayor's office) that Mayor Nagin intended to resurrect the BNOB planning committee and ask it to turn its plan into an ESF #14 project list, thereby short-circuiting both the city council and the Rockefeller efforts.[52] Most sources, however, believed the mayor intended to cooperate with the LRA but simply did not understand the role of planning and the importance of public involvement in urban development. Even before Katrina, he had discounted the significance of the planning commission and looked directly to the private sector for development initiatives. It was this void in planning leadership from city hall that had empowered neighborhood organizations to act on their own. Thus, the planners we spoke to saw the neighborhoods as leading the process, and the goal of the next phase of planning would be to provide information to neighborhoods so they could decide where and how to rebuild.

But implementing an overarching planning effort remained a challenge, and the proposed Rockefeller-funded process was still a mystery to everyone. How would the citywide plan interact with the neighborhood plans? Logically, it should be a sequential process, starting with neighborhood planning (guided by a consistent citywide framework), followed by integration and review at the citywide level, and concluding with a review and confirmation at the neighborhood level. But was there time to complete such a process by the end of the year? Who would oversee the plan's content? Who was really driving it? The LRA? GNOF? The City Planning Commission? Baton Rouge business interests led by the Baton Rouge Area Foundation? One evening that week, we were invited to the home of the Japanese consul general, Masaru Sakato, to have a long conversation about how New Orleans might benefit from Kobe's 10 years of experience recovering from its disastrous 1995 earthquake. Although the two cities had many experiences in common, one fundamental difference was clear. Sakato was very interested in knowing who was in charge of the reconstruction, and we could identify no such person.[53]

But surely the mayor would play an important role in rebuilding his city. We arranged to meet the cochair of the mayor's "100-day committee"—set up to advise the mayor in the first days of his second term—who indicated that the mayor was fully on board with the incipient planning process, which was a continuation of the process he had begun. In fact, she said she had a hand in drafting the work scope in the RFQs. She said the mayor appreciated that the city council had started a neighborhood planning process, but he sought a way to move it into a more established structure within city government, namely the City Planning Commission, and bring it in line with the city charter. The official planning procedure must first be approved by the planning commission after several public meetings, then go to the city council, and finally to the mayor. She characterized the CSO as an independent board that would direct the consultants. Its responsibility was to ensure the plan was developed and approved in a manner that reflects the city charter, is accountable to the citizens, and includes outreach to the displaced. The plan's content, in contrast, would be under the purview of the City Planning Commission. She emphasized that the CSO was an advisory group and the City Planning Commission was the client for the plan. Finally, she said the mayor's goal was to rebuild New Orleans over the next three years, before completion of his term. All of this seemed plausible and genuine to us.

The next day, we attended the monthly LRA board meeting in Baton Rouge, where Governor Blanco announced that Congress the previous day had approved the additional $4.2 billion the president had asked for in February, and the president had signed it into law.[54] The bill also appropriated $3.7 billion to strengthen levees.

The state expected these funds and had already worked out the details of what was now called the "Road Home" program, which would pay estimated damage costs to home owners up to $150,000, less insurance and other disaster-related payments, based upon the pre-Katrina assessed value of their homes. Home owners could choose to use the money to rebuild, or they could sell their property to the state and use the money to relocate. The state would accumulate the purchased properties in a land bank for

Fig. 4.6. The June 2006 meeting of the LRA board

subsequent redevelopment.[55] The state had already registered 90,000 home owners for the program but was unable to begin until the full amount of funding became official. The state could now begin to hire staff for this enormous effort. A pilot program would begin in August. The state would also begin developing a program for rental housing at that time.[56]

Next on the agenda was a report from the Louisiana Speaks consultants. The Calthorpe team presented the results of a survey of southern Louisiana citizens, which showed a strong consensus for several rebuilding priorities, such as coastal protection, stronger levees, safer buildings, and retaining the special qualities of the area. With regard to the planning process to date, however, most respondents were confused by the situation and were not convinced the process would be fair. Peter Calthorpe then unveiled the schedule for completing the Louisiana Speaks long-term regional plan for southern Louisiana, which he described as an important complement to local planning efforts. The regional planning effort would begin with a series of workshops over the summer and produce a draft regional planning document around March 2007.

We saw a stunning disconnect in this: if New Orleans intended to complete its recovery plan and send it to Washington by the end of 2006, then what was the intended use of this Louisiana Speaks framework, which would, three months later, lay down broader urbanization and economic development principles for all the cities in the region? The purpose of this multiyear regional plan—typical of many such efforts around the country in regions experiencing environmental stress due to rapid growth—was never made clear. The LRA suddenly switched to the topic of New Orleans as if the problem were not there.

LRA board member David Voelker and Carey Shea from the Rockefeller Foundation reported on the planning process in New Orleans. This was the first progress report to the LRA on New Orleans planning since the presentation of the BNOB report in January. Voelker announced an organizational chart for the planning effort existed, but it was not yet ready to be made public. He gave credit to the city council and the neighborhoods for starting to develop their own plans but said the city needed to quickly "put it all under one tent, so it makes sense."

Voelker described the six-member NOCSF. Shea announced that the planning teams for New Orleans would be selected by a review committee consisting of a planning commission representative, a nationally recognized neighborhood planner, a citywide planner, a disaster recovery planner, and a regional planner who would be selected largely on the advice of APA. They would sift through the RFQs for professional planning teams to lead the recovery planning. According to Voelker, the mayor had accepted this structure "through intermediaries," and the details would be solved in the coming week during meetings with the mayor and city council. Voelker emphasized that the "LRA's job [was] not to plan the City of New Orleans" but to ensure the plan was done properly, openly, in a nonpolitical manner, and quickly so New Orleans would be right in line when it was time for the federal government to give aid to the state. The *Times-Picayune* account of this meeting also confirmed that Oliver Thomas, the city council president, "after a recent meeting with Blanco about the issue, said council members favor letting the LRA take the lead in the planning and that the varied efforts would be brought into line."[57]

Thus, the stage was set for the finale of our mystery week: a board meeting of the NOCSF.[58] The agenda for the meeting, scheduled for 8:30 a.m. on a Saturday, had been innocuously taped to the door of the GNOF office 48 hours earlier. Jeff Thomas, a local attorney involved in post-Katrina planning issues, saw the agenda, noticed that it included matters such as the composition of the CSO and the planning consultant review panel, and immediately sent out an email to notify local neighborhood planning networks of the meeting. Not only was this going to be a good place to get some answers, but it might also be an opportunity to influence some important decisions. The New Orleans cyber community was soon abuzz with the news. We arrived at the meeting to find an overflow crowd of about 50 observers squeezed into a conference room barely adequate for such a turn-out. And this was no ordinary crowd. In the audience were several promi-nent neighborhood organization leaders, two city council members, at least one City Planning Commission member, planning faculty from UNO, a representative from LRA, FEMA ESF #14 staff, and representatives of sev-eral citywide nonprofits. This is how murder mystery weekends end: all the usual suspects are assembled in one place.

The NOCSF chair, Wayne Lee, described the expected membership of the CSO, which would include a nominee from citywide organizations and five representatives from neighborhood organizations throughout the city. He said they were working along with neighborhood groups to ensure their input to the process, but the presence in the room of so many confused neighborhood representatives suggested they had not progressed very far. Joining the meeting by telephone, David Voelker affirmed that the LRA was very supportive of a process in which New Orleanians would create their own plan. He also emphasized the need to raise additional funds for public communication in order to reduce confusion.

Lee and Steven Bingler then went on to describe how they would con-struct the CSO and reiterated that the NOCSF would manage the funds

Robert B. Olshansky

Fig. 4.7. The June 2006 meeting of the NOCSF board

whereas the CSO would interact with the community and the planning consultants. The agitated crowd showed concern about only a few anointed public groups having seats at the table. In response, the conveners emphasized that the NGO and neighborhood members of the CSO would represent all the city's NGOs and neighborhood organizations. Even so, attendees were full of questions about how the representative groups would be nominated and selected. Voelker stressed that while a commitment to open meetings was important, so was keeping the process moving forward. An overly large CSO could slow things down. In this discussion, we could see the leaders were sincere about having open public meetings, and in the end the exact composition of the CSO, which was really just an advisory oversight body, was probably not that important. But many in the audience felt their communities were at stake and had suspicions about what this mysterious planning thing was all about. They were driven by a lack of trust and fear that some entity was going to hijack the reconstruction they had begun. Attendees seemed to be overly concerned about the process for selecting representative groups yet insufficiently concerned about the substantive aspects of what the CSO would do or what the plan would accomplish. No one in the room was able to articulate what this plan would do besides guide the LRA in spending the remaining CDBG funds.[59] Voelker reiterated that the LRA wanted a plan for the whole city, but he also reported that the citywide planning guidelines were not yet ready, underscoring the still fluid nature of this process.

The more Lee, Bingler, and Voelker spoke, the more difficult it became to imagine exactly how this innovative structure in this unprecedented situation would actually function. In part, this confusion stemmed from the RFQ being issued before the public knew this process was moving forward. Many complained that they had not received the RFQ. Bingler reminded them that the RFQ sought qualified professional planning teams from all over the nation and that it had gone out through channels such as APA and AIA. Attendees also expressed concern about giving excessive power to planners from outside the area. Bingler replied that the RFQ explicitly asked for teams to include local planners and that neighborhoods would have a voice in selecting teams from the list of neighborhood planners the evaluation committee would recommend.

Some attendees expressed frustration that the mayor and council were not strongly supporting this opportunity provided by the Rockefeller Foundation to plan New Orleans without using taxpayer dollars. Voelker responded that the mayor authorized the RFQ, was "supportive of the process," and would meet next week with the city council. However, as noted at other points in the meeting, the mayor had not officially signed off on the planning process, and it was for this reason no official announcements had been released. GNOF and LRA representatives were describing their intention to create a transparent planning process, but in the absence of an official city endorsement they were forced to inform the public through disconnected pieces: the RFQ, the June 15 LRA meeting, occasional *Times-Picayune* articles, and this meeting.

What about the Lambert planning process? Bingler said this was up to the city council. Are the processes in competition with each other? Bingler answered, "We don't control the Lambert process. We're not going to walk away from it and demand everyone to start again." In other words, should the Lambert process continue, this new process would use the results as best it could.

Finally, attendees questioned the relationship of this plan to the legally recognized planning processes and documents of the city. Specifically, would this become the new city master plan and replace the one that was created but never officially adopted in the late 1990s? Bingler responded that it would not be the master plan, although "it would be the best of all worlds if this process could drive the completion of the citywide master plan."[60] Furthermore, this plan would involve city planning staff, and it would need City Planning Commission approval before going to the city council and then to the LRA. Arnie Fielkow, one of the two at-large members of the city council, agreed it was important that this plan have a legal component and be aligned with normal planning procedures. He offered to have a hearing and enact a council resolution to officially endorse the process.

Bingler concluded by saying the plan was going to bring together everything done so far, use consultants to fill the gaps, and lift all neighborhoods up to the same level. But he also reminded everyone that the situation was unprecedented and "there is no book on how to do this."

Later in the day, we visited a meeting in Lakeview that was presenting the status of the Lambert planning process in that area. We spoke with Paul Lambert. He stated clearly that he had a contract with the city council to complete a plan and that he had no intention of submitting his qualifications to the unified planning process.

Thus, for the moment, we had figured things out. We understood what the LRA hoped the plan would accomplish. We understood Voelker's role and could see that he was close to making it all come together. We had an officially unofficial statement from the mayor's spokesperson regarding his support for the project. We saw Steven Bingler and the NOCSF. We spoke to Carey Shea of Rockefeller about the consultant selection process. And we also knew that there were still many things that were ill defined, such as the relationship between New Orleans's planning process and Louisiana Speaks. It took a week of hard work, but we finally had a moment of clarity regarding the status of post-Katrina planning as of June 17, 2006.

It turns out that we were not the only patrons of this mystery weekend. The *New York Times* published an account of the state of planning efforts in New Orleans.[61] Using President Bush's signing of the funding bill the previous Thursday as the news hook, the article focused on the continuing uncertainty surrounding the rebuilding of the city. It described Ray Manning's resignation, the lack of clear signals from the mayor, and his expectation that individuals would make the right decisions. The article quoted the mayor as saying there would be a structure in place in the "next day or so" that would start the process of creating a master plan. We had learned more of the details than the *Times* reporter but still had no idea what would happen next.

SELECTION OF THE CONSULTANTS

Sixty-five teams responded to the RFQ by the June 26 deadline, but the city still was not formally on board.

On June 20, David Voelker and Steven Bingler met with the mayor and three key city council members in city hall.[62] Voelker and city council president Oliver Thomas reported they made significant progress at the meeting, but no one clarified what issues remained. The mayor's office had no comment. At a June 28 press conference, the mayor and President Thomas promised an announcement within a week.[63] Two days later, Thomas said the city council was happy to have the Rockefeller-funded process, so long as it did not prevent the completion of the Lambert plans. He stated all planning, including planning initiated by neighborhood, should continue. Paul Lambert said that his plans would be done by late August and would overlap the Rockefeller process by only a few weeks.[64]

Finally, on July 5, the mayor, the city council, and LRA officials announced an agreement to support a single comprehensive recovery and rebuilding planning process, thus "ending months of political wrangling that confused residents and put future grant requests at risk," according to the *Times-Picayune*.[65] The press release describing the agreement said the planning process would get $3.5 million from the Rockefeller Foundation and $1 million from GNOF. It would try to tap other funding sources as it went along.[66]

"The City Council is proud of the work that we have accomplished in helping our constituents get the information they needed when they needed it most," commented City Council President Oliver Thomas. "We have laid a solid foundation for the final phase of the planning process to build on. We are all looking forward to a single comprehensive recovery and rebuilding plan for New Orleans."

The structure of the CSO was described this way: "The nine members of the Community Support Organization, still to be named, will include one representative appointed by Mayor Nagin, one by the City Council, one by the City Planning Commission, one by the Greater New Orleans Foundation, and five citizens selected from the five council districts."

The announcement went on to say that the process of selecting consultants who responded to the RFQ was well under way. The finalists would

> work closely with the New Orleans City Planning Commission to begin planning in some neighborhoods or to provide additional support to independent planning efforts currently underway. In either case, every neighborhood organization will have the option of selecting their own planning teams from the [prequalified] pool of planning consultants or continuing to work with previously retained planners. Neighborhood plans will be prepared with consistent, adequate, and equitable resources to assure the city of a comprehensive and balanced master plan. Infrastructure needs will be identified and incorporated into the neighborhood plans as part of the [citywide] master plan.[67]

The press release also stated the final phase of the planning process would "incorporate and build upon the work of the Lambert Group." The deal would be sealed when Mayor Nagin signed a memorandum of understanding to officially create this integrative planning system. In short, the press release outlined everything almost everyone had hoped for. It portrayed a unified front, described the approach the planning process would take, addressed its relationship to the Lambert planning process, and made it clear that the purpose was to present a comprehensive plan to the LRA in order to receive recovery funding.

Unfortunately, such statements did not turn out to mean very much.

THE UNIFIED NEW ORLEANS PLAN (UNOP)

With a comprehensive planning process now apparently on track, optimism returned regarding the potential of planning to help shape recovery investments. The LRA hoped not only that a completed UNOP could guide spending of the CDBG community recovery and infrastructure funds but also that the process could guide individual decisions to relocate or rebuild under the state's CDBG-funded Road Home program. These individual decisions, in turn, could help to inform other public infrastructure investments. Although coordination between public and private decisions would be difficult—the Road Home program would begin in the fall, whereas the plan would not be completed until the end of the year—David Voelker observed that the neighborhood planning efforts could still help home owners struggling to decide what to do. And, according to Steven Bingler, decisions by residents could affect infrastructure investment plans: "If there are certain neighborhoods that decide they won't rebuild, then it wouldn't make sense to rebuild the infrastructure in those parts of town."[68]

Around July 11, 23 groups that had submitted RFQs were informed they had made it past the first stage of the selection process. They were told they would be interviewed the following week by the review panel, which was chosen by Concordia and Rockefeller in consultation with APA.[69] The panel consisted of former Pittsburgh planning director Bob Lurcott, former Berkeley mayor Gus Newport, City Planning Commission director Yolanda Rodriguez, and recovery planning expert and former Los Angeles planning director Ken Topping.[70]

The NOCSF announced the winning teams on Friday, July 21, having just completed the interviews over the preceding days. They announced five teams to be the district planners and 10 teams as qualified to conduct neighborhood planning.[71] New Orleans residents would help assign teams to specific neighborhoods during the next several weeks. The review panel selected Villavaso & Associates and Henry Consulting to do the citywide planning work. In the words of the *Times-Picayune*, "The team includes Laurie Johnson, a disaster mitigation specialist from San Francisco, and Duncan Associates, from Austin, Texas, but is mostly comprised of locals. It includes, notably, urban planners from the University of New Orleans, including Jane Brooks. Bingler said he expected the coordinating task to be handed to a team led by a non-Louisiana firm with a national reputation. But he said the expertise assembled by Villavaso was stunning, making that choice an easy one."[72] Local officials had been primed for the arrival of "world class planners" who would apply their worldwide expertise to the unprecedented task of rebuilding an entire city. In contrast, this was a local team, and their proposal was more about infrastructure and finance rather than urban design.

For professional planners who had been observing the post-Katrina circus, this was a remarkable moment: it unveiled a systematic public process that would be run through the City Planning Commission and guided by a steering council representing all the key political groups in the city. The reality, however, was that it was easier to fast-track a selection process than jump-start an enormous planning effort involving scores of consultants. The first few weeks of this new planning effort were marked by considerable confusion. But one thing was clear: the planning process was now officially called the Unified New Orleans Plan (UNOP), according to its new website, logo, and letterhead.

On July 27, Councilmembers Hedge-Morrell and Fielkow organized a city council "informational forum" to answer questions from citizens about the plan and provide clarity to the process.[73] It included several representatives of the UNOP team, including GNOF, Concordia, and Villavaso. Several points of confusion and concern became apparent. Foremost was the question of how UNOP related to the city council–Lambert neighborhood planning process. The council members' concern was that neighborhoods that had been actively planning—either on their own or through the Lambert process—would have to "start all over again."

A more substantive concern was the timing of plan completion and its relation to the flow of recovery funds. Some neighborhoods, planning since October 2005, were impatient to receive their funds and asked why their plans could not be submitted immediately. One citizen protested, "Don't hold us hostage for the money." Another said, "We are concerned that the planning will delay recovery." This discussion reflected some fundamental misunderstandings about the relationship of planning to the various pots of recovery money. In fact, the lion's share of the federal recovery dollars was in the Road Home program, which would flow to individuals, regardless of the plans. But mistrust remained: people were still convinced that the government would tell them where they could or could not rebuild, despite all city and state public claims to the contrary.

Many residents also had developed a misconception, perhaps dating back to the moratorium proposals of the previous December, that a sequential relationship existed between planning and rebuilding and that any actions would need to await completion of the planning process. In fact, the recovery funds for homes and infrastructure were already in process, albeit slowly. The Road Home money would pay for home reconstruction, several programs were in process to subsidize rental housing construction, and the FEMA Public Assistance program would pay for restoration of infrastructure and public buildings. The frustration was understandable, but it was not planning that was holding up these essential funds. The most substantive purpose of the planning process was to release the remaining CDBG funds: that would augment the FEMA money, support economic development and housing improvements, and catalyze private investment.

Finally, council members questioned GNOF representatives about the composition of the CSO. The representatives reported that they were currently interviewing candidates and expected to announce the selections within two weeks. The discussion focused on the neighborhood representatives to the CSO. GNOF explained there would be one representative from each city council district. Together, these representatives would constitute a majority of the CSO. The tension rose in the room as the discussion subtly became about the power to control this plan, the funding, and the direction of the rebuilding. Clearly, the councilmembers believed that they should be the ones to appoint the CSO representative from their district, and they were uncomfortable with a private, mostly white entity from uptown—GNOF—deciding who was an appropriate neighborhood representative. It was clear that some city council members did not trust GNOF, and they were insulted that GNOF would imply they were not familiar with the neighborhood-scale needs of their constituents. Conversely, GNOF was afraid city council members would make raw political appointments in an attempt to take over the process. GNOF and Rockefeller were external civic organizations concerned about government corruption, political favoritism, and influence trading. Perhaps sensing this, city council members often brought up their status as the only democratically elected representatives of the residents of New Orleans involved in UNOP.

Soon after this muted confrontation, the UNOP team announced it would hold two kickoff meetings. The first one would be held on Sunday, July 30, in City Park. Bobbie Hill of Concordia outlined the three purposes of this meeting: it would (1) help residents start organizing within their districts; (2) define the boundaries of neighborhoods; and (3) develop a set of criteria to select neighborhood planners. The second meeting was on August 1, the following Tuesday, also in City Park. At that meeting, all the planning firms would present their qualifications and philosophies and answer questions from residents.

The announcement of these meetings stoked great confusion. For one, it renewed concerns about how this was going to affect the ongoing Lambert process. The public announcements and flyers were unclear. For example, the notice published in *City Business* stated, "The meeting will begin involving community members in selecting technical assistance teams to support communities in neighborhood, district and citywide planning. Attendees will establish criteria for working with the assistance teams, define neighborhood boundaries and confirm projects for 13 planning districts."[74] Hence, many residents were concerned that they would have to start all over again and that if they did not come to the Sunday meeting, they would be left out. City council members were inundated with phone calls from confused and angry constituents. If residents were happy with the Lambert process in their neighborhood, did they have to pick a UNOP planner? What did it mean, "residents would select their planner"? Which residents would be involved, and how would they make the selection? On what basis would residents know how to set criteria for selecting planning consultants? How could a few people in a room on Sunday possibly be able to redefine their neighborhood boundaries?

This reflected two main problems surrounding the launch of UNOP. The first was a lack of clear communication. It was essential to have a system that would use multiple means to communicate clear and consistent messages to address citizen concerns, given that residents were still unsettled. In addition, there was confusion over the planning processes, uncertainty regarding what all the plans would lead to, and profound levels of mistrust.

The second problem was that the process itself was still unstable and ambiguous. Some aspects defied clear communication because no one knew what would happen.[75] The UNOP team members stated they could not predict the results of the two kickoff meetings, the timeline for the process, or the structure of the plan. They emphasized that the plan would be citizen driven and that this situation was unprecedented in American history. They expected citizens would buy into it in the end because they would be a part of it from the beginning. This meant that the UNOP team was relying on residents to trust that the process truly would be citizen based, in a city in which trust was in short supply. As for the residents, many expected expertise to guide them so long as experts did not tell them what to do.

By all accounts, the first UNOP meeting on July 30 was a disaster. The good news was the level of interest was much higher than Concordia anticipated. Around 500 people attended the meeting whereas they only expected 200. The bad news was the facility was too small to easily accommodate everyone. It was the largest room they could obtain on short notice, and it just wasn't big enough. Hundreds of people were waiting in a long line to register after the meeting had already begun. When they arrived, the room was crowded, noisy, and full of angry people. No one could adequately hear either their district discussions or the general announcements. Often, people couldn't even hear the person next to them. Needless to say, this impeded the ability to have meaningful discussions and increased the potential for miscommunication and frustration. Arguments erupted over neighborhood boundaries.[76] For example, in District Eight—the Lower Ninth Ward—the Holy Cross neighborhood argued for continuing its own planning process, whereas activists from other parts of the district argued for planning as one district. This argument was fueled by old tensions and bad feelings that became more pronounced over the next few months.

The poor organization of the meeting reflected badly on the new planning team even though the actual planning had not yet begun. In such an environment, the participants needed crystal-clear instructions. But Concordia and GNOF themselves did not know how the planning teams would be organized. They expected meeting participants to help them to decide how to structure the district plans, but the allotted time was insufficient for such open-ended deliberation. Bingler described how the neighborhood plans would come together into district plans in November and said that they would "stitch all the plans together into one citywide plan" in December so that "all the plans would become part of the whole." But participants had trouble envisioning this process and the result. The very existence of this large gathering suggested to participants that their decisions were important, but no one understood the meaning of this meeting or what the consequences of their decisions might be. UNOP leaders asked them to "talk about how you want to plan" and to decide whether they needed a "technical assistance team" to help them, as well as how many neighborhood plans would constitute their district plan. But participants had no basis for making these decisions.

The second City Park meeting on August 1 was a much smoother, albeit smaller, event. Each of the 15 consultant teams made a 10-minute presentation. Each attendee was asked to cast a vote for the teams they would prefer for their district or neighborhood. For the benefit of people who were unable to come, the presentations were also streamed on the UNOP website. People could vote online until the following Monday. Bingler urged everyone to tell their neighbors to vote. They were also told that if they were happy with the planning efforts already happening in their neighborhood, they didn't need to vote for a new neighborhood planner. But this process still seemed confusing. What did it mean to vote for both a district planner and a neighborhood planner? Should people who were already satisfied with their neighborhood planning process vote anyway, in case the rest of their neighbors decided to choose a new planning team? What about voting fraud? Many observers complained that it was misleading to call this "voting," since anyone could register an address on the website and submit a vote. Conversely, those without reliable Internet access were not able to view the presentations or submit their votes.

Two days later, Lambert took out a full-page paid advertisement in the *Times-Picayune* that made it clear he had no intention of being "folded in" to the UNOP process. The purpose of the ad, he claimed, was to "add clarity to a process that has become unnecessarily blurred by politics." Lambert argued his plans would lead to a faster flow of much-needed federal reconstruction funding:

> I am confident that the plan we have devised together will meet with your enthusiastic approval. Once it does, it should immediately be submitted to State and Federal funding agencies to spur the release of significant funding for neighborhood projects. It cannot and should not wait for the fledgling Unified New Orleans Plan which the principal organizers have indicated will not be ready until late spring, 2007.[77]

He also addressed the confusion being created by the UNOP:

> I am particularly distressed that we are receiving multiple inquiries from residents who have apparently been led to believe that if they do not select a planner from the UNOP list; their neighborhood will not receive funding. This is patently false and an abuse of community trust. You absolutely DO NOT need to choose a planner from the foundation's list to obtain funding for projects and investments in your neighborhood. It would be foolish

and wasteful if the Unified New Orleans Plan duplicates work already completed.

Instead, Lambert argued the UNOP should focus solely on the areas that his teams left untouched: the unflooded neighborhoods, the central business district, and large economic development projects, such as the port and the medical district.

He concluded by contradicting all the public messages made by the state and city with the claim that

> under the existing contract my company has with the City of New Orleans, I can assure you that the plans we have devised together will qualify for State and Federal funding. Our team works directly for the City of New Orleans, the entity which must submit plans to State and Federal funding agencies. Your continued participation at our planning meetings will only hasten the development of the plans, their approval and submission for funding.[78]

While it was true that he was under contract to the city, Lambert conveniently ignored the lack of support from the mayor and the City Planning Commission, as well as the council's recent statement of support for incorporating his work into the UNOP. More significantly, he ignored the wishes of state and federal funders, which had made it clear that Lambert's work addressed only one part of a larger building and recovery strategy. Lambert's work alone would not lead to the release of the most critical funding streams.

Some councilmembers and the press suggested Lambert was reacting personally to what he viewed as criticism of his planning team, a charge he denied.[79] Lambert argued that he placed the ad because he needed to communicate forcefully to residents who were genuinely confused. Many neighborhoods plans were almost complete, and people saw no need to put energy into another process. He thought it was in their interest to complete the plans they had started and was concerned they were getting the message to stop and wait for UNOP. Furthermore, he was afraid that the longer this process took, the less money the LRA would make available.

From his perspective, he was following the guidance of the federal recovery office, and it was frustrating that LRA had intervened. The only written guidelines regarding access to federal recovery funds were those related to the ESF #14 process and CDBG money. He believed that the federal government's own CDBG requirements said the funds could be used only for the areas with the most need, and the ESF #14 process was the way to identify recovery projects that deserved funding. Lambert had met with ESF #14 staff in March 2006, and they had jointly discussed FEMA's guidelines for parish plans and the format he should use for the final project lists.[80] Lambert's goal was to come up with a plan as quickly as possible that met the ESF #14 guidelines so the city could start accessing CDBG funds. To meet those guidelines, they needed to start from the bottom up, creating targeted lists of projects at the neighborhood level. In other words, Lambert reasoned his planning team was the one playing by the rules; the LRA's interference was just a power grab by the state shot through with the politics of race.

Both the LRA and city council quickly defended the UNOP approach. Councilmember Cynthia Hedge-Morrell emphasized, "The Lambert plan needs to be folded into the citywide plan. I don't think it can be done piecemeal." One councilmember even called for firing Lambert for being "divisive" and "confusing."[81] LRA chair Norman Francis reiterated that "the development of a comprehensive recovery plan, which brings together individuals, neighborhoods and the entire city, is a critical step on the road to rebuilding New Orleans."[82] In addition, the LRA indicated it would certainly be open to helping flooded neighborhoods get earlier funding for wet-neighborhood projects that clearly would be part of the final plan, thus rendering moot one of Lambert's arguments.

All parties were called into city hall on Friday and grudgingly emerged with a truce: Lambert and GNOF agreed that Lambert's work would be part of UNOP and that they hoped that the neighborhoods with head starts on planning would be able to access some funds without delay.[83]

Meanwhile, grumblings about the $356,390 no-bid contract for Concordia and Steven Bingler arose.[84] Why, some questioned, was this acceptable, when one of the rationales for UNOP was to have an open-bid process that contrasted with Lambert's contract? GNOF's response was that Concordia was managing the consultants, not leading the plan; they were simply an extension of GNOF's staff, which lacked the capacity to handle a project of this scope. Still, this was proving to be problematic during August: the CSO had yet to take the lead overseeing the planning process, and the consultants had yet to begin, which meant that Concordia and Bingler were effectively the public face of UNOP. His status rankled many, including Manning and Lambert, who were tired of scolding lectures from the LRA and GNOF about open-bid processes.

The real question was why the CSO had not yet been formed to take charge of UNOP? For that matter, why had the mayor and council not yet signed the memorandum of understanding to create UNOP? The sticking point seems to have involved the appointments to the CSO—or rather one appointment in particular. City council members assumed they would be entitled to appoint neighborhood delegates to the CSO to represent each of the five city council districts. Thus, not only would the council be involved in leading UNOP—as it should be, for a truly "unified" plan—but also each member would have what amounted to a voice in the planning process.

Cynthia Willard-Lewis was still dead set against UNOP because she perceived that it was delaying recovery funds to some of the city's most heavily damaged areas in New Orleans East and the Lower Ninth Ward. She
also still feared it would redirect some of the funds to less damaged areas.[85]
Reportedly, Willard-Lewis wanted to appoint Sherman Copelin as her representative to the CSO. Copelin is an outspoken developer, a leader of the
New Orleans East Business Association, a former longtime member of the
state legislature, and an influential politician with a controversial past.[86]
GNOF and Rockefeller balked at his appointment because Copelin was
obviously an opponent of UNOP and too controversial to serve effectively
on such an oversight body.

In a surprise appearance at the August 10 LRA board meeting in Lafay-
ette, Willard-Lewis and Copelin invited Charles Steele Jr., the president of
the Southern Christian Leadership Conference, to join them in presenting
their case. The three of them, who were also accompanied by Mtangalizi
Sanyika, spokesperson for the African American Leadership Project, "spoke
at length" during the public comments portion of the meeting.[87] According to people present at the meeting, Willard-Lewis and Copelin brought
Steele to help make the point that the LRA was a racist organization that
was delaying recovery assistance to the most needy African-American parts
of the city. The official minutes did not record the impassioned speech on
this point by Willard-Lewis, nor the stinging rebuke by Norman Francis.
As a longtime civil rights leader, Francis was deeply offended by the claims
of intentional LRA bias and expressed this in no uncertain terms. Francis
was not the only one offended by the accusation. The LRA board included
a number of other prominent African-American leaders, most notably the
Reverend Harry Blake, a legendary civil rights pioneer from Shreveport and
Freedom Rider in the 1960s.[88] Francis said that the LRA was trying to help
and that it was responding to the city's request for planning funds rather
than interfering. At one point, Francis suggested that perhaps the LRA had
gone too far in trying to help New Orleans and should give the Rockefeller
money back so the city could develop its own plan.[89] When Voelker offered
to meet with the Rockefeller Foundation to discuss this, Copelin and Willard-Lewis backed off.

Meanwhile, the UNOP memorandum remained unsigned. Throughout
the summer, the LRA—through point man David Voelker—continued to
work with the mayor and city council. Voelker was well suited to the role.
Of all the prominent members of the LRA from New Orleans, he was the
only one who did not take sides in the mayoral election. Thus, in late May
and early June, he had little political baggage and was able to engage all the
parties when he became the LRA's chief negotiator.[90]

On August 28, 2006, Voelker was holding all the cards. It was the eve of the first anniversary of Katrina's catastrophic landfall, and every major news organization was in town. New Orleans would be on the front page of *USA Today*, the *Wall Street Journal,* the *Christian Science Monitor*, the *New York Times*, and the *Philadelphia Inquirer*, and it was the subject of multiple articles and editorials in every major newspaper in the United States and Canada. The anniversary was covered by other major news outlets worldwide, including *China Daily*. Given all this attention, it is easy to imagine the conversation Voelker must have had with Nagin on August 28: save us the embarrassment of worldwide headlines that scream that not only do we lack a plan but that we are so inept and lacking in resolve that we cannot even agree on a planning process one year after the disaster.

Thus, on August 28, the mayor signed the "Memorandum of Understanding Between the City of New Orleans, New Orleans City Council, City Planning Commission, Greater New Orleans Foundation and New Orleans Community Support Foundation." It stated the agreement of all the parties to "advance a single [citywide] recovery and rebuilding planning process for the City of New Orleans, referred to as the Unified New Orleans Neighborhood Recovery Plan." It stated,

Jedidiah Horne

Fig. 4.8. Observers at a parade on the first anniversary of Katrina

The central goal of the planning process will be to create the Unified New Orleans Neighborhood Recovery Plan—which will consist of a comprehensive infrastructure plan and recovery plans for all of New Orleans' neighborhoods—as required by the Louisiana Recovery Authority as a pre-requisite to certain funding . . . the Unified New Orleans Neighborhood Recovery Plan will then be reviewed by the City Planning Commission, submitted to the City Council and Mayor C. Ray Nagin for approval, and forwarded to the Louisiana Recovery Authority for a final review and request for recovery funding for implementation by the appropriate governmental agencies. Public hearings will be held at the City Planning and City Council levels as required by law.

The memorandum also explicitly addressed the role of the Lambert planning efforts. One of the tasks of the CSO was to

monitor and coordinate the neighborhood planning and recovery and rebuilding planning process which includes but is not limited to the work currently underway by Lambert Advisory, LC [*sic*]. Lambert Advisory, LC will continue its work in the neighborhoods where the services/work product is substantially underway as determined through consultation between the CSO, the neighborhoods, and the City Council appointee. Any remaining work not started, incomplete and/or partially underway by Lambert Advisory, LC will be considered for inclusion in the planning process. The City Council appointee will ensure that all work products produced by Lambert Advisory, LC will be provided in a timely manner to the CSO and that Lambert Advisory, LC will participate in a cooperative and professional manner.

The announcement also included the names of the CSO members: Judith Williams would represent the mayor's office; the city council would be represented by Cynthia Hedge-Morrell; Poco Sloss, the City Planning Commission; Carey Shea, the Rockefeller Foundation; Albert Petrie Jr. would represent Council District A; H. M. K. Amen, Council District B; Tarence Davis, Council District C; Vera Triplett, Council District D; and Terrel J. Broussard, Council District E.[91]

Now that the memorandum was signed, the NOCSF would be able to sign contracts with the planning consultants, starting with the citywide team. Officials stressed individual neighborhoods were completely free to use their plans as a basis for obtaining government or private grants, but federal grants passed through the LRA required participation in this unified plan. When asked about the delays in signing the deal, Nagin responded, "There's always been a fundamental agreement, it's just that the lawyers were working on some final issues. It's signed, sealed and delivered."[92]

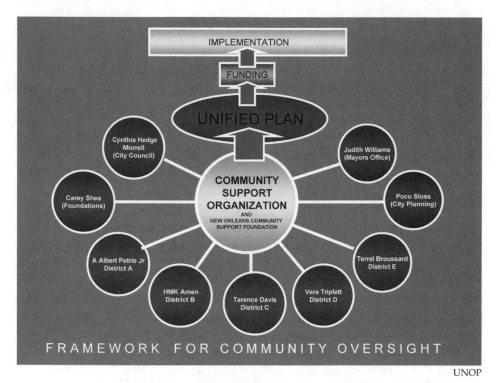

Fig. 4.9. The role of the Community Support Organization in the greater planning process

So, one year after Katrina struck, there was finally agreement on a planning structure—a plan for a plan—that was nominally acceptable to the city council, mayor, state, and federal government. But considerably more drama lay ahead.

What did New Orleans look like on the first anniversary of Katrina?

It depended upon whether one saw the glass as half full or half empty. According to the most reliable estimates, the city's population in July was about half of the pre-Katrina population, around 225,000.[93] As of June, as many as 150,000 evacuees remained in Houston, 84,000 in Atlanta, 50,000 in Baton Rouge, and 5,000 in Birmingham, Alabama.[94] Many evacuees were waiting for hurricane season to end, schools to open, a positive commitment from government regarding the provision of public services, or some signal that their neighbors would return.[95] Gas and electricity had been almost fully restored, though outages remained frequent; as of July, most residents had full postal service. The Army Corps of Engineers had almost finished removing the 300,000 refrigerators in people's yards and has begun work on the 250,000 wrecked cars still on the streets. In mid-June the Corps

Jedidiah Horne

Fig. 4.10. A parade on the first anniversary of Katrina

of Engineers completed its first-pass rehabilitation of the city's levee and pump system.[96]

Many of those who had returned to New Orleans were still evacuees in their own city and were without the jobs and homes they had had before.[97] Opinions were divided on what needed to happen first: the release of government funds, insurance settlements, restoration of government services, residents' return, private investments, job creation, or levee reconstruction. Views of the recovery also varied by neighborhood. According to the Brookings Institution, "A tour of the city today confirms that not all neighborhoods are benefiting from the recovery. While tons of debris have been removed, endless blocks in Lakeview, the Lower Ninth Ward, Gentilly, and New Orleans East look just as they did six months ago."[98] Large areas of Lakeview and the Lower Ninth Ward remained without gas and electric service.[99] Restoration of other public services continued gradually. Orleans Parish expected to open 56 public schools—far fewer than the 117 schools before Katrina but more than double the number open in the spring.[100] Eleven hospitals were open in Orleans Parish, about half of those available before Katrina.[101] The closing of Charity Hospital made medical care less certain for the uninsured, and large areas of the city, particularly New Orleans East, had no medical services at all. Ninety percent of the city's traffic signals were repaired, a significant improvement over the previous fall. The transit system was still devastated. Only 19,000 rode it daily, down from 124,000 before the disaster.[102]

The cost of living was much higher. Rents went up 39 percent, and electricity rates were up by 20 percent.[103] Home insurance was considerably more expensive, according to anecdotal evidence. According to the local representative of the National Association of Home Builders, home construction costs were up by 30 percent.[104] Although some lower-end jobs had higher wages in order to attract scarce workers, many households would be priced out of the housing market because of the increased building costs. The metropolitan area workforce was 30 percent smaller than before Katrina, and the unemployment rate was 7.2 percent—substantially higher than the 4.6 percent rate both in Louisiana and the nation as a whole.[105]

Still, the city's economy was improving, though unevenly across the city and its different economic sectors. Significant construction was taking place, but it was far from the boom one expects to follow a disaster.[106] The Brookings Institution found that "one year after the storm, the New Orleans area is both rebounding and stagnating, with much of the boon benefiting the least-impacted neighborhoods and parishes."[107] About 40 percent of the city's small businesses had reopened. Most of these were in the French Quarter or uptown. There were far fewer African-American businesses than before the storm. According to Richard Campanella at Tulane University, the level of flood depth was the main predictor of the rate of return for small businesses.[108] Only a third of restaurants and food stores were back in business.[109] Tourism was improving: 28,000 local hotel rooms reopened in Orleans and Jefferson parishes, compared to 38,000 before the storms. Louis Armstrong New Orleans International Airport was up to 12,000 passengers daily but still well below the 21,000 who traveled through it before the storm. Happily, convention business was back to normal. Cargo tonnage at the Port of New Orleans was at 94 percent of pre-Katrina shipments.[110] Finally, the city's finances were better than expected. Sales-tax revenues for the first six months of 2006 were at 77 percent of pre-Katrina levels, probably due in part to auto and construction material sales.[111] The city also expected 2006 property taxes to be about 80 percent of its pre-Katrina revenue.

Even though there was some improvement in the situation, Senator Landrieu reminded the press the city still had enormous needs one year after the flood:

> It needs a massive, massive—not just throwing money at the situation, but a Marshall Plan—effort to get this great city and region back up and running. . . . It's not because people don't have the will here, it's not because they don't want to work. But as the cameras will show the viewers this morning, it is overwhelming to people to come back to a neighborhood that was

basically destroyed to this level. It's just unprecedented, as I've said constantly this year, that needs an unprecedented response.[112]

To make the region whole, Landrieu said the Gulf Coast might need an additional "few billion dollars a year." Donald Powell admitted the possibility of meeting additional funding requests, but "should there be more requests, our job is to be sure it's based upon good data."[113]

The federal government would not provide even the authorized funds until local officials could present them with detailed recovery plans to explain how the funds would be spent. "They have to tell us what the needs are. Those needs need to be reduced to paper and verified," Powell reiterated.[114]

The federal government had committed significant resources to the region for both immediate relief and long-term reconstruction. President Bush declared the government had committed $110 billion to Katrina relief, though he admitted the money was taking longer to get to Louisiana than to Mississippi.[115] According to FEMA, the agency had provided nearly $6 billion directly to Hurricane Katrina victims for housing and other needs, which was the most ever provided by FEMA for any single natural disaster.[116] In all, nearly 950,000 Gulf Coast applicants were determined eligible for assistance under the Individuals and Households Program. As of August 2006, 64,150 Louisiana households were living in FEMA-provided mobile homes or travel trailers, and over half of these households would continue to depend on federally funded temporary housing through August 2009.[117] Bush predicted that the effect of federal funds would become much more evident as the $16 billion in CDBG money began to flow to the Gulf Coast in the coming months.[118]

For Orleans Parish, FEMA's Public Assistance program had, through August 2006, obligated a total of $455 million for damaged public facilities, including schools, hospitals, community centers, playground, and utilities.[119] Still, little of the appropriated money had reached New Orleans, which was still waiting for federal approval of much of the $1 billion requested for infrastructure. Although the city received two $120 million Community Disaster Loans from FEMA and $100 million to reimburse some infrastructure costs, it still lacked funds for architectural, engineering, and basic services and other start-up costs to repair damaged facilities before the Public Assistance reimbursements were received.[120]

It is difficult to interpret these numbers. It is true that the federal government had authorized significant funds for Katrina relief and reconstruction. But from the perspective of New Orleans residents, it mattered how much of this money was designated for Louisiana, how much of it was designated for permanent recovery and reconstruction, how much was for essential city services, and how much was for those most in need. The answers to these questions were unclear. Most of the $110 billion had been spent on emergency relief, and two-thirds of the housing money was for temporary housing, such as trailers and short-term rental assistance.[121]

For permanent reconstruction of affected communities, probably the two most important funding categories were the FEMA Public Assistance reimbursements to repair damaged public facilities and the CDBG dollars, which were negotiated between HUD, the LRA, and the affected parishes. These totaled approximately $35 billion for the Gulf Coast.[122] Because the funds from both of these sources were mired in bureaucracy—bogged down at every point in the pipeline from FEMA and HUD, through the LRA, through the legislature and governor, through state agencies and to local governments—residents had not seen the money yet, and it was difficult to know which joint in the pipeline was most to blame. Similarly, out of $10.4 billion in low-interest loans approved by the Small Business Administration, only $2.5 billion had found its way into people's hands by August.[123]

In FEMA's Public Assistance Grant Program, more than 17,000 "project work sheets" had been filed in Louisiana. They first needed to be approved by FEMA, a time-consuming and often contentious step. Then they were sent to Baton Rouge for the state to review. In August 2006, there were 60 grant managers each handling 20 to 25 requests to repair damaged public facilities.[124] Reportedly, state offices in Baton Rouge were being extremely thorough in their reviews because they were sensitive to the state's national reputation for waste, fraud, and corruption. This high level of care further slowed the flow of most federal funds. As of August, New Orleans had submitted 833 project worksheets to FEMA with a total value of $394.2 million, and FEMA had paid nearly $117.5 million for 239 of these.[125] And, again, these funds were being disbursed only when the city could show a receipt for the costs incurred; these funds were not provided in advance of repairs.

As for the CDBG funding, the Road Home program was going to use the bulk of the $10.4 billion provided by Congress. A pilot program was initiated in August, and the first Road Home office opened in New Orleans on August 22 with 147 staff members.[126] More than 100,000 households had applied for assistance by this time, and the governor hoped the money would soon start to reach home owners.

In other words, the city had made remarkable progress in one year. But enormous uncertainties remained, and, for tens of thousands of households, the nightmare was not over. Completing a plan for recovery would not solve the problems of these households. But a public planning process could go a long way toward providing the public with information and helping people and organizations communicate their intentions to one another, which would help everyone make better decisions.

5

The New Orleans Neighborhoods Rebuilding Plan

While almost everyone else waffled about the UNOP memorandum, Paul Lambert's process had been proceeding since April. The project assumed an official name: the New Orleans Neighborhoods Rebuilding Plan. Lambert and Sheila Danzey's firm, SHEDO, managed the project; the firms Bermello-Ajamil & Partners and Hewitt-Washington coordinated the planning work. From the beginning, Lambert wanted to emulate the plan developed in Miami-Dade County, Florida, after Hurricane Andrew and had brought in Bermello-Ajamil and others who had worked on it. To accomplish the plan, they dispatched seven neighborhood planning consultants to 49 flooded neighborhoods in 10 of the city's planning districts (see table 5.1).[1]

Between May 17 and September 12, the teams led a total of 66 neighborhood planning meetings, most of them during the summer. In late August, Lambert also held meetings in Baton Rouge, Atlanta, and Houston for New Orleanians still living outside of the city. According to Lambert, more than 7,500 residents attended the neighborhood meetings and roughly 400 to 500 people participated in the meetings outside of the city.[2]

The stated purpose of the plan was to

provide an assessment of what is required to return neighborhoods to the state that existed prior to Hurricane Katrina or to a level of revitalization beyond where the community was prior to Hurricane Katrina. This enhanced revitalization goal is particularly true for those neighborhoods with a high

TABLE 5.1. THE LAMBERT PROCESS'S PLANNING CONSULTANTS

PLANNING DISTRICT	CONSULTING FIRM	RESPONSIBILITIES / NEIGHBORHOODS
	Lambert Advisory	Project Management
	SHEDO	Project Management
	GCR	Data Collection and Mapping
	Dr. Silas Lee and Associates	Research Strategist
2	Cliff James / Byron Stewart	Central City, Milan
3	Billes Architecture	Hollygrove, Dixon, Leonidas, Marlyville-Fountainbleau, Broadmoor, Freret, Audubon*
4	Zyscovic, Cliff James / Byron Stewart	Bayou St. John, Tremé/Lafitte, Seventh Ward, Fairgrounds, St. Bernard Area, Mid-City, Tulane/Gravier, BW Cooper, Gertown, Iberville
5	Bermello, Ajamil and Partners / Villavaso & Associates	Overall Planning Consultants, Lakeview, West End, Navarre, City Park, Lake Shore*, Lake Vista*, Lake Wood
6	Hewitt-Washington Architects	Overall Planning Consultants, Fillmore, St. Anthony, Milneburg, Pontchartrain Park, Gentilly Woods, Gentilly Terrace, Dillard, Lake Terrace*, Lake Oaks*
7	St. Martin-Brown and Associates	St. Claude, St. Roche, Desire Area, Florida Area
8	Stull and Lee Architects	Lower Ninth Ward, Holy Cross*
9	St. Martin-Brown and Associates	Little Woods, Pine Village, West Lake Forest, Plum Orchard, Read Blvd East, Read Blvd West
10	St. Martin-Brown and Associates	Village de l'est
11	St. Martin-Brown and Associates	Viavant / Venetian Isles

*Partially flooded neighborhood

degree of blight, public facilities in poor condition, and generally where population and housing values were decreasing at a slow but steady pace over the past several decades.[3]

Not covered by the plan were citywide infrastructure issues, the school system, public housing, the overall flood protection system, or zoning. The resultant neighborhood plans were "generally consistent with" the City Planning Commission's Neighborhood Planning Guide.[4] The plan also describes the focus on the flooded neighborhoods, as the rationale for this planning process:

As early as October 2005, the Urban Land Institute and some members of Congress were advocating the establishment of policies to ensure that large areas in the flooded sections of the City not be rebuilt. The City Council made

Jedidiah Horne

Fig. 5.1. Paul Lambert

a decision to focus the planning effort on the flooded neighborhoods first-and-foremost in order to provide residents of the flooded neighborhoods a process that would allow them to formally voice and define what would become of their communities.[5]

The first of the planning meetings asked residents to evaluate the information consultants had gathered on the current conditions of their neighborhood. During the next phase, residents were asked to scrutinize the planning concepts the consultants were in the process of developing for each neighborhood. In the final phase, residents selected the best or most appropriate options for their neighborhoods. They also determined which of these projects were needed immediately, which could be done during the next several months, and which were long-term community improvements. This became the basis for each neighborhood's final plan, which included a matrix that estimated costs and identified potential funders for each project. Each phase involved a formal neighborhood meeting, but dozens of informal meetings reportedly took place between residents and consultants. These meetings also helped residents find out more about recovery resources. (This was especially true of the meetings held outside of New Orleans, which included representatives from FEMA, the U.S. Army Corps of Engineers, and the state's Road Home program.)[6] According to some observers, the performance of the consultants was uneven across the neighborhoods, but this is not surprising given that each consultant team was responsible for several neighborhoods, was given relatively little guidance in the early stages, and was under pressure to complete the plans within a fairly short period of time.

At a second-phase meeting on Saturday, August 12, in New Orleans East, hundreds of people showed up, exceeding the capacity of the room. The crowd was captivated by visions of "three major bicycle paths, each stretching at least five miles; landscape buffers between homes and businesses; a French Quarter–style mixing of commercial and residential properties at most major intersections along the interstate; a revitalized Lincoln Beach; a family entertainment district; an open-air, pedestrian-friendly town center for upscale shopping; and restrictions on dense apartment complexes."[7]

Realistic short-term goals included "repairing levees, major streets and drainage; replacing street signs; opening health care facilities, schools, supermarkets, drugstores, gas stations and banks; revitalizing Joe Brown Park; and organizing more neighborhood associations."[8] According to the *Times-Picayune*, audience members' reactions ranged from excitement to skepticism about project feasibility and financing. This meeting was characteristic of the Lambert team's way of facilitating citywide reconstruction, which was to create a sense of optimism about rebuilding all the neighborhoods in order to encourage residents to come back to the city. But it also may have been fanciful to have expected such significant new investment in areas like New Orleans East, given its low-density sprawl and its retail and entertainment decline before the storm.

Most of Lambert's community meetings were held between the July 5 announcement of a tentative agreement to integrate the planning processes and the August 28 memorandum of understanding that officially created the UNOP. While the Lambert planners were operating in high gear, the mayor and council were giving mixed signals regarding their support for the two simultaneous planning processes. There is still dispute about why Lambert and the city council never fully agreed to subsume their plans under the UNOP umbrella during that time, although most agreed the case of the dueling planners was the oddest, most politicized planning phenomenon any of them had ever seen.[9] As for Lambert, he believed the purpose of post-Katrina planning was to bring residents back to all the neighborhoods, and he never believed UNOP was a clean break from the BNOB plan, which never entirely lost the taint of encouraging New Orleans to shrink its footprint. To Lambert and some members of the city council, it was not a matter of asking whether people would return or projecting who would return; it was a matter of enabling all of them to do so. It was not about determining whether or not neighborhoods would be viable but helping them become viable. Even though many things had changed by late summer, the sense of this difference between the two strands of neighborhood planning never went away. The city council was never interested in stopping its neighborhood planning process, because it saw it successfully engaging residents and providing them with hope. For his part, the mayor did not challenge the council by asking it to stop the process or redirect its funding.

After the UNOP MOU was signed, Lambert's team was not certain whether it was expected to continue its work. The problem was less the MOU itself—which clearly stated that it should—but the widespread public perception that Lambert's process had been rendered irrelevant by the formalization of UNOP.[10] The two processes had little active cooperation and continued to operate completely independently. Given the extraordinary time pressures each was under, it is not surprising that neither proactively reached out to the other, especially with each assuming antagonism from the other.

The New Orleans Neighborhoods Rebuilding Plan was unveiled to the public on the afternoon of Saturday, September 23, at a five-hour meeting at city hall.[11] Lambert's team presented plans for 46 neighborhoods, which "feature[d] a dizzying array of ideas," ranging from the basic restoration of streets and sidewalks to bold ideas for linear parks, town centers, recreation amenities, and senior housing.[12] The summary of the completed plan stressed that the neighborhood plans were led by the residents, with the consultants there to assess only pre-Katrina and current conditions, funding sources and restrictions, the broader context, and potential pitfalls. "Professional guidance . . . was built based on trust. This was particularly important given the fact that two prior and related post-Katrina initial planning efforts, by the Urban Land Institute and Bring New Orleans Back Commission had ended with the perception among many of the community's residents that urban planning or recovery planning was something to fight rather than embrace."[13]

The District Five neighborhood plans were representative of the neighborhood-level plans. The district includes the City Park, Country Club Gardens, Lakeshore, Lake Vista, Lakeview, Lakewood, and Parkview neighborhoods. They were organized through the seven neighborhood associations, under the purview of an overall District 5 recovery steering committee. Several faculty and staff from the University of New Orleans College of Urban and Public Affairs were also part of the planning efforts because of the campus's location nearby.[14]

The plans were organized into six sections. They described the neighborhood, its condition before Katrina, the impact of the storm, neighborhood rebuilding scenarios, a neighborhood recovery plan, and strategies for implementation and funding. The proposed projects included reconstructing

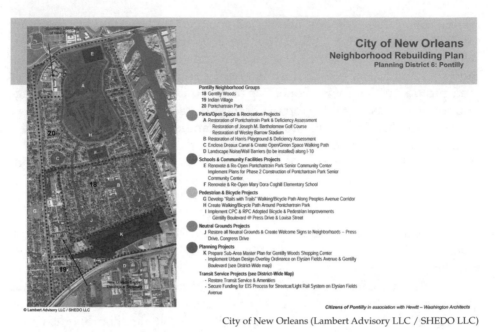

City of New Orleans (Lambert Advisory LLC / SHEDO LLC)

Fig. 5.2. The Lambert plan for Planning District 6, Pontilly

parks, creating a community center, reconstructing the Harrison Avenue retail district, and improving access to City Park. They also called for repairs to public facilities, improving drainage and transportation (including public transit and bicycle routes), and plans for two school sites. The total estimated cost of the projects was $236 million.

Lambert Advisory also created a summary citywide report that recommended policies on housing, economic development, and land use that were supported by all the neighborhoods. One of the most important recommendations was a "lot next door" program, in which neighbors would get right of first refusal to buy neighboring lots that entered into public ownership via voluntary sale through the Road Home program. This approach had several advantages: it would facilitate the transfer of Road Home properties into the hands of responsible owners; it would allow for older neighborhoods to include larger lot sizes than previously permitted; and it would maintain wealth in the community. However, if this program was widely applied, the lowered densities it would create might reduce the efficiency of restored citywide services.

Another housing proposal was to allow elderly home owners who were unwilling or unable to rebuild a stand-alone house to apply their Road Home grant toward a multistory condominium project. The summary report also proposed using the proceeds from lot sales in high-value areas to subsidize housing costs in areas with low-value lots.

The economic development priority for most residents was the return of neighborhood retail centers, especially grocery stores and pharmacies. To accomplish this in a depopulated city, the plan recommended first using aggressive enterprise-zone incentives to draw businesses to two or three areas near Interstate 10. After that, CDBG funds would be used to support more traditional neighborhood retail areas.

The plan's highest-priority land-use initiative was demolition and debris removal, which was still a significant problem in the early summer of 2006. It also stressed the importance of code enforcement and demolishing blighted homes as quickly as possible. The plan suggested rezoning in a few specific locations, in order to create an exclusive industrial zone, consolidate commercial areas, allow development of a town center, permit big-box retailers along Claiborne Avenue, and replace multifamily buildings in New Orleans East with single-family homes. The community also expressed broad support for a new comprehensive zoning ordinance, a process that the city was about to begin just as Katrina struck. Neighborhoods also were interested in having more of a role in project approval processes, especially when it came to historic preservation.

Finally, the plan expressed the residents' concerns about the lack of enough staff at city hall to process project approvals and cooperate across departments and agencies. The plan called for each part of the city to have dedicated staff who would be responsive to local concerns.

The price tag for all projects proposed by the Lambert plans was $4.4 billion: the most critical projects would cost $2.5 billion, less urgent projects would take $705 million, and the long-term community-improvement projects would cost an estimated $1.2 billion. The total cost concerned some people, but as city council member Hedge-Morrell pointed out, "If you don't put everything on the table, how would the federal government and the state know what the needs are?"[15]

At this event, the mayor was very supportive of the city council's planning process.[16] He cautioned the crowd, "Do not listen to these out of town folk," and claimed that he was succeeding in fighting off those who would deny recovery funding until the completion of UNOP. He said that the city would complete an ESF #14 format version of its plans within the month and that the Lambert plans would qualify to release CDBG money.

Soon after their public unveiling, the final plans for most, but not all, of the neighborhoods appeared on the New Orleans Neighborhoods Rebuilding Plan website, and the presentations were posted on the *Times-Picayune*'s site. However, the plans were taken off the NOLANRP site on October 15, just as UNOP was beginning to analyze earlier neighborhood planning to determine what else needed to be done. In other words, Lambert's plans were suddenly unavailable just at the moment they were needed most by UNOP.[17] Lambert says the plans were taken down because they were not yet complete. This was true: some of the neighborhoods did not yet have any plan at all. The revised, final plans were posted on November 1.[18] They included a set of citywide housing initiatives that were not in the earlier version. This suggested Lambert and the city council did not intend to cooperate with UNOP because the plan's scope was now citywide.

In other words, the Lambert group completed its plans as if UNOP did not exist, and UNOP was forced to begin without the benefit of the plans. But the real question was what the city council intended to do next: simply hand off the completed plans to the UNOP team or continue insisting that the plans for flooded neighborhoods by themselves met the criteria for a parish recovery plan?

At a special Thursday night meeting on October 27, the city council voted to accept the Lambert plans.[19] It was a surprise item added to the agenda for this meeting. (Its original purpose was to hold a vote on a gas and electric rate increase for Entergy New Orleans.)[20] There is nothing surprising about the council accepting Lambert Advisory's plan "as satisfactory completion of its contractual obligation to the City of New Orleans." But the council went much further, claiming that the plan fulfilled "the neighborhood planning requirements outlined by the City Planning Commission, FEMA, and the ESF 14 format as required by the Louisiana Recovery Authority." The council promised to

> immediately transmit the Neighborhood Rebuilding Plans, inclusive of the projects and their estimated funding requirements, to the City Planning Commission and to the Louisiana Recovery Authority for funding consideration. No further planning processes or documents are required by the Council to comply with its neighborhood planning initiative, nor are there any further requirements to submit the plans of the most devastated neighborhoods to the LRA or other funding sources.

To most observers, this action was baffling. The council declared that it would be delivering the plan that the LRA and FEMA asked for, even though FEMA's ESF #14 program had been handed off to the state months earlier, and the LRA had explicitly not asked for this plan. The motion made no mention of UNOP and denied the need for any other plan, despite the council's direct participation in UNOP since August 28. (Cynthia Hedge-Morrell, the council's representative to the CSO, had even sat with the CSO in the council chambers the previous night.)

Another part of the motion accepted "as a formal element to Lambert Advisory LLC's submissions the three peer reviews respectively submitted by: Dr. Ed Blakely, International disaster specialist, regional, urban and neighborhood planner; Dr. Phil Clay, Chancellor of MIT, and Professor of Urban Planning; and Dianne Rodriguez, Hurricane Andrew recovery specialist." The reviews all attest to the soundness and professionalism of the plans.[21] Although the reviews supported the credibility of the Lambert plans, they did not speak to the LRA's request for a more systematic and citywide process.[22] The council's motion also asserted its claim to New Orleans's fair share of all the state's CDBG funds, based on the city's 65 to 70 percent share of the state's storm damages. The council also asked for any leftover CDBG money following completion of the Road Home process.

Because they had not known about the October 27 motion until after it was passed, Broadmoor residents were upset that their plan had not been included in the motion, thereby possibly excluding them from a share of the money. As a result, they packed the council chambers for the regular meeting on November 2, and the council voted to amend the previous week's motion to include them. But this meeting also served to reopen the discussion of the October 27 meeting. With the Broadmoor amendment under consideration, some councilmembers also wanted to recognize that the plans would route through UNOP (according to the MOU) and then through the City Planning Commission (consistent with the city charter). The proposed amendment added "all neighborhoods' and agency plans" in the list of plans to be sent to the LRA.[23] Most members appeared confused by the proceedings, conflating different proposed amendments, sometimes including Broadmoor, sometimes UNOP.[24] In the end, however, there appeared to be a consensus to keep the motion as is—plus the amendment for Broadmoor—send the completed plans to the LRA, and postpone other questions.[25] The council continued to claim that more planning would just slow down the flow of money and that, with the completion of its neighborhood plans, planning was complete.

Immediately after the meeting, we spoke with city council president Oliver Thomas. We asked if he realized there was no way the LRA would accept the plans on their own. We also pointed out to him that there was not much CDBG money left and that the delays in infrastructure repair were all due to delays in the FEMA Public Assistance process and had nothing to do with these planning processes. He recognized all of this and responded that the council was simply providing an opportunity for members of the public to air their concerns.[26]

According to news reports the following day, the mayor and Thomas were going to go to the LRA on Monday, submit the plans, and request expedited funding for infrastructure projects.[27] The LRA stated its willingness to listen to the requests. According to an email sent out by Lambert Advisory, the city would try "to obtain a commitment from the state to both ensure that the city receives its fair share of recovery funds and obtain the state's commitment to immediately go back to Congress to ask for additional funds." The next day, however, the mayor said he did not intend to attend the LRA meeting, and Thomas was unsure as well. They both observed the city did not yet have a specific list of priority projects for funding.[28] The weekend was rife with rumors about who would attend and for what symbolic and strategic reasons. In the end, President Thomas, Vice President Arnie Fielkow, and councilmembers Cynthia Willard-Lewis and James Carter represented the city council at the LRA meeting on November 6.[29]

Contrary to all expectations, the showdown produced peace, harmony, and mutual admiration, which was no doubt the product of intensive negotiations over the weekend. Thomas began by stating that the purpose of their visit was to submit the neighborhood plans that were accepted by the city council. Significantly, he added that these plans would be "woven into the master plan for one New Orleans" and that they were just one piece of the puzzle for obtaining infrastructure funding. Fielkow clarified that UNOP would be the "overall master plan," that it was well on its way to completion, and that it would be submitted to the City Planning Commission, city

Jedidiah Horne

Fig. 5.3. New Orleans city council members presenting their plan to the LRA

council, and mayor. He claimed UNOP leaders were glad the Lambert plans were being presented to the LRA, and they were all in agreement about making requests for infrastructure funding as soon as possible. Willard-Lewis praised residents for their hard work and reminded the LRA that residents had been ahead of politicians in seeking a better, stronger, and safer city. David Voelker confirmed that there was no conflict between the Lambert plans and UNOP, and he expressed respect for the work of the city council. LRA chair Norman Francis praised everyone for doing their best under trying circumstances. He also clarified the funding situation, saying infrastructure funds from FEMA were not coming as quickly as they could. Francis reminded them New Orleanians needed to stand together in order to seek additional funds from Washington and private sources. "But we aren't going to get a dime without a plan. . . . We won't get the money if we are divided." He also stressed the importance of following all the rules, even though it could slow down the process: "Don't give anyone the excuse to close the doors when we go back for more." The LRA board then passed a motion to "receive and accept the plan," and the councilmembers all went up and shook hands with every board member. This effectively ended the city council's insistence that UNOP was the obstacle blocking the infrastructure money, and UNOP was now able to move forward, confident that it was the final process for drafting the parish's recovery plan.

Jedidiah Horne

Fig. 5.4. The November 6 LRA meeting

As if to underscore the real issue—the slow and bureaucratic flow of federal funds—the next item on the LRA's agenda involved allocation of the $4.2 billion approved by Congress in June.[30] This appropriation had more requirements than the first tranche of disaster recovery CDBG funds. The funds couldn't be used to match other federal government programs; $811,907,984 had to be used for affordable rental-housing stock; 50 percent of the funds had to benefit low- to moderate-income families; $400 million had to go specifically to the Housing Authority of New Orleans (HANO) for restoration of public housing; and 70 percent of the funds had to target the New Orleans–Metairie-Bogalusa Metropolitan Area. Thus, the state needed to carefully allocate its needs into each of the two appropriations. The board recommended allocations to the governor and legislature and called for the state to draft the official CDBG Action Plan for public comment, which would subsequently require LRA approval and its recommendation for approval by the governor and legislature.

Thus, by early November 2006, the planning duel had ended. It was recognized that the Lambert plans were a highly valuable planning contribution at the neighborhood level, but a more comprehensive parishwide plan provided by UNOP was still needed to satisfy the LRA and the federal government. The Lambert plans had helped to empower residents in the rebuilding effort, and they proposed some policies that were later implemented. But the larger UNOP effort would, in the end, provide a more persuasive foundation for outside funders. Furthermore, it was also increasingly clear that neither planning process was responsible for delaying what continued to be a frustratingly slow flow of the lion's share of federal recovery dollars.

6

The Unified
New Orleans Plan

Shortly after the second UNOP kickoff meeting on August 1, UNOP planning coordinator Steven Bingler and his Concordia staff met with City Planning Commission director Yolanda Rodriguez and city planner Dubravka Gilic to assign district planning consultants to neighborhoods.[1] Bingler says it was like playing a board game on the city planning maps; their moves were based on the votes cast by residents at the kickoff meeting, what they knew about the city, and the strengths of the consultants. They kept at it until they had solved the puzzle. (See table 6.1.) As it turned out, all districts got one of their top three choices for district planner and one of their top two choices for neighborhood planner, based on the 2,000 votes cast. Concordia and city staff made these decisions in mid-August but couldn't announce them until the memorandum of understanding had been signed to officially start UNOP.

In preparing for the UNOP process, the first task was to develop the overall structure of the citywide and district teams and draft a schedule of milestones. Equally important were to develop work scopes for the district and citywide teams and to design how all of the levels of planning and plan products would fit together. City planning staff and UNOP's citywide team started this work in mid-August.[2] The citywide consultants were starting work prior to authorization, but in developing the work scopes they were in effect working as an extension of city planning staff.[3]

On August 28, the same day that the MOU was signed, UNOP sent out a press release and a chart of the schedule of meetings.[4] They announced the members of the Community Support Organization, which would meet

TABLE 6.1. UNOP DISTRICT PLANNING CONSULTANTS

PLANNING DISTRICT	DISTRICT TEAM	NEIGHBORHOOD TEAM
District 1—CBD, French Quarter, Warehouse District	Goody Clancy	Duany Plater-Zyberk
District 2—Garden District, Central City	H3 Studio	Davis Brody Bond
District 3—Uptown, Broadmoor	Frederic Schwartz Architects	Now
District 4—Mid-City, Gert Town	Frederic Schwartz Architects	Now, HDR, and HOK
District 5—Lakeview	EDSA	
District 6—Gentilly	Goody Clancy	Duany Plater-Zyberk
District 7—Bywater	ACORN Housing	EDAW
District 8—Lower Ninth Ward	ACORN Housing	Williams Architects
District 9, 10, 11—New Orleans East, Village de L'est, Venetian Isles	EDSA	KL&M/CHPlanning, Torre Design Consortium
District 12—Algiers	EDSA	
District 13—English Turn	H3 Studio	

every two weeks and was intended to be the working group that would ensure that UNOP's planning goals were met. As originally envisioned, the CSO was to design the planning process and select the consultant planning teams. Unfortunately, due to the delay in signing the MOU and the crucial importance of completing the plan as soon as possible, GNOF and Concordia had, out of necessity, already accomplished these initial tasks, in close collaboration with City Planning Commission staff. To have waited for the CSO would have taken an additional two months. The release reiterated that "the Unified New Orleans Plan is also committed to working with Lambert Advisory to incorporate the planning work that they are doing and have done thus far" and included strong statements of support from the mayor and council president Thomas.

The citywide and district planning was to consist of three phases. The first would be a recovery assessment that described the current conditions of the neighborhoods. Among other things, the assessment would evaluate the levee plans of the U.S. Army Corps of Engineers and the costs of flood protection. Using this information, the second phase would involve scenarios that laid out possible developments and projects that might help districts recover. The third phase would include the recovery plans and a prioritized list of recovery projects. (See fig. 6.1.) The three phases would be punctuated by a series of four district and neighborhood meetings and three citywide "community congresses." The district meetings would begin in early October and end in early January. This was an ambitious schedule, designed to create and integrate all the plans and deliver them to the City Planning Commission and city council shortly after the end of the year. The CSO would hold a public meeting every two weeks to ensure that UNOP's planning goals were met.

One plan would be developed for each district, except for districts 9, 10, and 11, which would be combined into one. (See fig. 6.2.) The neighborhood planners were not yet assigned to specific neighborhoods; instead, each

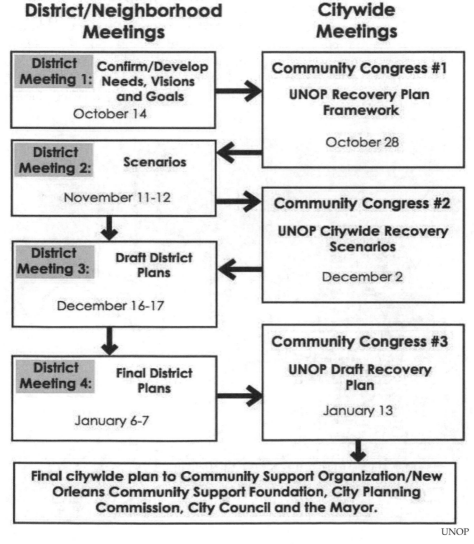

UNOP

Fig. 6.1. The UNOP meeting calendar as of September 2006

district planning team would wait to see where the greatest needs were. This flexible structure solved several problems. It allowed the district teams to use what was in the Lambert and resident-driven plans to identify gaps and then fill them using the neighborhood teams. It also neatly avoided the contentious issue of neighborhood boundaries. Instead, the planning teams would identify areas that needed help—whatever their boundaries might be—and work with them to boost the overall district planning effort. This hierarchical structure would help the citywide team to integrate all the work into one plan, since it would have to interact with only five teams of district consultants.

The NOCSF board met on August 31 to approve of the CSO appointments and consultant selections. The board also approved the $4.5 million budget but made it clear it was still seeking additional funding. It tentatively approved the contract of the citywide team, which consisted of Villavaso, Henry, and 12 subcontractors, but still needed time for GNOF staff to review budget details. It postponed the review of the district planner

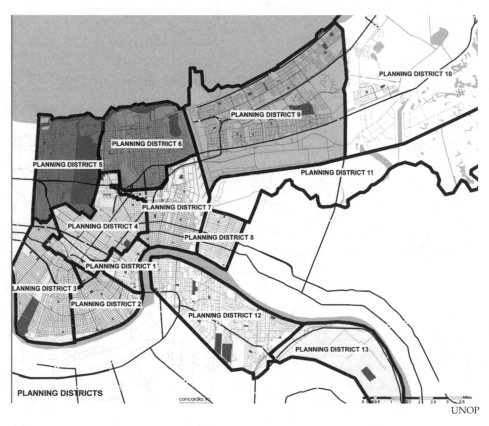

Fig. 6.2. New Orleans planning districts

contracts until the next monthly meeting. With this initial emphasis on describing and budgeting the planning tasks, the crucial matter of communication—to and from residents, among neighborhoods, and to and from the diaspora population—would be a continuing challenge for UNOP. As a first step, the CSF board approved contracts for a website manager (Whence: the Studio) and public relations and communications consultant (Peter A. Mayer and Associates). The board—Voelker in particular—stressed the critical importance to this planning effort of reaching out to the diaspora.

CITYWIDE TEAM ORIENTATION

The first meeting of the entire citywide team was held on September 6. More than 30 people participated, including the hired consultants and GNOF and city planning staff. This was a unique assemblage of consultants, who had

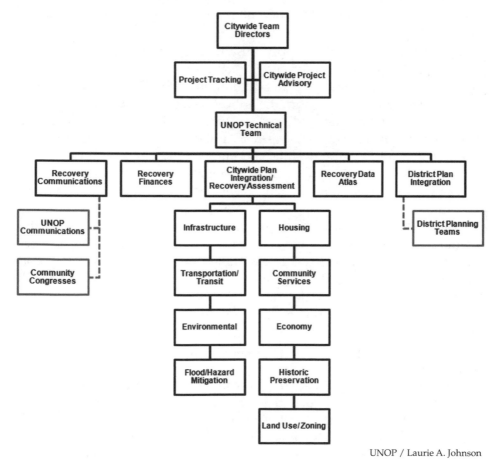

UNOP / Laurie A. Johnson

Fig. 6.3. The UNOP citywide team structure

to organize quickly and efficiently to accomplish an unprecedented task in less than four months. Troy Henry reminded them all, "We are on an aggressive time schedule." There was a sense of excitement in the room, a feeling of purpose and possibilities, but the discussion quickly centered on critical, practical matters, as well as unsettled issues the team would have to resolve quickly.

For one, the planning efforts so far in New Orleans made it clear that, in the absence of clear, regular, and consistent communication, residents would fill the void with rumors informed by mistrust. It was important for UNOP to convey consistent messages in all their public interactions. The challenge was to create a coordinated communication system with very limited resources. In order to attract participants to meetings, they hoped to harness the communications resources of local nonprofits. They also were hoping to engage America*Speaks*, a public engagement organization, perhaps best known for its post-9/11 "Listening to the City" meeting of 4,300 people in New York City in July 2002.[5] Bobbie Hill from Concordia announced she had contacted America*Speaks* about conducting the community congresses live from several cities simultaneously, all wired together by America*Speaks*'s network of telecommunications equipment. America*Speaks* would raise its own funds to accomplish this. In addition, the NOCSF had hired a public relations consultant to carry out the critical task of communicating to New Orleanians via flyers, statewide newspaper ads, and media advisories. The team also discussed using its website as a place to post all meeting notices, documents, and FAQs, as well as conduct polls, surveys, and respond to questions. Still, some citywide team members expressed concerns about reaching people who don't come to meetings, don't follow the news, and lack Internet access.

Another challenge was the management of the avalanche of data that would soon overwhelm the planning teams. There would be multiple meetings to record, previous plans to assemble in one place, an army of consultants both providing data and using it, and a need for clear and timely maps for public meetings. The group agreed that GCR & Associates, a New Orleans planning and technology consulting firm charged with providing basic data to the team, would take on this task, and its first job would be to produce a "recovery data atlas," with basic data to be used by all the planning teams.

The team also had to decide how it would deal with the significant flood uncertainties that still plagued New Orleans. What would be the underlying assumptions about the level of flood protection that would ultimately be provided? To what degree could UNOP planners discuss differential flood risk across the city? To what degree could they discuss a range of alternative mitigation strategies, such as levees, elevation, and relocation?

Bingler made it clear that they could not talk about "shrinking footprints" and that, technically, FEMA had established the acceptable risk, based on its elevation standards. But no one knew whether private insurers would continue to provide basic residential coverage and, if so, what the rates would be, which could have profound effects on individual rebuilding decisions. Similarly, no one knew exactly how many households intended to rebuild or where, because the Road Home program was just beginning. Further, it was already apparent that that program was a complicated, unwieldy, and bureaucratic process. As a result, neighborhood planning would have to go on at the same time individuals made their decisions to either rebuild or sell. Because of this, the citywide team decided that a primary role of UNOP would be to present data on risk and its costs and help community members understand this information. It would be left up to the public to decide how to eliminate, mitigate, avoid, or accept risk. Some team members stated that considering flood risk would be a uniquely critical function of UNOP, which none of the other planning efforts had successfully been able to address.

Ironically, back in January 2006, it was widely assumed that the neighborhood planning process would proceed simultaneously with individual home owner decisions: neighborhood conversations would inform individuals about their neighbors' intended actions, neighborhood organizations about the intended actions of individuals, and individuals about the possible futures for their neighborhood. Redevelopment plans would then grow out of these discussions, with different approaches for each neighborhood. But as it turned out, the two processes—neighborhood planning and individual decisions to rebuild or sell out—were in fact proceeding simultaneously. But given the complexities of the Road Home process, it was questionable whether these two processes could inform each other, let alone in any sort of continuous-feedback loop.

The final item of business was deciding when to start the district planning work. Everyone agreed that the district teams needed basic information to inform their discussions with residents. They would need, at minimum, the initial reports from the citywide sector teams, the Lambert plans, and a fully functional website. Subconsultant Burk-Kleinpeter, led by Randy Carmichael, would coordinate the work of the sector teams and be responsible for plan integration, along with Villavaso. The "sectors" were topical fields, including housing, economic development, community services, historic preservation, infrastructure and public works, transportation and transit, environment, and hazard mitigation.

Given this, they agreed to hold the first district kick-off meeting on September 27, which gave them three weeks to prepare basic data layers and a first draft of a citywide recovery assessment. But this meant pushing the due date of the first draft of the citywide plan back to January 5 instead of the more meaningful December 29. In turn, this would move the project end date to late January. It was an unsettling way to begin an ambitious project that would require heroic discipline to be completed close to the end of the year, in order to satisfy political and public demands. But even this extra time proved to be insufficient for preparing and distributing all the materials the district and citywide teams needed.

OTHER CITY EVENTS

On September 12, Mayor Nagin reviewed the first 100 days of his second term. He had assembled a team, including his former rivals in the election, to help the city to move strategically forward, and now he was announcing the results of this initiative with great fanfare.[6] He declared progress had been made on a variety of fronts, which was true. And he announced he would create two institutions responsible for implementing the final recovery plans: he would set up a recovery department in the next two months, and, as had been widely expected, he would revive the New Orleans Redevelopment Authority (NORA) to help to develop thousands of blighted and abandoned properties.[7] One member of his team of rivals, Rob Couhig, said the mayor deserved credit for running a "squeaky clean government" and creating an environment friendly to private initiatives.[8] He pointed out that "doing business as usual in this city is in fact a step toward (improving) quality of life. We haven't had business as usual in a year."

On September 15, Bill Clinton came to town to announce the Bush-Clinton Katrina Fund would give $7.5 million in grants to local nonprofits.[9] This included $1 million to the GNOF for UNOP, which brought the total funding for the UNOP process to $5.5 million. This additional funding would go toward expanding communication and outreach efforts. While he was in the city, Clinton tried to be reassuring about the seemingly never-ending sequence of planning processes, saying, "I know how maddening this is. It takes time. But we have to have a plan and we have to execute it."[10]

Perhaps the most visible milestone that month was the reopening of the Superdome on September 25, for a Monday Night Football game between the Saints and the Falcons. A national TV audience watched George H. W. Bush toss the pregame coin in front of a crowd of more than 68,000 people. The message was clear: the stench and misery of the post-Katrina Superdome were history, New Orleans was rebuilding itself, and it was now open for business. The city was capable of safely hosting tens of thousands of visitors and the nation's media; if it could host Monday Night Football, then it could host anyone's conference or vacation. Although the allocation of federal funds toward the Superdome was not without controversy, there was no doubt that this was an important symbolic moment.[11]

CSO ORIENTATION

The CSO held its first meeting on September 14. Although the CSO had been designed to lead the planning process, the delay over the memorandum of understanding forced the group to convert its first meeting into an orientation. The train had already left the station, and the CSO would have to try to jump on. At its first meeting, Concordia and the citywide team had to bring CSO members up to speed. Unlike later CSO meetings, this one was not open to the public. Concordia presented the planning framework, the structure and goals of the citywide and district teams, a communication plan, a data collection process, and the schedule of meetings.

Concordia also made it clear that two deliverables were expected out of the UNOP process. The first would be a set of 11 district plans that covered all of the neighborhoods in the city. These district plans would identify what infrastructure needed to be rebuilt to help neighborhoods fully recover from the storms. They also needed to integrate all of the earlier neighborhood plans into their final planning publications.

The second deliverable was a citywide recovery and rebuilding plan that focused on large-scale, high-priority public facilities and services that would speed up recovery and guide public and private investment decisions. The citywide plan would also include a prioritized list of recovery projects from the district plans that would be submitted to the LRA in the city's request for remaining CBDG funds.[12]

Concordia described the six anticipated outcomes of the plans. They would:

1. Provide every neighborhood with a recovery plan, as detailed in the district plans
2. Justify the funding and implementation of the recovery projects through the development of a citywide plan
3. Encourage the redesign and reconstruction of the region's hurricane flood protection system
4. Provide information to citizens and investors to make personal and business decisions about recovery
5. Help the city achieve long-term economic sustainability
6. Identify and feature opportunities to strengthen the city's economy

Paul Lambert and Sheila Danzey also presented their work at this meeting. Lambert stated that the plans for flooded neighborhoods would be completed by the end of the month. He reiterated that the planners had followed the neighborhood planning guidelines and that the plans were in ESF #14 format.[13] He concluded by saying UNOP planners would need to work only in the neighborhoods that were not flooded, although he admitted his plans did not address neighborhood flood risks. Cynthia Hedge-Morrell, representing the city council, seconded Lambert and argued forcefully for submitting the existing neighborhood plans directly to the LRA. But city-wide team members maintained the importance of planning for the city as a whole and the need to make some tough decisions, because of limited resources, before sending the plans to the LRA.

DISTRICT PLANNING TEAM ORIENTATION

On September 27, all of the district planning teams, led primarily by out-of-town consultants, gathered for their first UNOP meeting. It had been nearly four months since the RFQs were issued, and the entire team was assembled at last, with the seemingly impossible task of completing district plans in less than three months. Approximately 45 people were in the room. About 30 people represented the five district planning teams, eight were from the citywide team, Yolanda Rodriguez and Dubravka Gilic represented the City Planning Commission, and four were from Concordia. Other visitors came and went during the day, including two city council members, Arnie Fielkow and Stacy Head.

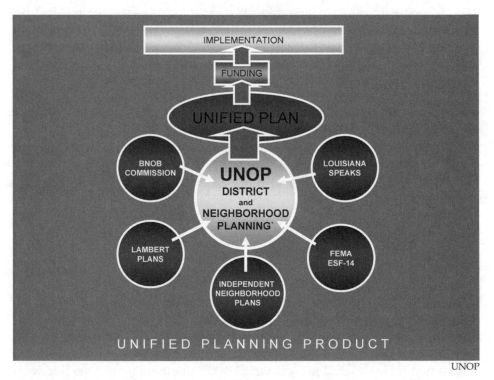

UNOP

Fig. 6.4. The role of UNOP in the overall planning process

The meeting was led by a combination of staff from the citywide team and Concordia. They presented an overview of the basic philosophy, process, assumptions, approach, and structure of the UNOP process. Each district team received a CD with 90 background reports, copies of earlier plans, government documents, and post-Katrina studies.[14] Steven Bingler laid out some of the ground rules. First, everyone would answer to the CSO. Second, timeliness and deadlines were nonnegotiable—a recurring theme of the day, appearing at times to be more important than content. Third, the district teams needed to appreciate their immediate audience for the deliverables, which was the City Planning Commission. Although GNOF would pay the bills, the UNOP planners were doing the work of the city.

This left some of the district consultants wondering who was actually in charge here. Concordia? The citywide team? GNOF? The CSO, as Bingler said? The City Planning Commission? The Rockefeller Foundation? The LRA? Clearly, this was a collective endeavor. The citywide team was creating content and working closely with City Planning Commission staff, who would ultimately take responsibility for the plan. Concordia, watched over by GNOF and Rockefeller, was managing the entire planning process. The CSO would be the conscience, the evaluator, and the watchdog as the process unfolded. But should problems arise, where does the buck stop? Who makes the tough calls? Who sets and maintains the key philosophical and policy principles guiding the process? Who is the chief planner, and who is their client? There was no clear answer.

The orientation also introduced the consultants to the politics and zeitgeist of New Orleans in 2006. Troy Henry reminded out-of-town consultants that many of the locals on the team, including him, were still not living in their homes. The planners need not go far to find people who understood the problems facing city residents. (In response to some complaints about last-minute changes in the meeting schedule and the late delivery of data, Henry said simply, "Welcome to New Orleans. It's going to get worse.")

Bingler and Villavaso also gave a brief introduction to post-Katrina life in New Orleans neighborhoods and what to expect at neighborhood meetings. They both emphasized that there would be no discussion of a smaller footprint for the city. People were trying to rebuild throughout New Orleans, and any suggestion to prohibit rebuilding would simply be unacceptable. This was now the official UNOP position, and they would do well to understand that before they set one foot into the neighborhoods. Bingler and Villavaso also instructed district planners to never refer to any of the previous plans as "failed" planning processes. Rather, UNOP would be building on the sequence of plans that preceded it. Villavaso reminded the group that all the previous planning efforts "had a kickoff meeting *just like* this one," and most New Orleans planners, himself included, had spent thousands of hours on the BNOB and Lambert plans. There was simply not enough time to start over, he said, and they needed to be grateful for the work that had been done by all the planners, as well as residents and others outside the formal planning process.

The citywide team and Concordia also acquainted consultants with the hard realities and challenges of the planning process itself, involving data management, district meetings, community congresses, two-way information flows, and tight deadlines. The district teams' contracts, for example, were not yet finalized and approved. The members of the citywide team explained that it was only recently that their own contracts had been executed and that this, in part, explained why some of the startup materials for the district teams were delayed. In fact, four firms had worked for a month without contracts.[15] Given the incomplete startup material, the citywide team suggested that district teams would do well to start with the neighborhood planning guide until additional materials became available. Despite the contracting delays, the citywide team and Concordia were inflexible about changing any of the calendar dates for the plan. Troy Henry explained: "Use your creativity to adjust accordingly. But the schedule is what it is." District consultants asked why the early January completion date was so critical. The answer was that there was no solid reason other than politics and public perception: the LRA wanted it by then, and there was intense political pressure for a draft plan before the "end of the year" and for the final product to be delivered early in January. Bingler promised the teams he would ask the NOCSF and CSO about changing the calendar but told them they shouldn't count on it. The only way to meet the deadline would be for the citywide and district teams to work simultaneously, even on planning tasks that would normally need to be sequential. The plan would need to be done simultaneously from the bottom up and the top down, and they would have to deal with this as best as they could.

The key to this would be team communication and coordination, which would be managed by GCR. The firm was quickly developing a data management strategy that would involve providing data to the district teams as well as receiving the data the teams collected. It was also creating a "recovery data atlas" with basic data important to the work of all planning teams. GCR promised to get this atlas to district teams by October 13. The district planners in turn would funnel their data up through GCR. GCR also designated one individual, Raphael "Rafe" Rabalais, to be the key point of contact between citywide and district teams. He would lead a biweekly conference call among all district teams and core members of the citywide team; it soon became a weekly call. Within each team, someone was designated the point person to coordinate with Rabalais about project management.

Everyone recognized the importance of communication and outreach, but development of a public outreach and communication plan was still in process. Joe Butler of Concordia described how they would work with various nonprofits to do "old-fashioned community organizing" to bring people into the process. Peter Mayer and Associates would do traditional media messaging, such as press releases. America*Speaks* was expected to help with the community congresses, although the details were not finalized. A call center would be set up to answer questions.

For the community congresses, the citywide team and Concordia would create the content of public messages with help from America*Speaks*. But considerable discussion revolved around the substance of the messages the district teams would be presenting to their communities. The website would play an important role as a content organization tool and would present the information that district teams would need to convey to residents. The website would also help communicate to residents, but in addition the district planners would need "street teams" to distribute flyers and newspapers developed by the citywide team. The teams designated one of their members to become responsible for these external communications and another to post content to the website.

The city planning team also explained what sort of planning product it expected from the district teams. The citywide team would focus on high-priority, large-scale "infrastructure" (defined broadly as public facilities and services) projects for jump-starting community recovery. Although "land-use planning" would be beyond the expected content, district teams were invited to include project ideas that extended beyond the recovery and rebuilding phase. And, although "reducing the footprint" was off the table, discussions about flood risk were not. The recovery assessment would describe current flood-risk conditions and costs of flood protection throughout the city, to form the basis of needed decisions. They were also encouraged to submit recommendations for zoning and plan implementation. The LRA's CDBG money was not the only source of funds they would eventually tap, and so they need not limit themselves to the LRA requirements alone.

In fact, an LRA representative confirmed later in the meeting that relatively little of the CDBG funds remained for community and infrastructure recovery projects. About $645 million of the CDBG remained uncommitted, and the governor was expected to commit some of it to Entergy. Nor was it known how much money, if any, would be left over from the Road Home program until all home owner needs were met. The LRA had been making it clear since May that there was not enough CDBG money to fund all the projects the city needed. But this was news to the district planning consultants, leading one district planner to point out that they were "undertaking this strenuous planning process with no readily available pot of money to fund it." Others argued that UNOP would put the city in a good position to make a compelling case for more money, possibly from Congress or from other funding sources. Furthermore, many of the projects that UNOP would identify were already in line for funding under the FEMA Public Assistance program, which would likely spend on the order of $6 billion in New Orleans. Unfortunately, many in the room agreed that it would be difficult to collect this information for the plan, because Public Assistance was being negotiated directly among 112 local entities and FEMA.

The day also included presentations from representatives of FEMA and the school district, which clarified the current status of evolving policies. In this constantly changing bureaucratic landscape, no one knew all the answers, and reliable information was an elusive commodity. But having representatives from so many key entities in one room provided the opportunity to have substantive conversations backed by accurate, up-to-date information.

Finally, the meeting focused on the next steps in the planning process. The first district meeting would be on October 14. The next meeting of all the planning teams was set for November 3, after the first round of district meetings and the first community congress. It would be a critical opportunity for teams to exchange information and identify gaps and conflicts ahead of the second round of district meetings. They would set the dates for future meetings then, too. The process would need to be refined over time, based on the teams' experiences in the neighborhoods.

In fact, even before the first round of district meetings, the relationship between and expectations of the citywide and district planning teams continued to evolve. On October 6, UNOP released an internal guidance document, "Working Paper #1: Anticipated Outcomes," which described the two types of planning documents that would come out of the planning process: the district plans and the citywide plan.[16] The descriptions of these deliverables hewed closely to ideas presented earlier to the district and citywide teams, except for one thing: only the citywide plan would meet the needs of the LRA for a "recovery plan" that would identify a list of projects for funding priority. Thus, only the citywide plan need go through City Planning Commission and city council review as the city's official recovery plan. Eliminating the need for official city review and approval of the 11 district plans would help to speed up the process. The district plans, in contrast, were now seen as the important raw material that would form the foundation of the recovery plan. In addition, these plans would continue to serve as critical guides for neighborhood-level planning and development. The work of the citywide team would focus on recovery progress and needs in the areas of hurricane and flood-risk management, housing and historic preservation, community facilities and services, utilities and transportation, the economy, and environment. The citywide team would begin by emphasizing citywide projects, but once district plans were further along they would begin to incorporate the projects they detailed.[17]

UNOP GOES PUBLIC

The first round of district planning meetings was scheduled for Saturday, October 14. These had been announced via a press release on October 7.[18] Several days after the announcement, the *Times-Picayune* carried the first public announcement of the addition of America*Speaks* to the UNOP team, to provide keypad voting and diaspora outreach for the second community congress to be held on December 2: "AmericaSpeaks President Carolyn Lukensmeyer said the project will cost $3 million and that $2.3 million already has been committed by private foundations. . . . AmericaSpeaks was brought in to support the New Orleans planning effort because of concerns that many displaced New Orleanians, especially low-income African-Americans, have no voice in recovery decisions, Lukensmeyer said." The price tag for this one meeting, although provided by outside funders, raised some eyebrows. As a response, "Lukensmeyer said her group's data-gathering is exceptionally labor-intensive, requiring a small army of 'facilitators' who help residents in small groups."[19] Attracting diaspora residents to the meetings would also require considerable effort.

On October 12, the CSO held the first of its biweekly public meetings in the city council's chambers.[20] It included reports from Concordia, a review of the calendar and planning team assignments, a presentation of the public outreach strategy, and a presentation by the citywide team. Approximately 70 people attended, including two councilmembers who offered the city's full support to UNOP. The CSO now had an official chair, Vera Triplett. She was an early leader of the Gentilly Civic Improvement Association, and she and her family had been displaced by the severe flooding. She began the meeting by declaring that UNOP would include all planning done to date, including her group's work in Gentilly, and that it was designed to speed up federal assistance rather than slow it down.

Some of the audience members expressed doubts about this. The very first public comment on the presentations was a plea for action rather than more planning. Triplett responded that this was the plan that would produce action, and Cynthia Hedge-Morrell added that it was important to have a systematic infrastructure plan for the entire city. Another questioner asked whether the city would be rebuilt to its original size and form. Triplett responded that the people would decide what to do but that good planning would provide the information to help them decide. Someone else asked how the planners would decide what parts of the previous plans (such as BNOB) to use. Troy Henry said that it was not up to the citywide team to decide; this was also up to residents. One commenter was dubious of the outreach plan and the teams' abilities to reach everyone. Triplett responded that the outreach effort was evolving and that they were considering every means to get people involved, including using buses to bring residents to meetings. But she also reminded the audience that it was the responsibility of residents to bring their neighbors to meetings and that they needed to take ownership of the planning effort.

These sorts of questions continued throughout the first phase of the planning process. For the first round of district planning meetings on Saturday, October 14, Concordia secured six venues throughout the city to host the 11 district meetings. Approximately 1,500 residents attended.[21] The purpose of the meeting was to introduce the district planning teams and the UNOP process, go over earlier plans, and open up a discussion about the neighborhoods' needs and goals that had not yet been addressed. Some districts broke into sectors or subgroups to have discussions; in some cases these would persist throughout the process, whereas in others they were simply devices to facilitate the meetings. Not surprisingly, citizens continued to express concerns regarding the purpose of yet another round of planning meetings.

The second CSO meeting occurred on Thursday, October 26, less than two days before the first community congress. The CSO members were clearly much better informed by this time, and they were more assertive in their roles as overseers of the process, particularly with respect to outreach efforts to date. The district planning teams gave progress reports. They all explained how they had begun with the Lambert plans and then focused on gaining participation from the neighborhoods that had been less involved to date.[22]

ACORN HOUSING FIRED

On October 17, the NOCSF board announced ACORN Housing would be terminated as district planner. Goody Clancy would replace them in District 7, and H-3 Studio would take over District 8.[23] Rumors of this had been brewing for a few weeks. It was thought that ACORN Housing had a conflict of interest because it held properties in their two planning districts. In August, it had been selected as one of 22 developers given rights to pay back taxes and acquire the titles to up to 2,000 tax-adjudicated properties throughout the city for purposes of rehabilitating homes and bringing them back onto the market.[24] ACORN Housing received the rights to 250 lots in the Lower Ninth Ward and 150 lots in New Orleans East.

According to GNOF and others, six neighborhood organizations objected to ACORN Housing's role as both planner and developer in these districts; they could be one or the other, but not both. These organizations threatened to stay out of the UNOP process if something was not done. This put NOCSF and UNOP leaders in a difficult position. They had selected ACORN Housing in part because of ACORN's deep knowledge and experience in these parts of New Orleans. Nor did they want to alienate ACORN, an influential group with several thousand members in New Orleans, which had been vigorously trying to bring residents back to their homes.[25] In the end, however, the NOCSF board decided to terminate ACORN Housing in order to keep the planning process moving and free of any taint.[26]

The termination frustrated ACORN Housing because it had never tried to hide its role as a nonprofit developer or its development interests. In fact, it viewed its position as a positive: if one of the planning goals was to repopulate the neighborhood, it was in a unique position to achieve that goal and lead by example. The competition for the adjudicated properties had transpired in July, precisely when the UNOP planners were selected, and the announcement of ACORN Housing's successful bid for the properties was announced on the same day as the second UNOP kickoff event in August, where residents voted on preferences for district and neighborhood planners. The ACORN Housing team was subsequently assigned to districts 7 and 8. The UNOP leaders must have been well aware of ACORN Housing's role as a nonprofit developer. Besides, ACORN Housing's partners on this project—planners from Cornell University and the University of Illinois—were doing most of the planning work in these districts, and they had no development interests at all.

Shortly after the termination, legal teams for GNOF and ACORN became involved, effectively ending any possibility for bringing the various parties back together again for UNOP.[27] In the end, ACORN reacted by organizing even more vigorously to get its people involved in the process. They were visible at both the district meetings and community congresses. In part, they attended out of self-interest. For example, they were concerned about the Lambert plan's suggestion for creating a light industrial zone in what had been a residential area along the Industrial Canal—an idea they did not want to see in the final UNOP district plan.

The ACORN Housing team also decided to continue with its planning efforts and complete its own plan by early January.[28] The intent was to contribute another voice to the planning process and ensure that its detailed housing and citizen survey data were well publicized.[29] ACORN also took a broader planning approach and addressed local economic development, institutional development, and building code issues.

COMMUNITY CONGRESS I

It would be fair to say that the first community congress on October 28 was the low point of UNOP. It was on a Saturday morning at the New Orleans Convention Center in a huge room with a capacity of 1,000. A sparse crowd

Laurie A. Johnson

Fig. 6.5. The lightly attended Community Congress I

of 250 to 300 people showed up, and nearly half of them were UNOP staff, volunteers, outside observers, and students who came from as far away as the University of Iowa. Most of the actual participants were white, wealthy, and from mildly flooded areas.[30]

The citywide team presented a significant amount of data on the condition of the city's infrastructure, economy, population projections, flood risk, transportation, and community facilities. America*Speaks* played a limited role at this congress because the NOCSF had not signed off on its participation until about 10 days before. On such short notice, it could only provide keypads to each participant to record answers to basic questions about expectations and concerns about returning to live in the city. The citywide team was responsible for all the meeting content and planning-related presentations.

Despite the effective presentation of substantive information, the poor attendance was disappointing. UNOP's official coming-out party seemed like a press conference with a crowd. However, it would have been difficult for anyone to create a meaningful citywide meeting at that time given the delays, the breakneck pace of the planning process, and the limited budget dedicated to outreach and communication at that point. Furthermore, Community Congress I occurred the very week the city council endorsed sending the Lambert plans directly to the LRA, which may have discouraged some people from coming. Whatever the cause was, the poor attendance undermined the credibility of UNOP as the people's last word on recovery planning in New Orleans.

National Public Radio was at Community Congress I (which it termed "a kind of large-scale, focus group").[31] Several days later, in a program entitled "New Orleans Master Plan Stalled," it broadcast to the nation this account: "Local government has yet to commit to a blueprint for rebuilding the city. The lack of a plan has left hundreds of thousands of New Orleanians in limbo." The program further explained that the mayor had not promised to adopt UNOP and that, therefore, residents were operating under the assumption that the plan would have little effect on the plans they make for themselves. This was not the positive message that the UNOP team had hoped to send out.

Yet it also was apparent to us as we stood among the small, subdued crowd in the cavernous convention center that the reported demographics of this meeting in fact represented a significant moment in the post-Katrina planning. In no other planning meeting had participation been so well documented. Not only did we know the racial makeup of the crowd, but, through America*Speaks*'s keypad voting, we also had more information about their income levels, ages, and their pre-Katrina places of residence. We knew who was represented at this meeting and who was not. This allowed

Jedidiah Horne

Fig. 6.6. One of the keypad voting devices used at Community Congress I

Carolyn Lukensmeyer to say to the crowd, "We're missing young people. We're missing African-American people in as high of numbers as we should have. We're missing certain districts of the city. This city is going to work best when people from all groups are represented. We have to keep in mind who's not in the room today."[32] Armed with this knowledge, UNOP officials asked residents who did not attend to answer the questions by phone, and they announced that they planned to rebroadcast the meeting in New Orleans, Atlanta, Baton Rouge, Dallas, and Houston. The communication team followed Lukensmeyer's lead and used the attendance data as a way to encourage others to pack the hall the next time.

The UNOP communication team shifted into high gear the morning after Community Congress I, and America*Speaks* quickly became the centerpiece of the effort to achieve broader public participation. Lukensmeyer began seeking funds to ensure that displaced residents would have a voice. She announced that they would use widespread advertising, a mailing to 120,000 displaced residents, and contact with local faith-based groups prior to the second community congress. Given the LRA's subsequent affirmation of UNOP at its November 6 meeting (see Chapter 5), it became clear to residents that the best way to get a message to the LRA would be to participate in UNOP meetings.

BEGINNING PHASE TWO: RECOVERY SCENARIOS

The weeks following the first community congress were critical for UNOP, which needed to address important planning issues and make genuine progress toward developing a plan that would build on the earlier planning efforts. Given the shortcomings of Community Congress I and the high expectations of the LRA, the pressure was on the team to engage the community in substantive planning questions at both the next set of district meetings and the second community congress.

This pressure was evident at the second meeting of the citywide and district consultant teams, held at the Marriott Hotel on November 3. One purpose of this meeting was to figure out how to proceed with the next phase of planning, which focused on recovery scenarios. After every district planning team reported on its work, the meeting broke into two groups. In one room, leaders of the district teams and the core citywide team worked together on a strategy to move the scenario development process forward (see fig. 6.7). The rest of the team members met to identify the gaps in their data about housing, infrastructure, and the economy. The meeting reflected the top-down and bottom-up processes that had to emerge simultaneously in UNOP. The citywide team was trying to create a consistent framework but also depended on the reconnaissance of the district consultants. Conversely, the district consultants sought guidance from the citywide team, but they

Robert B. Olshansky

Fig. 6.7. UNOP core team members at the second meeting of the citywide and district teams

also insisted on sharing their field experiences and representing the views of the participants at their meetings. In fact, in many heated discussions, it was evident the district consultants had taken on the interests of their neighborhoods, and they argued loudly for their constituents.[33]

This created some tension between the citywide and district teams, and it reflected the long-standing tensions in post-Katrina planning in general. The citywide team was concerned with gathering information that would help it set investment priorities. It wanted to encourage residents to make difficult choices that took into consideration future flood risk and priorities for public facilities. Because all the indicators pointed to a smaller population for some time, the city eventually would need to refine its funding requests to focus on the highest recovery priorities. The district planners, however, resisted bringing this message to their local meetings. They preferred to present a framework around three generalized scenarios that grouped recovery activities into short-, medium-, and long-term time frames and let the residents set the direction of the meeting. They used descriptors such as "repair, rebuild, renaissance" and "repair, rehab, revise." But the district planners also knew they would have to confront participants with the realities of the funding situation, and they were very concerned about how to do this. The planners needed to respond to outcries of "tell them to fix our streets"—which always got the biggest applause at meetings— with the truth that this had nothing to do with the current planning process.

And they needed to explain that "taking the plan to the LRA" would only result in a limited amount of CDBG funds, whereas the plan needed to help the city make its argument to the federal government for more money. The planners understood the purpose of this planning effort but were not sure how to explain it to the public in such a way that they would retain their trust and would keep participants involved.

And then there were other difficult topics such as future flood risk and rate of repopulation. At the very least, the citywide team wanted the district planners to describe the actual flood risks in the city just like the citywide team had done at the first community congress. This presentation included a map that showed how current and future flood risk varied according to the city's five drainage basins (fig. 6.8). The U.S. Army Corps of Engineers' plans were to first repair and substantially improve the hurricane flood protection system in the central core of the city ("Drainage Area 1"). This would happen much sooner than it could raise and redesign the protection system in the other four basins. The map also showed that neighborhoods in all five basins shared the same level of flood risk, irrespective of neighborhood or planning district boundaries. For example, the Lower Ninth Ward and St. Bernard Parish (which was virtually all white) shared the same level of flood risk.

But not all the district planners were comfortable with presenting even this level of risk information. This concerned the citywide team. If the second round of district meetings could not begin to engage residents in some

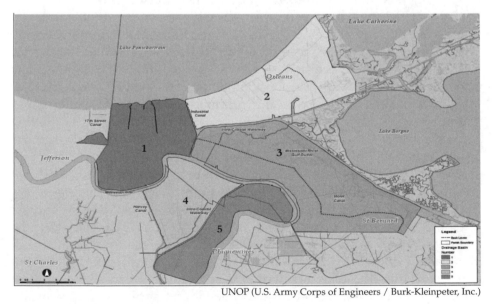

UNOP (U.S. Army Corps of Engineers / Burk-Kleinpeter, Inc.)

Fig. 6.8. Five drainage basins in New Orleans

discussion of flood risk, then when would that discussion take place? And it was clear to the citywide team that, whatever the Corps of Engineers would do, some residual level of flood risk would remain in each of the basins. Still, there was no choice but to keep moving forward and hope that, with all the district planning meetings and all the UNOP management meetings, sufficiently informed discussions would take place over the remaining six weeks to enable the team to identify appropriate recovery strategies.

The communication and coordination mechanism that had been established at the first meeting—Rafe Rabalais as the information funnel to and from the representatives of the district consultants—became the basis for what evolved into a planning content team that held weekly brainstorming conference calls between district team representatives and key members of the citywide team. Many of the recovery projects identified in the citywide plan had been brought up in a district planning meeting and then bubbled up to one of these group meetings, where it was debated and adopted. Thus, every important innovation had gone through a process that considered the perspectives of every part of the city as well as the citywide view.

The CSO meeting on November 9 echoed many of the themes of the previous week's team meeting regarding outreach to community and diaspora groups to ensure representation at the next community congress. In addition, the issue of public housing residents was raised by the Reverend Marshall Truehill, a longtime public housing activist who was also working for UNOP as part of the Goody Clancy team.[34] In a long and impassioned speech, Truehill asked the CSO to take public housing residents seriously and to adopt a policy regarding their needs. He observed that both the BNOB and Lambert plans ignored public housing residents but that they were participating in the UNOP process. He said that it was important for their voices to be heard and important for them to be welcomed back to the city, and he asked the CSO to support those efforts.

About 25 to 200 people attended each of the district meetings in the second round on November 11. Although it was getting increasingly difficult to draw large crowds to yet more planning meetings, the participants were engaged.[35] Generally, the meetings discussed some variant of the three scenarios developed by the citywide team on November 2. These scenarios ranged from basic repairs to reinvention of the district, with varying assumptions about the future levels of flood protection, population return, and reconstruction funds. Participants quickly understood they needed to temper their enthusiasm for major improvements with realism regarding funding sources.

The UNOP team was overwhelmed during the rest of November. Expectations were high, time was short, and the demands exceeded the teams' capacities. The number of meetings with community groups and steering

Jedidiah Horne

Fig. 6.9. District 4 meeting, November 11

committees, between planning teams, and with city and state officials all increased, and it was vital to make substantial progress before and after the Thanksgiving holiday. The volume of communication, information, and document exchange between the citywide and district teams exploded. At the same time, core members of the citywide team had to simultaneously work on their own products, such as scenario development and presentations for the upcoming second community congress. They had to attend as many district and neighborhood meetings as possible. They also had to develop the support materials for the district teams, which were overwhelmed with demands and expectations from residents. The demand for website postings and communication also increased. Unlike in most city planning processes, there was a high level of public interest in UNOP. The UNOP team was under the microscopes of watchdog groups and bloggers, all dogging their every step.

Victims of this relentless forward momentum included some fine publications written by the citywide sector teams. A document called "Working Paper #2 (City-wide Needs, Vision, and Goals)" appeared in draft form at the second joint team meeting on November 3. It was a snapshot of recovery efforts and information coming out of the first round of district meetings. This paper articulated, for the first time, the UNOP recovery vision, which had at its core the same fundamental philosophy that New Orleans leadership maintained throughout the first year of recovery: "Every citizen, regardless of current residence, has the right to return to New Orleans." It also stated UNOP was attempting to go a step further, so that "all citizens, businesses and investors of our Great City" also have "a right to return to a Safer, Smarter, Stronger City that enables a substantially higher quality of life, greater economic opportunity, and greater security against hurricanes than New Orleans had prior to Katrina."[36] Another document, *The Citywide Baseline Recovery Assessment*, was an extremely detailed report on the state of New Orleans in late 2006 and included well-informed projections of population and employment.[37] Although both of these documents were available in draft form to team members in November, neither one was completed and posted to the website until late December, long after the point where they would have been useful to residents involved in the process.[38] The recovery assessment was never widely distributed. A generalized summary appeared in the final citywide plan issued in late January, with the full assessment provided as an appendix.

COMMUNITY CONGRESS II

Given all the events of the previous month, the second community congress loomed as the critical moment for UNOP. For UNOP to have public

Laurie A. Johnson

Fig. 6.10. Community Congress II

legitimacy, it would need to erase all the doubts of the first congress, through the quantity and diversity of participants. And it was the UNOP team's last chance to get participants' answers to key policy questions that were needed to produce a viable plan.

The meeting lasted from 9:00 a.m. to 4:00 p.m. on Saturday, December 2. It was organized around six discussion topics. Each topic was framed as a discussion question, with a short list of suggested options and the pros and cons of each. These were given to each participant in the form of a "discussion guide." The topics were:

- Flood protection: What should we do to reduce the risk of flooding?
- Roads, transit, and utilities: How should we rebuild New Orleans's infrastructure?
- Neighborhood stability: What should we do to rebuild more stable neighborhoods?
- Rental and affordable housing: What should we do to create enough rental and affordable housing?
- Education and health services: What should we do to rebuild schools, hospitals, and clinics to meet our post-Katrina needs?
- Other public services: How should we provide vital services, like police, fire, and criminal justice, to meet our post-Katrina needs?

The citywide team and America*Speaks* crafted the choices and their wording together. They were also approved by city staff and the CSO, and they were tested with focus groups in New Orleans and Houston. The members of the team practiced all the presentations the night before, and they revised the text and slides well into the morning.

To prepare for the $2.4 million event, America*Speaks* had pulled out all the stops. Attracting New Orleanians who were still displaced required significant effort. In addition to the event in New Orleans, Lukensmeyer organized simultaneous meetings in Houston, Dallas, Atlanta, and Baton Rouge. They sent letters to 120,000 displaced New Orleanians, promising transportation, breakfast, lunch, child care, and translation services for Vietnamese and Spanish speakers.[39] They had coordinated outreach efforts through more than a dozen faith-based and community groups.[40] All of the tables were networked with laptops and keypad voting equipment. And the events were all linked by satellite to the New Orleans Convention Center for simulcast viewing in every city. The meeting would be broadcast live on the Internet in designated libraries and other public buildings in 16 other cities, including Chicago. America*Speaks* expected 500 people to attend each of these events outside of New Orleans and 1,000 attendees at the convention center.[41] They had trained facilitators for every table and additional staff floating throughout the event to solve problems, clarify the process, and counsel difficult participants. By November 21, about 3,000 people had registered; by the day before the event, nearly 4,000. America*Speaks* also met repeatedly with the mayor, city council members, and the press to explain the purpose and significance of the meeting and to review the draft discussion guides. As a result, the mayor and city council had urged people to attend, and the mayor had committed to spending the day at the meeting.

But how would the meeting turn out? Would it create useful information or simply rehash issues? A *Times-Picayune* editorial expressed the concerns of many:

> The questions that must be asked are what hard choices residents are willing to make, since rebuilding funds are limited. Which services and infrastructure should be rebuilt first and in which areas? What is to happen to neighborhoods that remain unpopulated in future years? Where exactly should those parks and schools be built? For their part, residents need to be productive in their participation. Katrina generated a healthy increase in civic involvement. But the anger and frustration many New Orleanians feel has often transformed public meetings into shouting matches that get little

Laurie A. Johnson

*Fig. 6.11. Carolyn Lukensmeyer of America*Speaks *at Community Congress II*

Laurie A. Johnson

Fig. 6.12. The "theme team" at Community Congress II

accomplished. Today's opportunity should not be wasted in such a manner. It's the least attendees can do for the tens of thousands of residents, across our region and in cities without scheduled sessions, who will not get the chance to be heard.[42]

If someone were to have arrived at the convention center shortly after noon, the quiet streets around it would have given no hint that anything of interest was happening inside the building. But after taking an escalator up to the meeting hall and stepping inside, anyone would have been impressed with the sight. About a thousand people clustered around 100 tables were all engaged in planning conversations with one another. The room was full, and it was buzzing. And it was clear that the participants reflected the real demographics of the city. Everyone was eating lunch together. Wires led everywhere.

Carolyn Lukensmeyer and the America*Speaks* team served as masters of ceremonies. The citywide team introduced each of the discussion topics with a brief presentation. At each table, participants discussed their views about each topic and the suggested options for each. The facilitator typed in these additional options and sent them immediately to the "theme team" table, where a small group of staff and community volunteers distilled the options into a new list that would be immediately available for voting. While the theme team worked, participants watched interviews with participants in the various cities on the big screens. The interviewees would often greet friends and family members back home in New Orleans. Lukensmeyer then reported the voting results, supplementing the data with quotes from participants. Facilitators in various color-coded shirts roamed the hall. Whenever a problem arose, someone was there to solve it. A film crew from Japan's NHK network spent the day filming table discussions and interviewing participants.[43]

In a city that supposedly was suffering from planning fatigue, most participants stayed all day, even though it was lovely and sunny outside. At the end of the day, Mayor Nagin spoke to the crowd, demonstrating his enthusiastic support. What politician wouldn't want to be associated with this obviously successful and festive event? A total of 2,366 keypads were used during the congress. Of these, 772 were used in New Orleans, which meant that two-thirds of the participants were displaced residents. Over 63 percent of the participants were African-American, nearly half had pre-Katrina household annual incomes that were less than $40,000, and every planning district was well represented. The only shortcoming was that there were only 39 participants under the age of 20, which meant youth were severely underrepresented. Other than that, the demographic composition of the participants closely mirrored the pre-Katrina population of New Orleans.

The meeting produced significant results on issues like flood protection. When participants were asked how the city should reduce flood risk, they were presented with several options ranging from simply letting people make their own decisions about where to live, to providing them financial incentives to move, to the construction of higher levees. The majority of participants, 57.8 percent, chose higher levees, although this choice assumed someone else would pay for them. The next three most popular choices were restoring wetlands (38.9 percent), providing standards and financial incentives to individuals (35.7 percent), and requiring flood insurance but keeping it affordable (32.8 percent). When asked to vote on the options prescribed by UNOP planners, 63.4 percent said they would strongly support financial incentives to reduce flood risk. Over 70 percent said they'd strongly support the creation and enforcement of standards and programs to reduce flood risk.

As for neighborhood rebuilding, 44.8 percent of the participants said they'd give a "very high level of support" to a policy that would allow well-informed home owners to make their own rebuilding decisions; 41.8 percent said they would strongly support financial incentives that would enable people to rebuild near one another. In other words, there was significant support for clustering development so long as it was based on incentives rather than regulation. As for the options submitted by participants at the congress, 57.2 percent of attendees indicated their favorite was to provide incentives for home owners to buy blighted property in their neighborhoods quickly and easily.

Nearly 59 percent of the participants also indicated they would give "low to very low support" to plans that rely on market forces to provide affordable and rental housing; 75.7 percent said they would strongly support financial incentives to build affordable housing. The participants were sharply divided over building more public housing.

For education and health care facilities, 72.7 percent of the participants favored opening and building facilities based on repopulation and recovery rates; 68.2 percent said they would strongly support combining facilities to reduce costs. Among the options submitted by participants, 64.3 percent said they would support making "schools 24/7 community centers in neighborhoods where people live" as well as rebuilding the community around schools. And 62 percent said they wanted school quality improved, better-paid teachers, and improved administration and facilities. Overall, this was a clear statement in support of rebuilding the school system with fewer facilities and in locations that also met community-planning objectives.

The biggest elephants in the room were issues surrounding reductions in future flood risk and population decline. The participants' clear preference was for the federal government to keep the floodwaters away from the city by strengthening the levees, which was no surprise. But they also said they would strongly support reducing flood risk via financial incentives and construction standards. They preferred to have someone else provide flood protection, but they indicated they were also willing to take personal responsibility for reducing their risk. Regarding neighborhood shrinkage, residents generally felt that home owners should make their own rebuilding decisions. But most also supported financial incentives for people to rebuild near one another. To an outsider, neither of these conclusions might seem like a breakthrough, but, in fact, they were. The subjects of risk and footprint shrinkage were now back on the table, and people showed a willingness to engage in these challenging issues thoughtfully and creatively. This, in turn, would increase the comfort of district planners to be more open to discussions about these difficult issues in subsequent neighborhood meetings. Finally, the results also made it plain that residents' opinions were varied and that the city was clearly divided on some issues, like public housing.

The *Times-Picayune* accounts of the community congresses in New Orleans and Atlanta stressed participants "rejected" the planners' options, but we were in fact very pleased that they produced their own preferred choices.[44] This was precisely the result the citizen involvement process was designed to produce. The participants also were quite satisfied with the day: on a scale of one to five—five indicating the highest level of satisfaction—73 percent gave the event a five, and only 2.9 percent gave it a one or two.

Abby Williamson, a doctoral student from the Harvard Kennedy School, interviewed 20 New Orleans community leaders one month after the community congress to evaluate its effect on the credibility and significance of UNOP. She concluded that the second community congress

> overcame significant obstacles to raise the credibility of UNOP in the eyes of public leaders. By bringing together a representative group of citizen participants and enabling meaningful discussion across lines of difference, Community Congress II engendered "buy-in" from both the public and their community leaders. Leaders were less clear about the role that public input played in influencing the substance of the plan. Looking back at previous planning processes, most community leaders felt that UNOP had managed to balance two crucial components in ways that earlier plans did not. Namely, leaders see UNOP as an effective marriage between citizen engagement and planner expertise, and believe that Community Congress II contributed to this balance. Looking to the future, leaders express hope that UNOP will pass quickly and New Orleans can attract the funds necessary to implement the plan.[45]

She quoted Councilmember Cynthia Hedge-Morrell, originally a skeptic of UNOP, as saying, "I think [it has] done more to bring credibility to the table than all of the little individual meetings that people go to. . . . It's brought the people who were displaced into the process. That's probably the one thing I would give UNOP real, real credit for. . . . [It] reminded me of true democracy like the town hall meeting."[46]

THE HOLIDAY SEASON

Community Congress II was a turning point. Participants felt planners were listening to them, and they believed this process would result in a plan that would influence funding decisions by the LRA and federal government. The UNOP team was relieved. It felt it finally had the public support it needed and had received significant, valuable input.

But, following a day of celebration, the cold, hard truth set in: the first draft of the plan was due in less than a month. The second draft was due January 5. Two more rounds of district meetings were scheduled for December 16 and January 6, with the final product to be unveiled at a third, final community congress on January 13. District planning teams would submit their preliminary project lists by December 15 and draft reports by December 22. It did not appear to be a very joyful holiday season for the UNOP team.

Two days after Community Congress II, Mayor Nagin announced Ed Blakely would be the director of the city's new recovery office, which would be in charge of implementing the city's recovery plans.[47] Slated to start work in early January, Blakely and his new office would be perfectly positioned to receive the results of UNOP and turn it into actions.[48] Furthermore, the city's fiscal situation had improved, and it was finally going to hire additional, much-needed planning and building staff.[49] In addition, Nagin announced the appointment of Becca O'Brien, formerly with Donald Powell's Gulf Coast Recovery Office, as Nagin's executive counsel. Nagin also appointed O'Brien to the last vacant seat on the CSO, at last linking him to UNOP in its final weeks.[50] This appointment would also be significant over the coming months, as O'Brien would play a key role in helping to position city hall for recovery implementation.

But UNOP still had a long way to go. This was an unprecedented planning effort in a difficult political environment, and UNOP members, with no examples to guide them, had to invent both the process and the products as they went. A common refrain—which relieved some and frustrated others—was that they were "building the airplane while flying it" or "drinking from the fire hose." These characterizations did not sit well with Carey Shea, the program officer from the Rockefeller Foundation, because she believed that they had paid for highly experienced world-class planners. But the reality was that there were no models for this, and no planners existed who could envision what such a plan would look like; to complete it in such a short time made it all the more difficult.

Many difficult decisions remained. The lack of a clear client-consultant relationship was problematic. Who would have the authority and credibility to make the tough calls? Not the mayor. The City Planning Commission was no longer taking an active role with UNOP because of the pace and the level of involvement it required.[51] The GNOF, the NOCSF, and Rockefeller were neither planners nor policy makers. The CSO took its oversight role seriously and guarded the integrity of the process, but it lacked the experience and perspective to make planning decisions. Concordia had been more involved than originally intended, but it, too, lacked planning authority. The citywide team was a committee effort, and even Villavaso, as the designated planning leader, had never led a project of this magnitude.

Searching for some credible expert advice and guidance, Steven Bingler reached out again to the group that had initially interviewed the planning teams in July. Now called the "resource team," the group—Ken Topping, Gus Newport, Robert Lurcott, and Yolanda Rodriguez, plus the newly appointed Rob Olshansky—was quickly called upon to meet with the UNOP core team of citywide and district team leaders on December 5.

The meeting provided a good opportunity to evaluate the status of all the planning activities so far and to refocus them for the final push. This meeting was also the first opportunity for the entire team to review the polling results from Community Congress II. But the biggest challenge was to figure out how to integrate risk reduction into the reconstruction process at both household and neighborhood levels. Put another way, how could they actualize the LRA motto of "safer, stronger, smarter" in New Orleans? According to the planners for New Orleans East, for example, residents of that area resisted discussions of risk and mitigation, and the citizen planning committees were distrustful of the citywide team and its data, believing that it was intent on depicting their area as unsafe in order to undermine their ability to return and receive public services. It was going to be very difficult to reduce risk in New Orleans East because of the prevalence of homes with slab-on-grade construction, which makes it difficult and costly to elevate homes. Thus, it seemed likely that home owners would re-create the pre-Katrina flood risk in this part of the city, and there was little that planners could do but support the ongoing return of residents.

Robert B. Olshansky

Fig. 6.13. A typical slab-on-grade house in New Orleans

Several district planners asserted residents understood the need for mitigation, but they simply had no means to pay for it. At the time, the Road Home program did not include sufficient funding to elevate homes, especially slab-on-grade homes. Some residents had expressed a willingness to elevate or relocate to higher ground if given additional incentives and better guidance regarding viable relocation sites within their district. At one meeting, some were open to the idea of a buyout option that would give them 130 percent of a home's pre-Katrina market value so that they could relocate somewhere else within the planning district. But they were skeptical such a program could actually occur, and even if it did they would need better guidance on sites. UNOP planners also lacked the information they would need to help residents relocate. They did not have access to detailed data from the Road Home program about home owners' stated intent to return or sell, though the parishwide data indicated about 10 percent had chosen to sell at that point. It seemed that all the planning teams could do was inform people about better and safer ways to come back to the city. Incremental safety achievements would be better than nothing at all.

One district planner observed that the risk reduction issue highlighted a fundamental tension between the citywide and district teams. The citywide team was driven by concerns about citywide facilities, whereas the district teams had become the advocates for households and neighborhoods. To planners, the tension between local desires and citywide physical and fiscal realities is nothing new. But the speed of this planning process meant there would be very little time to integrate the two levels. Thus, the citywide team would have to accept all the recommendations from the district plans to assure residents that they were helping to shape the overall plan, without actually promising the recommendations would be implemented. But this posed a fundamental problem in creating the final plan because a goal of the process was to create a specific list of recovery projects. One possible approach would be to have several tiers of projects, with some simply listed as proposals for further study.

The second major issue at the resource team meeting was how to continue neighborhood-based planning after UNOP ended. The topic was urgent now that the end of the official post-Katrina process was in sight. Suggestions included creating community development corporations, providing funding for neighborhood advocates, or supporting other forms of planning assistance. One district planner observed that the district focus had proven so successful in UNOP (by grouping together adjacent, though often dissimilar, neighborhoods) that it might be worthwhile to consider districtwide community boards. Team members agreed it would be good to be able to announce a longer-term structure before the end of UNOP to underscore the need for continuing citizen involvement. Yolanda

Rodriguez agreed it was important that ideas kept on coming from neighborhoods to ensure more effective plan implementation than had been seen in the past. She suggested designating a team of planners to work with each district. But this, of course, would require additional funding for the City Planning Commission.

The resource team also acknowledged that the city's new recovery office would play a huge role in financing, coordinating, and communicating with any neighborhood-based planning efforts. And it would need to manage federal funds and contracts in a transparent manner. At the time, there was a widespread expectation that the Road Home program would not need all the CDBG funds allocated to it. Thus, the resource team suggested two possible ways in which to redirect these surplus housing funds: affordable rental housing and use of incentives beyond the $150,000 maximum benefit limit set by the Road Home program. These proposals would need to be adopted by the LRA and approved by HUD.

After the resource team meeting, Ken Topping sent out a memo laying out the most important goals of UNOP at this point: prevent future flood losses, guide private investments, and encourage equitable resettlement patterns. His chief recommendation was a "proactive, incentive-driven, organized system of buyouts to assemble land for reorganized use [that] respects natural hazards and citizen interests and desires to return to their communities." He also recommended "an empowered City Planning Commission with adequate staff to address needs for revision of the City Master Plan in light of Katrina and for planning reform." He also stressed that the plan would need to be familiar with the countless federal recovery programs and should clarify which city agencies would implement each program. For example, considerable funds would eventually be available through FEMA's Hazard Mitigation Grant Program. Finally, he pointed out the government hearings related to the adoption of the UNOP were expected to extend into March. They needed additional funding if UNOP planners were expected to be there for the hearings and carry the plan through to the very end.

Later in the month, he issued another memo that emphasized the practical and strategic nature of the citywide plan. The "vision" and specifics about neighborhood design and physical needs would come out of the district plans. The citywide plan would focus on bureaucratic strategies. For example, the citywide plan could lay out a set of policies for land assembly, whereas the district plans would identify specific locations and how they might be used to meet the needs of the community.

But while the UNOP teams were rushing toward the finish line, one of their worst fears was confirmed on December 14 at an LRA board meeting. Very little of the $10.4 billion in CDBG funds would be available for community and infrastructure recovery projects.[52] Out of the $445 million in uncommitted CDBG funds, the LRA designated $135 million for state buildings, $40 million for public and private schools, and $20 million for the fishing industry. This left $200 million to the parishes for projects in their ESF #14 plans and only $50 million completely undesignated. Based on a formula derived from each parish's share of statewide damages, New Orleans would receive 58 percent of the funds, or $116 million.

The larger pot of recovery money, from FEMA's Public Assistance program also continued to pose problems. For one, $135 million of CDBG funds were designated for state buildings because FEMA had deemed these projects ineligible for the Public Assistance money. Second, the Public Assistance money continued to flow too slowly. According to Mayor Nagin, by the end of 2006 the city had received only about $100 million out of the $900 million it had requested in approved project worksheets.[53]

But FEMA was not the only bureaucratic bottleneck in town now. The state's Office of Homeland Security and Emergency Preparedness was also slowing down the flow of federal funds. It was the intermediary between FEMA and Public Assistance applicants and was responsible for processing applications and providing funds.[54]

All of this was bad news but not a complete surprise. It confirmed there was going to be an enormous funding gap to fill if the city wanted to meet the needs that the planning process was identifying. Most people were beginning to appreciate the value of UNOP in attracting private investments, but it was still sobering to realize that the only assured public funding amounted to just $116 million. Still, some people thought new opportunities for funding might emerge from the recent national elections. Democrats had taken control of both the House and Senate, and many local officials believed that a Democratic Congress, with Democratic committee chairs, would listen much more sympathetically to Louisiana's requests for additional financial assistance. The burden, of course, would still be on the state to document the need for additional funds. Because UNOP had the potential to provide such documentation, its potential role in advocacy had grown.[55]

In addition to these funding uncertainties, the UNOP team still had to deal with several outstanding questions regarding how parts of their plan might actually be implemented. How would they identify priority recovery areas? How would properties acquired through the Road Home program be managed? How could a program be implemented to help residents cluster together but avoid a patchwork development pattern? Should they promote development in particular locations (and, if so, which?)? Further, the structure of the plan itself was still in flux, and it was not yet clear how the final list of projects would be determined. In an interview with the *Times-Picayune*, Steven Bingler said the final UNOP product would be a recovery plan focusing on nuts-and-bolts infrastructure projects, not a visionary plan for the city's transformation. But, in fact, the UNOP team had yet to decide what the difference was between a "recovery" plan and a "vision." Nor had they finalized what the relationship would be between the district plans and the citywide plan. Internal discussions were pointing toward using the citywide plan to focus on recovery priorities, with the district plans as vehicles to carry bigger, long-term ideas toward a new master plan and comprehensive zoning ordinance for New Orleans.

But they had to present a consistent front to residents. Immediately before the third round of district meetings in mid-December, the citywide team developed an internal set of responses to 22 of the thorniest questions that district planners might be asked at their final meetings. It included questions like "What is our definition of high, medium, and low risk areas for development?" Another was "Does the citywide team have a conceptual idea of how an incentive-based program for voluntary relocation would work? Would this, in combination with strategic elevations and hardening of facilities, be the cornerstone of our hazard mitigation efforts?" And yet another was "Is there a citywide position on affordable housing, public housing, and gentrification?" And "Do we have a firm or tentative position on key economic development proposals?" As with previous meetings, the citywide team also developed a set of standardized slides covering the status

Laurie A. Johnson

Fig. 6.14. Meeting of the UNOP District 4 sector captains

of the planning process, its next steps, and its positions on future flood risk, for each of the district planning teams to use at their meetings.

The district planning meetings on December 14 and 15 went smoothly. Attendance had increased, and a *Times-Picayune* reporter attended each one. The meetings were more pragmatic than before, and they focused on tangible projects and specific land-use concepts.[56] The meetings also provided opportunities for UNOP planners to float some recovery strategies and project ideas being discussed internally at UNOP.

Around this time, the planning schedule had to be adjusted because an NFL playoff game hosted by the New Orleans Saints was scheduled for the weekend of January 13, which was the original date for Community Congress III. The NOCSF decided to reschedule it to January 20. Although it would require other schedule changes, there was simply no way the event could compete with Saints fever, which would undoubtedly captivate residents and visiting fans for the entire weekend. Fortunately, no games were scheduled for January 20, and the convention center was available for the day.

The schedule change provided a bit more time for the district planners to meet with their steering committees (although their contracts were to end on January 15). The NOCSF and UNOP teams allowed district planners some flexibility in scheduling their final district meetings sometime between January 6 and 13 to allow residents to review final drafts of the district plans. But the NOCSF stayed firm in its commitment to deliver the final document to the City Planning Commission by January 30. Afterward, it would dissolve, its mission accomplished. This would mean that the citywide team would need to complete its revisions to the plan within 10 days after Community Congress III.

Adding to the stress of this rigid timetable, all the teams were overspending their budgets. This was understandable, given the enormous demands on them. GNOF extended loans to the NOCSF, hoping that subsequent donors could reimburse them. And in December, with little fanfare and no press coverage, the Louisiana Office of Community Development awarded the NOCSF $2 million for UNOP, paid for with federal disaster recovery CDBG funds.[57] This was expected to cover the additional expenses incurred to date, as well as costs to carry the plan through the City Planning Commission review process. Thus, the total cost of UNOP was now up to $7.5 million, plus the $3 million raised by America*Speaks*.[58]

SECOND MEETING OF THE UNOP RESOURCE TEAM

On January 4, the resource team met for a second time. This meeting gave all the UNOP consultants a chance to present their nearly complete drafts and concepts, and it provided an opportunity to consider how best to strategically position the process for a successful completion. The meeting, held at

Robert B. Olshansky

Fig. 6.15. The UNOP resource team, meeting with UNOP core team members

the Concordia office in downtown New Orleans, focused on citywide issues in the morning and district planning in the afternoon.[59] The citywide team reported it had reviewed all the sector reports and the district plans, and it was pulling them all together. But it was also drowning in details. It hadn't had a chance to package the plan into a concise set of messages for the public, nor had it scripted Community Congress III, which was only 16 days away. For these reasons, the communication team was a key part of this meeting. In the afternoon, representatives of the district planners joined the meeting (one by phone), and, as with the previous resource team meeting, this doubled as the weekly citywide/district coordination meeting.

This all-day meeting was in many ways the high point of thinking about how New Orleans would not only recover from Katrina but thrive. Of course, the attendees had been thinking about these ideas for months. Attendees included highly experienced New Orleans natives, consulting planners, disaster recovery planners, and communications specialists. The group had all the information, all the ideas, and all the experience at its fingertips. It was time to wrestle with the big issues and resolve some key problems. They included the relative functions of citywide and district plans, what constituted a "recovery project," how detailed and specific the citywide plan should be, what the most important elements of the plans were, and what would happen after UNOP.

A single question lurked behind all of these issues: What is "recovery," and what goes beyond recovery? In Japan, the term *fukkyu* refers to restoration to the predisaster state, while *fukko* refers to a condition better than the one before the disaster. Our federal policy essentially uses this same distinction: the FEMA Public Assistance program pays only to restore public facilities to their predisaster state. The CDBG funds, however, can do more, though after Katrina CDBG funds were primarily used to supplement insurance in order to restore private facilities. But, by their very title, CDBG funds are also designed for community development projects. And because these were the very funds that required the guidance of a unified New Orleans plan, this means that UNOP stepped directly into this murky territory: recovery, in this instance, meant something more than simple restoration. Unless New Orleans could solve some of its long-standing problems of social and economic inequity and political corruption, then some people would be less willing to come back. And if the purpose of recovery is to bring back the city's pre-Katrina residents, then these "improvement" projects would in fact be critical elements of the recovery process.[60] For example, downtown revitalization projects, even if they did not necessarily fix flood damage, would enhance the overall economic recovery and viability of the region. As another example, improving the school system would increase the probability that people would choose to return to their neighborhoods.

One thing had become clear to the team over the course of the past months: the project-based methods that were the core of the ESF #14 approach and the heart of what UNOP was going to deliver to the LRA were inherently unworkable for such a large-scale disaster. The project-based approach of the Public Assistance program (as defined by the Stafford Act) is an inefficient way to rebuild an entire city. It would be better to give a block grant to the city, which would then have the flexibility to group actions into logical bundles and to appropriately apply combinations of Public Assistance and CDBG funds over time. Even the existing CDBG process was too project-specific and tied the city's hands. It was nonsensical to think of the recovery as a list of discrete projects, and it didn't shed any light on how such projects should be prioritized. Furthermore, the UNOP team appreciated that it really had no political legitimacy to dictate where everything should go or what should be done first. To counter the shortcomings of the project-based approach, the UNOP planners all agreed they needed to propose a broader strategic approach for managing all the proposed projects. The answer they were working on was a strategic framework—a citywide recovery strategy.

Although most people think a plan looks something like an architectural diagram, urban planning does not actually work this way. Because urban planning is a process over time, the citywide plan needed to create a mechanism that would help the most appropriate entities make the most appropriate decisions; groups projects into bundles; phases them over time; and puts responsible people in charge of their development. It should be a flexible framework, capable of confronting the uncertainties of population-return rates and markets over time. And it should be adaptable, strengthened by constant review and adjustment to the list of projects. In the ongoing meetings with city and NORA staff, all agreed that such an approach was the best way to meet their needs. Ed Blakely's office, for example, had asked for a structured program to support more effective use of existing agencies.

The citywide team proposed creating a "recovery council" to serve as a "recovery voice" for the city and guide the planning framework. It suggested that the mayor appoint the chair and recommended it be Blakely. They also recommended that the council consist of representatives from key public agencies in Orleans Parish that were managing core aspects of the city's recovery. The team suggested modeling it on the ongoing biweekly "institutional leadership meeting" that had become part of UNOP. These meetings had grown to include 14 representatives from federal, state, and local agencies, as well as staff from the mayor's office and City Planning Commission. Another model was the September 27 district planning team orientation, which demonstrated how efficient communication could be if all the agencies were represented in one room. Emergency managers are familiar with Emergency Operations Centers (EOCs), which facilitate information flows in a hectic, fast-paced environment. Recovering from a huge urban disaster is also hectic and fast-paced and therefore needs a similar body. This is not a new discovery.[61] A coordinating body makes fundamental management sense.

A recovery council could use the recovery framework to enable relevant government agencies to set priorities and make and coordinate decisions over time. Recovery decisions, such as clustering and phasing, would require interaction and cooperation among agencies. For example, if the city's Sewerage and Water Board were to do repairs randomly over time and not tell other agencies about its plans, it would impede the ability of other agencies to elevate or cluster new buildings. The UNOP team certainly appreciated that such a body would require some effort to establish with an appropriate level of authority and several MOUs. But, at a minimum, an organization that had no charge other than to meet regularly and promote communication would make an important contribution to the recovery process. UNOP would provide the framework, and recovery council members would discuss and make decisions within it.

The UNOP team also appreciated the need for a parallel system that would communicate with community groups, help them talk to one another, improve the quality and flow of information between residents and city government, and give those who are displaced by the disaster a voice. There was consensus that UNOP would not design such a system or systems, but it would recommend that something like it be created in the near future.

The group had a long discussion about what they would eventually call the plans. If the citywide plan was not a master plan or a blueprint, what was it? A framework? A project? Was it about recovery, or did it go beyond that? In the end, the team agreed it would call the citywide plan a "citywide recovery strategy." Given that most New Orleanians would expect it to be called a "plan," however, they decided that the best title should be something like "citywide strategic plan for recovery and rebuilding." As for the district plans, they would be called just that: district plans.

So, what about the district plans? What was their function, and what would be their role in the future? For one, because of the ESF #14 framework, the only plan that needed to be approved by the LRA was a list of recovery projects. Thus, the role of the district plans was to develop local lists of recovery projects, which would then be rolled up into the citywide plan as the official parish recovery plan submitted to the LRA. Furthermore, as the "recovery plan," according to the New Orleans' City Charter, the citywide plan would also need to be approved by the City Planning Commission and city council. Thus, the citywide plan had to go through public hearings in front of the City Planning Commission and a public review period of at least 30 days. The district plans, in contrast, required none of this. In formal terms, they were no more than working documents used as background for the recovery plan. Because they did not need to go to the City Planning Commission, they did not require the approval of the NOCSF or the advisory blessings of the CSO. As a courtesy, they needed to be approved only by the districts and the neighborhood steering committees.

District planning participants, however, would obviously expect some sort of formal recognition of the plans to give them meaning and stature. Residents should be able to see that their hard work in the district planning meetings resulted in projects listed in the citywide plan. The reality was that the district plans, in the public's mind, were the most important product of UNOP. Citizens created them, they were tangible, they conveyed specific information about the places where people lived and worked, and they embodied citizens' visions for the future. The district plans also deserved wide distribution and at least 30 days in public view. And the citizens should have their ideas recognized in some way by the city council.

However, it would be important to make it clear that district plans would not be static documents. The team agreed the district plans were really the first step toward the city's overdue revision of its master plan. Furthermore, most districts wanted to remain engaged in planning issues and wanted a continuing voice in future city planning decisions. The group agreed that UNOP should ask the city council to officially adopt the citywide recovery plan but also validate in some official way the important work their constituents had done in the district planning efforts.

The process and structure of the citywide and district planning framework were important, but UNOP also needed to address substantive issues such as housing, neighborhood repopulation and development, long-term flood mitigation, and economic development. To accomplish this, the citywide team proposed that the strategic recovery framework should balance the city's recovery vision—to fairly and equitably bring back the entire city and enable all citizens to return—with the two key risks that could undermine the city's future and any recovery investments: the pace of repopulation and the risk of future flooding. Using this framework, recovery projects would be phased across the city according to the combination of these two risks. Furthermore, the team agreed that all policies that had anything to do with private property had to be based on incentives rather than regulation. Individuals would make voluntary choices based on information and incentives provided by governmental agencies. Some of these incentives might also consist of strategic public investments made by the agencies.

Focusing on repopulation and flood risk allowed the team to categorize neighborhoods according to what kind of help they would need to recover. They would first determine whether these areas had a low, medium, or high risk of flooding. Then they would determine how quickly it would take for these areas to repopulate. These two factors taken together would determine what kind of recovery policies should be pursued in the neighborhood. (See fig. 6.16.) In reality, however, only three "policy zones" emerged from this process, because repopulation was not independent of flood risk as of that date; residents of the lowest-lying neighborhoods were the slowest to rebuild.[62] Thus, the three zones bore a troubling similarity to the three zones of the BNOB plan. The difference, however, would lie in the policies applied to the zones.

For example, under the UNOP strategic recovery framework, areas with the slowest repopulation rate and highest future flood risk would require the most money and active policy intervention, especially in the short term. They would also take the most time to fully recover. Clustering developments and elevating structures would involve considerable time and money. The city's new recovery office and NORA would need to work together to coordinate a resettlement program, refine its strategies, and start bundling properties in these zones. In fact, NORA's first task would be to clear the backlog of pre-Katrina blighted properties and turn them into areas that

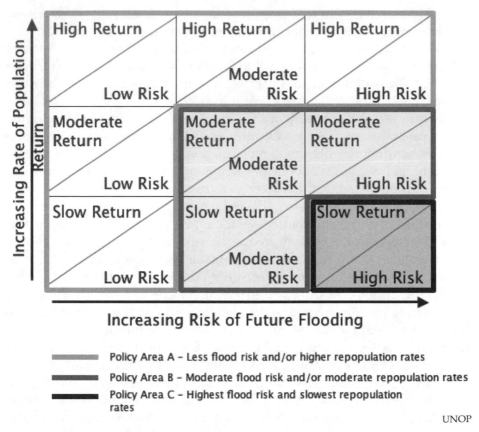

Fig. 6.16. Defining recovery policy areas

could be a start on "receiving zones" for resettlement programs. The city of Kobe did something similar to this after the 1995 earthquake. The most severely damaged areas were given the most money and intensive planning attention, but they took the longest to rebuild. Many of Kobe's residents complained about this approach at the time, but today those areas are more desirable than the adjacent areas that did not receive such special treatment.

The group discussed possible policies and projects for the Lower Ninth Ward in order to try out this risk-based recovery framework. The reality was that the area would take a long time to rebuild, and the city would need to commit to the area for just as long. So the framework needed to be flexible enough to withstand the uncertainties inherent in such a long time frame but still help the community immediately with technical assistance, public investments, and incentives for private investment.

The UNOP team anticipated that describing these policy zones to the public would be a challenge because of the tainted legacy of the BNOB plan. They would have to emphasize that all neighborhoods would be funded and the areas with the highest flood risk would receive extra help rather than be last in line for it. They would get more money, but it would take more time to help them recover. Second, the UNOP team decided to avoid the term "zones," which implies a regulatory approach. Instead they would call them "policy areas." The actual content of these policies would not surprise those who had been involved in the district planning meetings. These meetings had been discussing how to vary reconstruction incentives based on flood depth and extent of blight. In contrast to the incentives in the high-risk areas, the medium-risk policy areas would be the recipients of focused, strategic actions, and the low-risk areas would be repaired, densified, and used for siting some of the major regional economic drivers.

One critical question facing the team was this: should the citywide plan include a map of these policy areas? Some team members said that the public would not consider this a real plan without a map of the policy areas. Some argued that because no neighborhood fell entirely within one of the three levels, a map might be politically acceptable. Others argued that no matter how well meaning, a map of policy areas would mean the death of the plan. Any property-specific map would instantly become the focus of attention, dwarfing everything else in the plan. Furthermore, once a map was released to the public, the team would lose control over it. A map published in the *Times-Picayune*, for example, might take on a life of its own. Furthermore, creating a single map would be technically difficult. Because the three colors would be sensitive to threshold values selected for the two risk variables, policy area designations would be subjective. In addition, the repopulation variable would change over time, and so would the maps. Others proposed a compromise: publish a series of maps and the risk matrix. The argument was that this issue was at the heart of UNOP's purpose, which was to give people all the information that was available so they could make their own decisions. In the spirit of educating and informing the public, UNOP should produce a series of detailed maps accompanied by the matrix. They would be typical planning data overlays but with no set way of combining them. The team did not resolve this contentious issue at the meeting.

Policy and process questions aside, the primary requirement of UNOP was to deliver a list of projects to the LRA, but the team was still not sure about what constituted a "project." The team agreed that it would be good to include activities that would enhance the effectiveness of reconstruction projects, such as outreach to displaced households, governance reforms, citizen participation programs, and procedural strategies to maximize FEMA

Public Assistance reimbursements. As it was, the team was developing a list of projects prioritized according to their perceived importance to recovery efforts and scale of impact (national, state, region, city, district). This was consistent with the ESF #14 process. However, one key difference between the UNOP and the ESF #14 lists was that UNOP was also including projects already in the FEMA Public Assistance pipeline, in order to place these projects into context.

The citywide team and the district teams were working with each other to identify, define, and prioritize recovery projects. After identifying the high-priority projects, the team would then group them into sectors and different time frames. Over the coming weeks, defining "projects" and "recovery" would continue to challenge planners. It was also clear that these lists would continue to change. District planners also noted that residents' project choices in some districts had changed over time, too. Although, where Lambert plans had been completed, district planners began with them and continued to work with the same neighborhood steering committees, residents reevaluated their project priorities, and not all of the Lambert projects made the final list.

The UNOP team also discussed two concrete strategies to mitigate flood risk and rebuild neighborhoods. One strategy would be to elevate structures or rebuild them on higher ground. The second would be to cluster land use into nodes that could catalyze neighborhood revitalization. These activities would have to be undertaken voluntarily, but incentives would help. The solution, if there was one, depended on local involvement, money, and information. The UNOP team decided that it would ask for these resources through an "enhanced Road Home" program. In district meetings, planners had asked residents whether they would relocate or elevate and what might induce them to do so. Most expressed a willingness to consider this. For example, District 2 residents indicated they would be willing to relocate at 150 percent of home value and would be willing to elevate existing homes for full cost plus a small premium. District 6 residents showed support for the idea of clustering, but they were skeptical of its feasibility. Fred Schwartz proposed a citywide voluntary home-lifting program, with graduated subsidies based on level of risk (see fig. 6.17b). In some cases, pioneers who rebuilt quickly and then saw that their neighbors were relocating might wish that they could change their minds and relocate, too. Team members concurred that such pioneers should not be penalized and that funds should be available for voluntary relocation under such circumstances.

UNOP planners felt that the basic Road Home program was not doing enough for many home owners, even if they had flood and wind insurance. The money would fall short of what the home owner needed to move or rebuild. Low-income home owners needed full compensation for their homes, not just the loss on the pre-Katrina assessed value of their home less insurance payments. Additionally, the cost of elevating homes was much higher in areas like New Orleans East, where most homes were slab-on-grade. Finally, the Road Home program did nothing to help residents decide where to move if they were able to afford it or give neighborhoods the chance to collectively decide where they might want to reassemble properties. In order to do this, people would need to know what their neighbors were doing, and they would need continuing technical advice.

Team members agreed that the most appropriate way to address these problems would be through a modified Road Home program tailored specifically for New Orleans. Revising the program would also present UNOP with an opportunity to spend the Road Home money on neighborhood stabilization and elevation programs. This was consistent with the team's opinion that, given the level of devastation and urban complexities, New Orleans needed more flexibility in its use of CDBG funds.

Another troublesome issue was public housing. The city had asked UNOP not to get involved with the issue of how to reuse the sites owned by the Housing Authority of New Orleans (HANO). HANO was operated by HUD, and decisions about the sites' future were all being made in Washington, D.C., independent of actions by the City Planning Commission. But the residents weren't buying this. The district planners saw that public housing was a central issue in many neighborhoods, and they chose to confront it by advocating to the citywide team that public housing issues needed to be included in UNOP. Residents disagreed with HUD's approach and wanted their opinions in the district plans. This was an unusual opportunity to rethink public housing because the land was available and neighboring residents supported the rights of public housing residents to return. Another significant issue was the maximum density of 15 units per acre mandated by HUD's nationwide HOPE VI program. The HANO areas were built with 45 units per acre. To rebuild these HANO sites at such low densities would make it very difficult to rehouse all the residents who wanted to return. The UNOP team agreed that public housing was in fact an appropriate topic for the plans.

The UNOP team also described how it was putting more effort into engineering a smooth handoff to the city and ensuring city staff would have a plan that would meet their needs. UNOP now had a much better-defined set of clients in city hall now that it was beefing up its planning and recovery staff. For one, there was Ed Blakely at the city's new recovery office. There was also a new director for NORA, Joe Williams. (Members of the UNOP team had been meeting weekly with Blakely's new staff and with Williams.) In addition, the City Planning Commission now had more staff members. In addition, it would be critical for all the key players—especially higher-level officials who were parties to the memorandum of understanding—to be briefed on the contents of the plan prior to Community Congress III. If the process was done properly—extensive meetings in the planning districts, frequent communication with city staff, numerous meetings with state and federal officials, and briefings with key officials—there should be no public surprises at either Community Congress III or the final CSO meeting.[63]

The UNOP team expected that one of the major topics of discussion would be the expected cost of the plan.[64] Although financial estimates were still incomplete, the UNOP team was able to say that an incentive-based program for neighborhood stabilization would be, by far, the biggest cost. They had met with Blakely and Williams the previous week to alert them to the magnitude of the costs. The team agreed that one of the biggest media sound bites following the announcement of the plan would be the total cost of the plan, so it would be important to indicate how much of it would be borne by the state, city, and private investors. In many ways, the city and state had never fully recovered from the effects of the very first request to Congress after Katrina for a whopping $250 billion, and so it was crucial to demonstrate how much of the funding would come from local public and private sources.

Given all of the issues above, how should the UNOP team present the plan to the public? One concern was that many people were expecting a blueprint for the future. Indeed, many UNOP leaders had, earlier in the process, promised just that. Now, $10 million later, the product would instead come in multiple parts and be more nuanced than most people had expected. Instead of coming with a ribbon wrapped around it, it would be a framework for further action, a milestone along the long road to recovery. Nor would it bring limitless recovery funds from Washington, as had been implied back in April. Furthermore, some aspects of it looked suspiciously like BNOB.

So, was this really the "end of planning," as so many had promised? Was it time for planning fatigue to end and rebuilding to begin? Clearly, one type of planning was over, and it would be fair to announce to the public, "You won't be asked to do a recovery vision statement again." But it would also be honest to state that the implementation process would require continuous planning work in order to get the details right. It was not true that the residents were tired of planning. They were certainly tired of closing their eyes and envisioning the future, but participants in the district planning meetings were actively engaged in thinking about implementation details, and most expressed interest in continuing to meet over time. UNOP had created an opportunity for people to actually meet one another and talk, which was welcomed. For example, this process was the first time residents of District 2 met with their neighbors on the other side of St. Charles Avenue.

The participants in the Lower Ninth Ward had asked for frequent meetings and would likely continue to hold them.

In fact, Community Congress III would not be the end of planning but rather a launching pad to another kind of planning to build a smarter, safer, and stronger city. The planning baton would pass to city hall, but planning activities would continue. The plan would ask government agencies and citizen organizations alike to remain committed to achieve its goals.

FINAL DISTRICT PLANNING MEETINGS

On Saturday, January 6, ACORN released its "Peoples' Plan for Overcoming the Hurricane Katrina Blues."[65] This represented the product of the team from Cornell, Columbia, and the University of Illinois, which had continued its planning activities after being dismissed from UNOP in October. It was a valuable supplement to the findings and policies of UNOP and helped to augment and amplify important points. For example, it was consistent with the findings of the district planners from H3 Studio, which indicated that residents were eager to return if only they could fill the financial gaps left by Road Home and insurance. ACORN's team had surveyed 3,000 properties and interviewed 200 residents. The report concluded that, despite the slow visible progress, nearly 80 percent of Lower Ninth residents were in the process of gutting or renovating their homes. The message was clear: the Lower Ninth was coming back. At the end of the meeting, ACORN leaders encouraged residents to attend the UNOP district meetings later in the day to review the proposed plans.

The final round of UNOP district planning meetings was split over the weekends of January 6 and 13.[66] Participants finalized their project priorities, but they had questions about where the money would come from. Steve Villavaso reminded the public of the importance of the plan in making the city's case for its share of recovery dollars: "There's just a lot of competition for this money. Without this plan, we go nowhere." The 120 participants at the New Orleans East meeting were astute enough to realize they needed to identify a small list of high-priority projects to ensure they would rise to the top. All the planners reiterated the forthcoming citywide plan would not determine which neighborhoods were "viable" and which were not. And they tried to prepare the public for a strategic plan, rather than a blueprint: "What you won't see in the plan (are) directives that prioritize certain neighborhoods or districts over another, because we believe that they're all viable."[67]

THE LAST STRETCH

The final three weeks were hectic, to say the least.[68] Now that the conceptual approach was clear, it was critical to communicate it accurately and in readily understandable terms to the media, local officials, UNOP participants, and the public at large. At the same time, the team needed to prepare the plan, the maps, tables, analyses, financial projections, project lists, and so on.

The citywide team began to circulate draft copies of maps of the three proposed recovery policy areas to UNOP staff. By this point, Villavaso, Henry, and other core team members were in agreement that these maps would not be presented publicly. However, they still had to be created in order to determine what areas of the city fell into each policy category so recovery project costs could be accurately calculated. One version of the map broke up the city in three areas according to elevation. The lowest-lying areas were labeled "safer," the moderate-elevation areas (which were most of the city) were "smarter," and the highest-elevation areas along the river were "stronger." Its simplicity, however, was a double-edged sword. In one sense, it could be seen as a simplified diagram of the range of policy approaches. Seen another way, however, it was a cartoon of what was in fact a subtle and complex strategic plan. And it looked rather like the BNOB map, except that much of Lakeview and only a small part of the Lower Ninth were in the "safer" category.

Over the next weeks, the briefings with officials went well. No one expressed objections to the content of the plan, though several had opinions regarding its presentation at Community Congress III. But getting the message out to residents took much more work. UNOP core members were being pushed by resource team members to do more public outreach and communication, and the core members agreed that was critical. But there weren't enough hours in the day, or the night, to complete all that needed to be done.[69]

Further, the people who wrote and produced the communications material and the people who disseminated it were separated, and this created some problems. One problem with the public messages was that the team was working so hard on lowering people's expectations for a shiny new blueprint for the future ("it's a recovery plan, not a vision"), they neglected to promote public excitement for what in fact were some rather visionary strategies. By January 20, the day of Community Congress III, the positive message began to appear in the press:

> A New Orleans recovery plan to be presented to a four-city citizen "Community Congress" today suggests tackling flood threats and thinly populated neighborhoods with an ambitious mix of financial incentives for people to raise their homes or move to more-populated areas. . . . The plan's architects hope the document will serve as a lobbying tool to get the needed billions from the federal government and private donors. The plan gives few details about how the incentives would work, but planners want to see a bold

initiative that would, for example, provide enough money for owners of slab-on-grade New Orleans homes, a group that saw wholesale devastation during Katrina flooding, to demolish and build an elevated home at the same site. Such a program would seek to "make people whole," several organizers said.[70]

This article also highlighted the proposals to create an "Elevate New Orleans" incentive program, expand streetcar lines, build new libraries, create new investments for the downtown medical district, build a downtown theater district, repair water and wastewater systems, and construct a secondary levee system in selected locations.

City council president Oliver Thomas was enthusiastic about the plan content: "Generally, I liked what I saw, and it seemed to be very inclusive in that a lot of the ideas that we heard from different parts of the community were included in their suggestions."[71] But, not surprisingly, he was also wary of the bureaucratic obstacles that could get in the way of the financial incentives because such problems had plagued the Road Home program.

COMMUNITY CONGRESS III

Community Congress III was a great success. It was a well-organized event, designed to unveil a plan that was consistent with the desires of most of the people who had participated in the process. Nearly 1,300 people attended or watched the event in New Orleans, Atlanta, Dallas, and Houston. (Approximately 450 of these were in the diaspora cities.) Participants living in Baton Rouge were bused to New Orleans.

Vera Triplett started the congress by describing her initial skepticism of this planning process. But, she said, UNOP turned out to be "an historic undertaking." For most of the day, citywide planners summarized key aspects of the plan. America*Speaks* led table discussions and keypad polling. And the event was punctuated by musical and poetic interludes. Every table had a 20-page discussion guide, organized as follows:

How the Plan Responds to Input from Community Congress II
    Safety from Future Flooding
    Rebuilding Safe and Stable Neighborhoods
    Affordable Housing
    Public Services

Action and Implementation
    Moving from Planning to Action
    Government's Role
    The Public's Role

America*Speaks* polled participants to determine the demographics of the group, which generally reflected the ethnic and economic diversity of pre-Katrina New Orleans and represented every planning district.[72] After the poll, Mayor Nagin spoke. He congratulated participants for their hard work, said he would sign the plan after it was approved by the city council, and promised that by quickly "taking this comprehensive master plan and turning it into a comprehensive zoning ordinance, . . . we will codify all your hard work into the law of the land." Although he got his talking point a bit wrong, it was clear that he intended to support the City Planning Commission's intent to immediately follow up UNOP with a master plan and zoning ordinance update.

Troy Henry identified the top priorities of the plan:

- Safety from flooding
- Empowering and stabilizing neighborhoods
- Opportunity for all residents to return
- Equitable services, access for all to education and health care

He talked about the systems approach in identifying projects for each neighborhood, based on the variations in flood risk and repopulation rates across the city. He also emphasized the need for phasing these projects over time, because everything could not be done at once. As a result, he said that the plan designated a series of policy areas that reflect different conditions across the city, and plan policies would address the needs of each one. "We address every area of the city in a comprehensive fashion," in order to have flood protection, stable neighborhoods, paved streets, an education system that works, affordable housing, and an economy that thrives.

Next, the UNOP "core programs" were presented by a succession of speakers, who were importantly not just UNOP team members: neighborhood stabilization was covered by Vera Triplett, housing by Darren Diamond (financial analyst and partner at Henry Consulting), other priority sectors by Steve Villavaso, and implementation by Cynthia Hedge-Morrell. Triplett explained the "Elevate New Orleans" program, saying it would enable neighbors to voluntarily move together to higher ground, one of the things that people asked for in Community Congress II. Hedge-Morrell talked about the need for a recovery council to see these sorts of programs through to their completion.

The discussion guide described what would happen next: the City Planning Commission would hold public meetings on the plan on February 22 and March 7. It also explained that after the city council and mayor approved the plan, it would be submitted to the LRA. It also summarized the government's role in implementation and highlighted several key entities that would be responsible to execute it. Carolyn Lukensmeyer urged participants to continue putting pressure on these entities to keep the process going, and she emphasized the importance of residents taking personal responsibility for the recovery.

With the Saints playing in Chicago the next day for the NFC championship, virtually every speaker either used a football metaphor for rebuilding the city or simply ended their speech with "Go Saints!"[73] When Ed Blakely spoke near the end of the meeting, he was given a Saints jersey—the quarterback's—to underscore his role as quarterback of the recovery team. Blakely promised not to lose this game and laid out five directives that would guide his work: (1) continue the healing, (2) improve safety and security in all communities, (3) develop a diverse and robust economy (by promoting the port and health care in particular), (4) build a 21st century infrastructure, and (5) establish smart and sustainable development patterns while also rebuilding every neighborhood. He stressed that they needed to improve the flood safety of every neighborhood because the levees might not necessarily hold.

Kim Boyle, member of both the NOCSF and LRA boards, concluded the meeting. The plan, she admitted, was not perfect, but it reflected the will of those who participated and would be a useful guide to agencies and private investors. She described UNOP as being more about opportunities for rebuilding lives than about rebuilding infrastructure. It made her confident enough to tell people she sees all over the country that "this is truly our plan." "But we will be confronted by skeptics," she said, and frustrated by the political process. She urged the crowd to "use the same faith that brought you here today. . . . This is what we will use to show Congress what our vision for rebuilding the City of New Orleans is."

This community congress, like the second one, appeared to have met its goal of getting people to listen to one another. The tables mixed people of all races and ages from all parts of the city. And participants were supportive of the overall approach and recommendations of the plan. The strongest support was for strengthening levees and restoring wetlands. Residents also showed very strong support for creating health centers in communities and making schools into community centers. At the end of the day, 91 percent of participants agreed or strongly agreed that UNOP should go forward, and 92 percent said they were committed to remaining engaged with the effort to rebuild New Orleans.[74]

This was clearly a bright moment in the UNOP process, and participants were excited about the direction of the plan. Even the *Times-Picayune* account was positive, reporting the lack of conflict to be newsworthy.[75] But participants also were realistic, and they expressed very practical fears about what might stand in the way of implementing all these good ideas: bureaucracy, politics, government incompetence, insufficient resources, and the potential for inequities. Many noted that neither the federal government nor the city governments had very good track records on important issues like flood control, affordable housing, or controlling blight.

FINAL CSO MEETING

The final meeting of the CSO was on January 25. The meeting was a full one. Troy Henry presented the highlights of the citywide plan, repeating his performance from Saturday. He also said that the planning team would like the city to get more direct delivery of the CDBG funds. Bobbie Hill reported on Community Congress III and what would happen next. She said the UNOP plan would be released on Monday, January 29. After it was approved by the NOCSF, it would be officially transmitted to the City Planning Commission and become available immediately on the website and in libraries for review. An additional 50 copies of all the plans would be distributed to community centers a few days later. The planning commission would review the plan at its normal February 13 afternoon meeting and would hold special evening sessions to hear public comments on February 22 and March 7. The intent was to adopt the plan in March and expedite its delivery to the LRA.

The public comments portion of the meeting lasted for two hours, during which a very diverse group of 17 New Orleanians expressed a range of concerns about UNOP. Sherman Copelin complained about the proposal to initially provide temporary services to underpopulated areas, claiming that real recovery meant every place needed to have full and permanent services. UNOP's Errol George, who had lived in New Orleans East, responded by saying neither the residents nor the funds would show up tomorrow and that the provision of services to everyone required a strategic approach; the plan shows a way to do this, but not all at once. The temporary facilities were a way to help people come home. Becca O'Brien, from the mayor's office, reminded the audience that "shrinking the footprint" was no longer an active conversation and that services would be provided to all parts of the city.

A comment from a French Quarter resident implied public housing was a breeding ground for crime, which led to a spirited discussion about the need for affordable housing, the need for public housing, and the complex causes of crime. Both H. M. K. Amen and Vera Triplett took the opportunity to compliment the accomplishments of UNOP to date on this matter. One of them pointed out that UNOP "provided a forum where people who had never sat at the same table came together and shared ideas. . . . You would start off with stereotypes, but somewhere in the process you begin to understand each other and hear each other." And they asked for this spirit to continue, saying, "If we don't have a human connection to each other and are able to work with one another, it's all for naught."

Vanessa Gueringer, president of ACORN's Lower Ninth Ward chapter, expressed several fears. She was concerned that the neighborhood's infrastructure needs would not be addressed promptly and about the cost of elevating homes. She also feared that those who chose not to cluster would lose city services. Cynthia Hedge-Morrell responded that the city had a plan to help finance home elevations to reduce home insurance costs. Becca O'Brien reiterated that basic services would be available everywhere in the city but agreed some areas still needed attention. Carey Shea reminded everyone that these recommendations were in the plan, but residents would need to continue to advocate for them because the funding in fact did not yet exist. She also complimented ACORN on the People's Plan and encouraged the ideas to keep coming. O'Brien reported that the city was not waiting for federal funding but was actively talking to other funding sources.

Keith Twitchell, the organizer of a movement for a permanent citizen participation program in the city, commented that increased citizen involvement was one of the greatest benefits of this process, and he was glad to see the plan call for a formal citizen participation program. A public housing resident made an eloquent plea for affordable housing, police services, and schools. A few residents from English Turn, an upscale golf-course subdivision on the West Bank, stated their opposition to all of the proposed projects in their area because they wanted to retain their rural character. A dissenter argued that the footprint issue should still be on the table, that there was not unanimity on this issue, that the plan needed to identify high flood-risk areas, and that it needed to include a neighborhood viability index. Other comments touched on schools, news coverage, crime, affordable housing, building codes for modular homes, supporting the local construction industry, tutoring programs near schools, an idea for implementing clustered development, and translation of the planning documents into Vietnamese.

This meeting was a fitting way to conclude the services of the CSO. Vera Triplett complimented Concordia's Joe Butler, who, under so much fire from them about communication and outreach deficiencies in November, "met every single challenge put before him." She also complimented the citywide team for sincerely trying to rebuild the city for everyone and attempting to do something they knew would put them in the line of fire. In closing, she made a plea for everyone to work together to solve the social problems that cause crime and keep an open mind to change and new possibilities in New Orleans.

OFFICIAL HANDOFF

By all accounts, city officials were ready to give the plan a warm welcome. They all spoke well of the outreach efforts and broad participation, and Oliver Thomas praised the clustering and elevation ideas. Yolanda Rodriguez, now with a planning staff of 16, welcomed the opportunity to analyze the document. According to the *Times-Picayune*, city hall would first consider the citywide plan and then the district plans as background for a new city master plan.[76]

The final action of the UNOP process was for the NOCSF board to approve the planning documents, which it did on Monday morning, January 29. Several CSF and CSO members, Concordia staff, and Carey Shea met at the GNOF offices, among several large stacks of plans (six copies of the plan, the baseline recovery assessment, and the citywide financial analysis).[77] The NOCSF's purpose was to confirm that the planning process was transparent, had community input, met the requirements of the LRA and the City Planning Commission, and met the terms of the contract. The substantive content of the plan would be reviewed by the City Planning Commission and would be subject to revision. The participants all thanked one another for the hard work, reflected on the leap of faith each one had taken when they joined on to this unprecedented experience, shook hands, and moved on.

The next morning, Bobbie Hill and Joe Butler carried three boxes of city-wide and district plans to city hall and delivered them to the City Planning Commission, directly into the hands of Yolanda Rodriguez, thereby concluding the process devised with Rockefeller and GNOF the previous spring. The NOCSF held a press conference later in the day to publicly pass the planning baton to city staff. Steven Bingler reminded attendees that the intent all along was to help the City Planning Commission. Troy Henry, as he had done so many times this week, summarized the key elements and concepts of the plan. Laurie Johnson emphasized that a key contribution of UNOP was that it tried to bring two critical issues back to the public dialogue: the importance of flood protection and the recognition that everyone might not come back to their original homes. The citywide plan took a risk-based approach, to ensure that future investments (including by home owners) would be safe and viable. Darren Diamond then presented some information that had not yet been revealed to the public: the plan's price tag. He argued that the way to rebuild New Orleans would be to persuade people inside and outside the city that it was worth their investment. The three major initiatives—"Elevate New Orleans," the slab-on-grade program, and the clustering program—would cost $4.3 billion. He argued these initiatives were the most cost-effective, sensible, and sustainable way to rebuild the city.

The total cost of implementing the plan was $14 billion over 10 years, which included the money the federal government would have to pay to improve the levees. The UNOP team knew this bottom-line total would become headline material, so they chose it carefully. The "total" depended on variables such as time frame and the agencies and government funding streams they chose to include. If one of the purposes of the plan was to make an argument for more funding, then the terms of this argument were critical. For that reason, the $14 billion total was a decision made with city and LRA staff.

The press in attendance asked pointed questions. Probably the central question involved whether all of New Orleans would come back and how the plan could help make this happen. The planning team reiterated that the plan proposed incentives to help people make the right choices, and it set up a framework to vary application of the tools over time. From surveys, district meetings, and the community congresses, the team had identified the top four reasons for residents not to return: (1) fear of future flood risk; (2) lack of the full amount of funds needed to rebuild; (3) lack of neighborhood services, particularly schools; and (4) lack of knowledge about what their neighbors were doing. The plan was designed to address all four. Responding to a question regarding what the plan would mean to citizens, Vera Triplett said that, as a resident of a flooded neighborhood, it meant that she had choices for her future.

The press brought up the unimpressive records of NORA and the Road Home program in actually helping New Orleans's home owners and neighborhoods. This was a good point, UNOP conceded, but it was time to look to the future. The new Office of Recovery Management was starting up that week, and NORA had a new board and new executive director. As for the Road Home program, it was a work in progress, and the state was trying to fix it. Finally, one reporter reminded the team that, just the day before, Senators Lieberman (I-Conn.) and Obama (D-Ill.) had come to town and stated that no new federal funds would arrive until the currently allocated funds were spent. Johnson responded that the neither the FEMA Public Assistance money nor its associated mitigation funds had a preset limit. Both of these programs would continue to fund projects as they were approved. She cautioned this system was working slowly due to the size of the disaster, but there was still a chance to redesign and unblock the pipeline of these funds.

The release of UNOP was covered the next day in the *Times-Picayune*, the *Baton Rouge Advocate*, and the *New York Times*.[78] As expected, all three of them prominently reported on the $14 billion price tag and the financial challenges that lay ahead. But they also noted the plan called for rebuilding all neighborhoods through voluntary incentives for rebuilding, elevating, and clustering.

THE PLAN

So, what did the plan look like? The 510-page *Citywide Strategic Recovery and Rebuilding Plan* consisted of five chapters and five appendixes.

The executive summary said the plan's purpose was to focus on "strategic recovery investments and implementation strategies that aim to encourage robust investments, both private and public, so that the City can reasonably and equitably do more than rely on market forces alone, or face debilitating debt or tax increases to fund rebuilding."[79]

It explained the strategic framework in this way:

> The strategic recovery framework focuses first on equity and stabilizing every neighborhood to ensure that heaviest damages to infrastructure are repaired, blight is combated, and residents are provided with voluntary incentives that will help protect the investments that many have already made in rebuilding their homes and businesses, and also meet the needs of others to encourage them to return. It then phases recovery projects over time, to ensure that public and private investment in the recovery and rebuilding match the pace of resettlement while also making strategic upgrades in infrastructure, public facilities, and public services throughout the City to ensure that we rebuild Safer, Stronger, and Smarter.

As for the substantive programs, they would "focus on providing enhanced flood protection, stabilizing neighborhoods, providing affordable housing for all, enhancing public services, and providing state-of-the-art education and health care systems throughout the City." The initiatives and programs were listed as follows:

- "Elevate New Orleans" Program
- "Slab-on-Grade" Remediation Program
- Neighborhood Cluster Program
- Provide Housing Solutions for All to Return
- Rebuild a Premier, Regional, and Neighborhood-serving Health Care Network
- Re-vision the K-12 Public Education System
- Restore and Upgrade the Physical and Social Infrastructure of the Entire City

Section 1 of the plan was a summary of the citywide recovery assessment, which summarized conditions in New Orleans with respect to flood protection, neighborhood stabilization, housing, economic development, infrastructure and utilities, transportation, health care, education, public safety, environmental services (such as waste management, brownfields, and green building), recreation facilities and libraries, cultural resources, and historic preservation and urban design. The entire citywide recovery assessment was included in the plan's appendix.

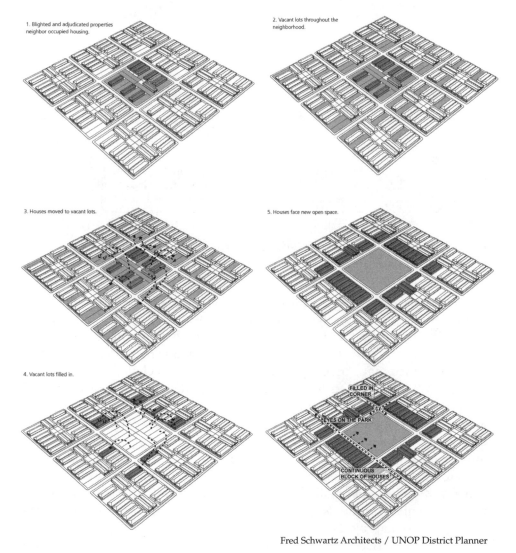

Fred Schwartz Architects / UNOP District Planner

Fig. 6.17a. Illustration of one way to achieve UNOP's neighborhood cluster program

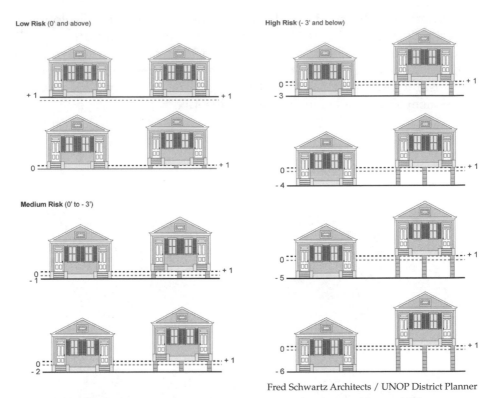

Fred Schwartz Architects / UNOP District Planner

Fig. 6.17b. Illustration of Fred Schwartz's proposed voluntary home-lifting program, with graduated subsidies based on level of risk

Section 2 covered the citywide recovery framework. It described the flood characteristics of each of the city's drainage basins and it included population estimates and future forecasts. This section also presented the various recovery scenarios, the plan's goals, and the strategic planning framework, which included maps of repopulation rates and flood elevations.

Section 3 summarized the recovery projects. For each sector described in section 1, the UNOP team proposed programs, policies, and projects across the three policy areas. It also laid out an implementation time line for each sector and a set of criteria that identified 91 high-priority projects. The authors were careful to explain that the list of these projects should not be used to determine funding or phasing. The project sheets for all 91 recovery projects were included in the appendix, as was a tabular list of the approximately 550 district projects and showing how they were incorporated in the 91 citywide plan projects.

Section 4 described the roles of key agencies and proposed the creation of a parishwide Recovery Council. It also strongly endorsed the creation of "a formal process for citizen engagement . . . to facilitate neighborhood

District 4 Recovery Planning Projects

1. District-wide Street / Infrastructure Repair and Replacement Program
2. Fund Study and Removal of I-10
3. Pumping Stations Upgrades and Associated Flood Protection Projects
4. Program and Develop Interim Use Strategies for Public Facilities / Schools
5. Bayou Road / Governor Nicholls Cultural Corridor
6. New Open Spaces Connections within Network (including Bike Paths)
7. Create New Connections between Zion City / Booker T. Washington / B.W. Cooper
8. Develop LSU / VA Regional Medical Center
9. Improve Louis Armstrong Park and Surrounding Area
10. Revitalize St. Bernard Avenue Commercial Corridor
11. Revitalize Tulare Avenue Commercial Corridor with Emphasis on Biosciences District
12. Revitalize Broad Avenue Commercial Corridor with Main Street Program
13. North Claiborne Avenue Corridor Study
14. Revitalize Galvez Street Commercial Corridor
15. Redevelop Blue Plate Node (Earhart / Washington Ave. / Jeff Davis Pkwy. Intersection)
16. Revitalize Canal Street Commercial Corridor from Claiborne Ave. to Broad Ave.
17. Revitalize Earhart Boulevard Commercial / Industrial Corridor
18. Develop Sustainable Industrial Park in partnership with Gert Town and Zion City
19. Revitalize Gert Town: New Town Center and Community Facilities
20. Redevelop the Lafitte Corridor as an Urban Mixed-Use District with a Central Greenway
21. Develop Neighborhood Specific Design Guidelines for Rebuilding and Flood Protection
22. Program and Develop Neighborhood Recovery Resource Centers
23. Neighborhood Green Block and Housing Moving Program
24. Home Elevation Program for High and Medium Risk Areas
25. Affordable & Rental Neighborhood Housing Renovation Program
26. Redevelop and Improve St. Bernard Housing and Adjacent Areas
27. Redevelop and Improve Lafitte Housing and Adjacent Areas
28. Redevelop and Improve B.W. Cooper Housing and Adjacent Areas
29. Redevelop and Improve Iberville Housing and Adjacent Areas

UNOP

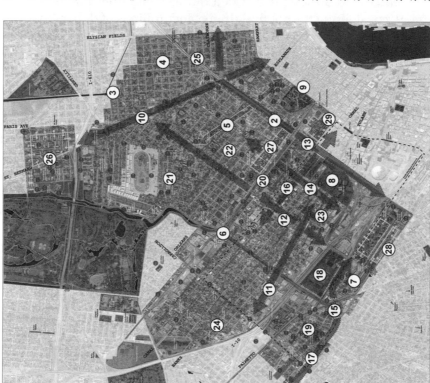

Fig. 6.18. UNOP's District 4 Recovery Planning Projects

recovery and future development, and to ensure that citizens continue to have a voice in the City's future." It proposed ideas for working with the federal government to enhance the flow of funds to meet the goals of the plan. It also recommended the city should begin immediately to update its master plan and the Comprehensive Zoning Ordinance, and it recommended some major goals for this update.

Section 5 covered financing. It summarized the costs of the programs and projects by sector and time frame. It also suggested several financing strategies. The plan's appendix also included a detailed assessment of the financial conditions of the Port of New Orleans, Regional Transit Authority, Armstrong International Airport, New Orleans Public Belt Railroad, and City of New Orleans (including the separate Sewerage and Water Board). It also identified sources of financing and included a list of approximately 40 private projects proposed or under way in the city.

The 11 district plans were also submitted, all in full-color, 11" x 17" format. All were organized roughly the same way and included consistent introductory material, a description of the planning process, a recovery assessment, a statement of visions and goals, recovery scenarios, descriptions of a planning framework or recovery projects, and a conclusion.

In the end, the citywide plan turned out to be a rather modest-looking document, considering the political drama and millions of dollars that went into producing it. In contrast, the district plans were dynamic, colorful, and full of maps, diagrams, and exciting planning ideas. This was probably as it should be. The district plans are the direct products of active citizen involvement. Of all the products of UNOP, they are the most familiar to the residents who attended the planning meetings. But most observers still expected a blueprint and did not fully appreciate the function of the citywide plan, which was a more abstract, strategic document intended to guide various agencies in their decisions about financing and managing recovery activities. It was more a public administration document than architectural diagram and was designed for audiences in Baton Rouge, Washington, and New Orleans's city hall, rather than the general public. As such, it met its goal of providing a rational basis for funding recovery projects. Sometimes it is the planner's lot to provide administrative guidance rather than colored maps and diagrams.

Passing the Planning Baton

ED BLAKELY COMES TO NEW ORLEANS

In September 2005, Hurricane Katrina caught the attention of Ed Blakely, even though he was half a world away from New Orleans.[1] The chair of the Department of Urban and Regional Planning at the University of Sydney, Australia, Blakely was particularly interested in sustainable urban development and disaster recovery. Within days of the storm, he was in contact with Paul Farmer, the executive director of APA. In October 2005, Blakely traveled from Sydney to Shreveport, Louisiana, to participate in the Katrina recovery sessions at the Louisiana APA chapter conference. He also visited New Orleans in January and July of 2006, on the latter occasion to attend the summit of the African American Leadership Project (AALP), where he urged the city to appoint an impartial recovery director with no prior ties to the city.[2] From September 27 through 30, the AALP hosted an extended visit to New Orleans for Blakely and Phillip Clay, the chancellor and a professor of urban planning at the Massachusetts Institute of Technology. As part of this visit, both Blakely and Clay formally reviewed the Lambert plans and concluded that the plans were of professional quality and suitable for conducting neighborhood recovery.[3]

In early November 2006, two months after Mayor Nagin announced he would create a "recovery office," Blakely was tapped by city hall to lead it. With his submission of the 2007 budget in November 2006, the mayor proposed a major reorganization of city government and established the Office of Recovery Management (ORM), the first management organization in the city government that focused on disaster recovery. The mayor directed it to deliver technical solutions to the city and neighborhoods, manage the recovery effort, and oversee the financing and implementation of all public recovery initiatives.[4] In early December, the city council's recovery committee held hearings on the need for a recovery management ordinance and the structure of a recovery office. They invited Ken Topping, former director of city planning for Los Angeles, to describe that city's recovery and reconstruction ordinance and the APA model ordinance for recovery management, both of which he helped develop.

Blakely appeared to be the perfect candidate to lead the ORM. He was a longtime urban planning professor and administrator at the University of California at Berkeley, the University of Southern California, the New School for Social Research, and the University of Sydney. He had also been a power broker and mayoral advisor in Oakland, California, where he had once been a serious candidate for mayor himself. He immediately commanded respect in New Orleans for his combination of planning expertise and experience in urban politics in one of the nation's centers of African-American political power. He was endorsed by APA and the AALP. Many community and business leaders from the uptown, white community were asking for world-class planners, and Blakely appeared to be just that. Similarly, politicians in Washington, D.C., believed that New Orleans needed a good dose of outside expertise, and Blakely had that. Moreover, Blakely is an African-American, so it was thought his appointment might help African-Americans in New Orleans feel more enfranchised in the recovery process. Blakely seemed to be the answer to New Orleans's prayers at this critical juncture.

But some key questions remained both for Blakely and for city hall. What powers would he have? Would he control the recovery funds? What would his relationship be with NORA and the LRA? Would his Oakland experience translate to New Orleans? And, finally, given the city's centuries-deep cultural traditions and inbred politics, would New Orleans, in the end, accept the authority of Ed Blakely?

Nagin and Blakely apparently settled these questions during their negotiations, and on Monday, December 5, at a press conference at city hall, Nagin introduced Blakely as the new recovery chief. Few details were offered about the position, but Blakely said the mayor promised him he would have the authority to staff his agency. Blakely also said he would set up a coordinating council of local government leaders.[5] When asked why it took so long to appoint a recovery chief, Nagin said it simply took time to find just the right person for the job. The *Times-Picayune* reported Blakely alternated between being blunt, vague, and testy during the press conference, and this turned out to be an accurate description of his relationship with the press over the ensuing months. At the press conference, Blakely, an author of a textbook on economic development, repeatedly emphasized the importance of building the city's economic base by doing things like rebuilding the port with an eye to future trade with Latin America. Blakely also emphasized the importance of using "smart building techniques" to make the city safer and greener than before. Finally, he stated he hoped New Orleans's land-use plan, once completed, would carry the force of law and no longer be subject to the whims of the city council.

There was no way to miss Blakely's formal arrival on the job on January 8, 2007. He was quoted often in the *Times-Picayune*, as well as the *Christian Science Monitor*, the *Washington Post*, and other national news outlets.[6] He talked about using land swaps as a way to provide people with more choices when moving to safer areas, which echoed one of the key recommendations of UNOP.[7] In mid-January, he led a delegation from New Orleans to Wall Street to seek out private capital to help the city.[8] On February 10, he led the first in a series of monthly bicycle rides through city neighborhoods to take a close look at flood-damaged parts of the city and demonstrate to residents the city's interest in their area.[9] The *Times-Picayune* reported that during a ride through Gentilly, Blakely talked to the crowd, inquired about residents' needs, and answered some of their questions:

Robert B. Olshansky

Fig. 7.1. Ed Blakely, on one of his monthly bike rides around New Orleans

When asked for a timeline, Blakely said it could take 20 years for the recovery to be complete, but that he'd like to see cranes in the sky by September, working on what he called "trigger projects," community focal points such as schools and libraries that will attract residents and add to a sense of safety. He also prioritized the rebuilding of the criminal court complex, the sheriff's office and other civic structures.[10]

In a speech to city business leaders at the World Trade Club of Greater New Orleans in late January, Blakely proposed numerous specific initiatives, such as increasing port jobs, targeting biomedical research to the health care needs of the Third World, and promoting New Orleans as a great American city.[11] According to the *Times-Picayune*, "Blakely characterized the recently released Unified New Orleans Plan as a done deal, rather than as a working document, as it was presented Tuesday to the City Planning Commission," and he "spoke of the proposed citywide recovery council, a panel uniting agencies ranging from the Department of Safety and Permits to the Sewerage & Water Board, as a sure thing. Under Unified New Orleans Plan recommendations, he would serve as its executive director. And he didn't balk at the estimated $14 billion price tag of bringing the plan to life."[12]

This signaled Blakely's intent to use UNOP as his guide even before the City Planning Commission and city council approved it. He was closely involved in the lengthy handoff from UNOP during December and January, and he recognized the need for speed and the legitimacy of the broad participatory process that was just completed.

By early February, the ORM had a staff of 17, including Blakely, three office staff, a deputy director, and four managers. Dubravka Gilic transferred from the City Planning Commission to become ORM's manager of strategic planning and a link to the commission staff. Blakely's $500,000 annual budget was supplemented with $1 million in grants from the Rockefeller, Ford, and Bill and Melinda Gates foundations, which funded nine of the employees.[13]

In a presentation to the LRA board on February 12, Blakely released a preliminary document that described the elements of his recovery strategy.[14] These included elevating buildings, land swaps, neighbors sharing green space, clustered communities, transit-oriented communities, integrated neighborhood commercial centers, new forms of public housing and civic design, leveraging public dollars with private financing, working with NORA to create affordable housing, retaining the young adult population, improvements for neighborhoods, a city park master plan, and riverfront development. He also told the LRA that the city hoped to have a new master plan and comprehensive zoning ordinance in place by the end of 2007.

Blakely's document also provided a snapshot of the city's recovery progress as of January 2007. Recovery funds were still flowing slowly into the city. For example, of the $843 million in FEMA Public Assistance funds requested by the city to repair damages to infrastructure and buildings, only $107 million had been obligated and only $9 million had been paid to the city. The CDBG money was also slow: the Road Home program was supposed to disburse about $3.7 billion to New Orleans home owners, but virtually none of it had arrived yet. Nor had the LRA officially pledged any of its remaining CDBG funds for infrastructure and community recovery to the city.

At the LRA meeting, Blakely laid out his desire for ORM to control both the FEMA and CDBG funds for New Orleans. He said that NORA should take the lead in redeveloping both blighted properties and Road Home properties sold to the state by converting them to cluster housing developments or green space.[15] He offered that ORM would provide the accountability and answer directly to the LRA. LRA board members were pleased to finally see a clearly articulated vision for New Orleans and an organization designed to accomplish it. They were not quite ready, however, to sign a blank check.

THE TARGET AREAS PLAN

On February 24, Blakely announced an action-oriented strategy designed to strategically jump-start reconstruction.[16] In a meeting with the NORA board of directors, he described his intent to identify several areas for targeted redevelopment, for which NORA would play a key role. These targeted areas would be the focus of the first parishwide recovery council meeting on March 23, which would involve about three dozen agencies.[17]

As it turned out, Blakely was not quite ready to unveil the exact locations of these areas before March 23 because city council members and leaders of neighborhood organizations were still vetting them.[18] The original idea was to single out a few small areas suitable for quick, clustered development. According to Blakely, New Orleans couldn't "afford to rip out the same streets two times. . . . We don't have the money, and more importantly, businesses looking to reopen or locate here will not tolerate a patchwork approach. When you're in the condition we're in, it doesn't take much to frighten a developer."[19]

Ultimately, the purpose of the target areas was to leverage the still meager flow of public funds with much more substantial private investments. Blakely said the target area program would cost $1.1 billion, which the city could access fairly soon—only a small part of the $14 billion envisioned over 10 years by UNOP—but it would attract up to four times that amount in private investment. This, in turn, would convince developers, residents, and business owners of the viability of New Orleans. The idea was to create successful neighborhoods in the large parts of the city that were otherwise dead.[20] The measure of its success would be "cranes on the skyline" by September.[21] He cautioned for patience, however, as there was neither enough construction capacity nor money to do everything at once.

This systematic, rational economic-development strategy, however, had some political and bureaucratic challenges ahead of it. First, it was still in the vetting process. The second and probably larger challenge was bureaucratic. The $1.1 billion may have been the cash most readily available to New Orleans, but "available" was a relative term. In fact, only $117 million in CDBG funds were truly close to being "in hand," assuming UNOP's approval. And even these would eventually be required to be cleared, one project at a time, with the LRA and the Louisiana Department of Housing and Community Development. An additional $324 million of anticipated CDBG funding was part of a pending request to Congress to waive Louisiana's required 10 percent match of the FEMA Public Assistance funds. Furthermore, one of the larger pieces, $300 million, was to come from the sale of "blight bonds"—bonds Blakely claimed he could sell to outside investors against the city's holdings of blighted properties, although no one in the redevelopment community seemed to know how they would work. Nor would the rest of the $1.1 billion be immediately accessible: $260 million in infrastructure bonds authorized by voters before Katrina in 2004 and approximately $60 million anticipated in FEMA hazard-mitigation grants.

At a news conference on March 29, Blakely, who was flanked by Nagin and community leaders, unveiled a detailed map of the 17 target areas (fig. 7.2).[22] In fact, only 40 percent of the $1.1 billion would be used in the target areas; the remaining 60 percent would be spread over much of the city for projects such as blight removal, parks, streets, and housing incentive programs. Three types of areas were shown on the map: "rebuild," "redevelopment," and "renew." The two "rebuild" areas were in devastated parts of the Lower Ninth Ward and New Orleans East. The six "redevelopment" areas were flooded locations at major commercial intersections that had promise for attracting investment. The nine "renew" areas were locations that had been recovering since Katrina but could benefit from some additional public investments. Blakely emphasized this was only the strategic first phase of what would be a 15-year recovery plan; as zones succeed, others would be added.

Blakely described these nodes as logical places to catalyze the rebirth of the city because they were the long-standing retail centers on which the city was built. A city does not simply grow everywhere at once; rather, it grows outward from transportation nodes. Thus, said Blakely, these areas were selected based on what was known about the growth of cities rather than

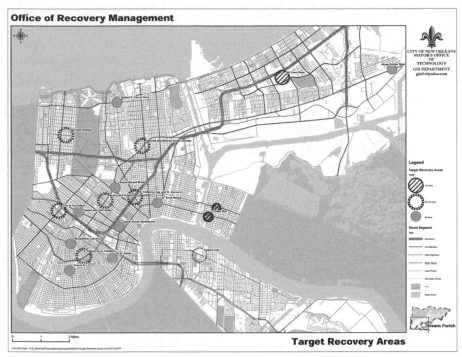

City of New Orleans, Mayor's Office of Technology, GIS Department

Fig. 7.2.

politics.[23] According to ORM staff, these target areas came directly from the UNOP district plans, which were the most detailed neighborhood-scale plans the city had ever had.[24] And these district plans were consistent with previous plans. In other words, there was broad consensus that these areas were important and worthy of special attention.

But it would be naïve to think that the target area designations were free of political considerations. Every council district contained at least one target area, and the two costly "rebuild" areas designated a disproportionate amount of the funds for the two African-American neighborhoods most fearful of being marginalized or "green dotted" out of existence. In fact, Councilmember Cynthia Willard-Lewis said Blakely's plan would help clear up "questions and doubts and fears" about the future of these areas. The two "rebuild" area designations reversed "all of the previous discussions of green space and wastelands and toxic soil."[25]

The target areas did not appear to be controversial, unlike previous plans unveiled in New Orleans over the previous 18 months. At the press conference, Nagin stated that the plan had the support of council members, neighborhood leaders, LRA officials, and the local business community, though it would still need formal approval from the City Planning Commission and the council.[26] Presumably, the goal was to make this an official recovery plan under the city's charter. Numerous parties spoke favorably of the plan in subsequent interviews. Significantly, Donald Powell supported the emphasis on private investment—but he said the administration would not support waiving the state's obligation to provide a 10 percent match of FEMA funds.[27]

Although the vision was clear, the maps were a bit vague. The target areas did not have definitive boundaries. Furthermore, neither the mayor nor Blakely was ready to identify specific projects.[28] These details would come later, though Blakely declared that all of the areas—not just a few pilot projects—would begin construction by September. And target area redevelopment was still expected to include land swaps coordinated by NORA. Blakely also reiterated his intent that this plan, as well as the UNOP district plans, would soon form the basis of a formal master plan, codified into law.[29]

PLANNING COMMISSION HEARINGS FOR UNOP

Blakely's new implementation plan was ostensibly based on a completed UNOP, but the legal reality was that UNOP was still officially under review by the City Planning Commission. The first public hearings were held on March 7 and 13, and several issues awaited resolution.

On March 6, the Bureau of Governmental Research (BGR) released a scathing critique of the UNOP citywide plan entitled *Not Ready for Prime Time*.[30] The crux of its argument was that the document was not a clear roadmap:

> In the end, the document fails to deliver a cohesive, workable roadmap for recovery. Instead, it proposes a sweeping list of 91 projects, without placing them in a realistic financial context. As for recovery strategy, it offers a continuation of the indecisive and confusing approach that has characterized New Orleans' recovery for a year and a half. . . .
>
> The Citywide Plan is enigmatic on key issues. It does not detail or provide a map showing where its programs and policies would apply. This makes it difficult or impossible for citizens to use it as a guide to understand the proposals applicable to their neighborhoods.

The most eye-opening conclusion was that the entire plan needed to be redone: "Unfortunately, the problems with the current Citywide Plan are so fundamental that they cannot be addressed through minor adjustments. Addressing them properly will require a return to the basic data, fresh analysis and an overhaul of the planning document." To do this, BGR recommended the City Planning Commission take charge and, in close collaboration with ORM, "create a clear, data-driven and practical recovery plan based on realistic financial considerations" and "useful data and concepts from the 13 District Plans, the Citywide Plan (particularly the Citywide Baseline Recovery Assessment) and other post-Katrina planning efforts."[31]

The BGR report appeared to be a purposeful reopening of the "footprint" issue, arguing for focusing recovery resources on the city's higher ground. For example, BGR observed:

> The plan does not openly confront certain critical issues. For example, it explains at length the higher vulnerability of eastern New Orleans. It also espouses safety as a guiding principle. But, having set off alarm bells, it does not follow its findings through with comprehensive remedies for that area or its residents. In fact, it recommends significant funding for resettlement of people living in areas at a high risk of future flooding without requiring that the resettlement areas be located at lower-risk sites.

Many of BGR's comments were welcomed by the UNOP team, which appreciated that the draft report, completed under great time pressure, could use improvement. Besides clearer priorities and timelines, BGR also asked for a more systematic project-scoring system and identified some contradictions and inconsistencies in the plan.

On March 7, the City Planning Commission played to a full house, with approximately 200 people in attendance at the city council's chambers. The chair, Tim Jackson, introduced the ground rules for the hearing: only the citywide plan was under consideration, and comments would be limited to three minutes. Over the next two and a half hours, more than 40 people presented testimony. Despite Jackson's admonition, many of the comments were related to details in the district plans. Relatively few were critical of the citywide plan. Many comments lauded UNOP's broad citizen involvement and the need to move forward. Such was the testimony of Charles Jenkins, bishop of the Episcopal Diocese of Louisiana:

> We have done what some have said we could not do. We have come together as one voice in this city to end the disparaging of New Orleans that strangles the flow of resources for our recovery. . . . The plan that the citizens of this city have come to is more adaptive than technical and actually provides a greater sense of hope and vision for the long-term future of the city than would a plan at this point that is burdened with technical details. In other words, we want to look more to the adaptive, not simply to the technical solutions.

The most frequent complaints involved the need for more explicit recognition of the district plans, as well as the need for a policy statement supporting a charter change to give the city's master plan the force of law. Numerous speakers declared their support for a statement issued by the Planning Districts Leadership Coalition, a new group claiming to include community leaders from all 13 planning districts that advocated for a more formalized and permanent system of community involvement in the city's planning decisions. Thus, the most common themes of the evening were support for the broad citizen involvement engendered by the UNOP process, a desire for such involvement to continue, and an explicit request for formal recognition of the district plans.

In response to BGR's concerns, Troy Henry said the UNOP team was working with planning commission staff to address inconsistencies and lack of clarity, but that it would not change the basic philosophy that every neighborhood deserves to be preserved while also reducing the threat of flood damages. When asked for a map of the three policy areas, Henry responded that UNOP's role was to provide the framework and that the ORM and the recovery council would be the appropriate entities to develop maps. Henry agreed that residents have the right to know the characteristics of their home's location but stated that all this basic information was already in the plan.

The BGR critique drew considerable attention but no support from any influential players, who were generally interested in continuing to move the process forward and saving the details for the subsequent master plan effort. Ed Blakely issued an official response:

> While the UNOP plan was not designed to provide an absolute blueprint for all of the actions necessary to complete our recovery, it does provide useful data based on a process driven by the people. . . . [We] have already begun working with the planning commission to craft a recovery plan with a budget and timeline. We are developing a clear path for the recovery of the great city of New Orleans, and the UNOP plan is a critical part of this process. . . . We applaud the Bureau of Governmental Research for its analysis and we welcome their constructive comments.[32]

David Voelker, a member of both the LRA and NOCSF boards, stated in a letter to the *Times-Picayune* that he was

> concerned about the message that the Bureau of Governmental Research's recent report about the Unified New Orleans Plan sends to our citizens and the nation about the progress of New Orleans' recovery. I think it's important to understand how UNOP fits into the rebuilding process and why it is critical to move without delay. The extensive outreach that led to development of UNOP was unprecedented, making it one of the largest and most important citizen engagement initiatives in U.S. history. . . . Now that the people have

spoken, the work of bringing this vision to life can begin. UNOP will serve as the foundation for a new master plan that will move New Orleans beyond recovery and further into the 21st century.[33]

Thus, the plans continued to move expeditiously toward approval. The purpose of the next planning commission hearing on March 13 was to hear from participants in other neighborhood planning efforts, so that the commission could evaluate to what extent UNOP reflected them. The commissioners were particularly interested in identifying any overlooked aspects of these plans that needed to be incorporated into UNOP. Around 40 people attended the hearing—a much smaller crowd than the previous week. The commission listened to presentations by the three groups that had created the ACORN plan for the Lower Ninth Ward (which had been presented to the city council in early February), the Broadmoor plan, and the Lambert plans.

For ACORN, Ken Reardon agreed that the general goals of UNOP were in concert with those of the ACORN plan. But he also suggested that repopulation rate might not be the only way to measure a neighborhood's reconstruction potential because some people, although committed to returning, may need more time to find the right resources. He also emphasized the ACORN position that plans should address what would happen to areas outside of clustered development.

Three representatives from Broadmoor described how they began planning in earnest in January 2006 "after being slated to become a green space." They described the planning effort as their fight for survival in response to a rumor at the time that some parts of the city would be abandoned if more than 25 percent of home owners chose to sell. They also were aware of the intent to start neighborhood planning in February 2006, and, seeing no one coming to help them, they chose to do it themselves. The result was a 323-page comprehensive document that was completed in July with student help from Harvard, MIT, Bard, and Purdue. Every property in their neighborhood was included in a photographic database that was linked to Google Earth. And thanks to repeated surveys of all 2,400 properties, they knew exactly what each property owner intended to do. Their effort was totally self-organized, though Harvard faculty helped them structure their message in the plan and organize the data to attract grants, which they ultimately obtained to help fund the restoration of their library. They focused on repopulation, housing renovation, and attracting funding for an "education corridor" linking the Keller Library, Wilson School, and St. Mathews School. Finally, they stressed the importance of their method of actively involving the entire community and avoiding divisiveness. In the end, they were pleased with the way that UNOP honored their ideas, and, in turn, they stated their support for the needs of other neighborhoods.

Finally, Paul Lambert, Sheila Danzey, and several of their neighborhood planners reported that the UNOP district plans were generally consistent with their neighborhood plans, except with regard to flood protection. They stated they did not really look at flood protection because they viewed it as a regional and federal issue. In the citywide plan, however, they identified some deficiencies and points of disagreement. They listed several problems with population and damage data (although Lambert and UNOP had used the same contractor, GCR, for data collection and mapping). And they felt that the plan did not sufficiently emphasize the need for systemwide federal flood protection, although the citywide draft plan explicitly called for "a federal and state commitment to provide Category-Five levee protection and wetlands restoration to protect all citizens and property in the Parish."[34] Surprisingly, they argued strongly that the UNOP plan should include maps of the areas with the highest flood risk, but for reasons opposite from those who wanted to use the maps as a basis for reducing the city's footprint. The Lambert team wanted to use the maps to hold the U.S. Army Corps of Engineers accountable for the protection of the entire city. They also disagreed with the project scoring criteria, which, in their opinion, overvalued regional economic drivers and undervalued neighborhood projects. Lambert viewed Katrina as a destroyer of neighborhoods. Thus, the project list should emphasize recovery projects in the flooded areas, whereas citywide economic development projects would more logically belong in a new master plan. They also argued that a neighborhood approach was more sensitive to the fact that recovery needs vary across the city, so one set of rules would not be appropriate for the whole city.

Several public comments followed these presentations. The developer Sherman Copelin asked for priority funding for infrastructure projects in the flooded neighborhoods. He also took the opportunity to state that "an amendment to the city charter [to give the master plan the force of law] will never pass" because it is un-American to give such power to a planning process over the authority of elected city council members, who are always available to talk to constituents. Others asked for action on their neighborhood plans. A leader from Central City pointed out that, because their planning area consisted of both wet and dry neighborhoods, UNOP allowed them to expand neighborhood representation and create a more comprehensive plan. Commission staff member Leslie Alley asked Lambert whether any of his proposed initiatives such as the "lot next door" program, the elderly Road Home initiative, and the urban enterprise zones conflicted with UNOP's clustering policies. He responded that there were no inherent conflicts among these policies.

Following this meeting, the commission expected to finalize the plan by March 30, make it publicly available by April 2, and hold final public hearings on May 8 and 22, when a final decision would be made. After sending the UNOP citywide plan to the city council, the commission intended to issue an RFQ for the master plan, which would incorporate the district plans and ultimately lead to a comprehensive zoning ordinance. Furthermore, after issuing the RFQ, they planned to start hearings on the district plans because they would relate to issues beyond recovery.

INTERLUDE: CONTINUING FEDERAL FUNDING ISSUES

By the first of May 2007, the Road Home program could finally report some measurable progress. More than 100,000 Louisiana home owners had completed initial interviews with staff, and 69,025 benefits had been calculated and mailed to applicants.[35] Of these, 35,178 had responded with their choice of one of the three options: repair their homes, sell the property and stay in Louisiana, or sell the property and leave the state. A total of 11,392 had closed and received their awards, which totaled $855 million. This had become the largest rehousing program ever attempted in this country, and it was an achievement of sorts to have completed so many closings less than 11 months after Congress appropriated the funds. But many residents were unhappy with the slow pace of the program, poor customer service, lost files, and obvious errors in benefit calculations.

Officials could now begin to evaluate the accuracy of their original budget estimates. A few months earlier, the sense was that there would be some CDBG money left over from the Road Home program—a belief that had made it easier for UNOP to propose additional incentives to move homes to higher ground. But by May, the numbers had a different story to tell. If the grants were to continue to average $75,000 per closing, the program would cost $9.75 billion.[36] Although the state received $10.4 billion in block grants, only $7.5 billion was designated for the home owner program. Moreover, $1.14 billion of that was expected to come from the FEMA hazard-mitigation funds to cover floodplain buyouts, relocations, or elevations, but this had been tied up for months in a series of disputes between the state and FEMA. Thus, the state was facing a shortfall of $2.25 to $3.39 billion, depending on the rate of new applicants to the Road Home program and the number of ineligible and duplicate applications. This was more than an accounting problem. The program had already sent out letters promising $5.1 billion in benefits, and it couldn't send letters promising money that did not exist; only 16,000 more letters would obligate the full $6.3 billion of CDBG funds available. Donald Powell indicated that the federal government would be willing to help if provided with sufficient evidence of need, but he also suggested the state could use its own resources to help to fill the gap.[37] In fact, the state had a budget surplus of $1.2 billion that was not yet designated, and some legislators suggested that it could help to meet the shortfall.[38]

On May 11, ICF International, the Road Home contractor, officially estimated a shortfall of $2.9 billion, or $4 billion if the hazard-mitigation money remained unavailable.[39] This announcement had repercussions beyond the Road Home program; it meant that the LRA had to cease designating CDBG funds for long-term infrastructure and community recovery projects until the deficit could be filled. Powell met with Governor Blanco and continued to indicate he was open to asking for more funds from Congress if the request was warranted by the data.

Andy Kopplin said that several faulty assumptions were the cause of the shortfall: more home owners were applying than expected, repair costs were higher, and private insurance was covering less.[40] He blamed this on housing damage statistics developed by FEMA. FEMA retorted that the state should not have relied on these estimates because they were not appropriate for such purposes. The state also blamed the insurance shortfall on insurers' refusal to pay for wind damages, a gap that was left to Road Home to fill.[41] Given how the Road Home program was set up, perhaps home owners were less likely to appeal low insurance settlements if Road Home might cover the difference. The federal government, in turn, criticized the state for wanting to cover wind damage at all. The state had done so because of the difficulty of determining what proportion of damage to a home is from hurricane flooding versus wind (which can lead to rainwater damage). As a result, Powell said it was unlikely the federal government would make up the difference.[42]

Blanco saw this as continued insensitivity on the part of the administration and was incensed: "It comes as no surprise to anyone in the administration that we believed our program should not discriminate between houses ruined by wind versus water. Insurance companies left many people shortchanged, and now our own federal government wants to do the same. I had hoped that we had grown past these evil political winds."[43] Both sides claimed that their positions had been clear from the beginning.

Although the state continued to maintain that the shortfall was the obligation of the federal government, the governor and legislators also stated a pragmatic willingness to contribute state funds if that commitment would sway Washington to provide the balance. A May 31 report by the legislative auditor now estimated the deficit at $5 billion. Despite the state's appreciation that blaming the federal government would hurt its position with Washington, it also continued to maintain that the administration had not treated Louisiana fairly relative to Mississippi. The state hoped that the new Congress would be more sympathetic to its view.[44]

At precisely this time, the state's urgent request to Congress to waive the 10 percent state match for the FEMA Public Assistance and hazard-mitigation funds finally came to the forefront. Debate over this issue had gone on for months, with the governor and LRA members repeatedly asking the administration and Congress for the waiver. For example, LRA board member Walter Leger testified to Congress in February. He described the history of the Road Home program and thanked Congress for the funds. But, he said, "those funds came down to us in Louisiana wrapped in red tape with strings leading back here to Washington." He also observed that

> the need to provide housing assistance after a truly catastrophic series of events like Katrina and Rita is different from garden-variety disasters. It's not just about helping people—it's about restoring neighborhoods and cultures through the redevelopment of housing. It's important to remember that we didn't have a few hundred or a few thousand homes impacted. We had more than 200,000 homes damaged or destroyed entirely. Entire parishes, entire cultures were devastated. To say that Louisiana faces challenges in its recovery is an understatement. Replacing 200,000 homes, rebuilding an economy, addressing the issues created by demographic and economic shifts, reconnecting people to their neighborhoods and cultures again—all complex problems that we need to address. . . . And we are learning lessons and changing our approaches to take into account the reality that the recovery from catastrophic disasters is fundamentally different than recovery from more typical ones. We aren't just rebuilding homes and infrastructure—we are rebuilding civil society and community.[45]

The funding became entangled with spending for the Iraq war because it required a supplemental spending bill from Congress, though war costs dwarfed those of Louisiana's needs. Congress finally passed an emergency war-spending bill on May 24, 2007, and the president signed it the next day.[46] The bill provided nearly $100 billion for the war and approximately $20 billion for several other needs, including Gulf Coast hurricane recovery. To pass the bill, many Democrats dropped their demands for a deadline to bring the troops home. (The president had previously vetoed a funding bill for containing a timetable for troop withdrawal.) But they tucked into the bill other priorities unrelated to the war, such as a $2.10 increase in the minimum wage, several billion dollars for farm drought relief and veterans' health care, $1.3 billion for New Orleans–area levees, $4.1 billion for FEMA's Disaster Relief Fund, $320 million to forgive disaster loans to Gulf Coast communities, $110 million for the Gulf Coast fishing industry, and $135 million for various other recovery needs.[47] But from Louisiana's point of view, the big prize was the waiver of the match, which made an estimated $775 million of additional funding available for the LRA to allocate to community needs.[48] Because the state had been planning to pay the $775 million with part of its $10.4 billion in CDBG funds, the waiver in effect provided Louisiana with an infusion of CDBG funding.

Because of the Road Home shortfall, however, the impact of this congressional victory was not clear. By June 2, Governor Blanco offered to contribute between $600 and 700 million in state funds if the federal government would provide the balance of the shortfall. Should the federal government continue to refuse, LRA board member Sean Reilly offered a multitiered solution starting with the "new" $775 million of CDBG money.[49] The next fallback would be money not yet allocated by the LRA, such as $135 million for state building repairs not covered by FEMA and $500 million for rental housing. The third step would be to cut more deeply into the state's operating budget surplus. Additional unspent LRA funds might also be available. Finally, the state was hoping that FEMA would eventually release the $1.1 billion in hazard-mitigation funds. Collectively, all these pieces could fill the $5 billion shortfall, albeit at the expense of a variety of much-needed recovery and economic development programs. The situation also put to a halt the home-elevation grants in the Road Home program. Thus, the state would be obligated to continue to spend billions on rebuilding homes but with no funding available for other forms of flood mitigation other than the levee improvements. This did not seem like a very satisfactory result from any point of view. Thus, the blame game between the federal and state governments continued into June, revolving around varying recollections of the agreements made over a year earlier in February through May of 2006.[50]

For New Orleans, this meant that virtually none of Blakely's $1.1 billion in supposedly available funds would in fact be forthcoming anytime soon. All the city had was its expectation of $117 million in CDBG funds, and this depended on the LRA's approval of UNOP, which was still under review by the city. The additional $324 million in CDBG funding that might have come once the state's match of FEMA funds was waived was now held hostage because of the Road Home shortfall. And Blakely's proposed "blight bonds" were also in doubt because of the city's continued shaky position with respect to all the public funding sources.[51] Virtually the only other viable piece was the $260 million bond issue that voters had approved in 2004. Blakely's office was actively working with the city's Board of Liquidation to authorize bond sales over the next year. It now seemed highly unlikely that cranes would be on the skyline in September.

INTERLUDE: LOUISIANA SPEAKS

May 2007 also saw the release of the state's Louisiana Speaks regional recovery plan. Originally scheduled for completion several months after UNOP (a timeline that perplexed many), the two plans ended up finishing at about the same time. In fact, the LRA approved Louisiana Speaks before UNOP.

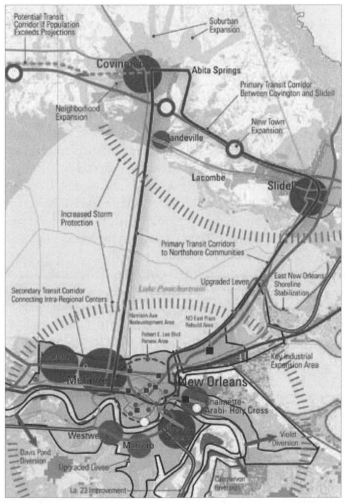

City of New Orleans Targeted Recovery Areas

● **Renew Area**—area or facility where trigger investments or administrative action will add to renewal

■ **Redevelopment Area**—area with some recovery, potential to spur future redevelopment, demonstrates key recovery strategies

■ **Rebuild Area**—area requiring major rebuilding and significant public or private investment

Louisiana Speaks

Fig. 7.3. The New Orleans portion of the Louisiana Speaks regional recovery plan, reflecting ORM's recovery target areas

By the time of the plan's completion, the structure and purpose of this effort were much clearer than in the confusing days of early 2006. *Louisiana Speaks Regional Plan: Vision and Strategies for Recovery and Growth in South Louisiana* was now officially a product of the LRA and was its "long-term community planning initiative."[52] As described in Chapter 2, the plan included several phases of citizen involvement, in the spring and summer of 2006, leading to a set of recovery and development scenarios. In early 2007, following the completion of the UNOP process, Louisiana Speaks conducted its most visible public process: the regional vision poll, to which more than 23,000 Louisiana residents responded.

The plan, released on May 3, 2007, had three vision goals: "Recover Sustainably" (build levees, restore wetlands, reinvest in communities, and meet immediate needs of workers and businesses), "Grow Smarter" (integrate coastal restoration with land use; build a range of housing and transportation options), and "Think Regionally" (link transportation and coastal protection investments; increase local and regional planning capacity). Although challenged by timing and coordination issues, LRA staff tried to reshape the final plan as an umbrella under which parish plans or topic area plans would fit. For example, the "Recover Sustainably" goal incorporated the near-term recovery goals of Blakely's target areas, as well as the master plan of the Louisiana Coastal Protection Authority.

The plan also laid out the guiding principles from the November 2005 Louisiana Recovery and Rebuilding Conference, which would be used as a basis for approving UNOP and, subsequently, the other parish recovery plans. Later in the summer, the LRA would begin to approve revisions of the parish ESF #14 plans in order to award the CDBG funds. These plans satisfied HUD's planning conditions for allocating the funds, and the CDBG funding turned out to be well timed to fund community projects on the ESF #14 lists that had not been covered by other programs, such as FEMA Public Assistance. In retrospect, the Louisiana Speaks, ESF #14 long-term community recovery planning, and CDBG processes seem as if they were consciously designed to work in a logical and coordinated sequence. In fact, all of them were invented on the fly, and any appearance of a systematic, sequential process is fortuitous. It is to the credit of LRA staff that it all came together.

The regional plan was to be followed by a more detailed strategic implementation plan in July 2007. Although the plan lacked specific funding mechanisms for projects, some initiatives were given priority by state officials. These included a stronger Office of State Planning, a high-speed public transit link between New Orleans and Baton Rouge (and to the New Orleans airport), trust funds for wetland conservation easements, incentives for urban reinvestment, and altered zoning laws to facilitate infill.[53]

At the May 10 board meeting, the LRA officially accepted and approved the Louisiana Speaks Regional Plan. One hope was that this coherent vision would help the state's case in acquiring federal funds for transportation and coastal protection, as well as immediate economic needs.

CITY PLANNING COMMISSION APPROVAL OF UNOP

On May 22, the City Planning Commission met to consider final approval of the revised UNOP Citywide Strategic Recovery and Rebuilding Plan. Because of the disputes over finances among the state and federal governments, the plan was about to gain official endorsement in an environment that would provide no support for its cornerstone mitigation and community development projects.

There was no question that UNOP had been awkward for the planning commission. Although staff members were involved in UNOP from the start, the commissioners were not. In fact, three of them were still displaced in other cities as of June 2006, when UNOP began. Now they were being asked to take ownership of the plan. How much of it was truly theirs? Arguably, it was grounded in their neighborhood planning guidelines, and it was based on a public involvement process that was broader than anything the commission had ever done. Some of the commissioners were looking for a perfect plan, but most appreciated that this was good enough and that it was time to move forward. In fact, if they did not approve it soon, the commission would begin to look irrelevant, since Blakely was already moving forward with his implementation of UNOP as if it had been approved months ago. Because of the fast pace of recovery, some commissioners were frustrated by how long the staff took to complete their comments. The chair wanted a vote in April, GNOF and the Rockefeller Foundation wanted a vote in March, and staff thought it could not be approved until June. The solution was to schedule a special public hearing on the revised plan on May 15 and to vote on it at the last meeting that month.[54]

For the May 22 meeting, the commissioners had received a 24-page report prepared by staff of both the City Planning Commission and the ORM, reflecting the views of the commission staff after reviewing the plan over the previous two months. The staff report concisely described its purpose: "While some have argued that the Plan should be rewritten, the Commission has taken a less drastic approach. This report will attempt to highlight attributes of the Citywide Strategic Recovery & Rebuilding Plan and identify procedural recommendations for implementing the Plan."[55] The report summarized the major recommendations of the citywide plan and identified the commission staffs' points of agreement and disagreement. Key disagreements included the citywide plan's recommendation to increase federal density guidelines under HOPE VI and the recommendation for unification of the Orleans Parish School Board. Staff also criticized the plan's integration: "city planning's review of the plan revealed that the revised document did not consistently integrate the information obtained from the neighborhood meetings and district plans. . . . The plan is disconnected from the district plans."

Nor was the staff convinced that all parts of the plan truly reflected public opinion:

> The Plan relied heavily on the discussion of recovery scenarios at the Community Congresses. While this information is informative, it is based on a very small sample using a non-scientific methodology, limiting the format and value of the questions and responses. The Plan includes editorial comments throughout the document that appear to be more indicative of the authors' personal and/or political views than representative of public input obtained in the planning process. The Commission does not support these statements and believes that they are inappropriate in a public policy document.

Still, they thought enough of the plan, as revised, to recommend that all Orleans Parish governmental entities administer their policies and programs in accordance with its recommendations. They also recommended a strong parishwide recovery council, "to ensure that all Parish governmental entities consult with and obtain from each other information and resources in order to develop prioritized and coordinated policies, programs, and projects in furtherance of the Plan." They suggested that this council model itself after the LRA in using "action plans for the priorities and use of [multi-agency] funds, including the potential prioritization and programming of key recovery funds, such as Public Assistance and Hazard Mitigation funds. The parishwide recovery council should also serve as the lead interface to State and federal recovery funding agencies so that priorities are clearly defined and funds optimized." Finally, the report described the roles of the City Planning Commission in leading the master plan effort and the ORM in implementing the 17 target areas.

The report summarized its position this way:

> The City Planning Commission recognizes that the Plan is not perfect. Many of the proposed programs are concepts in need of further development by others in the implementation phase, once funding is secured. The Plan is dependent on outside funding sources which are uncertain at this time. Several key elements such as flood protection are federally mandated initiatives outside the control of the City. The Plan does not specifically identify areas where it recommends that public investments be minimized until certain criteria are met.

However, the Plan does educate the public about hurricane flood protection and promotes a Category 5 level of storm protection. The Plan advocates the repair and upgrade of public infrastructure and gives a detailed list of needed projects. The Plan also emphasizes the need for intergovernmental communication, cooperation and coordination, traits that have been lacking throughout much of the recovery process.

It is anticipated that the Plan will move in positive direction [*sic*] and the Commission will support those efforts by collaborating with other key recovery agencies such as the Office of Recovery Management (ORM), the New Orleans Redevelopment Authority (NORA) and the Parish Wide Recovery Advisory Committee. The City Planning Commission will also pledge to further grass root planning efforts and work towards the implementation of community interest projects. An additional focus of the City Planning Commission will be the completion of the City's master planning efforts and totally revising the Comprehensive Zoning Ordinance. These documents are necessary tools to implement the Citywide and District Plans.

In conclusion, the staff report recommended approval of the plan, subject to 15 specified actions. It also recommended that the "district reports" be included as an addendum to the plan. Staff concisely stated two reasons for the recommendation: "The [Citywide] Strategic Recovery & Rebuilding Plan provides a strategic framework for future development decisions that will facilitate the rebuilding of New Orleans. The District Plans are the result of an unprecedented citywide planning effort and are supported by a broad coalition of citizens."[56]

The meeting itself was anticlimactic. Approximately 15 people were in the audience, most of them UNOP staff. The commissioners briefly discussed the plan and then voted their unanimous approval.

CITY COUNCIL APPROVAL

UNOP's next stop was the city council, specifically the June 13 meeting of the City Council Recovery Committee, consisting of councilmembers Carter, Willard-Lewis, and Midura. Councilmember Thomas also attended. They were not interested, however, in taking up the plan that the City Planning Commission had just approved. Rather, over the previous three weeks some councilmembers had clearly indicated to ORM staff that they wanted to approve all the plans—especially the Lambert plans—even though the UNOP district plans incorporated all these plans, a conclusion that had been confirmed by testimony at the March 13 City Planning Commission hearing. Furthermore, it was unclear how such an approach would reflect the council's duty to review and approve the disaster recovery plans prepared by the planning commission. Could the city council review and approve a recovery plan other than the one approved by the planning commission? And, if so, shouldn't that plan go back to the planning commission before returning to the council for final approval? But, of course, no one wanted to slow the process down. The solution, then, was something akin to a don't-ask don't-tell policy, in which each entity would believe that it got its way. The result would be a consensus to make it look like there was a consensus, even if there was not. In so doing, the city would send a message to the outside world that its factions had ceased bickering and were ready to move forward. But there was also a practical problem: the ORM was faced with deciding how big the bundle of plans should be. Should it include every plan done by every neighborhood since the storm? In the end, the ORM included the Lambert plans, the ACORN plan, the Broadmoor plan, all the UNOP district plans, and the ORM target area plan, along with the UNOP citywide plan.

The recovery committee meeting began with a presentation by Yolanda Rodriguez, who described the citywide plan's three critical elements. First, it was unified, because it included all the city's neighborhoods, thereby providing coherence to the planning process. Second, other planning efforts—the ESF #14, BNOB, Lambert, and neighborhood plans—were respected and integrated into it. Third, it was designed to be an action-oriented framework for carrying out recovery-related duties. The planning commission submitted its report that evaluated the plan and described how to use it.

Next, Jeff Thomas, attorney and ORM special assistant, asked the council for a motion to approve UNOP's strategic recovery plan and all the plans that led to its development.[57] This official approval, said Thomas, would signal the LRA to release the $117 million in CDBG funds. Thomas and Dubravka Gilic then presented the target area strategy and described how they would use these as guides for investing the $117 million in ways that would catalyze redevelopment in the most damaged parts of the city. They stressed the critical importance of the CDBG funds and the need to send the plan to the LRA for its next board meeting on June 25. In response to questions from the council, ORM staff confirmed the CDBG funds and the target areas were just the first strategic steps in rebuilding the city, that the ORM and the planning commission were working collaboratively with clearly defined roles, and that every major project would eventually be submitted to the council.

Approximately 15 members of the sparse audience provided comments. Mtangulizi Sanyika, in an impassioned speech, called the proposed action "a unifying motion . . . this unifies us, after months of struggle. . . . We can come to closure. Let it never be said by anyone that New Orleans does not have a plan." With this motion, he said, "We transcend all the criticisms from everywhere that they have come." He called it an integrative and guiding framework that includes all the plans produced since the flood and declared that the target plan represents "the deepest consensus we have had at any time." The plan is not perfect, he said, but it includes everyone; no one is suspicious, and no one is left out.

Finally, Sandra Gunnar, the LRA liaison to New Orleans, answered the councilmembers' questions regarding the details of how they should deliver the plan to the LRA. The mayor would not necessarily need to sign it, she said; rather, it would only need to reflect the cooperation of the mayor's office, which the ORM's involvement clearly represented. She also clarified that, although the draft of the proposed motion said that the LRA "approved" the Lambert neighborhood plans in November, in fact the board only "received" them, so the draft text would need to be revised. Councilmember Carter asked whether a plan approved by the full council on June 21 would make it to the LRA meeting on June 25. He also asked if such an action was the last act they needed in order to "get us the money." The answer to both questions was yes. Finally, Gunnar confirmed that Orleans Parish would be the first parish with a completed plan approved by the LRA. The council committee voted unanimously to send the plan to the full council.

During the meeting, Councilmember Willard-Lewis announced, curiously, that there would be public hearings on the plan, with dates to be announced later. The next day's news account elaborated that the council intended to hold public hearings on June 30 and July 1 and that they intended to endorse the plan only informally prior to the June 25 LRA board meeting.[58] Needless to say, this was not part of the conversation with Sandra Gunnar, and it was not at all clear that the LRA would accept this.

On June 21, the full New Orleans City Council passed the following motion:

> BE IT MOVED BY THE COUNCIL OF THE CITY OF NEW ORLEANS, on behalf of the Citizens of Orleans Parish, that it does hereby support and generally approve the Citywide Strategic (Orleans Parish) Recovery and Redevelopment Plan, inclusive of all of the neighborhood and public planning efforts that led to its creation, and the means for implementing said plans, as developed by the Mayor's Office of Recovery Management, including the specific use of seventeen (17) target recovery management zones that synthesize all of the previous plans into a coherent and comprehensive strategy to a) implement, direct, organize and manage the recovery, to b) determine the prioritized projects to be implemented based on the prior neighborhood planning processes and plans in consultation with neighborhood advisory committees, and to c) secure and manage public and private sources of capital for the recovery effort.[59]

Despite this motion, the council still intended to hold two public hearings, now slated for June 29 and 30, before voting on an ordinance in July.[60] The day before the two hearings, however, the council canceled them, with no public explanation.

LRA APPROVAL

On June 25, New Orleans presented its plans at the LRA board meeting in the state capitol building in Baton Rouge. First Carey Shea, Steven Bingler, and Joe Butler presented UNOP. Shea introduced it as "the most extensive and complicated urban redevelopment plan ever attempted." Bingler then briefly explained how the planning process was organized. He first gave credit to the "relay race" of the plans that preceded UNOP, each one contributing data and promoting community engagement. He stressed that UNOP was founded on best practices and sound planning principles, as articulated at the AIA/APA conference in November 2005. He said their goal was to pass the baton to the ORM, in the next step of the relay. With that, Ed Blakely presented the Strategic Recovery and Redevelopment Plan with Councilmembers Cynthia Willard-Lewis and James Carter. Blakely said that all of the plans had now been pulled together to make "an outstanding urban plan." He described the importance of continuing public involvement in the district plans and announced that the parishwide recovery council was due to have its second meeting later in the week. He then presented his target areas.

Willard-Lewis emphasized the urgency of the situation in New Orleans and declared, "This is the summer of decision making." Carter recounted the series of approvals of the plan and said, "The motion represents the collective will of the ORM, the recovery committee of the city council, the full city council, and the mayor's office." Then Blakely and LRA board chair Norman Francis engaged in a lengthy conversation regarding how to most quickly access the CDBG funds. Francis said that, to date, the state had to obtain approval from HUD for every action.

Before the vote, Andy Kopplin explained the meaning of the LRA's acceptance of the plan. Kopplin said the LRA's job was to verify that "each parish has a comprehensive recovery plan that has been developed with grassroots, broad-based input and has been adopted by the executive and legislative branch of that parish government." The LRA's role was to approve the plan. The parish would then need to go through the Office of Community Development to receive its funding on a project-by-project basis.

After a long wait for a quorum, the board voted unanimously in favor of the resolution, presented here in its entirety. (Astute readers will observe that the resolution appears to use various names to refer to the plan it is approving.)

A Resolution to approve Orleans Parish Community Recovery Planning

June 25, 2007

OVERVIEW: A Resolution recommending the official receipt and acceptance of the Unified New Orleans Plan (UNOP) and the official approval of the City of New Orleans Strategic Recovery and Redevelopment Plan.

WHEREAS, the Louisiana Recovery Authority (LRA) is charged with establishing policy and plans for the immediate and long-term recovery of regions of the state affected by Hurricanes Katrina and Rita;

WHEREAS, Hurricanes Katrina and Rita devastated the parishes of Louisiana and created long-lasting problems including, but not limited to those impacting; the economy, environment, housing, public safety, education, health care, and transportation among other problems;

WHEREAS, very robust planning efforts have been completed at the local, regional, and state levels to ensure a wise, forward-looking investment of very limited resources;

WHEREAS, these planning efforts have provided and continue to provide guidance to our recovery effort;

WHEREAS, prioritization of projects that drive local recovery must ultimately come from local communities;

WHEREAS, consistency between local priorities and projects and regional plans provides the best opportunities for wise recovery investments;

WHEREAS, on December 14, 2006, the LRA Board approved a resolution directing LRA and Office of Community Development (OCD) staff to develop and publish for public comment an Action Plan Amendment for the allocation of $200 million of CDBG funds for the implementation of long-term community recovery projects in the most heavily affected parishes;

WHEREAS, on February 12, 2007, the LRA Board approved a resolution recommending the Louisiana Parishes Allocation Plan Amendment for Disaster Recovery Funds to the Governor and Louisiana Legislature for approval;

WHEREAS, on November 6, 2006, the LRA Board officially received and accepted the New Orleans City Council commissioned Neighborhoods Rebuilding Plan (Lambert Plans);

WHEREAS, the Unified New Orleans Neighborhood Recovery Planning process was established by a Memorandum of Understanding between the

City of New Orleans, the New Orleans City Council, the New Orleans City Planning Commission, the Greater New Orleans Foundation, and the New Orleans Community Support Foundation;

WHEREAS, the Memorandum of Understanding, which was signed August 28, 2006, represents an agreement between all parties to advance a single city-wide recovery and rebuilding planning process for the City of New Orleans to incorporate all the community, professional, and volunteer planning processes that were previously completed and to establish a unified set of priorities for the recovery of New Orleans;

WHEREAS, the Unified New Orleans Plan (UNOP) represents a citizen-driven recovery vision for the entire city of New Orleans which has been developed with unprecedented participation and representation from every part of the city including displaced citizens currently residing in Baton Rouge, Houston, Atlanta, Dallas and the entire diaspora community and has consolidated and included all prior neighborhood recovery planning efforts;

WHEREAS, the UNOP was completed and presented to the New Orleans City Planning Commission and the public in January of 2007 for review and revisions prior to approval; WHEREAS, in May of 2007, the New Orleans City Planning Commission approved the revised UNOP plan and subsequently forwarded it to the New Orleans City Council for consideration;

WHEREAS, the UNOP now serves as the foundation of the Mayor's Office of Recovery Management's Strategic Recovery and Redevelopment Plan; and

WHEREAS, on June 21, 2007, the New Orleans City Council approved a motion to support and generally approve the New Orleans Strategic Recovery and Redevelopment Plan.

THEREFORE BE IT RESOLVED, that the Louisiana Recovery Authority Board does hereby officially receive and accept the Unified New Orleans Plan as the foundation for the Orleans Parish recovery plan.

THEREFORE BE IT FURTHER RESOLVED, that the Louisiana Recovery Authority Board does hereby approve the New Orleans Strategic Recovery and Redevelopment Plan as the official recovery plan for the parish of Orleans.

Thus, at long last, 22 months after Katrina devastated the city and 20 months after city, state, and federal officials first began to agree that it was critical to complete a plan, New Orleans finally had an officially approved recovery plan. The state could send the plan to Washington, D.C., and the city would receive what was left of the CDBG funding. The mood in the hallways was celebratory, full of TV cameras, smiles, and congratulations all around.

But what value, if any, had this process actually had?

CHAPTER

8

Conclusions

At the beginning of this book, we promised lessons for planners and local government officials facing a similarly large-scale disaster. Now, at the end of this complex story, what are the main lessons that we can take away from this experience?

Disaster recovery is a complex process, especially if it follows an urban catastrophe such as Hurricane Katrina in New Orleans. The long, complicated nature of the story is itself the first lesson. There is no easy way to rebuild after such devastation. Everything has to be done before everything else. Everyone is under stress, and preexisting conflicts intensify. It is complicated, confusing, and frustrating.

The case of New Orleans after Katrina teaches us these general lessons about postdisaster recovery, and they can help answer the question "What would I do if faced with a similar situation?" But the situation in New Orleans was also unique in many ways, and it offers more specific insights into the role of government after disaster. We hope we have prompted readers to ask themselves, "What would I have done if I were person X in September 2005?" This chapter will address both of these types of questions.

PLANNING TENSIONS: SPEED VERSUS DELIBERATION

To put it succinctly, recovery from a catastrophic disaster is about obtaining and spending large sums of money in a short period of time, as well as planning and managing processes to rebuild homes, livelihoods, and the economy as efficiently, equitably, and sustainably as possible. A large, immediate sum of cash is the essential ingredient in successful postdisaster recovery, but processing and coordinating its use in a short period of time are part of what makes it so challenging. It requires dozens of fast-track construction projects that all occur simultaneously.

As important as this is, it is only one aspect of a tension that characterizes all postdisaster work. A key challenge in recovery is balancing the need for both speed and deliberation. Communities must rebuild as quickly as possible in order to maintain existing social and economic networks. Recovery efforts after a disaster aim to swiftly return an area to its previous level of economic activity and replace the homes and businesses that were lost. But communities must also be thoughtful and deliberate in order to maximize the opportunities disasters provide for improving the city, and they must ensure that funds are spent as efficiently and equitably as possible. As noted by Kates et al., "Cities and regions seeking to reconstruct after a disaster seem to simultaneously pursue goals to rapidly recover the familiar and aspire to reconstruct in safer, better, and sometimes more equitable ways."[1] Stated another way, this tension is manifested as conflicting planning ideals: "There is already a plan for reconstruction, indelibly stamped in the perception of each resident—the plan of the pre-disaster city. The new studies, plans and designs compete with the old."[2]

In the case of New Orleans, this tension between restoration and change was severe. Many people, particularly outsiders, wanted the city to change, to abandon the areas at lower elevations, and to radically restructure its urban form. But most residents rebelled against this. Of the 44,000 Road Home participants in New Orleans, only 12 percent decided to sell their homes and leave.[3] The rest were determined to stay. Even in the lowest-lying, most flood-damaged areas, 50 to 80 percent of home owners are choosing to rebuild their homes.[4]

In New Orleans, this tension was exacerbated by racial mistrust, and it was impossible to disentangle issues of land-use change and race. The African-American community preferred the "plan" of the predisaster city not only because it was familiar and comforting (although not ideal by any means) but also because it was better than what they feared might take its place. Experience told them that change, when led by the white power elite, had never been a good thing for them. Their fears were indelibly influenced by decades of discrimination and neglect and fueled by comments made soon after the disaster that suggested it was an opportunity to cleanse the city of its poor. Furthermore, the slow disbursal of federal funds affected lower-income residents and businesses the most because they had no other resources. So, despite the opportunities the disaster provided for improving neighborhoods, the African-Americans at every income level wanted speed, above all.

Speed, however, causes many problems, such as incomplete analyses, insufficient consideration of all possibilities, and hasty decisions. Not only can speed cause mistakes, but it also allows no time to correct them. For example, the BNOBC was so intent on finishing its plan by the end of 2005 that it did not meaningfully involve neighborhoods or the people forced to leave New Orleans after the storm. Even toward the end of the Lambert planning process, some neighborhoods still had not been involved in it in any meaningful way. Nevertheless, all the plans were prepared and delivered by their deadlines. Likewise, UNOP planners, keeping to their tight schedule, held the first community congress less than two months into the process, without the public outreach and grassroots organizing necessary to get enough people to the meeting. The participants were so different from the city's pre-Katrina demographics that the public dismissed the meeting's results. If additional resources had not been committed to outreach later on, the damage caused by this community congress could have crippled the rest of the UNOP process.

Rebuilding too quickly can also be a mistake. The city's hasty issuance of thousands of building permits in the months following the flood has reduced the chances of rebuilding large numbers of structures in ways that reduce their vulnerability to flooding.

THE OPPORTUNITY TO CORRECT PAST WRONGS

In the aftermath of every disaster lies the opportunity to right the wrongs of the past and build a better city. Catastrophic disasters, in particular, may provide a chance to improve hazard mitigation, urban design, and infrastructure. It also offers an opportunity to distribute resources more equitably, restructure the economy, and reform government. However, we also know that such opportunities are often only partially realized, as observed by Haas et al. in their classic book, *Reconstruction Following Disaster*: "In general, the reconstructed city will be more familiar and less changed than inferred from the initial destruction and more safe and less vulnerable to recurrent hazard. But the achievement is inevitably less than the potential opportunity for change offered by the disaster." And planners and policy makers who are energized by these opportunities are usually disappointed:

> For the first time, adequate resources become available for thorough physical and design studies, albeit under pressure of time. . . . The impossible seems possible, and the various professionals are hopeful that the job can be done right; the opportunity for comprehensive study and major change is at hand. . . . Our review finds such hopes rarely fulfilled, and the characteristic finale to such expectation is bitterness and disappointment.[5]

In the case of New Orleans, the biggest historic wrong was racial discrimination, not something that could easily be righted by rebuilding the city differently. At the state level, the LRA recognized that economic and racial equity would be an issue, and they engaged PolicyLink—a well-known Oakland, California, nonprofit that advances economic and social equity—to help develop principles and policies that would integrate these concerns into the state's recovery actions from the beginning.[6] LRA staff believed they needed to embed equity in every policy. The Road Home program was crafted with the best of intentions and included a midcourse adjustment to add a grant program to help the most vulnerable residents. Still, an August 2008 PolicyLink report pointed out that most Road Home recipients did not receive enough to cover their construction costs, and this shortfall fell disproportionately on heavily flooded African-American neighborhoods. PolicyLink also reported that the rental component of Road Home replaced only a third of the damaged affordable rental units in New Orleans.[7]

At the city level, several groups organized to ensure the rights of all African-American residents. They were catalyzed by suggestions that a smaller city, with fewer low-income residents, would be an improvement, which implied a whiter city would be a desirable outcome. Organizations such as ACORN advocated for the right of all New Orleanians to return. They were successful in making this policy explicit in all the city's plans, although the continuing shortage of recovery funds has impaired this achievement.

Advocates for the poor and displaced have also had to fight for the restoration of public housing. Many public housing residents in New Orleans work in the hospitality industry, which is one of the city's biggest economic engines. The Housing Authority of New Orleans (HANO) has been under HUD receivership since 2002. Before the storm, HUD had been planning to redevelop all HANO properties into mixed income housing. The flood provided an opportunity to accelerate this controversial process. Public housing reconstruction is not a significant part of any of the city's plans because the city had limited control over this process. The Lambert plans, for example, explicitly refused to consider public housing reconstruction.[8] Although the UNOP process began with a similar intention, some of the UNOP district planners actively engaged public housing residents and their neighbors and proposed policies for reconstructing HANO properties. Based on these discussions, the citywide plan stepped into the fray with recommendations for HUD and HANO and asked HUD to provide "a sufficient number of public housing units to accommodate all displaced former public housing tenants in their own neighborhoods. In light of post-Katrina conditions, a housing strategy is required that accommodates all displaced former public housing tenants both in the short- and long-term."[9] The City Planning Commission, however, deleted these recommendations in its final review and approval of the plan.

While the city has not fully realized the opportunities to address these inequities, it has improved governance. Both the state and city have taken steps to improve transparency and initiate institutional reforms. The levee boards and the assessor's office of Orleans Parish are no longer fiefdoms. In late 2006, the city council created the Office of Inspector General to root out corruption in city hall. In 2008, voters gave the master plan the force of law in zoning decisions, to forestall ad hoc planning decisions by the city council. And residents have considerable optimism about the reinvention of the school system, in terms of both its organization and the new facilities that will be built over the next few years. Finally, the New Orleans Citizen Participation Project has been working to develop a permanent system to ensure ongoing, direct involvement of citizens in public decision making. Some residents and officials see this increase in political participation and reform as one of the most positive outcomes of the flood.

One of the most important improvements a city can make after a disaster is mitigation to reduce risks and vulnerability to the next disruptive event. In New Orleans, this has been a priority from the start (LRA's motto: "Safer, Stronger, Smarter"), but it will be years before we can evaluate the effectiveness of permanent mitigation efforts. In 2005, the U.S. Army Corps of Engineers received congressional approval to repair and enhance the flood hurricane protection system to withstand a Category 3 storm by 2011.[10] At the same time, Congress also ordered the Corps of Engineers to develop a plan that includes a "full range of flood control, coastal restoration, and [other] measures" to protect coastal Louisiana from Category 5 storms.[11] In November 2007, Congress passed the Water Resources Development Act (WRDA) of 2007, which included more than $3.7 billion in specific coastal restoration projects for Louisiana. This brought the total federal obligation to levee repair and drainage enhancements for the region to more than $15 billion, and the State of Louisiana has committed significant funding as well.[12] But the total cost needed for Category 5 protection is likely to exceed $40 billion.

Local mitigation efforts within New Orleans have also been proceeding slowly. The delays in gaining federal government approval to integrate the FEMA mitigation funds with the CDBG Road Home funds hampered the state's ability to integrate mitigation into the rebuilding process. UNOP's proposal to boost Road Home payments to help home owners elevate or relocate to higher ground also foundered because of the government's reluctance to help with the program's funding shortfall.

Despite all the obstacles, a number of homes have been elevated (although no one knows exactly how many).[13] Thus, there has been some incremental improvement in the city's ability to withstand a future flood, which is evident to visitors to New Orleans's flooded neighborhoods: little by little, one house at a time, the city is indeed rising up. But until FEMA mitigation funds become more accessible and home owners have resources to pay the high costs of elevating their homes, this success will not be widespread. In April 2009, the LRA announced that home owners could access up to $100,000 of FEMA mitigation funds to elevate their homes, above and beyond the $150,000 Road Home cap.[14] But the program has complicated requirements, and only time will tell how much of an effect it will have.[15] If it can, in fact, make it more possible for home owners to overcome the cost of elevation, then this new provision has the promise to spark a wave of reconstruction in the most devastated parts of the city.

To create a comprehensive flood-risk management program that is dramatically different from the incremental approaches of previous decades, a long-term and consistent commitment at all levels of government and by the general public will be required. If New Orleans is to become a safer place, billions of dollars must be invested in wetlands restoration, curbing regional subsidence, systematic levee rebuilding, home elevation, and other forms of hazard mitigation.[16] One risk management study declared,

> The city of New Orleans is at a cross roads. It can either embrace transparency around flood risk and flood risk management, or, as has happened on three previous occasions over the past century, it can simply resume business as usual and pray that the floods stay away. The terms of the next disaster are defined in the response to the previous catastrophe.[17]

In short, it remains to be seen whether or not New Orleans will fall in line with the observations of Haas et al., who write, "For most cities, most places, and most times, the balance of historical evidence suggests that reconstructed cities are better places to live for most people. But all cities lose some of the familiar and meaningful; injure more of the poor, the weak and the small among its citizenry and commerce; and fail to take full advantage of the opportunity that crisis represents."[18]

PLANNING WHILE IN THE FOG OF WAR

Planners often take the availability of planning information for granted. We usually know where to find what we need, can wait a while to get it, or make do when we can't get it all. If a planning situation is more complicated than usual, we gather primary data in the field, do web research, make some phone calls, or ask others for help. This was exceptionally difficult to do in post-Katrina New Orleans. State and city agencies, FEMA, neighborhoods, and individuals were all making significant decisions with inadequate information about what others were doing. It is well known that short-term disaster response processes have this "fog of war" characteristic. In the case of the catastrophic urban disaster in New Orleans, this fog lasted for many months and well into the recovery phase. In spite of urgent planning needs, neither individuals nor government agencies had enough information to make decisions. Planner John Beckman, in a news interview about his role in the BNOB plan, said, "I now know what it's like to be someone strategizing in the fog of war."[19]

When we visited New Orleans in February 2006, we found that none of the pivotal planning entities had a clear idea of what one another were doing. The situation was changing daily. Too many entities were making too many decisions at a speed that was too rapid for any of them to grasp the "big picture" or the decision environment in which they were working. Imagine having to make complex organizational and strategic decisions knowing full well that what little information you have is probably already wrong.

To a certain degree, this situation persisted in New Orleans for well over a year after Katrina. It was the planning equivalent of trying to travel faster than the speed of light. Everyone had to plan at a pace that was faster than the flow of the information the process needed. Likewise, decisions occurred so quickly that it was difficult for people to absorb this information. Planning takes time because individuals and groups need to acquire and comprehend information, build trust among parties, consider alternative courses of action, and feel some confidence in the decision. In the case of New Orleans, most of the planning processes kept moving ahead even in the face of discord.

PLANNING FOR THE WRONG BATTLE

Another, more dangerous effect was that people were developing strategies based on outdated information—that is, they were fighting previous battles in the war. Sometimes, even the previous week's information was perilously obsolete. Two groups would have arguments based on information from different points in time. In some instances, all of the parties' arguments and information were outdated. It was like the Battle of New Orleans—Andrew Jackson's great victory in the War of 1812 that came two weeks after the United States had signed a treaty with the British.

In this way, some strategic decisions were based on understandings from circumstances that no longer had any bearing on what was really going on. For example, in late 2006, Paul Lambert continued to rely on his conversations with FEMA staff from early 2006 while he attempted to meet the requirements of an ESF #14 plan. FEMA, however, had long since handed off ESF #14 to the state, and the LRA had become the body in charge of the parish planning framework. The requirements the LRA had set in mid-2006 were far more relevant than the earlier FEMA ones. Furthermore, Lambert believed that HUD's own CDBG requirements demanded that the funds be used only in the flooded areas. By mid-2006, however, the LRA had already been working with HUD on this, and the concept of parishwide plans had been published in an action plan amendment in April. While Lambert's interpretations were plausible in February and March, that was no longer the case by late summer.

Moreover, the federal requirement for a plan was itself a moving target. By the time UNOP began, the original reasons for it may already have been obsolete.[20] The imperative to plan began with BNOB, and one important reason for its prompt execution was to help the city tap into federal funds. The idea was that if New Orleans could document its needs, then appropriate funds would be forthcoming. This was the logic behind the ESF #14 process, too. Donald Powell's message at that time was quite clear and consistent with this as well: if you want more money, provide a plan that documents the need for it.[21] Thus, doing more planning became a dance—some might say an atonement, or even punishment—that New Orleans needed to perform in order to satisfy Powell, who would then convey his approval to the White House.

As a result, during the summer of 2006, the pressure to create a plan that met "LRA's requirements" was mostly about meeting Powell's requirements. And the punch line is that we suspect that by the end of the summer Powell represented no one but himself. The White House and Congress were focused on other matters by then, and Powell no longer had the same amount of power as he had had in February. But no one in New Orleans knew that. So the mayor and city council complied and agreed to do UNOP. In retrospect, it seems unlikely that Powell's superiors at the White House were overly concerned about the lack of a plan for New Orleans. Perhaps they simply did not want to send money to Louisiana or did not see any value in doing so.[22]

The imperative to plan in order to use the $10.4 billion in CDBG funds had taken on a life of its own, even as the Road Home process decoupled the housing money from the planning process, and the remaining CDBG pot for community development projects kept shrinking.[23] In July 2006, when city council member Cynthia Willard-Lewis asked repeatedly who, exactly, was asking for a single parish plan, she was asking the right question. The correct answer would have been that it was Powell, via LRA, via David Voelker. UNOP was a device to settle an argument in February 2006 that was no longer relevant by summer. By fall 2006, the issue wasn't the tiny pot of discretionary CDBG money but rather the billions in FEMA Public Assistance funds. And this money was not waiting for the completion of the multiple planning processes but was held up by FEMA and state bureaucrats in their processing of thousands of applications.[24]

The ACORN plan for the Lower Ninth Ward provides another example. Ken Reardon presented the plan in February 2007 and declared that "people in the press have demonized and vilified the neighborhood." But this was more descriptive of the press in the fall of 2005 than it was of subsequent media coverage, which was sympathetic to the challenges residents faced.[25] Since January 2006, all of the planning efforts emphasized rebuilding the whole city and rebuilding the Lower Ninth in particular. During this time, ACORN recruited hundreds of volunteers to gut houses, and foundations such as Make It Right were successfully raising millions to rebuild homes in the area. By the middle of 2006, the goal of reconstructing the Lower Ninth Ward was no longer a serious question.

It is only natural for people and organizations to strategize, form coalitions, and initiate campaigns based on a triggering event or events. But what happens in the rapidly changing world of postdisaster recovery is that the decision environment changes while the strategy is being implemented or even while the strategy is still being devised. The triggering events lose or change meaning over time. It is normal for people to operate according to their interpretation of how the world works, and conflicts arise over different interpretations of the same reality. But in post-Katrina New Orleans, conflict was compounded by the fact that reality itself was changing faster than the actors could adapt. Not only were they at odds over issues of race, class, risk, and responsibility, but the various parties were stuck in different points of the past. If the debates often seemed disconnected from reality and confusing to viewers, it's because they were simultaneous discussions about different points in history.

TIME COMPRESSION

Time compression—or, more accurately, the compression of a great many activities into a short period of time—is a phenomenon that creates unique challenges during disaster recovery. That actions proceeded faster than people could understand them caused a great deal of discord in New Orleans. This is not to say that a slower-paced environment would necessarily have led easily to peaceful resolution and consensus. But for planners at least, having more time makes it much easier to gather information, address the needs of a wide range of stakeholders, engage in negotiations regarding focused problems, and slow down for bumps in the road. Planning also needs time for stakeholders to absorb proposals and discuss them with others.

Consider UNOP. It involved approximately 200 consultant staff working full-time for about four months. Normally, such an ambitious plan would take two years and involve about 30 planning staff. But a two-year version of this $10 million plan would deliver much more than the same stack of documents. It would also allow for more public discussion and more time for new ideas to be developed. (Although it would probably receive less intense public attention.) Planning cannot simply be compressed in time by providing more planners. Could the same $10 million plan be done in one day by sticking 24,000 consultants in the Superdome? Clearly not, because there would be no time for fieldwork, no time to communicate with stakeholders, no time even to communicate with one another, and no time for stakeholders to ponder their options. Critical aspects of the planning process cannot be shortened. But postdisaster planning must overcome this challenge anyway.

COORDINATING AND IMPROVISING

Coordination is critical to recovery, due to many actors working in a compressed time environment and with constrained information flows. The only way to function effectively in a chaotic and uncertain environment is to provide information to actors systematically and coordinate with them regularly. This was the purpose of the New Orleans recovery council, for example, which was first proposed by UNOP and initiated by Ed Blakely. Although it never really fulfilled its promise, it was intended to facilitate information flows among agencies and provide opportunities for joint brainstorming and decision making.

In fact, several new institutions were created after Katrina because of the need for informed coordination. A particularly successful example is the Neighborhood Partnership Network (originally the Neighborhood Planning Network). The network was particularly helpful during the first two years of recovery as a way of quickly sharing resources and neighborhood-based strategies in a rapidly changing environment. Another early success was the Louisiana Recovery and Rebuilding Conference, which was cosponsored by the AIA and APA in November 2005. This was an important event because most of the planning concepts later used in several post-Katrina plans were introduced at this meeting. Many of the key participants in later planning efforts have said this conference was an important source of ideas and contacts. Similarly, the ACORN conference in Baton Rouge in early November 2005 provided a venue for rich exchanges among residents, politicians, community organizers, and academics.

The most appropriate plan in unpredictable environments is one that is strategic and adaptable to change. This was the idea behind UNOP's strategic planning framework, which established criteria and recovery implementation policies for three types of policy areas, the boundaries of which would change over time. Using the criteria, areas of the city could be monitored and policy approaches modified as the recovery progressed. However, officials never used this framework nor established monitoring systems.

Finally, the process of developing strategies, making decisions, and taking actions involves considerable creativity, which should be encouraged. Both the speed of the process and the unfamiliarity of the tasks may require planners and local officials to improvise. Planners who can be quick on their feet and organizations that allow such behavior are often the most successful in postdisaster recovery. In postdisaster New Orleans, we saw many professionals who met this challenge by demonstrating dedication, creative thinking, and an eagerness to work collaboratively with others to solve difficult problems. Many of these professionals discovered the "rush" of the fast pace, the opportunity to innovate on the fly, the instant recognition that follows, and the sense of doing something important and highly visible.

MONEY

Following a catastrophic disaster, the most urgent need is money. Big cities are built over centuries, and they are expensive to rebuild. To rebuild in a short period of time costs at least as much as it did the first time, but the money needs to flow much, much faster. Hence, recovery, above all, is a search for resources. All the struggles in New Orleans have centered on obtaining scarce funds for reconstruction.

In the case of Katrina, insurance was a major source of funds, whether it came through private carriers or the National Flood Insurance Program.[26] But from the beginning, Louisiana's primary funding target had to be the federal government. All throughout the world, it is expected that national governments step in to help after large disasters. Furthermore, because the flood was caused by the failure of the federal levee and floodwall system, Louisiana believed that the federal government was obligated to pay, especially for New Orleans.[27] By 2009, the federal government had committed a historically high level of assistance—more than $116 billion—in the form of grants, loan subsidies, tax relief, and incentives to Gulf Coast states for recovery efforts after the 2005 hurricanes.[28]

While the federal government acted quickly to provide relief funds in the first weeks following Katrina, it was slow to provide funds for permanent reconstruction planning and implementation. There were several reasons for this. First, Washington was reluctant to provide reconstruction funds to Louisiana. Congress has provided just enough money to address an immediate need on four separate occasions: December 2005, June 2006, May 2007, and November 2007. Each one of these appropriations was negotiated to gain support for a war-funding bill. Second, the FEMA Public Assistance program has excessively burdensome requirements that are particularly ill suited for a disaster of this size. Its funds are available only through reimbursement, meaning the city must pay in advance for construction, engineering, and architectural services. Cash-strapped New Orleans was not in a position to do this.[29] The reimbursement process is cumbersome, involving detailed review of every item. The program also has perverse incentives that work against replacing outmoded public facilities with newer and safer ones. Finally, the administration and Congress had considerable discretion they did not use. The federal government exhibited considerable flexibility and creativity in recovery programs following the 2001 terrorist attacks and during many other disasters. But, for some reason, it chose not to operate this way during Katrina's recovery.[30]

The State of Louisiana has been obligated about $72.5 billion in federal recovery funds—about $35 billion of which is for long-term rebuilding.[31] The state has also spent more than $4.6 billion of its own funds on the 2005 storm recovery.[32] According to UNOP, as of April 2007 approximately $47 billion in public or private recovery dollars had been obligated or spent in Orleans Parish. Twenty billion dollars came from private insurance; approximately $6 billion came from the National Flood Insurance Program; $5.7 billion went toward flood protection; and the remainder came through Small Business Administration loans, CDBG payouts (primarily from the Road Home program), highway funds, and FEMA reimbursements for damaged public facilities. Much of this assistance went to private owners, and relatively little has yet reached the city or other public agencies.[33] Of the $72.5 billion, the city is expecting to receive and control about $2 billion, far less than it needs for reconstruction.[34]

To illustrate the long, circuitous nature of the pipeline from Washington, here is how New Orleans finally gained its share of the CDBG funds, which depended on federal resolution of the shortfall in the Road Home program, several months after the state recognized the problem. The state was seeking a waiver so it would not have to provide a 10 percent match for all FEMA Public Assistance and hazard mitigation funds awarded within the state.[35] Louisiana had lobbied intensely for several months in the spring of 2007 and ultimately succeeded in getting the waiver attached to a $120 billion emergency war-spending bill in May 2007. However, this did not mean that the CDBG funds would become immediately available for reconstruction, because the state had to place this money in reserve to cover the shortfall in the Road Home program. After the state lobbied throughout the summer and fall, Congress approved $3 billion to address this shortfall as part of a $471 billion defense bill in November 2007. The state was able to confirm that this was sufficient because it coincided with the December 1 cutoff for individuals to register with the Road Home program. Thus, Louisiana was finally able to release the money it had originally designated for the state's 10 percent match and provide it to the parishes, including approximately $300 million for New Orleans in addition to the $117 million previously awarded. It would still be a long time, however, before any of this actually reached the city, because the state and HUD required detailed project-specific applications before releasing funds.[36] Even as we write this, four-plus years after the storm, the city still lacks much of the promised CDBG funding, which itself is substantially less than the documented need.

In recent months, many officials in Louisiana have come to believe that the slow pace of reconstruction has much more to do with red tape than with inadequate funds. They have scores of stories about contradictory policies, the lack of cooperation between FEMA and HUD, and unrealistic requirements demanded by federal agencies. This was a catastrophic disaster that required a monumental effort by the federal government, but for whatever reason—disinterest, distrust, political calculation, or neglect—Washington's responses generally came too slowly and were not easily amenable to requests for streamlined procedures. Bureaucracies are poorly suited for postdisaster recovery. For this reason, nongovernmental organizations always arise, as they did in New Orleans. Still, governments must provide funding, technical assistance, and basic information, among other things. But in this case the state and federal government's handling of the distribution of both the CDBG and the Public Assistance funds has excessively tied the city's hands.

Robert B. Olshansky

Fig. 8.1. A still vacant area in the Lower Ninth Ward, September 2008

Adapting the existing CDBG mechanism has become a useful way to fund postdisaster recovery in the United States. But because this program was not designed for disasters, its requirements are not always appropriate. Recovery works best when a national government provides funding and technical assistance but leaves considerable discretion to the local governments. Again, this did not happen in New Orleans after Katrina, an event that overwhelmed all the normal procedures. Recovery from catastrophic disasters requires greater flexibility and innovation, but these were stymied by a lack of resources and by excessive requirements. In the end, this highly bureaucratic, top-down process is not the most effective way to spend the nation's funds. The lack of timely funding has been the root cause of much citizen frustration over broken streets, inconsistent water supply, insufficient Road Home awards, the shortage of affordable rental housing, and plans that have not yielded apparent results.

PLANNING AND PLANS AFTER DISASTERS

Many organizations and individuals make plans after a disaster. City and state governments, utilities, community organizers, housing nonprofits, and others have been working since September 2005 to rebuild New Orleans and have used formal and informal plans to communicate their intentions. The process of recovery is one of obtaining funds and then applying them to the task of rebuilding as quickly, efficiently, effectively, and equitably as possible. Plans, then, are made by these various actors in order to help them to obtain and apply funds in order to attain recovery goals. The purpose of a plan is to influence decisions and persuade others to act. A recovery plan's persuasive power depends on the credibility of its authors, the information it contains, and the scope and equity of the process that creates it.

Government comprises only one set of actors making key decisions after a disaster. Given the fast pace required for recovery, new organizations always emerge, and they are necessary for successful recovery. In New Orleans, most of the work of community organizing, cleanup, and rebuilding to date have been done by emergent and nongovernmental organizations such as ACORN, Common Ground, Habitat for Humanity, the Enterprise Foundation, university groups, and scores of faith-based groups that have mobilized thousands of volunteers to gut flood-damaged houses and assist in rebuilding. The neighborhood planning process would not have occurred without the work of more than 160 neighborhood organizations, including both preexisting and emergent groups. These groups have also provided residents with information on financial issues and the evolving status of city services. The NPN, for example, provided information to neighborhood organizations and community activists through its weekly meetings and its monthly newspaper, which is distributed to 10,000 households throughout the city and among displaced households in Houston.

Government-led recovery plans, however, have several important functions. They can offer incentives to attract and steer private investors. They can establish public budget priorities. And they can provide certain kinds of definitive, publicly accessible information that will help other government entities, nonprofits, and individuals make more informed and rational decisions. Some of the main reasons for government-led planning after Katrina were to lead a public conversation about recovery goals, document reconstruction needs, provide information to help individuals and organizations make informed decisions, communicate the intended actions of the city, and develop strategies for financing public investments.

Recovery plans are also ways to provide the "vision" for how best to spend recovery money. Government-led plans focus on how to spend the government's recovery money to benefit the public and motivate the private sector to reinvest its recovery resources. In the case of New Orleans, there were plans instigated by the mayor, city council, and governor (via UNOP). In the end, the most significant of these was the governor's plan (UNOP) because it was linked to receiving federal money.

In reality, however, the plans played other roles as well. They were political symbols. Some might say that their purpose seemed to be to cause public confusion. Ideally, a recovery plan is a way to allocate recovery resources; for New Orleans, the plan was a starting point in arguing for the resources in the first place. Just as the Broadmoor neighborhood mobilized to develop a plan for its survival, the entire city developed a plan in order to fight for its existence. Unfortunately, the city lacked even the resources to do the plan. So they were faced with simultaneously needing to persuade the federal government for reconstruction funds, while also seeking planning funds. That FEMA refused to provide these funds was a frustrating disappointment. In this situation, planning felt like some sort of punishment inflicted by Washington upon the city.

INTO THE VOID:
LACK OF LEADERSHIP AND COMMUNICATION

Reconstruction called for strong local leadership to mobilize the city's stakeholders and make the case to Washington for funding. Unfortunately, such leadership was lacking during the crucial 16 months following the storm. Amy Liu of the Brookings Institution, an astute observer of post-Katrina New Orleans, offered advice to the mayor as UNOP was beginning in August 2006:

Government sets the rules for the marketplace. The market and the public are waiting for more signals and clarity of information from government. A plan is critical because it provides this clarity. It helps guide how and where the market invests and provides predictability for [decision making]. To this end, the mayor's voice matters greatly on the front end of such a plan to both motivate and inform market actors, including families. He needs to set a clear direction for the city and its neighborhoods, but also be honest about the tough choices ahead so the people of his community can weigh these choices together and put those decisions in the plan. . . . [T]he mayor needs to be a leader and partner in the planning process now. If he is not meaningfully engaged immediately, all of the efforts of the citizens will be wasted. But, the mayor still has time to be at the center of the planning process, and the players in the unified plan must work closely with him.[37]

There is considerable evidence to suggest that New Orleans's mayor was overwhelmed by and unfocused about his role in the recovery process. A greater problem, however, is that he did not seem to realize where to go for help. Nor did he appreciate the critical importance of city hall as a focal point for information and communication. In the chaos of those early months, citizens were looking for a central source of information that would provide clear, consistent messages regarding the recovery process. The mayor could have defused the negative response to the BNOB plan by explicitly accepting it as just a first step in the planning process. He could have encouraged citizens to continue making their own informed choices while aggressively seeking funds to continue the public planning process. He could have said, clearly and repeatedly, that it was the city's intent to rebuild every neighborhood but not necessarily every part of every neighborhood.

In this leadership void, misinformation flourished in the form of rumors and misinterpretations of the city's actions. The most popular and fast-spreading rumors were those that expressed people's worst fears. To stem this, city hall needed to become a trusted central source for information for residents and other levels of government.

The mayor's complacency resulted in what can only be described as a political free-for-all of self-interested turf battles. He established the BNOBC as a way to mobilize the city's stakeholders and then distanced himself from it when the recommendations caused controversy. Even though the City Planning Commission was officially designated as the lead agency to prepare and approve reconstruction plans, the mayor undercut its ability to fulfill this mission with the massive post-Katrina layoffs and by creating and diverting resources to other planning entities.

The mayor's absence left open the main question that was on everyone's mind: where would the city rebuild? Charles Mann, writing for *Fortune* on the first anniversary of the flood, put the issue succinctly:

> Deciding where to rebuild is thus the primary decision—it is pointless to ask utilities to reconnect neighborhoods that will not exist and cruel to invite homeowners and businesses to return to them. The obvious way to reduce New Orleans is to buy out evacuees from flood-prone areas and bring them to abandoned homes on higher ground. But because whites disproportionately live on higher ground, this would involve parachuting many African Americans into white neighborhoods. In few cities would this be an easy sell. Crucial to the success of any plan would be political leaders with a minimal reputation for color-blindness and competence. Unfortunately, southern Louisianans, black and white, rarely elect them.[38]

This core issue became everyone's crusade, and people lined up behind the plans they thought were sympathetic to their particular focus, be it racial equity, neighborhood rights, fiscal efficiency, or maintaining the power of New Orleans in Louisiana. Some members of the city council thought their plan represented a struggle against the state for control of the planning process and, ultimately, of the recovery funds. Nagin was sometimes swayed by this view. In their suspicion of the state, they seemed unaware of the crucial battle it was waging in Washington for federal money.

There were also residents and organizations in New Orleans that seemed interested primarily in rationalizing city governance to recognize the fiscal realities of what would undoubtedly be a smaller city. They had great hopes that rational planning would produce analytical maps that delineated which areas were suitable for reconstruction and which were not, and they believed that the plans had instead fallen into narrow, parochial thinking that would ultimately result in a reconstructed city that was as vulnerable as it was before.

Conversely, many neighborhood organizations from around the city insisted the neighborhood-based plans were the only ones that had any legitimacy and that all neighborhoods needed public support for their recovery. They were generally suspicious of all levels of government because they saw little evidence that they were actually helping. Even the Road Home program became a bureaucratic nightmare for many.

Finally, city council members often used one plan or another as a symbol of how effectively they were representing their constituents. If they could characterize a plan as representing their views—standing up to Washington, standing up to Baton Rouge, releasing the money sooner, supporting the rights of the people—then throwing their weight behind that plan demonstrated how they were fighting for their constituents.

The vacuum of local leadership created problems for UNOP as well. Normally, a plan belongs to the entity that creates it. The BNOB plan was the mayor's, although he never officially endorsed it. The Lambert plans were the city council's. The target area plans were Blakely's and by extension the mayor's, if he chose to say so. But UNOP belonged to no one in New Orleans. On one hand, it was the LRA's plan: it supported it, it made sure that the memorandum of understanding was signed, and it had a use for it—to ask for funding from Washington. On the other hand, it was never their plan because, unlike most clients, they were never very interested in the details of its contents. The mayor never saw it as his plan. The council certainly never saw it as theirs. And the City Planning Commission was ambivalent. Even though foundations paid for UNOP, the plan did not belong to them either. In the end, UNOP had the most public credibility of all the planning efforts, and it represented the city best to the outside world, but it had no authoritative local face behind it. Until Ed Blakely came along, the combination of a credible plan promoted by a credible leader did not exist.[39]

PUBLIC PERCEPTIONS OF PLANNING

The citizens of New Orleans are now arguably the best-educated citizen planners in the country. They participated in months of meetings. They have become accustomed to using planning jargon, do not appreciate planners talking down to them, and are a difficult audience to fool. Nevertheless, they still have disparate views and, in some cases, are confused about the purpose of their completed plans and of planning in general.

Most residents found the multiple planning processes perplexing because they were not quite sure what a recovery plan was, what one looked like, or what it would do for them. That the leaders of the planning efforts had multiple, evolving explanations did not help. Citizens were told various things in order to lure them to a given planning meeting. It would be a blueprint for the rebuilding of the city. It would be a way to "get the money." They could decide how to organize the rebuilding of their neighborhoods. They could advocate for the survival of their neighborhood. In various venues, UNOP was alternatively described as a "blueprint," "framework," "roadmap," and "strategy."[40] The Rockefeller Foundation's press release in April 2006 stated that its funding was to be used for "a comprehensive rebuilding plan."[41] The UNOP process was referred to both as an opportunity for citizens to be involved in planning the redevelopment of their neighborhoods and as a "recovery plan" with a limited scope and timeframe that was concerned primarily with infrastructure financing and coordination of recovery activities, not redevelopment.[42]

While it was never quite clear who would do the rebuilding, who would provide the money, or when it would all happen, residents often felt that they could not afford to miss a meeting, or else another participant with misguided opinions might prevail. So they continued attending, never quite knowing what the plan would look like but willing to give it a chance. For most, however, the strategic planning framework presented by UNOP's citywide plan was far from anything they had envisioned; it wasn't tangible and visual enough. As a result, most people felt best about the district plans, which were sensible representations of recovery actions near their homes.

In fact, citizens seemed to have very little trouble understanding the concept of neighborhood planning.[43] The notion of empowering all neighborhoods to rebuild was always at the core of the planning concept advocated by the city council and Paul Lambert. According to John Beckman, neighborhood planning was always part of the BNOB plan as well; the January 11 BNOB presentation described using a neighborhood center model to rebuild the city, as well as organizing neighborhood planning teams to complete plans by May 20.[44] Even the November 18 presentation of the ULI plan said quite a bit about neighborhoods and argued that Entergy should quickly "[reestablish] electrical service to all of the city's neighborhoods." It also supported the idea that New Orleans should be a city of neighborhoods and that planning grants and technical assistance should be provided to strengthen and empower them.[45] Thus, although citizens were often confused by the various claims of planners, the one thing they agreed on was the need for neighborhood-centered planning to rebuild the city.

PUBLIC INVOLVEMENT IN PLANNING

Citizen participation in hundreds of planning meetings was phenomenal. People spoke of planning fatigue, but we saw little evidence of it. Although many residents claimed to be confused by the planning processes, they were, in fact, no more confused than were many public officials. Eventually, most residents intuited the purposes of planning and the importance of their neighborhood planning efforts.

There are two anecdotal schools of thought about citizen involvement in planning after great disasters. The first is that involvement in planning meetings is good therapy. People need something to do to heal themselves and feel like they are taking positive action to improve their lives. Meetings provide other benefits as well, such as a chance to socialize and trade useful news and information. These were all true in post-Katrina New Orleans. Planning meetings served as recreation, entertainment, and empowerment all rolled into one. The second school of thought, however, says that victims of a recent disaster are too traumatized to make serious long-term decisions. Furthermore, they are too busy doing the hard work of rebuilding to waste their time on meetings. This was also evident in New Orleans. Many people were not ready to confront the reality that it would take a long time to rebuild the city and that, inevitably, it would be a different city than the one they remembered. And many people who were working long hours, taking care of children, and commuting long distances just to survive had no time or inclination to attend meetings. More significantly, public involvement in New Orleans was hampered by the fact that so many residents were not there.

It is certainly a challenge to conduct public involvement processes with people recently traumatized by disaster, but people should be involved from the beginning. They should be given enough information to begin to intelligently draw their own conclusions. Bringing in experts with quick and early answers for BNOB may have seemed like a good idea, but it was threatening to residents who already felt that they had lost control over their lives.

But it is extremely expensive to conduct such processes properly. It requires collecting accurate data, producing and providing meaningful information, transmitting clear and consistent messages to rise above the noise of rumors and fears, communicating in an environment where not all the normal channels are operating, and holding genuinely productive public meetings. The necessity of paying for all of these elements is an important lesson from New Orleans.

VALUE OF PRIOR PLANNING

The difficulties of postdisaster recovery are arguments for doing planning all the time. Planning anticipates how to manage change and prepares local government for decisions that will arise in the future. It is best to prepare for these things in normal times when heads are calmer. Planning also provides guidance for how to respond to crises.

The days and weeks following a disaster are not the ideal time to initiate planning. Without a basic planning infrastructure in place, postdisaster planning is more challenging and takes much longer. The best preparation for recovery planning is to have active planning processes beforehand that include networks of well-established community organizations, clear lines of communication, and a variety of planning documents and tools. This was not the case in New Orleans. Prior to Katrina, the city lacked a formal neighborhood planning program and was perceived to be insensitive to citizen views. Furthermore, it lacked an up-to-date comprehensive plan, and the zoning ordinance was obsolete. And while some of the planning superstructure (and parts of the 1997 master plan) did exist, the mayor's decision to reduce the city's planning staff from 24 to eight compromised the city's already limited planning capacity.[46] This undermined the city's ability to apply existing institutional resources to the challenges of post-Katrina reconstruction.

DID THE PLANS MAKE A DIFFERENCE?

Given all the planning efforts and the months of contention, it is perhaps surprising to observe that the plans, in their final forms, were not dramatically different from one another. All were based on rebuilding neighborhoods. All of them—even the January 30 draft of the BNOB plan—explicitly stated the right of all residents to return to the city.[47] All wanted to put extra effort and care into the most heavily flooded neighborhoods in order to give residents the best chance of successful reconstruction. They all focused on how to meet the needs of those who returned. And they all had somewhat similar price tags. Overall, there were no major conflicts between the plans, as was evident at the City Planning Commission's March 13, 2007, hearing.

The plans were similar because they were based on similar sets of facts, and all of them consulted with a wide range of stakeholders. The plans got better over time because the information improved and the range of participants broadened. The ULI and BNOB plans were not parts of an evil conspiracy by developers to take the city away from its traditional residents. Rather, they were rational, professional planning products that shocked traumatized residents when they called for land-use changes at the neighborhood level. The weakness of these early plans was that they did not reflect wide public input, particularly from displaced New Orleanians. Subsequent plans were better because they were more sensitive to the needs of more residents and they actively involved residents in the decisions. Many observers have commented that the target plan concept is not all that different from the conceptual BNOB map, both of which assumed that the city's rebuilding would begin at viable nodes and then grow outward. One difference was that the BNOB map explicitly showed more of its concepts, which got it into trouble. Conversely, the target area map went out of its way to highlight significant investment areas in New Orleans East and the Lower Ninth Ward, which allowed it to explicitly underscore its intentions to welcome everyone back and to direct resources toward the African-American areas most in need of assistance.

We see UNOP as the final plan in the sequence. Blakely's target area plan was actually the first implementation strategy following the planning process. So the question is, Was UNOP worth all the money and time that went into it? We think so, for several reasons. It was remarkably transparent, had broad involvement, and carried considerable credibility. Whereas BNOB took a broad citywide view and Lambert focused on the flooded neighborhoods, UNOP did both. Its citywide plan, while not the detailed blueprint that many hoped for, laid out the strategic principles that were needed at the time. And the district plans served to activate civic conversations that extended across historic neighborhood, racial, and economic divides. It also serves as the foundation for the subsequent master planning process. UNOP demonstrated that cooperation and collaboration were possible and that people really can learn to appreciate one another's points of view. UNOP certainly did not transform New Orleans, but it did successfully bridge some of the city's divides.

UNOP was an important planning milestone for the city. It improved the culture of planning in the city, and it also helped to improve New Orleans's image to the outside world. UNOP served the city well as a means of adapting to evolving circumstances and changing targets. UNOP began with the purpose of obtaining federal recovery funds, and it evolved into being a means of arguing for more funds and a first step toward a new master plan. It is difficult to say whether it added $10 million of value beyond previous plans, but a considerable part of this expense was for communication and outreach under difficult circumstances.

In late 2006, one of the primary goals of UNOP was to convince the new Congress to provide needed funds to the city. So it is fair to ask to what extent it succeeded at this.[48] On its face, it is difficult to see the effect of UNOP, but we know from LRA staff that it played a role in the various federal funding decisions in 2007. The fact that New Orleans had a plan was a part of the argument (imagine how not having a plan would have undercut it), and the documented $14 billion gap helped to underscore New Orleans's needs. UNOP appears to have helped make Congress and the White House comfortable enough to release additional funds. Its existence also facilitated negotiations with HUD for more community development funds.

THE FUTURE

At least three important plans follow the end of this account. One was the School Facilities Master Plan, which was begun in August 2007, completed a year later, and approved by the state in November.[49] It used $700 million in FEMA Public Assistance funds to completely redesign the city's school facilities and redesignate school locations. It made it clear that the system would need an additional $1.3 billion from other funding sources to improve facilities systemwide. On January 25, 2010, the City Planning Commission unanimously approved the new 500-page Master Plan, "Plan for the 21st Century: New Orleans 2030," which now awaits city council approval. A new Comprehensive Zoning Ordinance is also in process. As promised by the City Planning Commission, an RFP was issued shortly after the approval of UNOP, and a team led by Goody Clancy began work in the summer of 2008, funded by $2 million of the city's CDBG funds. In November 2005, the state established the Louisiana Coastal Protection and Restoration Authority and directed it to create a regional master plan for coastal restoration and future hurricane protection. Louisiana's Comprehensive Master Plan for a Sustainable Coast was released in April 2007.[50] It is the first document to completely incorporate hurricane protection projects with plans to rebuild Louisiana's rapidly eroding coastal wetlands. It will be the guide for all coastal restoration and hurricane protection efforts in Louisiana over the next several decades.

Although it has taken a while, the federal funds have finally begun to flow, and a variety of large public and private projects have moved closer to fruition in New Orleans.[51] These include the redevelopment of HANO sites, new park facilities, and theater renovations. Negotiations are under way for an enormous new medical campus of LSU/Tulane and the VA hospital (though the planning process surrounding this complex project will require a book of its own). Providence Community Housing and Enterprise Community Partners have broken ground on an ambitious project to construct 900 subsidized rental homes and apartments and 600 for-sale homes both on the site of HANO's Lafitte public housing development and in the surrounding neighborhoods of Tremé. Finally, NORA has been proceeding systematically with several housing redevelopment projects throughout the city.

New Orleans is still struggling to address long-standing problems of crime, a sluggish economy, and poor public schools. The aftermath of the storm initially exacerbated these issues, but there are signs that things are improving. In 2009, the local economy was showing signs of recovery and strength as the bulk of construction work shifted from home rebuilding to infrastructure repairs.[52] According to *Money* magazine, the city had the sixth-fastest-growing real estate market in United States in late 2008. There was healthy local lending activity at banks and a low number of subprime-related foreclosures.[53] Also, in 2008, *BusinessWeek* named New Orleans one of the "20 Best Cities for Riding Out a Recession."[54] In 2009, the city earned an investment-grade bond rating from each of the ratings agencies for the first time since Katrina.[55] There are also signs that residents are optimistic about the city's future. A 2008 survey conducted by the Brookings Institution found that 56 percent of New Orleanians believed rebuilding and recovery activities are moving the city in the right direction. Another survey by the Kaiser Family Foundation reported that 75 percent of New Orleanians say they are hopeful about the future of the city.[56]

A major challenge is blight, which continues to be the most visible evidence of Katrina's wrath. Dealing with blight is a major priority for the city, particularly in its code enforcement department and NORA.[57] NORA is also focusing limited resources on inspections and enforcement in and around the 17 target areas and its own project areas, acquiring more abandoned

Robert B. Olshansky

Fig. 8.2. Streetcars—and a degree of normality—have returned to some parts of New Orleans.

properties and bundling them for large-scale redevelopment projects, and instituting a new lien foreclosure program.[58] In addition, NORA is the designated receiver of all properties voluntarily sold to the state through the Road Home program. It is expected to receive approximately 5,000 parcels in Orleans Parish.[59] NORA estimates the New Orleans market can absorb only 3,000 residential units per year, so it will have to hold on to many of these properties to avoid flooding the market and lowering home values. In the meantime, these properties will need to be managed and kept in good condition, which is expected to take up a significant portion of NORA's budget in the coming years. While NORA's work is just beginning, it is poised to become one of the largest and most powerful land banks in the United States.[60]

Recovery following a catastrophic disaster takes a long time. It is never easy, and it is never fast enough for affected residents. In the fall of 2005, many experts said the recovery of New Orleans would take five to 10 years. Geographer Robert Kates predicted it would take eight to 11 years.[61] In early 2010, these predictions seem about right. The city has about 75 percent of its pre-Katrina population, the streetcars are full, and most parks have reopened.[62] Many of the city's neighborhoods now look much like they did before the storm, especially in the areas that did not flood. These areas now have as many residents as they did before the storm, if not more. Still, some areas are not recovering as quickly. Portions of the lowest-lying neighborhoods in Lakeview, New Orleans East, and the Lower Ninth Ward, for example, have less than half of their pre-Katrina populations. Many of the residents and businesses who intend to return to these heavily flooded areas still lack the necessary resources to rebuild.

It may be that in 2010 the city will round the final bend and move entirely out of the recovery planning phase and into recovery implementation. As we write this in early 2010, the city has a new incoming mayor, Mitch Landrieu.[63] We predict his top challenge will be to keep funding flowing into the city and developing the economy to continue the recovery. Publicly funded construction is still far from complete, and a remaining challenge is to help the large number of households that have been left behind. New Orleans also still faces uncertainty about its long-term safety from future flooding. Hanging over the city's future economic

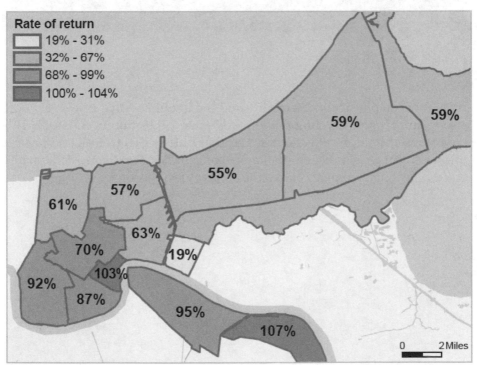

New Orleans 2030 / GNO Community Data Center analysis of Valassis Residential and Business Database

Fig. 8.3. Share of June 2005 residences active in September 2008, by planning district

Robert B. Olshansky

Fig. 8.4. New Orleans

viability is its physical vulnerability and the likelihood that it will see more strong storms and flooding without adequate protection from either. This enormous and unprecedented task requires patience as well as tolerance of missteps. But we also believe that more concerted actions by the federal and city governments to date could have better eased the way.

Acknowledgments

Above all, we thank Ken Topping, George Mader, and Martha Blair-Tyler for introducing us to the field of recovery planning and for being such great mentors. Special thanks are also due to Professor Haruo Hayashi from the Disaster Prevention Research Institute at Kyoto University, Japan, for being so supportive of our research.

Rob is grateful to the Public Entity Risk Institute, the Mid-America Earthquake Center, and the Lincoln Institute of Land Policy for supporting his travel to New Orleans. He also thanks Jed Horne and Jane Wholey for providing him a home away from home and so much more. Laurie is grateful to the staff of the Greater New Orleans Foundation and fellow members of the UNOP project management, citywide, and district teams. She also thanks Yolanda Rodriguez and the City Planning Commission staff for support of and collaboration on UNOP.

We also owe special thanks to the Concordia gang (especially Steven Bingler, Bobbie Hill, Joe Butler, Claudia Kent, Brenda Cho, Ximena San Vicente, and Jacqueline Newman), Jeff Thomas, Jeff Hebert, Scott Davis, Jedidiah Horne, Brendan Nee, Dubravka Gilic, Ed Blakely, Rebecca Mann, Steve Villavaso, the UNO crew (Jane Brooks, Renia Ehrenfeucht, Marla Nelson, Shirley Laska, Bob Becker, and Jim Amdahl), the Henry Consulting gang (Troy Henry, Darren Diamond, Errol George, and Gary Odland), the BKI team (especially Randy Carmichael, Paul Waidhas, Ralph Thayer, and Ellen Soll), the GCR team (especially Rafe Rabalais, Greg Rigamer, and Robert Edgecombe), America*Speaks* (especially Joe Goldman and Carolyn Lukensmeyer), Mark Romig and Peter A. Mayer Public Relations, Blake Haney and Whence the Studio, Luisa Dantas, Ken Reardon, Doug Meffert, Charles Allen, Keith Twitchell, David Dixon, Vera Triplett, Melissa Mitchell, Ikuo Kobayashi, Kazuyoshi Ohnishi, Yoshiteru Murosaki, Hisako Koura, Norio Maki, Shig Tatsuki, Yoshimi Amakawa, Toyoku Shimizu, Yukiko Nishimura, and Masaru Sakato. We also thank William Anderson for supporting our research in so many ways. And we are grateful to APA's Sylvia Lewis for having faith in us and Timothy Mennel for helping us to hone our message.

In addition, this book would not exist without our conversations with Leslie Alley, Scott Ball, Gill Benedek, Ed Blakely, Steve Bradberry, Beth Butler,

Hal Cohen, Pam Dashiell, Fred DuPlantis, Dominique Duvall-Diop, Donna Fraiche, Kate Gillespie, James Gilmore, Ramsey Green, Tanya Harris, Alvin Harrison, Richard Hayes, Janet Howard, Tim Jackson, Nadine Jarmon, Ben Johnson, Patricia Jones, K. C. King, Adam Knapp, Andy Kopplin, Reed Kroloff, Mel Lagarde, Paul Lambert, Walter Leger, Ray Manning, John Marshal, Earthea Nance, Jean Nathan, Mark Newberg, Father Nguyen, Becca O'Brien, Angela O'Byrne, Tom O'Rourke, John Paige, John Pine, Ezra Rapport, Robin Rather, Wade Rathke, Peter Reichard, Sean Reilly, Yolanda Rodriguez, Gordon Russell, Victoria Salinas, Ommeed Sathe, Carey Shea, Nathan Shroyer, Gary Solomon, Robert Tannen, Boo Thomas, Keith Villere, David Voelker, Darren Walker, Rick Weil, Joe Williams, Judith Williams, and Glenn Yancy.

We also want to express our heartfelt appreciation to our families for their tolerance and support through the years, especially during the most tumultuous times of our research and writing. Rob dedicates this book (especially Chapter 8) to the memory of his sister, Jaigne, whose time on earth was far too short.

Finally, we also dedicate this book to the residents of New Orleans, some of the world's best citizen planners. May your resilience, perseverance, and courage help you and your communities survive whatever future storms, natural or otherwise, come your way.

It is now early 2010, and the most intense part of our journey has ended. We understand that we are the lucky ones with homes and lives in cities that are still whole. We also know quite well that we are outsiders, though we have made many friends in New Orleans. But our professional and personal interests in the continued recovery of the city will extend for many more years. We will be watching how the city actually rebuilds.

Notes

PREFACE

1. Albert Crenshaw, "Surviving Katrina's Huge Damage Claims," *Washington Post*, sec. Financial, September 7, 2005, final edition; Jennifer Bayot, "First Estimate Puts Storm's Economic Toll at $100 Billion," *New York Times*, sec. C, September 3, 2005.
2. Jed Horne, "Carving a Better City; in Seconds, Buildings Collapsed, Bridges Toppled and Thousands Died When an Earthquake Hit Kobe, Japan, 10 Years Ago. Despair Was Rampant. But with Dogged Determination, the City Rebuilt, Repopulated and Rebounded.," sec. National, *New Orleans Times-Picayune*, December 4, 2005.

CHAPTER 1

1. Richard D. Knabb, Jamie R. Rhome, and Daniel P. Brown, "Tropical Cyclone Report, Hurricane Katrina, 23–30 August 2005" (National Hurricane Center, National Oceanic and Atmospheric Administration [NOAA], August 10, 2006), www.nhc.noaa .gov/pdf/TCR-AL122005_Katrina.pdf.
2. Paul Rioux, "Meeting the Challenge, Storm-scarred Buras Still Struggles to Recover, but," *New Orleans Times-Picayune*, West Bank Bureau, sec. Metro Real-time News, August 26, 2009, www.nola.com/news/?/base/news-2/1251264698267740 .xml&coll=1.
3. Knabb, Rhome, and Brown, "Tropical Cyclone Report, Hurricane Katrina."
4. The city first used the Superdome as a "refuge of last resort" seven years earlier when Hurricane Georges passed near the Louisiana coast before making landfall in Biloxi, Mississippi, as a Category 2 storm on September 28, 1998. John L. Guiney, "Preliminary Report, Hurricanes Georges, 15 September–01 October 1998" (National Hurricane Center, NOAA, January 5, 1999), www.nhc.noaa.gov/1998georges.html.
5. Sally Forman, *Eye of the Storm: Inside City Hall During Katrina* (Bloomington, Ind.: Anchor House, 2007).
6. Knabb, Rhome, and Brown, "Tropical Cyclone Report, Hurricane Katrina."
7. Joe Hagan and Joseph T. Hallinan, "Why Levee Breaches Were Late-Breaking News," *Wall Street Journal*, September 12, 2005.
8. U.S. House of Representatives, *A Failure of Initiative, Final Report of the Select Bipartisan Committee to Investigation the Preparation for and Response to Hurricane Katrina* (Washington, D.C.: U.S. Government Printing Office, 2006), www.gpoaccess.gov/ congress/index.html; U.S. Office of the President White House, *The Federal Response to Hurricane Katrina—Lessons Learned* (Washington, D.C.: White House, 2006).
9. Independent Levee Investigation Team (ILIT), *Investigation of the Performance of the New Orleans Flood Protection Systems in Hurricane Katrina on August 29, 2005*

(Berkeley, Calif.: University of California, July 31, 2006), www.ce.berkeley.edu/~new
_orleans; Interagency Performance Evaluation Task Force (IPET), *Performance
Evaluation of the New Orleans and Southeast Louisiana Hurricane Protection System*,
IPET Risk and Reliability Report (Washington, D.C.: U.S. Army Corps of Engineers,
2009), http://nolarisk.usace.army.mil.

10. Hagan and Hallinan, "Why Levee Breaches Were Late-Breaking News."

11. Federal Emergency Management Agency (FEMA), *Hurricane Katrina in the Gulf
Coast: Mitigation Assessment Team Report, Building Performance Observations, Recommendations, and Technical Guidance* (Washington, D.C.: FEMA, July 2006), www
.fema.gov/library/viewRecord.do?id=1857.

12. ILIT, *Investigation of the Performance*; IPET, *Performance Evaluation of the New
Orleans*.

13. Richard D. Knabb, Daniel P. Brown, and Jamie R. Rhome, "Tropical Cyclone Report,
Hurricane Rita, 18–26 September 2005" (National Hurricane Center, NOAA, August
14, 2006); www.nhc.noaa.gov/pdf/TCR-AL182005_Rita.pdf.

14. Ibid.

15. John McQuaid and Mark Schleifstein, *Path of Destruction: The Devastation of New
Orleans and the Coming Age of Superstorms* (New York: Little, Brown, 2006), 334.

16. Government Accountability Office (GAO), *Preliminary Information on Rebuilding
Efforts in the Gulf Coast: Testimony Before the Committee on Homeland Security and Governmental Affairs, U.S. Senate* (Washington, D.C.: U.S. GAO, June 29, 2007), www
.gao.gov.

17. Ibid.

18. R. W. Kates et al., "Reconstruction of New Orleans after Hurricane Katrina: A
Research Perspective—PNAS," *Proceedings, National Academy of Sciences* 103, no. 40
(October 3, 2006): 14653–60.

19. GAO, *Preliminary Information on Rebuilding Efforts in the Gulf Coast*.

20. Donna Fraiche, Testimony of Donna Fraiche, Member of the Board of the Louisiana
Recovery Authority: Before the Subcommittee on Disaster Recovery, Committee on
Homeland Security and Governmental Affairs, U.S. Senate, April 12, 2007, www
.gao.gov.

21. FEMA, "Recovery Planning in Louisiana: 18 Months Along. ESF #14, the Recovery
Support Branch and Emerging Recovery Planning Initiatives. Hurricanes Katrina
and Rita, FEMA-DR-1604/1607-LA" (April 2007).

22. Fraiche, Testimony.

23. Unified New Orleans Plan (UNOP), "Citywide Strategic Recovery and Rebuilding
Plan, Final Draft," April 2007, www.unifiedneworleansplan.org/index.php.

24. FEMA, *Hurricane Katrina in the Gulf Coast*; Kates et al., "Reconstruction of New
Orleans after Hurricane Katrina."

25. UNOP, "Citywide Strategic Recovery and Rebuilding Plan, Final Draft."

26. "Katrina's Diaspora," *New York Times*, August 23, 2006, www.nytimes.com/
imagepages/2006/08/23/us/24katrina_graphic.html.

27. Knabb, Rhome, and Brown, "Tropical Cyclone Report, Hurricane Katrina."

28. Raymond J. Burby, "Hurricane Katrina and the Paradoxes of Government Disaster
Policy: Bringing About Wise Governmental Decisions for Hazardous Areas," *Annals
of the American Academy of Political and Social Science* 604, no. 1 (2006): 171–91.

29. Richard Campanella, "Above-Sea-Level New Orleans: The Residential Capacity of
Orleans Parish's Higher Ground," white paper (New Orleans: Center for Bioenvi-
ronmental Research [CBR] at Tulane and Xavier universities, April 2007), http://
cbr.tulane.edu/PDFs/campanellaaslno.pdf.

30. McQuaid and Schleifstein, *Path of Destruction*.
31. Ibid.
32. Ibid.
33. Michael Grunwald and Susan B. Glasser, "The Slow Drowning of New Orleans," *Washington Post*, October 9, 2005, www.washingtonpost.com/wp-dyn/content/article/2005/10/08/AR2005100801458.html.
34. ILIT, *Investigation of the Performance*; IPET, *Performance Evaluation of the New Orleans*.
35. National Research Council (NRC), *Lessons Learned Between Hurricanes: From Hugo to Charley, Frances, Ivan, and Jeanne–Summary of the March 8, 2005 Workshop of the Disasters Roundtable* (Washington, D.C.: National Academy Press, 2005), www.nap.edu/catalog.php?record_id=11528.
36. Risk Management Solutions (RMS), "Flood Risk in New Orleans: Implications for Future Management and Insurability" (RMS, 2006).
37. Al Naomi and Jack Fredine, *District Works to Tame Ol' Man River*, engineer update (New Orleans: U.S. Army Corps of Engineers, New Orleans District, February 2000), www.hq.usace.army.mil/cepa/pubs/feb00/story14.htm.
38. Campanella, *Above-Sea-Level New Orleans*.
39. FEMA, *Answers to Questions about the National Flood Insurance Program* (Washington, D.C.: FEMA, 2004), www.fema.gov/nfip.
40. U.S. House of Representatives, *Failure of Initiative*; U.S. Office of the President, *Federal Response to Hurricane Katrina–Lessons Learned*.
41. FEMA, *Hurricane Katrina in the Gulf Coast*.
42. FEMA, "National Flood Insurance Program, Policy statistics," 2005, http://bsa.nfipstat.com/reports/1011.htm#LAT.
43. Burby, "Hurricane Katrina and the Paradoxes of Government Disaster Policy."
44. U.S. GAO, Comptroller of the Currency, *Cost, Schedule, and Performance Problems of the Lake Pontchartrain and Vicinity, Louisiana, Hurricane Protection Project* (U.S. GAO, August 31, 1976).
45. Burby, "Hurricane Katrina and the Paradoxes of Government Disaster Policy."
46. UNOP, "Citywide Strategic Recovery and Rebuilding Plan, Final Draft."
47. City Planning Commission (CPC), *Consideration of the Citywide Strategic Recovery & Rebuilding Plan, Final City Planning Commission Report* (City of New Orleans, May 22, 2007).
48. Burby, "Hurricane Katrina and the Paradoxes of Government Disaster Policy."
49. Ibid.
50. Campanella, *Above-Sea-Level New Orleans*.
51. UNOP, "Citywide Strategic Recovery and Rebuilding Plan, Final Draft."
52. Ibid.
53. Shirley Laska and B. H. Morrow, "Social Vulnerabilities and Hurricane Katrina: An Unnatural Disaster in New Orleans," *Marine Technology Society Journal* 40, no. 4 (2006): 16–26.
54. Christina Finch, Christopher T. Emrich, and Susan Cutter, "Disaster Disparities and Differential Recovery in New Orleans," *Population and Environment* (submitted manuscript, 2009).
55. McQuaid and Schleifstein, *Path of Destruction*.
56. UNOP, "Citywide Strategic Recovery and Rebuilding Plan, Final Draft."
57. Elliot Blair Smith, "Wave of Debt Sweeps over New Orleans," *USA Today*, May 1, 2006, nation edition; UNOP, "Citywide Strategic Recovery and Rebuilding Plan, Final Draft," Appendix E: "Preliminary Citywide Financial Assessment."

58. UNOP, "Citywide Strategic Recovery and Rebuilding Plan, Final Draft," Appendix E.
59. UNOP, "Citywide Strategic Recovery and Rebuilding Plan, Final Draft."
60. D. Robert, "Junk Bond Rating Prevents N.O. from Borrowing Recovery Cash," *New Orleans City Business, Dolan Media Newswires*, December 11, 2006.
61. Ibid.
62. UNOP, "Citywide Strategic Recovery and Rebuilding Plan, Final Draft," Appendix E.
63. NRC, *Lessons Learned Between Hurricanes*.
64. Laurie A. Johnson was one of the attendees and felt this way.
65. NRC, *Lessons Learned Between Hurricanes*.
66. John Harrald, "Emergency Management Restructured: Intended and Unintended Outcomes of Actions Taken since 9/11," chapter 6 in *Emergency Management: The American Experience 1900–2005*, 2d ed. (Fairfax, Va.: Public Entity Risk Institute, 2007), 179.
67. U.S. Office of the President White House, "Homeland Security Presidential Directive/HSPD-5," February 28, 2003, www.whitehouse.gov/news/releases/2003/02/20030228-9.html.
68. U.S. House of Representatives, *Failure of Initiative*; Harrald, "Emergency Management Restructured," 167.
69. Harrald, "Emergency Management Restructured," 171.
70. Melanie Gall and Susan Cutter, "2005 Events and Outcomes: Hurricane Katrina and Beyond," chapter 7 in *Emergency Management*, 195.
71. NRC, *Lessons Learned Between Hurricanes*.
72. Ibid.
73. McQuaid and Schleifstein, *Path of Destruction*.
74. NRC, *Lessons Learned Between Hurricanes*.
75. Ibid.
76. McQuaid and Schleifstein, *Path of Destruction*.
77. Ibid.
78. Michael Grunwald and Susan B. Glasser, "Louisiana Goes After Federal Billions," *Washington Post*, sec. A, September 26, 2005.
79. Ibid.
80. U.S. House of Representatives, *Failure of Initiative*; U.S. Office of the White House, *Federal Response to Hurricane Katrina–Lessons Learned*.
81. U.S. GAO, "Disaster Recovery, Past Experiences Offer Insights for Recovering from Hurricanes Ike and Gustav and Other Recent Natural Disasters," report to the Committee on Homeland Security and Governmental Affairs, U.S. Senate (Washington, D.C.: U.S. GAO, September 2008), www.gao.gov.
82. Harrald, "Emergency Management Restructured," 178–79.
83. Gall and Cutter, "2005 Events and Outcomes," 192.
84. Harrald, "Emergency Management Restructured," 180.
85. Jed Horne, *Breach of Faith: Hurricane Katrina and the Near Death of a Great American City* (New York: Random House, 2006); U.S. House of Representatives, *Failure of Initiative*; Forman, *Eye of the Storm*.
86. Michael Brown, *ABC This Week*, ABC-TV, August 27, 2006.
87. U.S. GAO, "Gulf Coast Rebuilding: Observations on Federal Financial Implications," testimony before the Committee on the Budget, U.S. House of Representatives (Washington, D.C.: U.S. GAO, August 2, 2007), www.gao.gov. The appropriations came through P.L. 109-61 on September 2, 2005, and P.L. 109-62 on September 8, 2005.

88. President George W. Bush, "President Bush's Speech in Jackson Square after Hurricane Katrina," televised address to the nation (Jackson Square, New Orleans, September 15, 2005), www.hurricanekatrinanews.org/Bush.html.

CHAPTER 2

1. Jennifer Bayot, "First Estimate Puts Storm's Economic Toll at $100 Billion," *New York Times*, sec. C, September 3, 2005.
2. Michael Grunwald and Susan B. Glasser, "Louisiana Goes after Federal Billions," *Washington Post*, sec. A, September 26, 2005.
3. Ibid.
4. Ibid.
5. Kim Cobb, "Katrina's Aftermath; Spending; Ex-governors Urge Outside Oversight of How Funds Used; Louisiana's Past Is Prompting Fears of Waste and Fraud," *Houston Chronicle*, sec. A, September 14, 2005, 3-star edition.
6. Ibid.; Peter Applebome and Jeremy Alford, "History of Corruption in Louisiana Stirs Fears That Aid Will Go Astray," *New York Times*, sec. A, October 1, 2005, late edition–final edition.
7. Bruce Alpert, "Relief Bill Seen as Grab for Cash; Corrupt La. Past Has Some Fearful," *New Orleans Times-Picayune*, sec. News, October 3, 2005.
8. "Louisiana's Looters," editorial, *Washington Post*, September 27, 2005.
9. Alpert, "Relief Bill Seen as Grab for Cash."
10. Spencer S. Hsu and Terence O'Hara, "A Bush Loyalist Tackles Katrina Recovery: Officials Hope Wealthy Texas Banker Has the Skills to Manage Reconstruction," *Washington Post*, November 21, 2005, A-8.
11. This quickly became known in state government circles. Paul Alexander, "How Karl Rove Played Politics While People Drowned," www.salon.com/books/excerpt/2008/06/06/rove_katrina; Jed Horne, *Breach of Faith: Hurricane Katrina and the Near Death of a Great American City* (New York: Random House, 2006), 357.
12. Patrick Waldron, "Hastert Says Rebuilding Isn't Sensible," *Chicago Daily Herald*, sec. News, September 1, 2005.
13. Daniel Schorn, "New Orleans Is Sinking; New Orleans May Sit in the Gulf of Mexico in 90 Years," *60 Minutes*, November 20, 2005, www.cbsnews.com/stories/2005/11/18/60minutes/main1056304.shtml.
14. Bill Walsh, "Idaho Senator Says Fraud Part of La. Culture; More Lawmakers Join Debate on Storm Relief Plan," *New Orleans Times-Picayune*, sec. National, October 15, 2005.
15. Ibid.
16. Peirce F. Lewis, *New Orleans: The Making of an Urban Landscape*, 2nd ed. (Santa Fe, N.M.: Center for American Places, 2003).
17. John M. Barry, *Rising Tide: The Great Mississippi Flood of 1927 and How It Changed America* (New York: Simon & Schuster, 1997).
18. Brod Bagert, "Hope VI and St. Thomas: Smoke, Mirrors and Urban Mercantilism," master's thesis, London School of Economics, 2002, http://cwsworkshop.org/katrinareader/files/Katrina-II-C-Housing6-Public-31.pdf; Horne, *Breach of Faith*, 357.
19. Jonathan Alter, "How to Save the Big Easy," *Newsweek*, September 12, 2005; Robert Travis Scott, "Racial Tension Mars Initial Discussions: Rebuilding Plans Confront Turf Wars, Political Strife," *New Orleans Times-Picayune*, sec. News, September 18, 2005.

20. The following account comes primarily from two interviews: Andy Kopplin, Baton Rouge, La., October 31, 2006; Sean Reilly, Baton Rouge, La., October 27, 2006.

21. Governor Kathleen Blanco, "Executive Order KBB05-63: Louisiana Recovery Authority" (Governor's Office, State of Louisiana, October 17, 2005).

22. Louisiana Revised Statutes Title 49, 220.1. It also expanded to 33 members. Its primary functions are:

    • Securing funding and other resources
    • Establishing principles and policies for redevelopment
    • Leading long-term community and regional planning efforts
    • Ensuring transparency and accountability

    Louisiana Recovery Authority (LRA), "Louisiana Recovery Authority Quarterly Report, June–August 2006" (Baton Rouge, La., 2006).

23. Reilly, interview; LRA, "Minutes, LRA Board Meeting of October 26, 2005."

24. FEMA, "Emergency Support Function #14—Long-Term Community Recovery and Mitigation Annex," in *National Response Plan* (Washington, D.C.: FEMA, 2004), 6, www.fema.gov/pdf/rebuild/ltrc/nrp_esf14annex.pdf.

25. The LTCR process was discussed publicly on October 7 in Shreveport at the annual meeting of the American Planning Association's Louisiana Chapter, which had added special sessions on post-Katrina recovery planning. The authors, Ken Topping, and Ed Blakely were among the recovery planning experts invited to participate in these special sessions. FEMA began to staff up its LTCR office with consultants and reservists who had planning experience, and this team, with collaboration from the LRA, designed the framework of the LTCR process for Louisiana. At the same time, FEMA prepared a step-by-step guide, *Long-Term Community Recovery Planning Process*, and published it in December. FEMA, "Long-Term Community Recovery Planning Process: A Self-Help Guide" (FEMA, December 11, 2005).

26. In addition, they held one coordinated event: "Louisiana Planning Day," on January 21. More than 3,000 citizens participated in 32 Louisiana Recovery Planning Day open houses held in the 20 affected parishes, five other locations in Louisiana, and 12 out-of-state locations with large evacuee populations. According to the LRA press release following this event, "The parish level planning process will result in the development of initial parish recovery plans, which will be used to set funding priorities for the recovery effort. The final plans will include a community baseline, a needs assessment, a recovery strategy including principles, vision, goals, a set of high value recovery projects and a strategic recovery timeline. LRA, "Louisiana Recovery Planning Day Participants Declare: Safety Is Top Priority."

27. Many local officials were confused and frustrated by the frequent rotations of FEMA staff. Furthermore, the implicit authority of FEMA confused them regarding the purpose of ESF #14; many of them expected substantive help (including funding) from FEMA, rather than just technical advice.

28. For example, the FEMA recovery "storefront" office in Plaquemines Parish opened in November, rapidly increased its staff, and began its work by meeting with approximately 40 key leaders on December 12. They also held several open houses. At its peak, the office had more than 20 people on staff who were from a variety of disciplines. About half of them were locals and several others were on loan from various federal agencies. By late February, the office began to wrap up its work, and by the end of March it completed its project list and shut down. The final

list consisted of 31 projects totaling $877 million, grouped into of the following categories: economic and workforce development, education, flood protection and coastal restoration, community and economic development, human services, public health, public safety, transportation, and infrastructure.

29. The plan detailed 36 recovery projects, totaling $2.1 billion and each ranging in projected cost from $40,000 to $650 million. They were categorized according into high, medium, and low priority. High-priority projects included improving transit, restoring port operations, developing medical schools, redeveloping Canal Street, and promoting business incubators. This document, prepared with no public input, has generally been ignored, although the mayor's office in September briefly considered using it to speed the flow of federal money to Orleans Parish (see Chapter 5); www.louisianaspeaks-parishplans.org/default.cfm.

30. Almost immediately after the storm the American Planning Association and other professional organizations began working to identify a multitude of educational, training, and advocacy avenues through which they might help New Orleans. APA hosted an audio/web conference on September 19, and by October 7 and 8 it had organized a recovery workshop in Shreveport, Louisiana. Ken Topping and APA's Jim Schwab organized the workshop, and Laurie organized a visioning exercise and made a presentation on recovery financing. Ed Blakely, FEMA representatives, and colleagues from Japan also gave presentations, and Rob assisted in the visioning exercise. This turned out to be a rather chaotic event, organized too soon after the storm, but it was a useful opportunity to gather intelligence, present information to local planners, and begin to brainstorm.

31. American Institute of Architects (AIA), "Louisiana Recovery & Rebuilding Conference," 2005, http://lrrc-prod.aia.org/lrrc_agenda; American Planning Association (APA), "Louisiana Recovery and Rebuilding Conference," 2005, www.planning.org/louisianarecovery/index.htm.

32. According to the conference report, 71 percent of attendees had suffered damage to their homes and 7 percent had lost their homes entirely. Of these, 35 percent were displaced somewhere else in the state and 31 percent outside Louisiana. Most were long-term residents: 68 percent of participants had lived in the state more than 20 years. And "they included a wide range of citizens as well as leaders in civic, community, church or faith-based organizations; public officials and government employees; educators and school professionals; healthcare workers; corporate and business representatives; architects, engineers, designers and other planning professionals." Still, the attendees seem to have consisted disproportionately of professionals and elites, as they would necessarily have been those who were able to attend a three-day meeting and have a home or other place to stay in and near New Orleans in early November 2005. APA, "Louisiana Officials to Participate in Recovery and Rebuilding Conference," press release, November 8, 2005, www.planning.org/newsreleases/2005/ftp110805.htm.

33. Louisiana Recovery and Rebuilding Conference, *Starting Point: Report from the Louisiana Recovery and Rebuilding Conference* (AIA, 2005), http://lrrc.aia.org/SiteObjects/files/lrrc_startingpoint_crf.pdf

34. LRA, "Minutes, LRA Board Meeting of December 1, 2005" (Baton Rouge, La.).

35. Most of this account comes from an interview with the president of the Center for Planning Excellence, Elizabeth "Boo" Thomas, Baton Rouge, La., February 5, 2007. Thomas also provided several supporting documents. Key elements of the story were corroborated by interviews with LRA staff members, including Jeff Hebert and Melissa Landry.

36. LRA, "Minutes, LRA Board Meeting of November 11, 2005."

37. See the LRASF website, www.lrasupportfoundation.org.

38. This selection process has always appeared a bit murky to us. Many area planners have whispered that the process was set up for Calthorpe right from the start and cite the quick turnaround on the RFP and hiring decision. Because we have been unable to locate documentation of the proposal review process, it is difficult to refute these suspicions.

39. LRA, "Gov. Blanco and the LRA Introduce La.'s Long-Term Planning Team: Calthorpe, Duany and Gindroz to Lead the Planning Process for South Louisiana" (Baton Rouge, La., January 19, 2006).

40. DPZ had already conducted a charrette in Mississippi the week of October 11–18, at the invitation of Governor Haley Barbour. And UDA had completed a pattern book for Governor Barbour's *Commission on Recovery, Rebuilding and Renewal* in November 2005.

41. To manage the consultants, LRASF hired the Center for Planning Excellence (C-PEX), which, as of January 2006, was the new name for the broadened version of what had previously been Plan Baton Rouge.

42. UDA, *Louisiana Speaks: Pattern Book* (Baton Rouge, La.: LRA, 2006).

43. UDA, *Louisiana Speaks: Planning Toolkit* (Baton Rouge, La.: LRA, 2006).

44. Calthorpe Associates et al., *Louisiana Speaks Regional Plan: Vision and Strategies for Recovery and Growth in South Louisiana* (Baton Rouge, La.: LRA).

45. The timing of the regional vision planning process was confusing to many. The LRA's January 2006 press release announcing the planning teams emphasized the importance of doing a long-range plan, in order to "build a better, safer place," in the words of the governor. Yet, on virtually the same day, citizens were being asked to attend FEMA LTCR meetings in their parishes because the project lists needed to be complete by March. And, as we will see, New Orleans was under great pressure to complete its recovery planning within months, well before the regional vision planning process would be done. The relative purpose of these planning processes was confusing to citizens and professional planners alike. Despite this, however, citizens attended the meetings. In New Orleans in 2006, that was simply what people did: attend first, ask why later. The only time we witnessed public acknowledgment of this contradiction in timing was at a September 2006 meeting of the LRA Long-Range Planning Task Force in New Orleans, at which the chair was pressing the consultants to speed up their process so as to be ready for the state to deliver to Congress as soon as possible, to which they responded that this was already the fastest regional planning effort they had ever done. This is another example of the lack of coordination to be expected in a fast-paced, postdisaster environment: several planning efforts were initiated simultaneously by different entities, and it was simply not possible to design them to all link to one another.

46. LRA, "Governor Blanco, Coaches and Community Leaders Speak Up on Regional Vision" (Baton Rouge, La., January 23, 2007).

47. Louisiana Speaks was largely funded by the LRASF. As of January 2007, the LRASF had paid $1 million to DPZ, $718,000 to UDA, $2.5 million to Calthorpe Associates, and $1.3 million for advertising, communications, and the "One Voice" campaign to develop a unified message to convey to Congress. John Davies, President, Baton Rouge Area Foundation, letter to LRASF contributors, January 29, 2007; Calthorpe Associates et al., *Louisiana Speaks Regional Plan*; LRA, "Minutes, LRA Board of Directors Meeting of May 10, 2007" (Baton Rouge, La.).

CHAPTER 3

1. Metropolitan Policy Program, *New Orleans After the Storm* (Washington, D.C.: Brookings Institution, 2005).
2. Anne Rochell Konigsmark, "New Orleans Universities Seeing Real Homecoming; Students Back in Greater Numbers Than Expected," *USA Today*, sec. News, January 10, 2006, final edition.
3. James Varney and Frank Donze, "N.O. Fires 3,000 City Workers; and That Could Be Just the Start, Nagin Says," *New Orleans Times-Picayune*, sec. News, October 5, 2005, New Orleans edition.
4. Varney and Donze, "N.O. Fires 3,000 City Workers"; City of New Orleans, *One New Orleans 100 Day Report*, www.cityofno.com.
5. Deon Roberts, "Junk Bond Rating Prevents N.O. from Borrowing Recovery Cash," *New Orleans City Business*, December 11, 2006.
6. Federal Emergency Management Agency (FEMA), *Disaster Assistance: A Guide to Recovery Programs*, www.fema.gov/txt/rebuild/ltrc/recoveryprograms229.txt.
7. Metropolitan Policy Program, *New Orleans After the Storm*, 28, 38.
8. New Orleans Planning Assessment Team, *Charting the Course for Rebuilding a Great American City: An Assessment of the Planning Function in Post-Katrina New Orleans* (Chicago: APA, 2005). The APA team was organized under a contract with FEMA; FEMA and APA were in communication immediately in the wake of Katrina, though the team's arrival was delayed by Rita.
9. Robert Travis Scott, "Racial Tension Mars Initial Discussions: Rebuilding Plans Confront Turf Wars, Political Strife," *New Orleans Times-Picayune*, sec. News, September 18, 2005.
10. Frank Donze, "Council Wants Own Rebuilding Panel; with Governor's, Mayor's Committees, That Makes Three," *New Orleans Times-Picayune*, sec. Metro, October 1, 2005.
11. Frank Donze and James Varney, "Nagin Introduces His Own Rebuilding Team for City; Move Comes Day after Governor Unveils Her Version," *New Orleans Times-Picayune*, sec. News, October 1, 2005.
12. We are not aware of any written charter or guidelines for the BNOB commission, nor did its website provide systematic documentation or minutes of its meetings.
13. It is not clear when the ULI visit was arranged, but it may have predated the inception of the BNOB, as ULI's impending business was listed under "old business" in the minutes for the second meeting of BNOB on October 24.
14. Urban Land Institute (ULI), "A Rebuilding Strategy: New Orleans Louisiana" (Washington, D.C.: ULI, 2005); ULI, "A Strategy for Rebuilding New Orleans, Louisiana, November 12–18, 2005; Draft Report for Review" (Washington, D.C.: ULI, 2005).
15. ULI, "A Strategy for Rebuilding New Orleans," 50.
16. Martha Carr, "Rebuilding Should Begin on High Ground, Group Says," *New Orleans Times-Picayune*, sec. National, November 19, 2005.
17. ULI, "A Rebuilding Strategy: New Orleans Louisiana."
18. Frank Donze, "Don't Write Us Off, Residents Warn; Urban Land Institute Report Takes a Beating," *New Orleans Times-Picayune*, sec. National, November 29, 2005.
19. Martha Carr, "Experts Include Science in Rebuilding Equation: Politics Noticeably Absent from Plan," *New Orleans Times-Picayune*, sec. National, September 26, 2005.
20. Working with ACORN and LSU, Ken Reardon from Cornell University organized the Community Forum on Rebuilding New Orleans in Baton Rouge. This hosted

an unusual mixture of planning academics, housing and community development nonprofits, national policy organizations, local politicians, and community
organizers. The conference's daylong bus tour of the devastated city was a highly
memorable event for the participants. Kenneth Reardon et al., "Overcoming the
Challenges of Post-Disaster Planning in New Orleans: Lessons from the ACORN
Housing/University Collaborative" (presented at the 48th Annual Conference of
the Association of Collegiate Schools of Planning, Milwaukee, Wisc., 2007).

21. Bring New Orleans Back Commission (BNOBC), "Bring New Orleans Back Commission Draft Meeting Minutes," October 24, 2005, www.bringneworleansback
.org.

22. Anabelle Garay, "New Orleans Evacuees Attend Town Hall Meeting on Rebuilding," Associated Press, sec. Domestic News, December 6, 2005; Mae Gentry, "Evacuees Frustrated With Nagin; New Orleans Official's Upbeat Talk Irks Many," *Atlanta
Journal-Constitution*, sec. Metro News, December 4, 2005, Home edition.

23. Jeffrey Meitrodt and Frank Donze, "Plan Shrinks City Footprint; Nagin Panel May
Call for 3-Year Test," *New Orleans Times-Picayune*, sec. National, December 14,
2005.

24. Ibid.

25. Although this accurately describes much of today's New Orleans, the question is
whether three years is long enough to assess the long-term future of a neighborhood. Some of the neighborhoods that still suffer from post-Katrina blight and
vacant lots may yet be able to rebuild, as the CDBG and FEMA funds continue to
flow and the biomedical complex generates jobs over the next five to 10 years.

26. Gordon Russell and Frank Donze, "Proposal: Let Residents Decide; Well-Populated
Areas Wouldn't Get Buyout," *New Orleans Times-Picayune*, sec. National, December
19, 2005.

27. Ibid.

28. Allan Turner, "Katrina's Aftermath; Some New Orleans Evacuees Homesick, Some
Sick of Home," *Houston Chronicle*, sec. A, December 9, 2005, three-star edition.

29. Reardon et al., "Overcoming the Challenges of Post-Disaster Planning in New
Orleans."

30. Hovering over this debate was the specter of an upcoming mayoral and city council election. Prior to Katrina, it was generally thought that Nagin would coast to an
easy win in the February 4 mayoral primary. But now all bets were off, including
whether the election could even be held. As the December 14 deadline for candidate
filing approached, many began to argue that it made no sense to hold an election
in a city that, for the moment, did not really exist. As the most important election in the city's history, it would need to proceed carefully and with the full participation of all New Orleanians. This would require not only the repair of voting
machines and polling places but also a massive absentee voting system with some
means of identifying, informing, and verifying displaced residents. As a result, on
December 2, responding to the secretary of state's recommendation that conducting an election so soon after the flood would be onerous, the governor declared
the election would be postponed for as long as eight months, possibly coinciding
with a September 30 statewide election, with the runoff to be held on November 7.
One week later, the governor signed an executive order to this effect even though
several New Orleans citizens had filed a lawsuit against the postponement. The
business community was generally in favor of going ahead with the February 4
election as scheduled because of the importance of selecting officials to lead the city
and the need for certainty about who would be in charge of the recovery. Mayor

Nagin also preferred to have the election sooner because he did not want the city to suffer under continued uncertainty or give opponents too much time to organize. The underlying issues in the debate surrounded race, class, and power: an earlier election would be dominated by the white, wealthier voters who had been able to move back to the city quickly and those who had been able to register their temporary addresses in order to submit absentee ballots. In a December 22 settlement, both parties agreed to an April 29 election date, which put some pressure on New Orleans to appropriately manage the election and provide for absentee voting. At the time of the settlement it was unclear who would eventually run against Nagin, but several potential candidates had already expressed their interest.

See Doug Simpson, "La. Gov Agrees to Postpone Feb. Elections," Associated Press Online, sec. Domestic News, December 2, 2005; Frank Donze and Robert Scott, "Officials May Stay on Past Normal 4 Years; Feb. 4 Election Is Latest Storm Victim," *New Orleans Times-Picayune*, sec. National, December 3, 2005; Adrian Angelette, "Group Files Suit Against Blanco; Residents Say Governor Wrong to Halt Elections," *Baton Rouge Advocate*, sec. B., December 10, 2005, main edition; editorial, "Delaying Elections Only Slows Progress," *New Orleans City Business*, sec. Commentary, December 12, 2005; Robert Travis Scott, "Deal Calls for N.O. Elections by April 29," *New Orleans Times-Picayune*, sec. National, December 23, 2005.

31. Bureau of Governmental Research, "Wanted: A Realistic Development Strategy," www.bgr.org/BGR_Reports_Realistic_Development_Strategy_12_22_05.pdf. BGR is a "private, non-profit, independent research organization dedicated to informed public policy making and the effective use of public resources for the improvement of government in the New Orleans metropolitan area." It analyzes local government policies and finance and, since Katrina, has issued approximately a dozen reports each year.

32. Gordon Russell, "City's Rebuild Plan Draws Criticism; Smaller Footprint Needed, BGR Says," *New Orleans Times-Picayune*, sec. Metro, December 23, 2005.

33. Karen Shalett, "To Raise or To Raze . . . That Is the Question; Experts Look at the Issues Involved in Homeowners' Decisions," *New Orleans Times-Picayune*, sec. Inside Out, December 10, 2005.

34. Adam Nossiter, "Sparing Houses in New Orleans Spoils Planning," *New York Times*, sec. 1, National Desk, February 5, 2006, final edition.

35. Bruce Nolan, "Support Builds for Rebuild Plan; Official Says Blueprint Will Be 'Good Enough,'" *New Orleans Times-Picayune*, sec. National, January 5, 2006.

36. Gwen Filosa, Gordon Russell, and Bruce Eggler, "Lower 9th Ward Activists Chase away Bulldozer Crew; Razing of Homes after Storm Disputed," *New Orleans Times-Picayune*, sec. Metro, January 6, 2006.

37. BNOBC, "Bring New Orleans Back Commission Draft Meeting Minutes."

38. This was the third supplemental appropriation for hurricane relief, P.L. 109-148.

39. U.S. Government Accountability Office (GAO), *Gulf Coast Rebuilding: Observations on Federal Financial Implications, Testimony Before the Committee on the Budget, U.S. House of Representatives*, GAO-07-574T, April 10, 2007; Andrew Kopplin, *Written Testimony of Andrew D. Kopplin, Executive Director of the Louisiana Recovery Authority, Before the U.S. Senate Homeland Security and Governmental Affairs Subcommittee on Disaster Recovery, May 24, 2007*; Bruce Alpert, "$29 Billion Aid Bill Wins Senate OK; $6 Billion in Coastal Restoration Money Is Lost after Alaska Oil Drilling Is Defeated," *New Orleans Times-Picayune*, sec. National, December 22, 2005; U.S. GAO, *Preliminary Information on Rebuilding Efforts in the Gulf Coast: Testimony Before the Committee on Homeland Security and Governmental Affairs, U.S. Senate* (Washington, D.C.,

2007). The first two supplemental appropriations were for emergency expenses: P.L. 109-61 on September 2, 2005, and P.L. 109-62 on September 8, 2005. Much of this assistance was directed to emergency and short-term needs, such as emergency housing, relocation assistance, immediate levee repair, and debris removal.

40. *Louisiana Recovery Corporation Act*, HR 4100, 109th Cong., 1st sess., 2005.

41. Bill Walsh, "Plan Would Buy Homes, Ease Mortgage Payment Fears; Baker's Redevelopment Bill Wins Endorsements," *New Orleans Times-Picayune*, sec. National, November 18, 2005.

42. Bill Walsh, "Plan Would Pay for Ruined Houses; in Baker Bill, Bonds Settle Mortgage Debts," *New Orleans Times-Picayune*, sec. National, December 2, 2005.

43. Gwen Filosa and Michelle Hunter, "Rental Quandary; Scarce Units, Costly Repairs and Surging Rents Hit Tenants and Landlords Hard," *New Orleans Times-Picayune*, sec. National, December 12, 2005.

44. Wallace Roberts & Todd (WRT), "Action Plan for New Orleans: The New American City" (New Orleans: BNOBC Urban Planning Committee, 2006).

45. Ibid., 9, 11.

46. Ibid., 12.

47. Ibid., 13.

48. Ibid., 14.

49. Gordon Russell and James Varney, "New Flood Maps Will Likely Steer Rebuilding; But FEMA Says It's Still Too Soon to Guess What They Will Look Like," *New Orleans Times-Picayune*, sec. National, January 15, 2006.

50. WRT, "Action Plan for New Orleans," 16. The plan further stated that a citywide plan "also can be the place where conflicting desires and tough decisions are fairly and equitably discussed—based on facts."

51. Frank Donze and Gordon Russell, "4 Months To Decide; Nagin Panel Says Hardest Hit Areas Must Prove Viability; City's Footprint May Shrink; Full Buyouts Proposed for Those Forced to Move; New Housing to Be Developed in Vast Swaths of New Orleans' Higher Ground," *New Orleans Times-Picayune*, sec. National, January 11, 2006.

52. Ibid.

53. WRT, "Action Plan for New Orleans," 19.

54. Donze and Russell, "4 Months to Decide."

55. Wade Rathke, "A New Orleans for All," January 12, 2006, www.tompaine.com/articles/2006/01/12/a_new_orleans_for_all.php. Rathke was actually referring to the BNOB plan.

56. Miguel Bustillo, "A Will-to-Rebuild Deadline Proposed for New Orleans," *Los Angeles Times*, sec. A, January 12, 2006.

57. Gordon Russell and Frank Donze, "Rebuilding Proposal Gets Mixed Reception; Critics Vocal, but Many Prefer to Watch and Wait," *New Orleans Times-Picayune*, sec. National, January 12, 2006.

58. Ibid.; Manuel Roig-Franzia, "Hostility Greets Katrina Recovery Plan; Residents Assail Eminent Domain and Other Facets of New Orleans Proposal," *Washington Post*, sec. A., January 12, 2006.

59. Bustillo, "A Will-to-Rebuild Deadline Proposed for New Orleans."

60. Russell and Donze, "Rebuilding Proposal Gets Mixed Reception."

61. WRT, "Action Plan for New Orleans," 3.

62. Roig-Franzia, "Hostility Greets Katrina Recovery Plan."

63. Russell and Donze, "Rebuilding Proposal Gets Mixed Reception."

64. Gary Rivlin, "Anger Meets New Orleans Renewal Plan," *New York Times*, sec. A, January 12, 2006, final edition.
65. Elisabeth Bumiller, "In New Orleans, Bush Speaks with Optimism but Sees Little of Ruin," *New York Times*, sec. A, January 13, 2006, final edition.
66. James Varney, "President Avoids Endorsing Baker Bill; Bush Cites Progress in Recovery, Remains Coy on Category 5 Levees," *New Orleans Times-Picayune*, sec. National, January 13, 2006.
67. Laura Maggi, "Blanco Panel Backs 4-Month Process; State Authority Will Control Purse Strings," *New Orleans Times-Picayune*, sec. National, January 14, 2006.
68. Ibid.
69. Gwen Filosa, "Nagin Says He'll Oppose Building Moratorium; Any Homeowner Can Rebuild, Mayor Vows to Residents During Lakeview Appearance," *New Orleans Times-Picayune*, sec. National, January 22, 2006.
70. Maggi, "Blanco Panel Backs 4-Month Process."
71. Russell and Donze, "Rebuilding Proposal Gets Mixed Reception."
72. WRT, "Action Plan for New Orleans."
73. We have spoken to Kroloff and Manning about this and have no doubt they prepared the systematic work plan they described. But it is also true that they never distributed this document. We know of no one who has seen it, and the city's planning community was full of rumors at the time regarding the plan's cost, the individuals designated to lead the planning teams, and how the process would roll out.
74. Gordon Russell and Frank Donze, "Planners Anticipate a Better City; but Residents Must Guide Rebuilding," *New Orleans Times-Picayune*, sec. National, January 22, 2006.
75. Ibid.
76. Ibid. In fact, Kroloff's stay in New Orleans was short. In September 2007, he took a new position in Michigan. Furthermore, in contrast with the quotes in the January 2006 *Times-Picayune* article, he subsequently lamented to one of the authors in 2007 that New Orleans squandered a great opportunity in 2006 because world-class architect-planners were prepared to offer free help in redesigning the city and were turned down in favor of local teams.
77. Jed Horne, *Breach of Faith: Hurricane Katrina and the Near Death of a Great American City* (New York: Random House, 2006), 342–43.
78. Bill Walsh, "Louisiana Feeling Shortchanged; Mississippi's Clout Gives Its Residents an Edge," *New Orleans Times-Picayune*, sec. National, January 20, 2006; Emily Wagster Pettus, "Barbour: Miss. Could Owe Hundreds of Millions of Katrina," Associated Press, January 4, 2006; Emily Wagster Pettus, "Barbour Says Grant Proposal Crucial to Coast Homeowners," Associated Press, December 18, 2005. In fact, the basic structure of Mississippi's program had been decided much earlier, prior to the congressional approval of the funding bill.
79. Bill Walsh, "White House Against Baker Bailout Bill; Bush Point Man Says Block Grants Enough," *New Orleans Times-Picayune*, sec. National, January 25, 2006.
80. Frank Donze, Gordon Russell, and Laura Maggi, "Buyouts Torpedoed, Not Sunk; Leaders Still Looking for Ways to Rebuild," *New Orleans Times-Picayune*, sec. National, January 26, 2006; Bill Walsh, "Ball Now in La. Court, Bush Says; State Needs a Plan for Recovery, He Says," *New Orleans Times-Picayune*, sec. National, January 27, 2006.
81. Ibid.
82. Donze, Russell, and Maggi, "Buyouts Torpedoed, not Sunk."

83. Keith Darce, "New Orleans Has Plan, Nagin Says; Strategy for Rebuilding Ready to Be Released Soon," *New Orleans Times-Picayune*, sec. Metro, January 28, 2006.
84. Horne, *Breach of Faith*, 345–46.
85. Bill Walsh, "No New Promises for N.O. from Bush; Speech Focuses on Foreign Policy, Addiction to Oil," *New Orleans Times-Picayune*, sec. National, February 1, 2006; Elisabeth Bumiller and Adam Nagourney, "Bush, Resetting Agenda, Says U.S. Must Cut Reliance on Oil," *New York Times*, sec. A, February 1, 2006, final edition.
86. Donald E. Powell, "Rebuilding Wisely," *Washington Post*, sec. A, February 2, 2006.
87. Horne, *Breach of Faith*.
88. Ed Anderson and Robert Travis Scott, "'It's Time to Play Hardball'; Blanco Rebukes Bush, Challenges Lawmakers," *New Orleans Times-Picayune*, sec. National, February 7, 2006.
89. Gordon Russell, Frank Donze, and Laura Maggi, "Buyout in Works; Five Parish Leaders Agree to Make Thousands Whole; First Phase of Voluntary Program Focuses on Owner-Occupied Homes," *New Orleans Times-Picayune*, sec. National, February 13, 2006.
90. Walsh, "Louisiana Feeling Shortchanged"; Pettus, "Barbour: Miss. Could Owe Hundreds of Millions of Katrina"; Pettus, "Barbour Says Grant Proposal Crucial."
91. Walsh, "Louisiana Feeling Shortchanged." Louisiana officials later became much more publicly explicit about the disparity, e.g., *Written Testimony of Walter Leger, Member of the Board of the Louisiana Recovery Authority, Before the U.S. House of Representatives Financial Services Committee*, February 6, 2007, http://financialservices.house.gov/pdf/htleger020607.pdf.
92. Ibid.
93. Ibid.
94. James Dao and Christopher Drew, "More U.S. Aid Will Be Sought for Louisiana," *New York Times*, sec. A, February 16, 2006, final edition.
95. Ibid.
96. Bill Walsh, "Bush to Seek $4.2 Billion More for La.; Proposal May Provide $150,000 per Home," *New Orleans Times-Picayune*, sec. National, February 16, 2006.
97. Ibid.
98. Gordon Russell and Laura Maggi, "La. Leaders Agree New Aid Should Be Spread Around; Nagin Says Homeowner Grants Could Start Flowing in 2 Months," *New Orleans Times-Picayune*, sec. National, February 17, 2006.
99. Ibid.
100. Gordon Russell, "6 Months Later, Recovery Gaining Focus; City May Be Near Turning Point," *New Orleans Times-Picayune*, sec. National, February 26, 2006.
101. Gordon Russell, "Nagin Panel to Hold Final Meeting; Next Phase to Focus on Residents' Visions," *New Orleans Times-Picayune*, sec. Metro, February 28, 2006.
102. Coleman Warner and Keith Darce, "Locals Not Waiting to Be Told What to Do; Neighborhoods Grab Building Bull by Horns," *New Orleans Times-Picayune*, sec. National, March 13, 2006.
103. Ibid.
104. These come primarily from our conversations with Andy Kopplin, Ray Manning, John Beckman, and Ralph Thayer, which, in turn, are based on their conversations with other involved parties.
105. Frank Donze, "Rebuild, but at Your Own Risk, Nagin Says; Recommendations from BNOB Come with Warnings and Worries," *New Orleans Times-Picayune*, sec. National, March 20, 2006; Joe Gyan Jr., "Nagin Rejects Limits on Rebuilding," *Baton Rouge Advocate*, March 21, 2006, main edition.

106. Donze, "Rebuild, but at Your Own Risk."

107. Sally Forman, *Eye of the Storm: Inside City Hall During Katrina* (Bloomington, Ind.: Author House, 2007).

108. Russell and Donze, "Rebuilding Proposal Gets Mixed Reception."

CHAPTER 4

1. Rob's first research visit to New Orleans was in February 2006. His goal was to get as close as possible to the center of planning decision making, to experience firsthand the challenges of creating planning strategies in such an uncertain and overwhelming environment. He met several local planners and was a guest at Jane Brooks's planning studio at the University of New Orleans. He spoke with key players at FEMA, the City Planning Commission, and the Bring New Orleans Back Commission. He observed that no one was fully cognizant of the decisions being made around them. Earlier studies had not fully prepared him for the realization that the chaos or "fog of war" after large disasters can extend for months into the recovery process. This was to continue in New Orleans for at least another year, making research challenging.

2. Kevin McCarthy et al., "The Repopulation of New Orleans After Hurricane Katrina" (RAND Gulf States Policy Institute, 2006), www.rand.org; Gordon Russell, "Comeback in Progress: Formal Numbers Are Hard to Come by, But One Thing's Certain: New Orleans' Population Is Coming Back More Quickly Than Expected," *New Orleans Times-Picayune*, January 1, 2006; Gordon Russell, "Exodus May Be Ebbing, Data Show; Fewer Forwarding Mail out of Region," *New Orleans Times-Picayune*, May 4, 2006; Coleman Warner, "Census Tallies Katrina Changes; but the Changing New Orleans Area Is a Moving Target," *New Orleans Times-Picayune*, June 7, 2006.

3. City of New Orleans, Mayor's Office of Communications, "Situation Report for New Orleans" (February 21, 2006), www.cityofno.com.

4. UNOP, "Citywide Strategic Recovery and Rebuilding Plan," Final Draft, Appendix E: "Preliminary Citywide Financial Assessment."

5. City of New Orleans, *One New Orleans: 100 Day Report*. The city also used these funds and insurance proceeds to create its own local revolving fund to start projects that it could then pay back with federal reimbursements when they came. Both the city's charter and state law require that funds be available before beginning work on capital projects.

6. Russell, "Comeback in Progress."

7. Ibid.

8. Anne Rochell Konigsmark, "New Orleans Universities Seeing Real Homecoming; Students Back in Greater Numbers Than Expected," *USA Today*, January 10, 2006.

9. City of New Orleans, Mayor's Office of Communications, "Situation Report for New Orleans" February 21, 2006; Jaquettta White, "Harrah's Capitalizes on Loyalty to Line Up Staffing to Resume 24/7 Operations Today," *New Orleans Times-Picayune*, February 17, 2006.

10. Jeff Duncan, "The Good Times Roll Again in New Orleans, as Carnival Is Deemed a Critical Success," *New Orleans Times-Picayune*, March 2, 2006.

11. Adam Nossiter, "New Orleans Election Hinges on Race and Not Rebuilding," *New York Times*, April 4, 2006.

12. Frank Donze and Gordon Russell, "Forman Runs Distant Third; Runoff Set for May 20," *New Orleans Times-Picayune*, April 23, 2006.

13. Coleman Warner, "Candidates Playing It Safe on Land Use; Nagin and Landrieu Are Equally Vague," *New Orleans Times-Picayune*, May 13, 2006.

14. Ibid.

15. Gordon Russell, Frank Donze, and Michelle Krupa, "It's Nagin; 'It's Time for Us to Be One New Orleans,'" *New Orleans Times-Picayune*, May 21, 2006.

16. Some diaspora voters also were bused in from Houston. Peter Whoriskey, "Nagin Is Reelected in New Orleans," *Washington Post*, May 21, 2006.

17. Frank Donze and Michelle Krupa, "Nagin Upbeat after Win; Victor, in a Conciliatory Mood, Says He's Ready for Rebuilding," *New Orleans Times-Picayune*, May 22, 2006.

18. Gordon Russell and Frank Donze, "Planners Anticipate a Better City; but Residents Must Guide Rebuilding," *New Orleans Times-Picayune*, January 22, 2006.

19. Ibid.

20. Ibid.

21. Vien The Nguyen, personal interview, New Orleans East, March 23, 2007.

22. Much of this section comes from an interview with Paul Lambert at his office in New Orleans, October 26, 2006, as well as a follow-up telephone interview on August 18, 2008.

23. Council of the City of New Orleans, *Motion M-05-592*, 2005.

24. Bruce Eggler, "Planning Contract Process under Fire," *New Orleans Times-Picayune*, May 9, 2006.

25. Coleman Warner and Keith Darce, "Locals Not Waiting to Be Told What to Do; Neighborhoods Grab Building Bull by Horns," *New Orleans Times-Picayune*, March 13, 2006.

26. Bruce Eggler, "N.O. Is Paying Consultants to Help Neighborhoods Plan; Advisers Will Work to Build Consensus," *New Orleans Times-Picayune*, April 10, 2006.

27. Ibid.

28. Warner and Darce, "Locals Not Waiting to Be Told What to Do."

29. Ibid.

30. This account comes primarily from interviews with Sean Reilly (October 27, 2006, in Baton Rouge), Donna Fraiche (February 8, 2007, in New Orleans), Andy Kopplin (October 31, 2006, in Baton Rouge; August 20, 2008, via telephone), Darren Walker (August 31, 2007, via telephone), Steven Bingler (September 10, 2006, in Poplarville, Miss.), Keith Twitchell (June 12, 2006, in New Orleans), Steve Villavaso (June 16, 2006, in New Orleans), and Carey Shea (June 5, 2007, in New Orleans).

31. GNOF operated out of the BRAF offices in Baton Rouge in the weeks after Katrina, at the same time that BRAF created the LRASF to fund the LRA's planning efforts.

32. These funds also supported New Orleans housing and community development activities by the Local Initiatives Support Corporation, Enterprise Foundation, Habitat for Humanity, and the Urban League of Greater New Orleans. Rockefeller had also helped to fund the Spike Lee film about New Orleans, *When the Levees Broke*. Rockefeller Foundation, "The Rockefeller Foundation Commits $3 Million for Housing and Economic Redevelopment in Response to Hurricane Katrina," news advisory, September 8, 2006.

33. These principles were best articulated in the February 2006 LRA Quarterly Report: "The LRA has focused on four main priorities: Securing funding and other resources, Establishing principles and policies for redevelopment, Leading long-term community and regional planning efforts, Ensuring transparency and accountability." LRA, "Louisiana Recovery Authority Initial Quarterly Report, February 2006" (Baton Rouge, La., 2006).

34. Bingler believes it started when Ralph Thayer, the retired dean of the UNO College of Urban and Public Affairs who was then working with FEMA, and Yolanda Rodriguez, director of the City Planning Commission, suggested that they start such sessions.
35. At some point during the previous month, Reed Kroloff—Manning's cochair—reduced his role in leading the neighborhood planning process.
36. The GNOF board has approximately 30 members, so it would be an unwieldy organization to guide the plan; hence the CSF, as a smaller task-oriented subset of GNOF board members.
37. It is unclear why Rockefeller chose this particular moment to officially commit its funds. Perhaps it wanted to make a statement prior to the election. Perhaps the negotiations were at an impasse that required Rockefeller to make a public statement to assure all parties that it was committed to following through. Perhaps this was the earliest moment at which GNOF felt prepared to receive the funds. Rockefeller Foundation, "The Rockefeller Foundation to Provide $3.5 Million to Accelerate Recovery Planning for the City of New Orleans," news advisory, April 20, 2006.
38. Janet R. Howard, "City Council Planning Contract Is Out of Bounds" (Bureau of Governmental Research, New Orleans, May 8, 2006).
39. Ibid.
40. Eggler, "Planning Contract Process under Fire"; Oliver M. Thomas and Eddie L. Sapir, "Planning Contract Was Awarded Appropriately," letter to editor, *New Orleans Times-Picayune*, May 11, 2006.
41. Janet R. Howard, "View Contract for Yourself," *New Orleans Times-Picayune*, May 15, 2006. Notably, the *Times-Picayune* account of the BGR report referred to the mayor's BNOB planning process as if it were dead ("failed to get off the ground") and replaced entirely by the council's Lambert process, although this was not yet quite true.
42. To allow the planning commission to issue the RFQ would have required the mayor's approval, which, according to our sources, he provided.
43. Coleman Warner, "State and City to Talk Recovery; Neighborhoods Begin Crafting Their Plans," *New Orleans Times-Picayune*, May 27, 2006.
44. Ibid.
45. Coleman Warner, "N.O. Plan's Chief Critical of Delay; He Warns City Could Lose Control to State," *New Orleans Times-Picayune*, June 2, 2006.
46. New Orleans Community Support Foundation (CSF), "Request for Qualifications for City-wide Planning Teams New Orleans, Louisiana" (GNOF, June 5, 2006).
47. Ibid., 1, 2.
48. Ibid., 8.
49. Ibid., 3.
50. New Orleans CSF, "City-wide and Neighborhood Planning Teams Request for Qualifications—Questions and Answers," June 15, 2006.
51. The RFQs for the Rockefeller-funded planning process were issued on June 5; applications were due on June 26. Ken Topping was on the selection committee. At the end of the week, some of the prospective teams contacted Laurie. As a result, she was included on two teams, including Steve Villavaso's winning one, so Ken temporarily ceased contact with us.
52. This was confirmed to us a month later by another highly credible inside source, who just happened to be sitting next to Laurie on an airplane. This all seems curious to us, however, for at least two reasons. First, given that planning funds were

in such short supply, how would the mayor pay to complete this effort? Second, and more important, why would the LRA accept the project list, given that it had clearly asked for a transparent public process and now had arranged to fund just that? Perhaps the mayor thought that he could bluff the LRA into backing down, accepting the BNOB process as having had sufficient participation (arguably more than any other parish), gain the support of the city council in having stared down Baton Rouge, and get those federal recovery dollars rolling.

53. The mayor certainly was not taking the kind of active leadership role that Kobe's Mayor Sasayama had in the aftermath of the M6.8 earthquake of January 17, 1995. Sasayama had been a planner charged with helping rebuild Kobe after World War II. He knew the city intimately and had a vision for the reconstruction from the morning the earthquake occurred; he literally lived in city hall for two months as his staff hammered out a reconstruction plan.

54. LRA, "Minutes, Louisiana Recovery Authority Board of Directors Meeting" (Baton Rouge, La., June 15, 2006). The description of this meeting is also based on our notes.

55. Timothy Green and Robert Olshansky, "Home Owner Decisions, Land Banking, and Land Use Change in New Orleans after Hurricane Katrina," working paper (Cambridge, Mass.: Lincoln Institute of Land Policy, May 2009).

56. This was, in fact, the beginning of another long and complicated saga, which is beyond the scope of this book. Suffice to say that we still find it disappointing that it took more than nine months for the federal government to provide a basic level of recovery funding for this catastrophe-stricken state. Nor did it surprise us that the program became so challenging to implement; it would have been better for everyone had it started sooner.

57. Coleman Warner, "Various Recovery Planners Might Coalesce; LRA Awaits Assent from Nagin, Council," *New Orleans Times-Picayune*, June 16, 2006.

58. The description of the meeting comes from our notes at the time. We would like to express our appreciation to Kimberly Solet from the Center for Hazard Assessment, Response and Technology at the University of New Orleans, who provided her description of the meeting, which corroborated ours.

59. This clarification regarding the fundamental purpose of the plan—to guide the city's CDBG funds—was articulated not by the convenors of the meeting but by Laurie and Jeff Thomas in comments to the group.

60. In fact, the City Planning Commission initiated a master plan process shortly after adoption of this plan in 2007.

61. Adam Nossiter, "In New Orleans, Money Is Ready but a Plan Isn't," *New York Times*, June 18, 2006.

62. Staff reports, "Progress Cited on Recovery Planning; Process Halfway There, N.O. Officials Affirm," *New Orleans Times-Picayune*, June 21, 2006.

63. Coleman Warner, "Council Wants Its Planners Retained; Foundation Shouldn't Halt Work, Officials Say," *New Orleans Times-Picayune*, July 1, 2006.

64. Ibid.

65. Coleman Warner, "N.O. Blazes Trail for Grant Money; City and State Agree on Planning Process," *New Orleans Times-Picayune*, July 6, 2006.

66. "Mayor C. Ray Nagin today announced the Unified New Orleans Neighborhood Plan, an agreement between his office, the New Orleans City Council, local leaders and the Louisiana Recovery Authority to advance a single comprehensive land use planning process for the City of New Orleans. The planning process will be implemented under the auspices of the New Orleans Community Support Foundation

(NOCSF), a newly established public/private partnership." Mayor's Press Office, City of New Orleans, "Mayor, City Council and Civic Leaders Reach Accord; 'Unified New Orleans Neighborhood Plan' to Guide Rebuilding Process for City" (City of New Orleans, July 5, 2006).

67. Ibid.

68. Warner, "N.O. Blazes Trail for Grant Money." In retrospect, it was perhaps naively optimistic to assume that the money would be in the hands of home owners in such a short time. In mid-July, the LRA announced an initial test of 500 home owners. As it learned the realities of the process, it slowly began to ramp up in order to accommodate the 90,000 home owners who had registered to date (eventually, twice this many registered). This was easily the largest public housing program ever attempted in this country, and so no one had any experience to guide them as to what would be needed to accomplish the task and how long it would take.

69. Following our June visit, Laurie was invited to join two of the citywide teams submitting qualifications. One of her teams was invited to be interviewed on July 18.

70. This situation was admittedly a bit uncomfortable for us because of our long relationship with Ken Topping. But Topping, once officially selected as a member of the team, ceased any substantive communication with us until the selection was complete. Furthermore, he was honest with the committee about his past working relationship with Laurie, this relationship involved no potential financial gain for him, and he was but one advisory voice on the committee. Bingler later reported that the committee was most impressed by Laurie's presentation, irrespective of Topping's having worked with her.

71. Staff, "Nonprofit Pushes New Orleans Planning Process," *New Orleans City Business*, sec. News, July 25, 2006.

72. Coleman Warner, "Teams OK'd for Recovery Plan; N.O. Neighborhoods to Get Tech Support," *New Orleans Times-Picayune*, sec. Metro, July 22, 2006.

73. *Times-Picayune* staff, "Council Forum Targets Recovery; Joint Effort Named Unified N.O. Plan," *New Orleans Times-Picayune*, sec. Metro, July 2006.

74. Staff, "Nonprofit Pushes New Orleans Planning Process."

75. Some of the confusion reflected some disagreement within the evolving UNOP team with respect to the overall structure of the planning teams. Some members felt that they had to plan at the neighborhood level, consistent with the expectations of the previous 10 months, and that district plans would be too large to address the level of detail needed. Others, however, such as the City Planning Commission staff, felt that it would be impossible to do scores of neighborhood plans, especially in such a short time. A more feasible way to create a citywide plan would be to combine 13 district plans based on the districts used in the city's master plan. The consultant review panel, which included Yolanda Rodriguez, had realized that the neighborhood plans would need to be rolled up into district plans first. Thus, they distinguished consultants qualified to be district planners from those best suited to work at the neighborhood scale. But at the time of the first City Park meeting, these concepts were still fluid.

76. In fact, questions about neighborhood borders were probably distracting and premature and proliferated here because of the lack of structure. How to delineate neighborhood boundaries was really not such a critical issue at this point. It was generally recognized that the existing definitions of the 73 neighborhoods were insufficient, since the boundaries no longer represented residents' perceptions of the city and there were now at least 180 identifiable neighborhood organizations. But what mattered was that there would be 13 district plans. These might well

include neighborhood-scale discussions and focused analyses of some particular neighborhoods. But, under the umbrella of a district plan, neighborhoods would obviously coordinate meetings and communicate with one another. Some neighborhood meetings could even have overlapping boundaries.

77. Paul Lambert, advertisement, *New Orleans Times-Picayune*, August 3, 2006, A22.
78. Ibid.
79. Coleman Warner, "Council Defends Plan for Recovery; Members Brush off Consultant's Criticism," *New Orleans Times-Picayune*, August 4, 2006; Stephanie Grace, "No Place for Egos," *New Orleans Times-Picayune*, August 6, 2006. We agree that Lambert probably felt disrespected by the LRA. He and his consultant team may have felt insulted by the release of the UNOP RFQ in June, with its goal of bringing "world class planners" to town when what was really needed were sensitive neighborhood planners who would listen to the residents. The appropriateness of Lambert's team for this role could have been recognized earlier in the year, and Lambert was still annoyed that he had never been able to meet with LRA staff at that time, so they could agree on how the council's planning effort could meet the state's goals.
80. It was probably Lambert's mistake to assume that this guidance, obtained from FEMA staff several months earlier, was authoritative. In fact, the New Orleans ESF #14 team in February and March was as confused as anyone at that time regarding the planning requirements for New Orleans to be able to access federal recovery funds. ESF #14 was a joint federal-state effort, with FEMA providing assistance to help Louisiana make recovery decisions. The policy decisions about what would or would not count resided with the LRA, and ultimately the decisions about funding requirements resided with Donald Powell and the White House. Those decisions had been made over the intervening months, and they called for a citywide plan.
81. Warner, "Council Defends Plan for Recovery."
82. Coleman Warner, "Consultant Slams Recovery Plan; It Delays Critical Grants, He Says," *New Orleans Times-Picayune*, August 3, 2006.
83. Steve Sabludowsky, "New Orleans Planners Call Cease Fire," *Bayou Buzz*, August 4, 2006, www.bayoubuzz.com; Grace, "No Place for Egos."
84. Coleman Warner, "Planner Seeks Chords of Unity; Major Grants for N.O. Depend on Consensus," *New Orleans Times-Picayune*, August 7, 2006.
85. Willard-Lewis got political mileage from her key role in standing up for her constituents. If UNOP could not get off the ground, so the reasoning went, then perhaps the LRA would simply give in and accept the Lambert plan as being sufficient, thereby finally putting BNOB's "viability" test to rest and unleashing federal funds focused on the most damaged areas. But she was not the only one who found it convenient to delay. Other councilmembers, although willing to accept UNOP, were generally pleased with the Lambert process and would have been glad to have their neighborhood plans anointed as the official New Orleans recovery plan, so that the city could get its money and move on.
86. A December 1993 article, for example, when Copelin was at the peak of his political power as speaker pro tem of the state house of representatives, describes both his power and his controversies (Dawn Ruth, "Profiles: The New Orleans Mayoral Race—Sherman Copelin," *New Orleans Times-Picayune*, December 30, 1993). He began his political life as "the unofficial leader of SOUL, an organization that groomed some of the city's most influential politicians." He was a close confidant of Governor Edwards, who subsequent to the article was convicted and imprisoned. The article succinctly states, "Even though friends and foes alike regard Copelin as

one of the most effective and diligent members of the House, only Edwards equals his flair for unfavorable attention." In the 1970s he testified under immunity that he had received a "consultant's fee" from the head of a family planning center who was later convicted of fraud. In the 1990s a substance abuse clinic he partly owned was under investigation for questionable practices. Copelin was powerful, wealthy, and mysterious.

87. LRA, "Minutes Louisiana Recovery Authority, Board of Directors Meeting" (Baton Rouge, La., August 10, 2006). One observer reported to us that they spoke for two hours, effectively holding the board hostage, insisting that the LRA allocate the recovery funds immediately. They suggested using the ESF #14 report for Orleans Parish as a basis to move forward. Some in the city had advocated submitting the city's ESF #14 project lists—which had been developed by FEMA staffers in February and March, based largely on BNOB and other New Orleans planning documents—to the LRA and insisted that the board approve them as meeting the parish planning requirement, thereby circumventing the other ongoing planning processes. This would bring both UNOP and the Lambert process to immediate halts. The minutes are not explicit about the board's response to this request, other than to say that Norman Francis and Kim Boyle discussed the New Orleans planning process to date and that Cynthia Willard-Lewis "emphasized the need for rebuilding rather than excessive planning."

   On its face, the request to move forward with the ESF #14 documents seems reasonable. FEMA paid for them, and the New Orleans project lists follow the same format as the planning documents from the other parishes. But this assumes that the LRA had approved the ESF #14 plans from other parishes as a basis for allocating the state's remaining CDBG funds. It had not, because it was not clear to what extent any of the plans represented the result of a well-reasoned, systematic, participatory process. In fact, the LRA would not accept any of these plans until mid-2007, after it had first approved the plan for the most important jurisdiction affected by the storm: Orleans Parish. Thus, it was premature for it to accept the Orleans ESF #14 plan at this point. Indeed, by its actions in promoting UNOP and asking for a data-driven plan with extensive public involvement, the LRA had clearly signaled that the ESF #14 project list for Orleans Parish was totally unsuited to this function.

88. In fact, Blake was the SCLCs first full-time field secretary, working closely with Martin Luther King Jr. in 1960, and so he had little patience to be on the receiving end of a sermon by Steele.

89. Michelle Millhollon, "Critics: Urgency Lacking in N.O.," *Baton Rouge Advocate*, August 11, 2006.

90. The most important thing to remember is that, given that all the fuss was about accessing federal funds, the most critical player was still the White House. The underlying reality for Louisiana, from September 2005 onward, was a continuing process of groveling for funds and seeking support from both the White House and Congress. Many in New Orleans chose to point fingers at Baton Rouge, but there is no doubt that the more potent adversary was in Washington. The LRA's goal was to play by Washington's rules in order to curry favor. And Donald Powell was the White House's agent in New Orleans—it was he who had nixed the Baker bill, fought for presidential approval of the additional $4.2 billion in CDBG funds, and insisted on a coherent plan as a basis for providing funding. Powell particularly wanted New Orleans to speak with one voice. To avoid getting mixed up in the city's internal politics, he wanted the various parties to sort out their differences

and present Washington with a single plan. So, in effect, Voelker—in pressing for a unified, citywide plan—was actually representing Powell. He had become acquainted with Powell over the preceding months and therefore had a clear sense of what type of planning arrangement would be acceptable.

91. "Memorandum of Understanding Between the City of New Orleans, New Orleans City Council, City Planning Commission, Greater New Orleans Foundation and New Orleans Community Support Foundation," August 28, 2006.

92. Coleman Warner, "Recovery Planning Pact Signed; 'Unified Plan' Is Designed to Ease Conflicts," *New Orleans Times-Picayune*, August 29, 2006.

93. Gordon Russell, "Entergy Data Shed Light on N.O.'s Population; with 219,000 Estimated Back, City Nears Half Its Prestorm Level," *New Orleans Times-Picayune*, August 23, 2006.

94. James Howell, "A Continuing Storm: The On-Going Struggles of Hurricane Katrina Evacuees" (August 2006), http://appleseeds.net.

95. But more than 30,000 families would be displaced in the long term, depending upon federal housing assistance from FEMA and then HUD and still unable to return to New Orleans before the programs ended in August 2009. U.S. Housing and Urban Development (HUD), Disaster Housing Assistance Program, Greater New Orleans Area, 2009, www.dhapneworleans.org/index.html.

96. Charles C. Mann, "The Long, Strange Resurrection of New Orleans," *Fortune*, August 21, 2006.

97. Ibid.

98. Amy Liu, "Building a Better New Orleans: A Review of and Plan for Progress One Year after Hurricane Katrina" (Washington, D.C.: Brookings Institution, Metropolitan Policy Program, August 2006).

99. Amy Liu, Matt Fellowes, and Mia Mabanta, "Special Edition of the Katrina Index: A One-Year Review of Key Indicators of Recovery in Post-Storm New Orleans" (Washington, D.C.: Brookings Institution, Metropolitan Policy Program, August 2006).

100. Coleman Warner, "Progess Report; Area's Rebound Slow but Steady," *New Orleans Times-Picayune*, August 26, 2006.

101. Liu, Fellowes, and Mabanta, "Special Edition of the Katrina Index."

102. Warner, "Progess Report; Area's Rebound Slow but Steady."

103. Rebecca Mowbray, "Wounded N.O. Economy Remains in Coma; Experts Say It's Still Too Early for Full Prognosis," *New Orleans Times-Picayune*, August 25, 2006.

104. Rebecca Mowbray, "Post-Katrina New Orleans Proves Pricey; Some Say New Economic Realities Will Reshape the City Permanently," *New Orleans Times-Picayune*, August 25, 2006.

105. Liu, Fellowes, and Mabanta, "Special Edition of the Katrina Index."

106. Mowbray, "Wounded N.O. Economy Remains in Coma."

107. Liu, "Building a Better New Orleans."

108. Leslie Eaton, "Failed Shops and Faded Charm Are Dual Worry in New Orleans," *New York Times*, August 25, 2006.

109. Liu, Fellowes, and Mabanta, "Special Edition of the Katrina Index."

110. Mowbray, "Wounded N.O. Economy Remains in Coma."

111. Gordon Russell and Bruce Eggler, "Financial Clouds Lift Somewhat for N.O.; New Federal Loan, Tax Uptick Ease Crisis," *New Orleans Times-Picayune*, August 28, 2006.

112. Alpert, "Bush Repeats Pledge to Aid Recovery; but Process Takes Patience, He Says."

113. Richard Wolf, "Katrina Cost Continues to Swell; Gulf States Likely to Get Billions More," *USA Today*, August 22, 2006.

114. Bill Walsh, "Billions in Federal Aid Stuck in System; Money Must Trickle Through Bureaucracy," *New Orleans Times-Picayune*, August 23, 2006.

115. Michelle Roberts, "Nagin Says Bureaucracy Slowing Rebuilding of New Orleans," Associated Press, sec. Domestic News, August 22, 2006; Alpert, "Bush Repeats Pledge to Aid Recovery."

116. FEMA, "Frequently Requested National Statistics Hurricane Katrina—One Year Later," August 21, 2006, www.fema.gov/hazard/hurricane/2005katrina/anniversary_factsheet.shtm.

117. Beginning December 1, 2007, HUD's newly created Disaster Housing Assistance Program (DHAP) replaced the FEMA rental assistance program; it continued until March 2009. In December 2007, there were 40,000 families affected by hurricanes Katrina and Rita in the DHAP. By March 2009 when the DHAP officially ended, 31,000 families were still participating in it. At this time, HUD initiated the Transitional Housing Closeout Program and worked to transition families to self-sufficiency or into HUD's nondisaster (Section 8) housing voucher program by August 31, 2009. U.S. HUD, DHAP.

118. Alpert, "Bush Repeats Pledge to Aid Recovery."

119. FEMA, "Orleans Parish Still Rebuilding One Year after Katrina," August 21, 2006, www.fema.gov/news/newsrelease.fema?id=29074.

120. Roberts, "Nagin Says Bureaucracy Slowing Rebuilding of New Orleans."

121. Liu, "Building a Better New Orleans."

122. Ibid.

123. Walsh, "Billions in Federal Aid Stuck in System." In some cases, recipients chose not to use the loans because of continued uncertainties regarding the business environment.

124. Ibid.

125. John Pope, "Leaders Hopeful about Recovery; but Restoring Coast Is the Key to Security," *New Orleans Times-Picayune*, August 29, 2006.

126. Bruce Eggler, "Blanco Launches Road Home Office on Poydras Street; but Appointments Must Be Made for One-on-One Grant Counseling," *New Orleans Times-Picayune*, August 23, 2006.

CHAPTER 5

1. Lambert Advisory, "New Orleans Neighborhoods Rebuilding Plan," July 2007, http://nolanrp.com. Lambert avoided using teams actively under consideration for the proposed neighborhood planning under BNOB, as that situation had not yet been resolved. Some planning teams were already working in certain neighborhoods, and Lambert simply assigned new planners to the other neighborhoods.

2. Lambert Advisory and SHEDO, "City of New Orleans Neighborhoods Rebuilding Plan, Summary" (Lambert Advisory, October 2006); interview with Paul Lambert, New Orleans, October 26, 2006.

3. Ibid., 6.

4. Ibid., 11. The Neighborhood Planning Guide was adopted by the City Planning Commission in June 2006; a draft version was available starting in March 2006.

5. Ibid., 7

6. Staff, "Rebuild Meetings Set for Displaced; Baton Rouge, Atlanta, Houston to Be Sites," *New Orleans Times-Picayune*, August 17, 2009.

7. Leslie Williams, "Family-friendly Eastern N.O. Seen," *New Orleans Times-Picayune*, August 12, 2006; Leslie Williams, "Eastern N.O. Plan Returns Area to Its Roots; Walkable Town Center, Bike Paths Included," *New Orleans Times-Picayune*, August 13, 2006.

8. Ibid.

9. This discussion is informed in part by interviews with Paul Lambert on October 26, 2006, in New Orleans and on August 18, 2008 via telephone. It is also informed by discussions with Steven Bingler, Carey Shea, and others in New Orleans during and after this time period.

10. One of the Lambert planners, for example, was Steve Villavaso, the lead planning consultant for the UNOP citywide team. Through September, while organizing UNOP, he also kept actively participating as a neighborhood planning consultant for Lambert.

11. Coleman Warner, "Schools, Streets, Trees Top Most Planning Lists," *New Orleans Times-Picayune*, September 23, 2006; Gwen Filosa, "N.O. Neighborhood Plans Unveiled; but Total Price Tag Exceeds $2 Billion," *New Orleans Times-Picayune*, September 24, 2006.

12. Warner, "Schools, Streets, Trees Top Most Planning Lists."

13. Lambert Advisory and SHEDO, "City of New Orleans Neighborhoods Rebuilding Plan, Summary," 12.

14. The college is now the Department of Planning and Urban Studies.

15. Filosa, "N.O. Neighborhood Plans Unveiled."

16. Mayor Nagin had also been recently quoted as saying quite the opposite, suggesting that some neighborhoods would be wise not to rebuild: "New Orleans east is showing some signs [of recovery], but it's so vast, it's going to hit the wall. . . . There's just such a big footprint. I don't think they're going to get the clustering they need. So I think you're going to have little pockets in the east. . . . I've been saying this publicly, and people are starting to hear it: low-lying areas of New Orleans east, stay away from. Lower 9th Ward. I said it in Houston; people are starting to hear it. That's what I'm telling people (in the Lower 9). Move closer to the river. That stuff from Claiborne to the lake—we can't touch that." Gordon Russell, "On Their Own; In the Absence of Clear Direction, New Orleanians Are Rebuilding a Patchwork City," *New Orleans Times-Picayune*, sec. National, August 27, 2006.

17. Fortunately, Jedidiah Horne and Brendan Nee had loaded the plans to their nola-plans.com website, and so they were still publicly accessible during this time period.

18. The final plans consisted of 42 plans covering 47 flooded neighborhoods. (Broadmoor did its own plan, and the 49th neighborhood consisted entirely of a Housing Authority project slated for demolition.)

19. New Orleans City Council, *Motion M 06-460*, October 27, 2006.

20. Pam Radtke Russell, "Council OKs 8% Boost in Utility Rates; Entergy N.O. Deal Dodges Big Increase," *New Orleans Times-Picayune*, October 28, 2006.

21. Edward J. Blakely, Phillip L. Clay, and Diana M. Gonzalez, "City of New Orleans Neighborhoods Rebuilding Plan Peer Review," October 2006.

22. Coleman Warner and Bruce Eggler, "N.O. to Take Requests to LRA; Cash Sought before Submitting City Plan," *New Orleans Times-Picayune*, November 3, 2006.

23. Ibid.

24. This meeting was a curious affair. The wording of the proposed amendment was not evident in supporting materials at the meeting or in the discussions of the councilmembers. It was not clear whether anyone knew what he or she was voting for.

25. Warner and Eggler, "N.O. to Take Requests to LRA."
26. This suggests that the council knew it was just posturing for New Orleans voters, given that the public did not fully appreciate all the funding subtleties. But it was a dangerous game, because New Orleans needed the good will of the LRA, as was about to become evident.
27. Warner and Eggler, "N.O. to Take Requests to LRA."
28. Coleman Warner, "Unprepared Nagin Lets Agency Wait; City Lacks Projects Info for Key Meeting," *New Orleans Times-Picayune*, November 4, 2006.
29. LRA, "Minutes, LRA Board Meeting of November 6, 2006" (Baton Rouge, La., November 6, 2006). This account also derives from a video recording of the meeting.
30. This was the key piece of funding promised by the president back in February, to replace the failed Baker bill and to assuage Louisiana's concerns about not receiving enough in the December 2005 appropriation. That these funds—dating back to the state's first requests for federal aid in the fall of 2005—were still not flowing in the fall of 2006 should have been the biggest news of the LRA board meeting.

CHAPTER 6

1. Most of the information in this chapter comes from our personal experiences, as well as interviews with participants. Where statements can also be supported by publicly available documents, we cite them. Descriptions of meetings come either directly from notes taken at the meeting or from video recordings. Most of the key meetings were filmed by Luisa Dantas, a filmmaker who has generously provided raw footage to us.
2. Laurie began work on the UNOP project in New Orleans on August 14, 2006.
3. Steven Bingler described it this way to the consultant team at the September 6 city-wide team meeting.
4. UNOP, "Community Support Organization Members Announced; Assignments for District and Neighborhood Planning," August 28, 2006.
5. America*Speaks* had been involved in New Orleans as early as November 2005, when it organized the communication for the AIA/APA Louisiana Recovery and Rebuilding Conference. That event sparked Carolyn Lukensmeyer, president of America-*Speaks*, to seek funding and opportunities to ensure that displaced residents would have a voice, and she specifically sought a role in the UNOP process. On August 30, immediately following the official signing of the UNOP MOU, the CSF sent a letter of intent to Lukensmeyer to coordinate "a six-site simultaneous town hall meeting," provided that she could raise the funds to support it. Shortly before the first community congress occurred, they agreed to organize the second community congress according to these terms (but reduced to five cities) and to accomplish it in six weeks' time. In addition, the group agreed, at the last minute, to provide the keypad polling and facilitation for the first community congress on October 28. According to an official at America*Speaks*, the scope of work involved "project management for the Community Congress, directing outreach to ensure diverse participation, leading the design and production of the Congress, managing the logistics, event and technical management of the events, recruiting and training volunteer facilitators, working with the planning teams to frame the content, participating in the communications/media strategy and deployment, managing the multi-site broadcast, setting up the webcast sites, facilitating the event itself, and presenting the results."

It was only after the second congress that they were retained to organize the third and final one.

6. Michelle Krupa, "100 Days in, Nagin to Discuss Progress; 3 Advisers not Sure What Mayor Will Say," *New Orleans Times-Picayune*, September 9, 2006.

7. Editorial, "Nagin's 100 Days," *New Orleans Times-Picayune*, September 13, 2006.

8. Krupa, "100 Days in, Nagin to Discuss Progress."

9. Laura Maggi, "Clinton Delivers Hope, Grant Money to N.O. Area; Ex-President Urges Patience with Process," *New Orleans Times-Picayune*, September 16, 2006.

10. Ibid.

11. David Barron, "A Timeout from the Aftermath: Louisiana Superdome Reopens," *Houston Chronicle*, September 25, 2006; Chris Rose, "Eternal Dome Nation," *New Orleans Times-Picayune*, October 3, 2006; Mark Bradley, "Spin Can't Obscure Vast Devastation in City," *Atlanta Journal-Constitution*, September 24, 2006.

12. Concordia, "Recovery and Rebuilding: Unified New Orleans Plan" (PowerPoint presentation, September 14, 2006).

13. This meant that the product was a list of projects and cost estimates, grouped into three levels of priority.

14. It included the Lambert plan maps from their September 23 presentations, but Lambert had not yet released the narratives, which he had promised to deliver to UNOP within seven to 10 days of this meeting. Because GCR had provided data support for the Lambert plans, all the relevant data were available to the UNOP teams.

15. Fred Schwartz and his team had also been on the ground since early September, which also meant that—unlike the other district teams—they were particularly frustrated by the lack of guidance from the top.

16. UNOP, "Working Paper #1: Anticipated Outcomes, Unified New Orleans Plan for Recovery and Rebuilding," October 5, 2006. This paper articulated the anticipated outcomes of UNOP:

- Providing every neighborhood in New Orleans with a recovery plan, as detailed in the district plans, and identifying infrastructure improvements necessary to implement neighborhood-level recovery
- Justifying the funding and implementation of the recovery projects through the development of a citywide plan based on the citizens' vision for recovery and the desire to rebuild a smarter, stronger, and safer New Orleans
- Encouraging the redesign and reconstruction of the regional hurricane flood protection system to reduce the risk of another disaster like Katrina befalling the city
- Providing information to citizens and investors to make personal and business decisions about recovery and rebuilding
- Achieving better long-term sustainability for the city—that is, to balance the city's long-term capital and operating expenses with its long-term revenue potential

17. Ibid.

18. The same day, no doubt coordinated by the UNOP communication team, a detailed article appeared in the *Times-Picayune*, summarizing the plans to date and describing how UNOP would work. It described the three phases of the process and explained the purposes of the meetings. Importantly, it noted that "the starting point for the Unified New Orleans Plan includes three main assumptions: that every New Orleans resident has the right to return and rebuild; that better levees and hurricane

protection will be built; and that New Orleans will receive 'its fair share' of federal dollars to finance the rebuilding process." Molly Reid, "Together at Last?; A Recap of the City's Rebuilding Plans," *New Orleans Times-Picayune*, sec. Inside Out, October 7, 2006.

19. Coleman Warner, "N.O. Planning Sessions Set for Saturday; Displaced Will Provide Feedback on Repair Blueprints from Afar," *New Orleans Times-Picayune*, sec. National, October 12, 2006.

20. Coleman Warner, "Panel Queried on the Future Of N.O.; 'Shrunken Footprint' Worries Residents," *New Orleans Times-Picayune*, October 13, 2006.

21. Michelle Krupa, "Planning Meetings Objectives Questioned; Some Say Challenges Differ by Neighborhood," *New Orleans Times-Picayune*, October 15, 2006; Brian Friedman, "Algiers Recovery Plans Aired in Meetings," *New Orleans Times-Picayune*, October 19, 2006.

22. Vera Triplett also reported on the recent trip of New Orleans community leaders—including council president Thomas—to Kobe, Japan, where they learned about rebuilding after a great disaster. This trip is described in Gordon Russell, "Lessons from Abroad; Japanese City's Rebuilding Began with a Plan That Was to Be Imposed on Its Citizens, but Ultimately Relied on Discussion and Compromise," *New Orleans Times-Picayune*, sec. National, December 5, 2006.

23. Coleman Warner, "ACORN Loses N.O. Recovery Consulting Jobs; Intent to Develop Properties Seen as Potential Conflict of Interest," *New Orleans Times-Picayune*, October 19, 2006.

24. Frank Donze, "Seized N.O. Houses May Alleviate Shortage; Developers Awarded Properties for Quick Rehab Or Demolition," *New Orleans Times-Picayune*, August 2, 2006.

25. ACORN organized a trip for 400 Katrina survivors to visit Congress and FEMA on February 8–9, 2006 (Petula Dvorak, "Hurricane Victims Demand More Help," *Washington Post*, February 9, 2006). They clearly caught the attention of key lawmakers, and it was less than a week after their visit that President Bush announced that he would ask Congress for the additional $4.2 billion of CDBG funding.

26. From Rob's point of view, this also affected students from his department, led by faculty member Lisa Bates, as well as colleagues and students from Cornell who were working as part of the ACORN Housing planning team.

27. Eventually it became clear that GNOF viewed ACORN Housing's development work as laudable. In February 2008 the foundation awarded ACORN Housing one of the first grants from its Community Revitalization Fund, which was created in October 2007. It provided $200,000 to ACORN Housing for predevelopment costs for the 150 homes planned for the Lower Ninth Ward. According to GNOF officials, if successful, they expected to give ACORN Housing $200,000 a year for two more years as well. Bruce Eggler, "$2.4 Million in Grants Awarded for N.O. Housing," *New Orleans Times-Picayune*, February 14, 2008.

28. Kenneth Reardon et al., "Overcoming the Challenges of Post-Disaster Planning in New Orleans: Lessons from the ACORN Housing/University Collaborative," presented at the 48th annual conference of the Association of Collegiate Schools of Planning, Milwaukee, 2007.

29. ACORN Housing/University Partnership, "A Peoples' Plan for Overcoming the Hurricane Katrina Blues" (ACORN Housing and Cornell University, January 6, 2007).

30. Michelle Krupa, "Survey Backs Plan for Smaller Footprint; but Demographics of Voters Questioned," *New Orleans Times-Picayune*, October 29, 2006. One possible

reason for the disproportionate showing from less-flooded areas was that these people had not participated in the Lambert plans, and so this was one of their first opportunities to be heard.

31. Martin Kaste, "New Orleans Master Plan Stalled," National Public Radio, November 5, 2006, www.npr.org.

32. Krupa, "Survey Backs Plan for Smaller Footprint."

33. Once the planners became more familiar with their districts, almost all of them decided to break their districts into smaller working groups before assembling them back into a whole. For example, the District 4 consultants had formed seven steering committees based on "emotional boundaries" and had held 16 meetings to date. Each group could begin with the Lambert plans as appropriate and sort out local issues before interacting with the larger group. Conversely, District 2 residents insisted that they needed to have one steering committee of neighborhood leaders, rather than fall back into the historic divisions, particularly the St. Charles Avenue dividing line. Another unique approach tailored to the needs of a district was the charrette run by Andres Duany and DPZ planners during the week before the November 11 district meetings, focused on design issues in the French Quarter and downtown. Their final presentations on Friday evening, November 10, became the focus of the District 1 meeting the next day, which discussed potential housing and tourist growth in downtown and the French Quarter.

34. Truehill had also been a member of the City Planning Commission, appointed in 1998. He received a Ph.D. in urban studies from the University of New Orleans in December 2008 and died suddenly that Christmas Day.

35. Michelle Krupa, "Recovery of N.O. Districts Pondered; High-ground Areas Want More Housing," *New Orleans Times-Picayune*, November 12, 2006.

36. Citywide Planning Team, UNOP, "Working Paper #2: Needs, Vision and Goals" (UNOP, December 18, 2006).

37. This was the title of the final version, published as part of the final UNOP report in 2007. Earlier working versions were called the Recovery Needs Assessment.

38. The final version of the Recovery Assessment is dated October but was not finalized until November 28 (Citywide Planning Team, UNOP, "Citywide Baseline Recovery Assessment" [UNOP, October 2006]). Working Paper #2 was not finalized and posted until around December 30.

39. Coleman Warner, "Rebuild Sessions Casting Wide Net; Thousands Expected In Five Linked Cities," *New Orleans Times-Picayune*, December 1, 2006.

40. ACORN, All Congregations Together, the Committee for a Better New Orleans, Community Initiative Foundation, Dallas Area Interfaith, the Episcopal Diocese, Faith in the City, Jeremiah Group, the Metropolitan Organization, NOLA Network, Northern and Central Louisiana Interfaith, the People's Organizing Committee, Peoples Hurricane Relief Fund, the Regional Council of Churches, and Renaissance Village. America*Speaks*, "Five-City Town Meeting Gives Displaced New Orleans Residents Voice in Rebuilding; Citizens to Prioritize Infrastructure Investments," press release, November 13, 2006.

41. Ibid.

42. Editorial, "Planning Our Future," *New Orleans Times-Picayune*, December 2, 2006.

43. NHK's program on New Orleans aired nationally throughout Japan on January 20 in prime time and again on February 4. It emphasized ways in which New Orleans had learned from the experience of Kobe.

44. Michelle Krupa and Coleman Warner, "Across South, Displaced Chime in with Own Ideas for Rebuilding N.O.; but Residents Hesitate on the Tough Calls," *New*

Orleans Times-Picayune, December 3, 2006; Bruce Nolan, "At Tables, Options Often Revised; Participants Tailor Plans to Their Liking," *New Orleans Times-Picayune*, December 3, 2006.

45. Abigail Williamson, "Citizen Participation in the Unified New Orleans Plan," unpublished ms. (Harvard University, Kennedy School of Government, March 21, 2007), 1. See also Coleman Warner, "Recovery Pledge Is Letdown for N.O.; City's Percentage Is Less Than Local Officials Expected," *New Orleans Times-Picayune*, December 15, 2006; LRA, "Minutes, LRA Board Meeting of December 14, 2006" (Baton Rouge, La., December 14, 2006).

46. Williamson, "Citizen Participation in the Unified New Orleans Plan," 20.

47. Frank Donze, "N.O. Recovery Chief Chosen; Planner Draws on Disaster Experience," *New Orleans Times-Picayune*, December 5, 2006.

48. Gordon Russell, "New Recovery Chief Sees Chance to Transform City; N.O. Must Remake Its Economy as Well as Its Housing, He Says," *New Orleans Times-Picayune*, December 8, 2006.

49. Bruce Eggler, "Panel Backs Raises for Two Agencies; N.O. Departments Plagued by Backlogs," *New Orleans Times-Picayune*, November 30, 2006.

50. Judith Williams, the original mayoral appointee, had been unable to serve.

51. Williamson, "Citizen Participation in the Unified New Orleans Plan," 8.

52. Coleman Warner, "Recovery Pledge Is Letdown for N.O."

53. LRA, "Minutes, LRA Board Meeting of December 14, 2006."

54. Warner, "Recovery Pledge Is Letdown for N.O." In all fairness, the delays may have been caused by state bureaucrats' fears of violating FEMA rules.

55. In fact, one outcome of the new Congress was the appointment of Senator Mary Landrieu as chair of a new Disaster Recovery Subcommittee of the Senate Homeland Security and Governmental Affairs Committee, a position she was to use over the next two years to watchdog the progress of recovery policies.

56. Michelle Krupa, Coleman Warner, and Gwen Filosa, "Problems & Solutions; Residents Offer Their Visions to Revitalize New Orleans Neighborhoods," *New Orleans Times-Picayune*, December 17, 2006. This account also comes from Concordia staff, who observed portions of all the meetings.

57. State of Louisiana Division of Administration, Office of Community Development, "Cooperative Endeavor Agreement Implementing Grant Under Community Development Block Grant Disaster Recovery Program by and Between New Orleans Community Support Foundation and State of Louisiana Division of Administration Office of Community Development" (December 2006).

58. The work of America*Speaks* in New Orleans was supported by the Case Foundation, the Carnegie Corporation of New York, the W. K. Kellogg Foundation, the Ford Foundation, the Louisiana Disaster Recovery Fund, the Mary Reynolds Babcock Foundation, the Rockefeller Brothers Fund, the Rockefeller Foundation, and the Surdna Foundation. The cost through Community Congress II was $2.4 million. Warner, "Rebuild Sessions Casting Wide Net." Community Congress III cost approximately $700,000 more, according to Joe Goldman of America*Speaks*.

59. Both of us were active participants in this meeting, and we subsequently viewed video recordings of it. Attending the morning session—in addition to the core members of the citywide team, Concordia staff (Steven Bingler, Bobbie Hill, and Joe Butler), and the resource team—were Carey Shea from Rockefeller; Carolyn Lukensmeyer and Joe Goldman from America*Speaks*; Sandra Gunnar, the LRA New Orleans liaison; and Carling Dinkler from Peter A. Mayer and Associates.

60. Both David Dixon, a district planning consultant, and Gus Newport, a member of the resource team, deserve credit for this astute observation.
61. See Robert Olshansky, "Planning after Hurricane Katrina," *Journal of the American Planning Association* 72, no. 2 (2006): 147–53; and Kenneth C. Topping, "A Model Recovery and Reconstruction Ordinance," in *Planning for Post-Disaster Recovery and Reconstruction,* PAS Report 483/484 (Chicago: American Planning Association, 1998): 149–67. APA also has incorporated this idea into its model recovery ordinance.
62. This has remained true since then, perhaps becoming even more pronounced.
63. Bobbie Hill of Concordia described the meeting schedule for January:

> January 11, morning: CSF
> January 11, afternoon: CSO
> January 12, morning: Blakely and his senior staff
> January 12, afternoon: mayor and staff, with selected city council staff
> Week of January 15–19: city council members, organized through the mayor's office
> January 17: City Planning Commission, requiring participation by district planners
> January 17: Donald Powell and staff
> January 20: Community Congress III
> January 25: Final CSO meeting
> January 29: CSF officially accepts the plan, then officially submits it to City Planning Commission, which will begin an official hearing process

64. Darren Diamond and Gary Odland of Henry Consulting were working on financial estimates by sector, based on review of the finances of each agency and on standardized costing of construction (provided by Randy Carmichael and his team at BKI).
65. ACORN Housing/University Partnership, "A Peoples' Plan for Overcoming the Hurricane Katrina Blues"; Gwen Filosa, "ACORN Offers Its Own Plan," *New Orleans Times-Picayune,* January 7, 2007.
66. Michelle Krupa, "Neighborhood Plans Wind Down; the Next Step Is City Planners," *New Orleans Times-Picayune,* January 14, 2007.
67. Ibid. The quote is from Joe Butler of Concordia.
68. Laurie can attest that the pressure the teams were under was extreme. Words cannot adequately depict the fast pace, pressure, and overwhelming sense of the enormous task at hand. Individuals handled the stress differently; it was a very difficult time for all the consultants.
69. A response by one of the UNOP core members to Rob's email plea for broader public communication was telling: "I know you are totally right on this. We're working hard to do just that. Joe Butler is doing a great job. All of us are on TV and radio, it seems like, every day. I think this can be refined, smarter and slicker and we're trying to do that on a crazy schedule and with limited resources. I'm still working on budgets to see if we can possibly do a video and if the timing even makes sense."
70. Coleman Warner, "Plan Calls for Drier, Denser City; Recovery Blueprint Review Set for Today," *New Orleans Times-Picayune,* January 20, 2007.
71. Ibid.
72. For example, 55 percent of attendees were African-American, compared to 67 percent pre-Katrina; 24 percent had incomes less than $20,000, compared to 35 percent pre-Katrina. The crowd, though, was disproportionately older than the general population. For example, 50 percent of the adults at the congress were older than

55, compared to 28 percent of the pre-Katrina adult population. All the districts were remarkably well represented, with only District 12 (Algiers and unflooded West Bank) being notably underrepresented compared to its share of pre-Katrina population.

73. Full disclosure: Rob is a Bears fan.

74. UNOP, "Preliminary Report, Updated, Community Congress III, January 20, 2007" (January 22, 2007).

75. Michelle Krupa, "Citizens Say Yes to Unified N.O. Plan; Recovery Director Calls for Streamlining," *New Orleans Times-Picayune*, January 21, 2007.

76. Coleman Warner, "Unified N.O. Plan Gaining Steam; Recovery Blueprint Impresses City Officials," *New Orleans Times-Picayune*, January 27, 2007.

77. The full collection of sector reports, summarized in chapter 3 of the plan, was never fully released. This compendium of data formed a critical foundation for all the UNOP plan products. But it could have also been more useful to agencies and the public if it had been more readily available.

78. Coleman Warner, "N.O. Planners' Vision Will Cost $14 Billion; City Approval, Money Source Hurdles Ahead," *New Orleans Times-Picayune*, January 31, 2007.

79. UNOP, "Citywide Strategic Recovery and Rebuilding Plan, Final Draft" (New Orleans CSF, January 29, 2007), executive summary, 2.

CHAPTER 7

1. We know Ed well, so we are not unbiased observers of him. Rob was a student at Berkeley in the 1980s when Ed was on the faculty; after Rob completed his Ph.D., Ed hired Rob for his first teaching job. We communicated with him during the year after Katrina. We also provided him with news and information regarding potential New Orleans political and administrative minefields while he was deciding whether or not to accept the job and on what terms. We joined him and Ken Topping for dinner the night he arrived in town. We saw Ed when he was overwhelmed by the enormity of the task before him. We watched him while he was unreasonably expected to be the city's savior. And we watched him as he rearranged the administrative structure at city hall in order to implement the recovery projects. Ed had credibility, but he also had a difficult job operating in the sometimes inbred and incestuous world of New Orleans governance. He at times created excessively high expectations for himself and from the public, he sometimes misspoke, and his office never produced results fast enough to satisfy the city council. We leave it to Ed to tell the rest of his own story.

2. According to its website, www.aalp.org, "The AALP is a 5-year-old network of about 50 New Orleans African-American community, business and religious leaders and representatives that focus on agenda building, policy analysis, strategic dialogue and consensus building. . . . Since Katrina, we have all been scattered to many locations, but through phone discussions, policy summits, e-mails, and other gatherings the broad outline of our response to the disaster has emerged. . . . We believe that the AALP, and numerous other groups are articulating the same position: Rebuild a New Orleans that is more just and equitable for the citizens who were displaced, and eliminate racial and class inequities." Its spokesperson and most visible member is Mtangulizi Sanyika, who knew Ed Blakely during his 13 years with the National Economic Development and Law Center in Oakland, California. Sanyika moved back to New Orleans in 2004. Gordon Russell, "New

Recovery Chief Sees Chance to Transform City; N.O. Must Remake Its Economy as Well as Its Housing, He Says," *New Orleans Times-Picayune*, December 8, 2006.

3. Although Blakely commended the council and appropriately agreed that the neighborhood plans met the council's requirements, he also noted that "the City of New Orleans will need to integrate infrastructure requirements with the neighborhood plans to provide a coherent and integrated delivery strategy." Furthermore, he also recognized that "there is recognition in the plans that the flood issues and many infrastructure requirements reach well beyond any single neighborhood or District. . . . A solid citywide infrastructure and a companion economic development plan—as called for by FEMA—will be needed to carry out the neighborhood plans." Edward J. Blakely, Phillip L. Clay, and Diana M. Gonzalez, "City of New Orleans Neighborhoods Rebuilding Plan Peer Review," October 2006.

4. City of New Orleans, "2007 Annual Budget" (November 2006).

5. Russell, "New Recovery Chief Sees Chance to Transform City."

6. Patrik Jonsson, "Big Easy Makes Way for New Recovery Czar," *Christian Science Monitor*, sec. USA, January 25, 2007; Peter Whoriskey, "New Orleans Repeats Mistakes as It Rebuilds; Many Houses Built in Areas Katrina Flooded Are Not on Raised Foundations," *Washington Post*, January 4, 2007.

7. Bruce Nolan, "New Nagin Aide Floats Land Swaps to Aid Recovery; Clusters of Neighbors Would Trade Together for Spots in Viable Areas," *New Orleans Times-Picayune*, January 5, 2007; Whoriskey, "New Orleans Repeats Mistakes as It Rebuilds"; Jonsson, "Big Easy Makes Way for New Recovery Czar."

8. Jonsson, "Big Easy Makes Way for New Recovery Czar."

9. Julie Bourbon, "Recovery Czar Rolls Through the Wreckage; He'd Like to See Real Progress in New Orleans by September," *New Orleans Times-Picayune*, February 11, 2007.

10. Ibid.

11. Michelle Krupa, "Grand Plan; City's Recovery Chief Envisions N.O. as a Hub for World's Growing Economies," *New Orleans Times-Picayune*, February 1, 2007.

12. Ibid.

13. David Hammer and Frank Donze, "Recovery Czar Throws Down the Gauntlet before LRA; He Wants Control over Money Coming into New Orleans," *New Orleans Times-Picayune*, February 13, 2007.

14. City of New Orleans, "Recovery in New Orleans, Background Document," February 12, 2007.

15. Hammer and Donze, "Recovery Czar Throws Down the Gauntlet before LRA."

16. Michelle Krupa and Frank Donze, "City to Select Targeted Recovery Zones; First Project Could Include 60 Houses," *New Orleans Times-Picayune*, February 25, 2007.

17. This meeting was followed the next week by an Employee Town Meeting to provide city employees and key personnel with the information to understand the city's recovery plan and an opportunity to discuss and deliberate their roles in rebuilding; this discussion was also focused around the target areas. America-Speaks, "Spotlight: Call for Facilitators—New Orleans, Philadelphia, and Chicago" (February 28, 2007), www.americaspeaks.org/spotlight/index.php?paged=3R.

18. Michelle Krupa and Frank Donze, "N.O. Lays Out $1.2 Billion Rebuilding Project; Citywide Spending Combined with Money for 16 Targeted Zones," *New Orleans Times-Picayune*, March 24, 2007.

19. Frank Donze, "Recovery Summit Kicks off Today; Disparate Agencies Unite to Brainstorm," *New Orleans Times-Picayune*, March 23, 2007.

20. Ibid.

21. Krupa and Donze, "N.O. Lays out $1.2 Billion Rebuilding Project."
22. Michelle Krupa and Gordon Russell, "N.O. post-K Blueprint Unveiled; Plan Puts Most Cash in East, Lower 9th," *New Orleans Times-Picayune*, March 29, 2007; Adam Nossiter, "All Areas Open in New Blueprint for New Orleans," *New York Times*, National Desk, January 31, 2007. Michelle Krupa and Frank Donze, "Leaders Stand United Behind Recovery Plan; Blueprint Addresses Fears of Abandonment," *New Orleans Times-Picayune*, March 30, 2007.
23. Krupa and Russell, "N.O. post-K Blueprint Unveiled."
24. This is based on several conversations with Jeff Thomas and Dubravka Gilic, the ORM managers who delineated the target areas.
25. Krupa and Donze, "Leaders Stand United Behind Recovery Plan."
26. Ibid.
27. Gordon Russell, "Financing for Plan Could Be Problematic; Federal Officials Resist Waiver of Fund Match," *New Orleans Times-Picayune*, March 30, 2007.
28. City of New Orleans, ORM, "Office of Recovery Management Target Areas" (PowerPoint presentation, New Orleans, March 29, 2007).
29. Krupa and Russell, "N.O. post-K Blueprint Unveiled."
30. Bureau of Governmental Research (BGR), *Not Ready for Prime Time: An Analysis of the UNOP Citywide Plan* (New Orleans, March 2007). Bruce Eggler, "N.O. Recovery Plan Called a Muddle; Watchdog Group Urges Fresh Analysis," *New Orleans Times-Picayune*, March 6, 2007.
31. BGR, *Not Ready for Prime Time.*
32. Bruce Eggler, "Planning Process OK, Speakers Say; Continued Public Participation Urged as Document Is Revised," *New Orleans Times-Picayune*, March 8, 2007.
33. David Voelker, "UNOP to Serve as Foundation," *New Orleans Times-Picayune*, March 17, 2007.
34. UNOP, "Citywide Strategic Recovery and Rebuilding Plan, Final Draft" (New Orleans CSF, January 29, 2007), 4.16.
35. Road Home Program, State of Louisiana, "The Road Home Week 43 Situation and Pipeline Report" (May 1, 2007), www.road2la.org/Docs/pipeline/Week%2043%20 Combined%20Report.pdf.
36. David Hammer, "Road Home Going Broke, Blanco Aide Says; at This Rate, Looming Shortfall Will Reach Billions of Dollars," *New Orleans Times-Picayune*, May 2, 2007.
37. Ibid.
38. Jan Moller, "Surplus Could Go to Road Home; GOP Leader Suggests $1.2 Billion to Fill Gap," *New Orleans Times-Picayune*, May 4, 2007.
39. David Hammer, "Road Home Short $2.9 Billion; Shortfall Could Grow to $4 Billion," *New Orleans Times-Picayune*, May 11, 2007.
40. Ibid.
41. David Hammer, "Blowing in the Wind; Federal Officials and the Louisiana Recovery Authority Disagree on What Caused a Projected $3 Billion Shortfall in the State's Road Home Program," *New Orleans Times-Picayune*, May 24, 2007.
42. Bruce Alpert, "Road Home Rescue Unlikely, Powell Says; but He Tells Congress He Is Willing to Discuss Options with Blanco," *New Orleans Times-Picayune*, May 25, 2007.
43. Hammer, "Blowing in the Wind."
44. Bill Barrow, "Road Home Gap Hits $5 Billion; State Feeling Pressure to Kick in Money," *New Orleans Times-Picayune*, June 1, 2007.

45. Walter Leger, "Written Testimony of Walter Leger, Member of the Board of the Louisiana Recovery Authority," U.S. House of Representatives, Financial Services Committee, Washington, D.C., February 6, 2007.

46. Bill Walsh, "Iraq War, Gulf Aid Are Funded; Congress OKs Waiver of Recovery Match," *New Orleans Times-Picayune*, sec. National, May 25, 2007; Leslie Eaton, "Gulf Region Gains Help in New Law on War Funds," *New York Times*, May 26, 2007.

47. Walsh, "Iraq War, Gulf Aid Are Funded."

48. Eaton, "Gulf Region Gains Help in New Law on War Funds."

49. David Hammer, "Governor Offers Cash for Gap in Road Home; Up to $700 Million in State Money Floated," *New Orleans Times-Picayune*, June 3, 2007.

50. Ibid.; David Hammer, "Blanco Move May Signal Cease-fire; Shortfall Had Set off Fed-State Bickering," *New Orleans Times-Picayune*, June 3, 2007.

51. Michelle Krupa, "Recovery Czar Revises Timetable to Launch N.O. Rebuilding Plan; City Lacks Enough Cash Until Later This Year," *New Orleans Times-Picayune*, June 4, 2007.

52. LRA, "Louisiana Speaks Regional Plan: Vision and Strategies for Recovery and Growth in South Louisiana" (Baton Rouge, La., May 2007). The planning team was led by Calthorpe Associates, but project management and coordination were provided jointly by the Center for Planning Excellence (CPEX) and the LRA. Although the LRASF paid for the consultants and for CPEX, the project was overseen by state employees at the LRA, and printing costs were covered by CDBG funds.

53. David Hammer, "Planners Unveil Vision for La.; Rapid Transit, Denser Development Urged," *New Orleans Times-Picayune*, May 3, 2007.

54. At this May 15 hearing, UNOP staff presented the revisions to the plan, in response to previous public comments. Thirteen individuals testified regarding various details of the revised plan.

55. City Planning Commission of New Orleans in collaboration with the ORM, "Consideration of the Citywide Strategic Recovery and Rebuilding Plan," May 22, 2007.

56. Ibid., 6, 7, 10, 16, 20.

57. Planners reading this will no doubt find this concept intriguing. Does this mean that they also approved the previous city master plans, which heavily influenced this plan? How about all the other agency plans over the years that, implicitly, led to the development of this recovery plan?

58. Bruce Eggler, "UNOP Citywide Plan Wins Approval; City Council Expected to OK It Next Week," *New Orleans Times-Picayune*, June 14, 2007.

59. City Council of the City of New Orleans, *Motion M-07-271*, "A Motion to Grant Acceptance and General Approval of the Citywide Strategic Recovery and Redevelopment Plan," June 21, 2007.

60. Bruce Eggler, "Council Endorses Recovery Blueprint; Move Could Unlock $117 Million in Aid," *New Orleans Times-Picayune*, June 22, 2007.

CHAPTER 8

1. Robert W. Kates et al., "Reconstruction of New Orleans after Hurricane Katrina: A Research Perspective," *Proceedings of the National Academy of Sciences* 103, no. 40 (2006): 14653–60.

2. J. Eugene Haas, Robert W. Kates, and Martyn J. Bowden, eds., *Reconstruction Following Disaster* (Cambridge, Mass.: MIT Press, 1977), 268.

3. As of April 13, 2009, the Road Home program had granted more than $7.9 billion to 124,119 home owners across the state. Of this, $3.7 billion went to about 44,000 Orleans Parish home owners. To receive the rebuilding grants, home owners must accept a number of covenant requirements. They include remaining on the property for three years, complying with FEMA Advisory Base Flood Elevation guidelines as necessary, and maintaining flood and hazard insurance. LRA, "Executive Director's Report, Paul Rainwater, August 19, 2009," http://lra.louisiana .gov/assets/docs/searchable/meetings/2009/Board%20Meeting%208-19-09/ ExecDirectorsReport8-19-09.pdf.

4. Timothy F. Green and Robert B. Olshansky, "Homeowner Decisions, Land Banking, and Land Use Change in New Orleans after Hurricane Katrina," working paper (Cambridge, Mass.: Lincoln Institute of Land Policy, May 2009).

5. Haas, Kates, and Bowden, *Reconstruction Following Disaster*, 263, 267.

6. PolicyLink participated in the September 2005 brainstorming sessions with Andy Kopplin in Baton Rouge.

7. Kalima Rose, Annie Clark, and Dominique Duval-Diop, "A Long Way Home: The State of Housing Recovery in Louisiana 2008" (PolicyLink, August 2008). Federal funds have been insufficient for reconstruction of permanent rental housing. Although 40 percent of Louisianans who lost their homes were renters, only 15 percent of the Road Home housing funds were designated for rental housing. Despite the rhetoric that New Orleans residents had a "right to return," it was very hard for those who were displaced to return to homes and jobs in New Orleans unless they were home owners covered by the Road Home program (many of whom could not afford actual construction costs of rebuilding).

8. "Not addressed in the Neighborhoods Rebuilding Plan, but required for the functional restoration of the flooded areas of the City are: . . . A plan for the reconstruction of the major public housing properties, including resident relocation and accommodation issues." Lambert Advisory and SHEDO, "City of New Orleans Neighborhoods Rebuilding Plan, Summary," October 2006, 6. (This list also includes flood protection, economic development, schools, and utilities.)

9. UNOP, "Citywide Strategic Recovery and Rebuilding Plan, Final Draft" (New Orleans CSF, January 29, 2007), Project Description Sheet #14.

10. Throughout late 2005 and the first half of 2006, the Corps of Engineers spent more than $350 million and worked nonstop to repair almost half (170 miles) of damaged levees and floodwalls in time for the 2006 hurricane season (Mark Schleifstein, "Flood Protection Plans Lacking. Changed Standards Mean New Strategies," *New Orleans Times Picayune*, August 28, 2006). It completely replaced 25 miles of levees and also began constructing storm surge gates and new pumping stations at the mouths of the three major canals that empty into Lake Pontchartrain. It also started strengthening other inadequately designed elements of the system in order to provide 100-year flood protection by 2011 (Mark Schleifstein and M. Grissett, "The Risk of Hurricane Flooding Today," *New Orleans Times Picayune*, June 21, 2007). The cost for these two efforts has been at least $4 billion (Anne Rochell Konigsmark, "Levees not Fully Ready for Hurricane Season. Holes Have Been Plugged, but New Orleans' System Won't Survive Major Storm," *USA Today*, April 24, 2006). The system underwent its first major test in September 2008 when Hurricane Gustav came onshore southwest of New Orleans and caused some wind and flooding damage in the city. The miles of repaired levees held even as water overtopped the floodwall along the Industrial Canal.

11. U.S. Army Corps of Engineers (USACE), "Information on Organization and Programs," 2008, www.usace.army.mil.

12. Gulf Coast Rebuilding Office of the Federal Coordinator and USACE, "Corps of Engineers Releases New Risk Maps for the New Orleans Area; Powell Releases New Costs for 100-Year Hurricane Protection," news release, August 22, 2007.

13. The "Advisory Base Flood Elevations for Orleans Parish, Louisiana," first released on April 12, 2006, are still in effect as of early 2010; www.fema.gov/pdf/hazard/flood/recoverydata/orleans_parish04-12-06.pdf.

14. LRA, "State of Louisiana Lifts HMGP Elevation Cap to $100,000," press release, April 7, 2009.

15. As of August 2009, the state had made 28,831 awards totaling $835 million for home elevation projects as part of the Road Home program. More than 29,000 additional home owners have reported expressed interest in the program. LRA, "Progress Report, October 2008," http://lra.louisiana.gov/assets/docs/searchable/Quarterly%20Reports/October08QuarterlyReport.pdf.

16. Allison Plyer and Amy Liu, *The New Orleans Index: Tracking the Recovery of New Orleans and the Metro Area* (New Orleans: Greater New Orleans Community Data Center and the Brookings Institution, July 30, 2009), www.gnocdc.org/NewOrleansIndex/index.html.

17. Risk Management Solutions (RMS), "Flood Risk in New Orleans: Implications for Future Management and Insurability" (Newark, Calif.: RMS, 2006), 29.

18. Haas, Kates, and Bowden, *Reconstruction Following Disaster*, 248.

19. Inga Saffron, "A Planner's Historic Opportunity, Impossible Task," *Philadelphia Inquirer*, sec. Domestic News, February 19, 2006.

20. The stated purpose of UNOP evolved: it was always to attract a variety of investors, but the primary target changed from the White House to private investors to the new Congress.

21. Frank Donze, Gordon Russell, and Laura Maggi, "Buyouts Torpedoed, Not Sunk; Leaders Still Looking for Ways to Rebuild," *New Orleans Times-Picayune*, sec. National, January 26, 2006.

22. An alternate interpretation is that Powell, understanding the administration's reluctance to fork over money to Louisiana, may have wanted an airtight plan to make it easier for him to go to the White House for more funding. Eventually, Powell began to appreciate the needs of New Orleans. He became an advocate for the state and worked, with limited success, to cut through some of the bureaucratic requirements that were slowing the flow of funds. As a result, he ultimately won the praise of Louisiana officials for his efforts. Bruce Alpert, "Powell Ready to Leave Gulf Coast; La. Leaders Applaud Recovery Chief's Work," *New Orleans Times-Picayune*, sec. National, March 1, 2008.

23. The mayor, among others, still hoped in late August that the planning process would help to inform these individual decisions. Gordon Russell, "On Their Own: In the Absence of Clear Direction, New Orleanians Are Rebuilding a Patchwork City," *New Orleans Times-Picayune*, sec. National, August 27, 2006.

24. In the words of one New Orleans official, state personnel, overly fearful of being audited by either FEMA or HUD, were being "more Catholic than the Pope." According to several officials, this problem has continued to this day.

25. For example, Felicia R. Lee, "Demme's Tales of Ordinary Heroes in New Orleans," *New York Times*, sec. E, May 28, 2007, late edition–final edition. Ann M. Simmons, "Bringing back Home in New Orleans," *Los Angeles Times*, March 28, 2007, www.latimes.com/news/nationworld/la-na-lowerninth28mar28,1,221138.story.

26. Private insurers paid out more than $53.7 billion in claims for the 2005 storms, about $38.1 billion of which was related to Hurricane Katrina, and the National Flood Insurance Program paid out $13.6 billion for flood-related claims. Insurance Information Institute III, "Issues Updates, Industry Financials and Outlook, Presentations and Latest Studies," February 25, 2009, www.iii.org/presentations/media. About $6.5 billion of NFIP payments went to insured entities within the city of New Orleans. LRA, "Louisiana Recovery Authority, Progress Report, October 2008."

27. An additional claim could be made that the surge height was exacerbated by the Mississippi River Gulf Outlet (MR-GO), which was excavated by the federal government. William R. Freudenburg et al., *Catastrophe in the Making: The Engineering of Katrina and the Disasters of Tomorrow* (Washington, D.C.: Island Press/Shearwater, 2009). In November 2009, a federal judge agreed with this interpretation, ruling that the Corps of Engineers was responsible for flood damage in St. Bernard Parish and the Lower Ninth Ward. Mark Schleifstein, "Corps Told to Pay MR-GO Damages; Ruling Applies to St. Bernard, Lower 9, But not Eastern N.O." *New Orleans Times-Picayune*, November 19, 2009.

28. Of the more than $116 billion in Congressional authorizations, $19.7 billion was allocated to the CDBG program for disaster recovery and rebuilding assistance and $13.6 billion was paid by the National Flood Insurance Program. U.S. GAO, *Gulf Coast Rebuilding: Observations on Federal Financial Implications, Testimony Before the Committee on the Budget, U.S. House of Representatives*. Many of the more than 200,000 displaced city residents had their housing costs supported by HUD emergency rental vouchers or FEMA's temporary housing program for four years. HUD made its last emergency rental voucher payments on August 1, 2009, and FEMA was in the process of closing out its trailer program then. As of then, the State of Louisiana was working with about 11,000 families who were still transitioning out of these programs to permanent alternative solutions. LRA, "Executive Director's Report, Paul Rainwater, August 19, 2009."

29. Recovery funds did not really start flowing into the city until early 2008. At the end of 2008, the city reported that it had been obligated about $1.1 billion in recovery funds. Nearly one-third of these funds came from federal loans. (Repayment was to begin in 2012, but Congress has since forgiven them.) One-third was expected to come from the FEMA Hazard Mitigation Grant Program ($31.8 million) and the Public Assistance program ($353 million had been obligated as of October 2008). Another third ($411 million) was expected in CDBG "disaster recovery grant" program funds. City of New Orleans, "2009 Annual Budget," www.cityofno.com/Resources/2008mayorsbudget.pdf.

30. There was unprecedented flexibility in federal spending after the September 11, 2001, attacks. On September 18, 2001, President Bush amended his disaster declaration and authorized 100 percent funding of all eligible costs (for both response and recovery), retroactive to September 11. FEMA headquarters approved of a broader definition of the Stafford Act of "what comprised a damaged system" and allowed the use of Public Assistance funds for enhancement of facilities that had not been directly damaged, as well as construction of new facilities (David Mammen, "Recovery Efforts in New York after 9/11," *Journal of Disaster Research* 2, no. 6 [2007]: 502–16). In February 2003, Congress authorized FEMA to conclude the Public Assistance program early; normally, close-out does not occur until all the work is completed and all costs clarified. This arrangement allowed FEMA to use $2.37 billion in remaining Public Assistance funds to reimburse local governments for formerly ineligible costs under the Stafford Act. U.S. GAO, *September 11:*

Overview of Federal Disaster Assistance to the New York City Area (Washington, D.C.: U.S. GAO, October 2003), www.gao.gov.

31. LRA, "Louisiana Recovery Authority, Progress Report, October 2008."

32. Andrew Kopplin, *Written Testimony of Andrew D. Kopplin, Executive Director of the Louisiana Recovery Authority, Before the U.S. Senate Homeland Security and Governmental Affairs Subcommittee on Disaster Recovery, May 24, 2007.*

33. City of New Orleans, "2010 Budget Presentation," www.cityofno.com/Portals/PublicAdvocacy/Resources/2010%20Budget%20Presentation%20FINAL.pdf.

34. Ibid.

35. Such waivers were issued following many other past major disasters.

36. Throughout 2008, the city worked with the state and HUD to complete the application process for the $411 million in CDBG funds that it had been allocated. But, as of December 2008, the city had spent less than $10 million of them. City of New Orleans, "2009 Annual Budget."

37. Amy Liu, "Building a Better New Orleans: A Review of and Plan for Progress One Year after Hurricane Katrina" (Washington, D.C.: Brookings Institution, Metropolitan Policy Program, August 2006), 26.

38. Charles C. Mann, "The Long, Strange Resurrection of New Orleans," *Fortune*, August 21, 2006.

39. In the end, even Blakely was not a credible and strong leader. In part, this was because he was an outsider and could not find a workable niche within New Orleans politics. What worked in Oakland did not work in New Orleans. In part, this was because he was the mayor's appointment and had to defer to the mayor's office.

40. Coleman Warner, "N.O. Blazes Trail for Grant Money; City and State Agree on Planning Process," *New Orleans Times-Picayune*, sec. National, July 6, 2006; Susan Saulny, "New Orleans Sets a Way to Plan Its Rebuilding," *New York Times*, sec. A, July 6, 2006, late edition–final edition; Michelle Millhollon, "Critics: Urgency Lacking in N.O.," *Baton Rouge Advocate*, sec. B, August 11, 2006; Molly Reid, "Together at Last? A Recap of the City's Rebuilding Plans," *New Orleans Times-Picayune*, sec. Inside Out, October 7, 2006.

41. Rockefeller Foundation, "The Rockefeller Foundation to Provide $3.5 Million to Accelerate Recovery Planning for the City of New Orleans," news advisory, April 20, 2006.

42. Coleman Warner, "Locals Key to N.O. Rebirth; Expert Says Residents Get 'Historic' Chance," *New Orleans Times-Picayune*, sec. Metro, July 20, 2006.

43. We tried unsuccessfully to trace the origins of the imperative to embed planners in each neighborhood. We were enthusiastic about this idea from the beginning, because city-paid neighborhood planners were one of the most positive features of the Kobe recovery process. It is possible that Kobe's experience might have influenced thinking in New Orleans in December 2005. Jed Horne, "Carving a Better City; in Seconds, Buildings Collapsed, Bridges Toppled and Thousands Died When an Earthquake Hit Kobe, Japan, 10 Years Ago," *New Orleans Times-Picayune*, sec. National, December 4, 2005, 1.

44. Wallace Roberts & Todd, "Action Plan for New Orleans: The New American City" (BNOBC Urban Planning Committee, January 11, 2006).

45. Urban Land Institute, "A Rebuilding Strategy: New Orleans Louisiana" (Washington, D.C.: ULI, November 18, 2005).

46. New Orleans Planning Assessment Team, *Charting the Course for Rebuilding a Great American City: An Assessment of the Planning Function in Post-Katrina New Orleans* (Chicago: American Planning Association, 2005).

47. ULI, "Rebuilding Strategy"; Wallace Roberts & Todd, "Urban Planning Committee: Action Plan for New Orleans, Executive Summary" (BNOBC Urban Planning Committee, January 30, 2006). E.g., "Because the Committee wants everyone to return and new people to come, we have to support and create great neighborhoods" (10); "Remember that the critical need is to provide housing for people who want to return" (12).

48. The LRA intensified its lobbying efforts in Washington throughout 2007 with frequent trips by numerous board members and staff. In the first half of the year—before the LRA approved UNOP—their goal was to convince Congress and the White House to waive the required state match for Public Assistance funds. It is likely that they then intended to lobby for enhanced Road Home funding, as outlined in UNOP, but, unfortunately, the Road Home shortfall intervened. So, from May to December, the LRA's lobbying efforts focused instead on addressing the shortfall, and it finally received $3 billion by the end of the year.

49. Concordia et al., "School Facilities Master Plan for Orleans Parish" (Recovery School District and Orleans Parish School Board, August 2008).

50. Coastal Protection and Restoration Authority, State of Louisiana (CPRA), "Louisiana's Comprehensive Master Plan for a Sustainable Coast," April 2007, www.lacpra .org/assets/docs/Comprehensive%20Master%20Plan%20(Main%20Report)%20 -%201.%20Executive%20Summa.pdf.

51. In October 2007, under Blakely's leadership, the city's Office of Recovery Management (ORM) merged with the city's Economic Development, Workforce Development, and Housing and Neighborhood Development agencies and was renamed the Office of Recovery Development and Administration (ORDA). ORDA focused on obtaining and packaging funds for priority recovery projects in the city's target areas. By early 2009, it was managing 394 capital projects throughout the city and was working to integrate these projects into the city's 2009 capital budget. ORDA was dissolved in mid-2009, and Ed Blakely returned to Sydney, Australia (City of New Orleans, "2010 Budget Presentation"). Since late 2009, the new Office of Community Development and a quasi-public New Orleans Economic Development Corporation have been in charge of the city's economic growth activities. Plyer and Liu, *New Orleans Index*.

    In October 2009, during his unveiling of the city's 2010 budget, the mayor claimed the city was managing construction projects worth more than $1.9 billion and estimated that, overall, construction projects being designed, being built, or recently completed in the city amounted to as much as $26 billion. The city also said more private investments were pouring into its 17 target areas (as well as the "housing opportunity zones" that surround them). In those areas, the city estimates that every dollar of public infrastructure investment is being matched by $188 in private funds. Outside of the target areas, that ratio is 1:98. City of New Orleans, "2010 Budget Presentation."

52. City of New Orleans, "2010 Budget Presentation."

53. City of New Orleans, "City of New Orleans 2008 Budget," www.cityofno.com/ Resources/2008mayorsbudget.pdf; CNNMoney.com, http://money.cnn.com/ galleries/2008/moneymag/0805/gallery.resg_gainers.moneymag/6.html.

54. City of New Orleans, "City of New Orleans 2008 Budget."

55. City of New Orleans, "2010 Budget Presentation."

56. Ibid.

57. A political corporation of the state, NORA was established to undertake community improvement projects consistent with city plans and policies. It is acquiring properties that were blighted before Katrina and will also acquire properties abandoned and blighted as a result of the flood. Working with the city council, the LRA, federal agencies, and others, ORDA and NORA rewrote the city's code to combat blight and give power to the city to make repairs if owners do not. Andrew Holbein, "Building a Recovery Department: New Orleans Attacks Blight Through Code Enforcement," Planning, February 2009.

58. Green and Olshansky, "Homeowner Decisions, Land Banking, and Land Use Change in New Orleans after Hurricane Katrina"; Holbein, "Building a Recovery Department."

59. LRA, "Executive Director's Report, Paul Rainwater, August 19, 2009." NORA's plan for disposing of the Road Home properties was approved by the LRA in December 2007 and contains 17 principles for property transfer and redevelopment that include job creation, bringing back displaced families, creating opportunities for affordable housing, and flood hazard mitigation. LRA, "Progress Report, April 2008," http://louisianarecoveryauthority.org/assets/docs/searchable/Quarterly%20Reports/April2008QtReport.pdf.

60. Green and Olshansky, "Homeowner Decisions."

61. Kates et al., "Reconstruction of New Orleans after Hurricane Katrina," 14656.

62. Plyer and Liu, *New Orleans Index*. It is a misnomer, however, to call the repopulation a "return of residents"; a considerable percentage is made up of new residents and workers who came to help with the rebuilding. In contrast to New Orleans, the regional population has reached about 90 percent of its previous level. Given a 2000 metropolitan area population of 1.29 million, this means that the region's population is down by about 130,000; approximately 110,000 of this loss is from Orleans Parish alone.

63. Troy Henry was a candidate in the mayoral race. Troy's former partner, Darren Diamond, withdrew from Henry Consulting effective April 17, 2009. Michelle Krupa, "Henry Sued by ex-Partner in Firm; Mayoral Candidate Calls It Merely Ploy," *New Orleans Times-Picayune*, January 16, 2010.

Index

Note: An *italicized f* or *t* following a page number refers to a figure or a table, respectively.

Discussion Questions

In what ways was New Orleans a disaster waiting to happen? What might have been done differently prior to Katrina to lessen the disaster potential? In what ways is New Orleans now more resilient should a similar hurricane strike? In what ways is New Orleans still at risk?

What were the multiple and systemic causes of the disaster in New Orleans? Who was responsible and how has each been addressed?

What are the specific strengths and limitations of private-sector and public-sector institutions in dealing with a large-scale catastrophe?

What are some of the unique characteristics of postdisaster recovery that challenge the typical practices of planning?

Why does a city need a plan after a catastrophic disaster? Why did New Orleans need a plan after Katrina? To what extent did the various plans serve these needs?

Who should pay for planning after a disaster? Should FEMA have paid for the neighborhood planning process in New Orleans? Should a city be able to use CDBG funds? What if other city entities, other than the planning commission, want to use these funds to do a plan?

After a large urban disaster, what do you think should be the relative roles of the federal, state, and municipal governments? If you had been the mayor of New Orleans in fall 2005, how might you have organized for recovery?

What should be the characteristics of a "recovery plan?" Should it differ from a typical comprehensive plan—and if so, how?

Following a great disaster, how would you manage the tension between needing to rebuild quickly and taking advantage of the opportunity to rebuild a better, safer city?

What are some of the reasons that information management and communications are so critical following a great disaster?

Is your community prepared for a disaster of its own? Is planning playing a role in preparation?